The
Mansion
on the
Hill

The
Mansion
on the
Hill

DYLAN, YOUNG, GEFFEN, SPRINGSTEEN,
AND THE HEAD-ON COLLISION
OF ROCK AND COMMERCE

Fred Goodman

TIMES ⓣ BOOKS

RANDOM HOUSE

All rights reserved under International and Pan-American Copyright Conventions. Published in the United States by Times Books, a division of Random House, Inc., New York, and simultaneously in Canada by Random House of Canada Limited, Toronto.

Grateful acknowledgment is made to the following for permission to reprint previously published material:

HAL LEONARD CORPORATION: Excerpt from "Stoney End," words and music by Laura Nyro. Copyright © 1966 (renewed 1994), 1968 by EMI Blackwood Music, Inc. All rights reserved. International copyright secured. Used by permission.
JOHN SINCLAIR: Excerpt from "Which Is the Real BS?" by John Sinclair (*Detroit Sun*, October, 1975). Copyright © 1975, 1996 by John Sinclair. All rights reserved by the author. Used by permission.
SPECIAL RIDER MUSIC: Excerpt from "Stuck Inside of Mobile with the Memphis Blues Again" by Bob Dylan. Copyright © 1965 by Warner Bros. Music. Copyright renewed 1993 by Special Rider Music. Reprinted by permission.
STRAIGHT ARROW PUBLISHERS, INC.: Excerpt from "Rock and Art" by Jon Landau (*Rolling Stone,* July 20, 1968); excerpt from "The Newport Folk Festival" by Jon Landau (*Rolling Stone,* August 24, 1968); excerpt from "So Hard to Make Arrangements for Yourself" by Cameron Crowe (*Rolling Stone,* August 17, 1975). Copyright © 1968, 1975 by Straight Arrow Publishers, Inc. All rights reserved. Reprinted by permission.
WARNER BROS. PUBLICATIONS, INC.: Excerpt from "For What It Is Worth" by Stephen Stills. Copyright © 1966 (renewed) by Cotillion Music, Inc., Ten East Music, Springalo Toones and Richie Furay Music. All rights administered by Warner-Tamerlane Publishing Corp. All rights reserved. Excerpt from "A Mansion on the Hill" by Hank Williams and Fred Rose. Copyright © 1948 (renewed) by Julian J. Aberbach, the Estate of Joachim Jean Aberbach and Milene Music, Inc. All rights o/b/o Julian J. Aberbach and the Estate of Joachim Jean Aberbach, administered by Intersong USA, Inc. All rights reserved. Reprinted by permission of Warner Bros. Publications U.S., Inc., Miami, FL 33014.

Library of Congress Cataloging-in-Publication Data

Goodman, Fred.
   The mansion on the hill: Dylan, Young, Geffen, Springsteen, and the head-on collision of rock and commerce / Fred Goodman.
      p.   cm.
   Includes index.
   ISBN 0-8129-2113-5
   1. Rock music—United States—History and criticism.   2. Rock music—Economic aspects—United States.   I. Title.
ML3534.G66   1996   781.66'0973—dc20   95-53216
                                                 CIP
                                                 MN

Text design: Levavi & Levavi

Random House website address: http://www.randomhouse.com/

Printed in the United States of America on acid-free paper

9 8 7 6 5 4 3 2

For Janet

Contents

Prologue: The Secret Language

> Tonight, down here in the valley,
> I'm lonesome and oh, how I feel,
> As I sit here alone in my cabin,
> I can see a mansion on the hill.
>> Hank Williams,
>> "A Mansion on the Hill"

I spent my high school summers working in the kitchen of a camp in the Poconos. It was dirty work but a great paying gig at sixty dollars a week. Of course, there wasn't a hell of a lot to do at night and that was a problem: What's the good of being sixteen and on your own if you can't go completely insane?

Sometimes we'd borrow a car and drive to New York, where the drinking age was still eighteen and we stood a better chance of getting served. But usually we'd just sit around the dilapidated shack we lived in behind the kitchen, getting loaded on whatever we could lay our hands on and listening to records. Among eight guys there were four stereos and over two thousand albums in that bunk: the bare necessities required for two months away from civilization. Music—rock and roll—was far and away the most discussed topic. (Girls and drugs were tied for second.)

As great as the music was, the ongoing conversation was really about something more than solos and songs. Listening to rock and roll was learning a secret language. There was something conveyed by the attitude of the bands and their records that stood apart from the music, and the way you spoke that language told people how you felt about the world. When you first met someone, the conversation turned immediately to music because once you knew which bands a person listened to, you knew if you were going to get along.

It was a lot like administering a psychological test. First you'd check to see if the basic language was there—the Beatles, the Stones, and the British Invasion bands; Motown and Stax; the San Francisco groups; Dylan. After that, you'd probe special interests for signs of sophistication or character flaws. For instance, a passion for a perfectly acceptable but lightweight group like Steppenwolf showed a certain genial rebelliousness but suggested a lack of depth; a girl who listened to a lot of Joni Mitchell could probably be talked into bed but you might regret it later; a single-minded focus on the Grateful Dead and the New Riders of the Purple Sage was a sure sign of a heavy dope smoker; anyone with a record collection that traced the blues further back than John Mayall and the Yardbirds was an intellectual. It was, I recall, a remarkably accurate system.

Nearly twenty-five years later, after spending much of that time as a music business reporter, I'm not sure that secret language still exists. The question—at least to someone my age—is no longer "Will rock and roll change the world?" but "How did the world change rock and roll?"

Rock went through a dramatic transformation in the mid-sixties. The folk-rock movement brought a new artistic, social, and political intention to the music that early rockers did not have. Chuck Berry, Little Richard, Elvis Presley, Jerry Lee Lewis—all were extraordinary and inventive performers, but they aspired to show business careers, not to creating lasting art. The same is true of the early Beatles, and it was folk artists—and Bob Dylan in particular—who changed the music's parameters and aspirations to include a quest for legitimacy, values, and authenticity—specifically an interest in populist folk forms and populist politics of the left. Folk was entertainment, but there was a real and right way to play it. "It was *musicology,*" Peter Wolf of the J. Geils Band remarked to me in recalling the spirit that infused the coffeehouse scene. That distinction set folk apart from what many of its fans viewed dimly as the junk culture entertainment that post–World War II consumer society produced solely for the sake of being sold. Considering the increasing rejection of those values in the early sixties, it's not surprising that folk found a new resonance, especially on college campuses, that led to the "folk boom" of that period. When Dylan and others created folk-rock, those aspirations were transferred to electric music, and the results proved far more popular and profound for the mass culture than folk had ever been. The most influential rock albums of the later part of the sixties were made by people who took themselves quite seriously—as did their listeners.

Just a few decades ago rock was tied to a counterculture professing to be so firmly against commercial and social conventions that the notion of a "rock and roll business" seemed an oxymoron. In 1962, the year before the Beatles' debut, the $500 million record business shunned rock music—"It smells but it sells" was the guilty refrain of those who stooped to recording and releasing rock records. With the rise of the popular rock culture in the sixties, as rock albums supplanted films and books as the most influential popular art form for young people, the mainstream entertainment industry embraced the music. At the better-run companies, the fiscal results were astounding: although largely unnoticed, the twenty-two-year history of Steve Ross's Warner Communications, Inc., reveals that the record operation was the firm's biggest, most dependable financial engine; the corporation widely considered the preeminent American media conglomerate of the age was literally fueled by rock and roll.

The entertainment industry has done more than survive its head-on collision with rock's antithetical culture—it has thrived. This year, largely on the strength of rock, the worldwide record industry will gross over $20 billion, and global media and technology giants like Time Warner, Sony, Bertelsmann, Philips Electronics, and Thorn-EMI will view rock bands as key assets. How did this happen? And what does it mean that bands accept it?

Seriousness and artistic intent were a key part of the growing appeal of the subsequent "underground" rock scene. But the success of that scene also revolutionized the music business. It's easy to forget that in the early sixties the sound track to *West Side Story* was the number one album in *Billboard* for fifty-four weeks—and that for certain rock stars today its sales figure would be considered disappointing. That commercial revolution had a huge and not necessarily positive effect on rock music. It bred financial opportunities for artists and a certain professionalism that has proven to be at odds with a quest for authenticity. I have nothing against commercial success, it's just not an artistic goal in and of itself. What I find most troubling is that the scope and reach of the business often make it impossible to tell what is done for art and what is done for commerce—which calls into question the music's current ability to convey the artistic intent that made it so appealing and different to begin with. And, if the acquisition of wealth and influence is rock's ultimate meaning, then the most meaningful figure it has produced is the billionaire mogul David Geffen. Indeed, it's more than ironic that Geffen's appreciation of the dollars-and-cents value of the music has placed him in a position to exert a greater influence and power over society and politics than the artists—it may be the measure of a profound failure by the musicians and their fans. Geffen is a visionary businessman and a generous philanthropist, but I never sat around the shack behind the kitchen when I was sixteen trying to divine the secret language of business, and I don't know anyone else who did. I wasn't looking for the mansion on the hill, and I didn't think rock and roll was, either.

Perhaps it is my own professional cynicism, but after years of covering the music business as a reporter, it is hard for me to believe that many of the performers who stake a claim to that old folk ethos—making music with conscience and meaning—are as interested in that message as they are in what it does for their careers as messengers. When Bob Dylan mounted the Rolling Thunder Revue in 1975, nothing about it suggested that it was a business or career move or, indeed, that it was anything other than an artist attempting to reconnect with his roots. I had a completely different reaction when Bruce Springsteen evinced a sudden interest in the plight of Vietnam veterans at precisely the moment that he was making a frank bid for commercial superstardom. Springsteen has given his time and attention to many charities and worthy causes, including Amnesty International, the antinuclear movement, and food banks, but—like it or not—his career has benefited from those associations at least as much as the causes themselves.

The point is not that Bruce Springsteen is a big phony and Bob Dylan has pure thoughts—I don't think that of Springsteen, and God knows I've read enough interviews with Dylan to conclude he'd prefer I have no idea what his thoughts are beyond what he puts in his songs. This book is about the relationship between the music and the business, and I believe that I could have made the same points by writing about the Rolling Stones or U2 or any number of performers. But I've elected to examine Springsteen for several reasons. The first is that his work and success are worth examining, both on their own and for what they say about a time in which the lines between art and commerce, altruism and self-interest, have been obscured. The second is that while I like and am moved by much of his work, the claims that have been made for him—particularly by people with a personal interest in his career—are extravagant and perhaps purposefully misleading. And the third reason is my fascination with his manager, Jon Landau, whom I find even more interesting than his client.

Prior to becoming a record producer and manager, Landau was one of rock's earliest and most successful professional music critics. He was also, in my estimation, the most brilliant. When I got to know him in the course of preparing a magazine story, I found him without doubt one of the brightest people in the music industry—and one of the most unapologetically mercenary. He enjoys business and making money at least as much as he likes music and brings the same keen eye to those endeavors. He has been instrumental in Bruce Springsteen's success: both the records he coproduced, beginning with *Born to Run,* and Springsteen's career since he became manager in 1978 are significantly different from what came before. I don't think anyone, including Springsteen himself, would argue that he would have had the same career or done the same work without Landau. Wanting to write about where art and business intersect in rock, I couldn't find a better subject than Jon Landau.

I believe it is possible to both achieve commercial success and rise above it, but that it requires an absolute faith and focus in the intrinsic value of the work itself rather than smart career moves. Over the years, I've developed a growing appreciation in this regard for the work of Neil Young, who I believe started out to be rich and famous and ultimately decided he'd rather be an artist. Young is as self-indulgent as any rock star, and the quality of his work has been uneven. But time and again he has been willing to fail in public—and that is not the mark of someone who is thinking only about his career. I also suspect he is the most admired artist among his peers: his influence is apparent on an extraordinarily broad range of musicians, including the singer/songwriters of the seventies, the country rock movement, such noise devotees as John Lydon and Bob Mould, and the Seattle bands of the nineties, such as Nirvana and Pearl Jam. That's my idea of success.

This book's title is partly a reference to three different songs: the Hank Williams ballad quoted above, as well as subsequent reworkings of the image by Springsteen and Young. Springsteen's composition, which appears on *Nebraska*, is certainly not one of his best; the lyrics borrow liberally from Williams's yet don't tally up quite the same way. There is, by contrast, a romance and grandeur to Young's "Mansion on the Hill" that is wholly original. His mansion is not an isolated house of privilege he pretends he doesn't live in but an idealized vision of the power of rock.

"In my own moments of greatest need," Jon Landau wrote after seeing Bruce Springsteen play in 1974, "I never give up the search for sounds that can answer every impulse, consume all emotion, cleanse and purify—all things that we have no right to expect from even the greatest works of art but which we can occasionally derive from them." I agree with that sentiment. But working as a reporter I began to wonder if my generation had done it more than lip service. The questions that would form the basis for this book were crystallized by a remark I heard while covering the Rock and Roll Hall of Fame induction dinner at the Waldorf-Astoria in 1988.

Perhaps the locale or the fact that it was a formal, industry-only affair made it particularly difficult to discern any difference between the diners who called themselves artists and the ones who called themselves businessmen, but I was struck that night by the way everyone was drinking and mingling easily and by the idea that what they really shared was a common bond of privilege. Money certainly wasn't an issue: a table for eight cost $10,000, and there was tight security to keep the public out. The roster of inductees who were on hand to acknowledge the accolade and entertain the crowd included such seminal rock performers as the Beach Boys, the Drifters, the Supremes, Bob Dylan, and Ringo Starr and George Harrison. Also inducted for his profound pre–rock and roll influence on popular music was folksinger Woody Guthrie. By tapping Guthrie, the Hall was both paying tribute to and basking in the reflection of the best and purest part of itself: music having nothing to do with making money and everything to do with integrity and simplicity, delivered without pretension or ulterior motive in the sole hope of uplifting any who might hear it. To accept the honor, the Hall had invited Woody's son, Arlo Guthrie.

It had been twenty years since the Vietnam War, the underground, and Woodstock had made Arlo a popular performer in his own right. No longer a star for Warner/Reprise Records, his relative lack of status and fame among such a financially successful crowd was palpable. Times, of course, had changed, and he had dealt with that by continuing to perform steadily, often with Pete Seeger, and by championing ecological and antinuclear causes. Stepping to the Waldorf podium to acknowledge his father's enshrinement in the Hall, the gray-haired songwriter looked out on the tuxedoed crowd that claimed Woody Guthrie as its own.

"I don't know where Woody would be tonight if he were alive," Arlo said with a small grin when the applause died down. "But I can guarantee you he wouldn't be here."

BOOK ONE

The

American Revolution

Exultation is the going
Of an inland soul to sea,

Past the houses—
Past the headlands—Into deep Eternity—

Bred as we, among the mountains,
Can the sailor understand
The divine intoxication
Of the first league out from land?

—Emily Dickinson

CAMBRIDGE
AND THE
BATTLE OF NEWPORT

PAUL ROTHCHILD WASN'T THINKING ABOUT BUSINESS WHEN HE WAN-
dered into Club 47 in Cambridge one night in 1962. A salesman for a
local record distributor, he'd been hearing about Club 47 and some of
the other small coffeehouses sprouting up around Harvard Square.
For fifty cents you could buy a mug of coffee and hang out all night
talking, reading, playing chess, or listening to the students who
brought along their guitars and banjos. Rothchild didn't know much
about folk music—he was a jazz and classical buff—but it sounded like
a nice way to kill an evening.

The group playing that night, the Charles River Valley Boys, was
the first bluegrass band Rothchild had ever heard, and something
about the music and the scene really grabbed him. Introducing himself to the band after the set, he said he wanted to sell their records
and was surprised to learn they hadn't made any. The next night he
heard the band again and offered to make the record himself.

Like the musicians, Rothchild was barely better than an amateur.
He jotted down the items he thought should be included in a contract
and—unaware that there wasn't any recording business to speak of in
Boston—went looking for a studio in the Yellow Pages. He found just

two. The first was limited to voiceovers for commercials, and the other was run by Steve Fassett, a hobbyist operating out of his mother's basement. That wouldn't do either, but Fassett obtained the use of a Harvard University library for two Sundays and improvised a control booth in a coatroom there. When folk fans around Cambridge quickly snapped up all one thousand copies of the Charles River Valley Boys' album, Rothchild began recording other Club 47 performers.

Making records by local coffeehouse musicians was a new wrinkle and an indication of just how popular the scene was becoming. When Cambridge's first coffeehouse, Tulla's Coffee Grinder, opened five years earlier, music hadn't even been on the menu. It was just a cheap, homey place to hang out. But with none of the Cambridge bars offering live music, or even encouraging students and other campus types to drink there, Tulla's became home to a small group of folk enthusiasts and would-be players who brought their instruments and took to trading songs. The following year, when Club 47 debuted a few blocks from Tulla's at 47 Mt. Auburn Street, it quickly developed into a showcase for local folk performers, particularly Joan Baez, an eighteen-year-old Boston University coed soon to become Cambridge's first nationally recognized folk singer. Other coffeehouses opened, and while the "open microphone" and "hootenanny" nights featuring local enthusiasts remained a mainstay of the clubs, the scene's popularity—and its rapidly rising level of musicianship—was soon reflected in regular appearances by established folk and blues artists like Theodore Bikel and Sonny Terry and Brownie McGhee, who were finding a new national audience as a result of what was being called "the folk revival."

Still, the Boston scene was small and rabidly anticommercial, due in large measure to folk's history. Earlier American folk artists like Woody Guthrie had achieved some commercial success, but fame and fortune was not their goal. It was, rather, to celebrate and express the struggles of plain people through plain songs. Folk's respect for popular and traditional forms was part and parcel of a similar respect for the struggles of the labor movement and populist politics of the left. By the late fifties, that approach and message held a growing appeal and veracity for many young intellectuals and middle-class college students who were increasingly uneasy with the country's postwar consumer society. Folk music was entertainment, but it was also serious stuff with legitimate American roots. For young enthusiasts like the Charles River Valley Boys, playing was fun, but folk was also a scholarly search for values and authenticity. It had to be treated with respect for its pedigree and aspirations—played the "real" and "right" way. But neither the scene nor Rothchild's modest success went unnoticed by a handful of players on the fringe of the commercial record business. Bob Weinstock, the owner of Prestige Records in New York, was willing to try folk or blues because there was a ready market and the records were cheap to make. For $135 a week, Rothchild became the label's one-man folk department.

Within six months he'd recorded thirteen albums, signing such Boston talent as Geoff Muldaur and Tom Rush. And they weren't just revivalists. As the scene came into its own, the young performers were making a natural leap from playing classic folk songs about coal mining, union struggles, and the dust bowl to writing new, topical songs about the civil rights movement and the cold war. Ironically, record companies found Boston particularly attractive precisely because folk enthusiasts viewed it as existing beyond the influence of Tin Pan Alley and the machinations of the music business. "Boston was a spawning ground and a trendsetter," says Jac Holzman, the founder of Elektra Records. "Something happening organically out of Boston was better than something out of New York. People always suspected that anything coming out of New York had some kind of manufactured zeal behind it." Ethos, it seemed, sold.

Holzman, who had started Elektra a few years earlier with $600 of bar mitzvah money, could truthfully call himself a folk fan. But he was also a businessman and would release just about any record to make a buck. Elektra's early albums included such ingenious gambits as *Wild Blue Yonder*, a collection of drinking songs popular in American air force officers' clubs in Japan, and a Morse code instruction course that allowed students to increase the speed from thirty-three to forty-five as their skills improved. Like Prestige, Elektra saw folk music as a cheap bet. "I loved classical music," says Holzman, "but it was too expensive and too competitive. Somebody else could do a recording of the same work. Whereas if I recorded Jean Ritchie and the songs of the Kentucky Mountain Family, I had a unique one. Plus, I could do it in the artists' homes and it was very inexpensive and a lot of fun. The record costs were never more than the cost of the tape. And that was it. I didn't pay an advance for the first six years I made records. And even then it was only one hundred dollars." Holzman hired Rothchild away from Prestige and gave him the freedom to sign any folk singer who could sell five thousand albums, which was Elektra's break-even point.

Just two years after Rothchild wandered into Club 47, he and Boston were in the forefront of a burgeoning commercial market for folk records. But unlike the pop and rock and roll markets, which relied on 45 rpm singles, it was based on selling albums. Part of the reason was that there was simply no outlet for 45s by folkies. The music's association with civil rights, labor, and the American left didn't invite commercial radio play, and *Variety* perfectly captured the mainstream entertainment industry's attitude when it wrote derisively of "folkniks." The rare exceptions were acts like Peter, Paul and Mary, who were built to commercial specification by their manager, or ultra-collegiate faux folk acts like the Kingston Trio and the Brothers Four. But folk itself had always favored the LP. During the fifties, Folkways and other traditional folk labels found the new format more appropriate for preserving and cataloging songs, performers, and styles, while its packaging allowed for extensive notes and commentary. In the early sixties, as the folk movement evolved to include a new generation of young songwriters and performers intent on extending rather than preserving the folk tradition, they gravitated naturally to the more serious LP.

Commercial radio looked down on folk, but the feeling was definitely mutual. In Boston, real folkies viewed Top 40 radio station WRKO and its teenybopper disc jockeys like Arnie "Woo Woo" Ginsberg with disdain. Although it was clear that many of the new British Invasion bands, including the Rolling Stones and the Animals, were fans of the same American bluesmen like Howlin' Wolf and John Lee Hooker, whom young folk fans were discovering on the revival circuit, few in the folk camp could see an affinity between Cambridge's intellectualism and the rock records spun by a disc jockey like "Woo Woo."

There were, however, glimpses of one. Harvard student and aspiring record producer Joe Boyd returned from England in 1964 excited about a rock band he'd seen in a pub in Birmingham, the Spencer Davis Group. It featured a fifteen-year-old organ player named Stevie Winwood and performed versions of Leadbelly songs. Boyd collared

Rothchild: Did he think there could be something called folk-rock? Rothchild said he'd already heard it at the Night Owl in Greenwich Village, where young folkies and jug band musicians like Jim McGuinn were starting to play electric instruments. Although McGuinn had been booed offstage for playing Beatles songs, Paul certainly believed something like this could work, and he and Boyd wrote up a list of their ideal group on the back of an envelope. It included harmonica player John Sebastian, guitarists Jesse Colin Young and Zal Yanovsky, and drummer Skip Butler. Although the band never came together— "too many jealousies," recalls Boyd, "they wouldn't come to rehearsals"—Sebastian and Yanovsky would soon form one of the most important and successful early folk-rock bands, the Lovin' Spoonful, and Young would go on to lead the Youngbloods. Others, like folksingers Richard and Mimi Fariña, were making records that also anticipated a mixing of folk and rock, but it would take another band that Rothchild signed to Elektra to tear down the walls between the rock and folk camps. On a trip to Chicago, Boyd had run into blues scholar Samuel Charters, who urged him to see "the best new blues band in Chicago."

"Sam, don't one-up me," replied Boyd. "I know about Buddy Guy, I know about Junior Wells, I know about Howlin' Wolf . . ."

"I'm not talking about them," replied Charters. "I'm talking about a white mixed blues band."

The best new blues band in Chicago turned out to be the Butterfield Blues Band, and it was an unusual amalgam of talent. The young white harmonica player Paul Butterfield wasn't just another college kid hanging around the blues clubs, he was a stone-cold fanatic who'd apprenticed with some of the world's greatest blues musicians, and his five-piece band featured two former members of Howlin' Wolf's group, bassist Jerome Arnold and drummer Sam Lay. Rothchild, who came out to Chicago to hear the band at Boyd's urging and immediately signed them, convinced Butterfield to add another young white Chicago guitarist, Michael Bloomfield, to handle the slide parts. Elektra arranged for the band to play a workshop at the 1965 Newport Folk Festival in Newport, Rhode Island, and the opening salvo was launched in folk music's about-to-be-declared civil war.

The ultimate bastion of folk purity, the festival was structured as a nonprofit foundation, and its board of directors included musicologist

Alan Lomax and performers Pete Seeger, Theodore Bikel, and Peter Yarrow. "The board was interested in the great and good of the folk movement," says Boyd, who became the festival's production manager. "Everybody played for scale: fifty dollars a day. Bob Dylan did it for the same money as the prisoners from a Texas chain gang."

In 1963, the festival received a huge boost from the twenty-two-year-old Dylan. He appeared with Peter, Paul and Mary, sang with Joan Baez, took part in Pete Seeger's workshop on topical songs and new songwriters, and performed a featured set that was greeted with near reverence. The Newport Folk Festival—which had struggled from its inception in 1959—was finally a hit, the folk movement was reinvigorated, and Bob Dylan was the shining star of both.

Just two years later, however, cracks were beginning to appear in the movement's foundation. In June of 1965, two months before the festival, Dylan had released an electric single, "Like a Rolling Stone." The notion that the artistic and social intentions of folk could be expressed through a blatantly commercial medium like rock and roll horrified folk's old guard. "There were lots of battles at that time about what a folk song was," recalls Peter Yarrow. "Whether urban singers like Peter, Paul and Mary were emasculating music. Whether we were too homogenized; who had the right to call themselves a folksinger. The battles about definition were fast and furious. In the midst of this there was a division between amplified instruments and acoustic. And that was a real line." The scene was set for a showdown. "This was the last outpost," says organist Barry Goldberg, who came from Chicago to perform with Butterfield at the '65 festival, "and the feeling was that the barbarians were at the gate." Introducing Butterfield's band, festival director Alan Lomax offered up a long-winded and snide rant to the effect that in his day *real* bluesmen didn't need a bunch of fancy electric hardware. Rising to the bait, Albert Grossman, who managed Dylan, Peter, Paul and Mary, and Butterfield, accosted Lomax as he came offstage. In an instant, the two men were rolling around in the dust, trading wild punches.

Butterfield's performance was just the excuse for a fight that had been waiting to happen. "There was a clear generational and cultural gap widening as the weekend went on," says Boyd. "The year before, Dylan had been the pied piper in blue jeans. This year he was in a puffed polka-dotted dueling shirt and there were rumors that they were smoking dope. The old guard—Seeger, Lomax, Bikel—were very upset. They had gotten to the point of having all their dreams come true two years before . . . having this gigantic mass movement of politically active kids. And suddenly they could see it all slipping away in a haze of marijuana smoke and self-indulgence. As far as they were concerned, Grossman was the money changer at the gates of the temple."

The fisticuffs would prove just the undercard for the festival's main bout. The next afternoon an obviously nervous Dylan took the stage with an electric guitar and band. Pummeled by the opening chords of "Maggie's Farm," the audience was struck dumb. "There was almost no sound," remembers Yarrow. "Then after the interminable two or three seconds, there were boos and whistles. Overwhelmingly, people were in shock."

Onstage, Barry Goldberg could hear both cheers and boos. Backstage, the world was coming to an end. "Goddamnit, it's terrible!" shouted Pete Seeger. "You can't understand the words! If I had an ax I'd cut the cable right now!"

Seeger, Lomax, and Bikel grabbed Boyd. "You've got to get the sound down!" they yelled. "It's far too loud!" Dashing to the mixing board where Yarrow and Rothchild were stationed, Boyd relayed the message. No one budged.

After three songs, Dylan walked off to continuing boos. "People were just horrified," says Yarrow, who, despite refusing to interfere with Dylan's music, sympathized with the crowd. "It was as if it was a capitulation to the enemy—as if all of a sudden you saw Martin Luther King, Jr., doing a cigarette ad. It was unimaginable that of all people this poet would abandon the touchy-feely intimacy of the music."

Dylan was badly shaken, but Yarrow and festival promoter George Wein convinced him to mollify the crowd by going back onstage with an acoustic guitar and playing two songs. But there was no turning back, and it was soon obvious that the inability of folk's old guard to accept the validity of the electric music would cost them. The following week Butterfield received an unheard-of $100 a night to play Club 47—an amount that forced club manager Jim Rooney to clear the coffeehouse after each set like a standard nightclub rather than allow people to loiter all night over a fifty-cent mug of coffee. The Cambridge folk scene was dead.

FEW WHO WITNESSED THE FOLK MOVEMENT'S SELF-IMMOLATION IN THE
summer of 1965 were able to see in it the birth of a new rock music
business. But over the next two years, some of Boston's more prescient
fans would measure the business ramifications of what the vast majority of devotees simply viewed as an exploding music scene. None
would do so with the intelligence, eagerness, and ultimate success of
Jon Landau, a history major at Brandeis University.

A music fanatic, Landau had grown up in the Boston suburb of Lexington; he loved the early rock and roll of Chuck Berry and Little
Richard and had pursued his passion throughout high school, playing
guitar in folk and rock bands. If there was a rock concert in the Boston
area—whether it was the Animals at Rindge Tech, Mitch Ryder and
the Detroit Wheels at Walpole Skating Rink, the Beatles at Suffolk
Downs, the Rolling Stones at the Lynn High School football field, or
just about anyone else at a host of equally unlikely venues—Jon Landau was there.

If rock and folk were important to many of Boston's other students,
Landau's interest could only be called obsessive. While his classmates
wrestled with the challenge of staying in school, he practiced banjo
and guitar five hours a day, prowled the coffeehouses and performed
at Club 47's open-mike hootenannies in the evenings, and still
achieved honors in history. Any remaining free time was spent listening to records—some of which, like those of Otis Redding—could
reduce him to tears.

His intelligence and passion were formidable and arresting, but it
was his pragmatism and sharply honed feel for opportunity that made
Landau a commanding presence. Just nineteen, he spoke with an authority tinged with arrogance and seemed a good deal older and more
worldly than his peers, who wondered how he could be so different
from them. Although his collar-length hair was cut with the straight
bangs worn by his favorite group, the Rolling Stones, he was clearly
not one of the guys. During school vacations he worked as a sales clerk
at Briggs & Briggs, the landmark music store in Harvard Square,
where he enjoyed arguing the merits and shortcomings of new rock
records with the shop's student clientele. His most spirited debates
were with Paul Williams, whose passion for music matched his own.

But unlike Landau, there was little about Williams that was pragmatic. He was an idealist.

Like many of the friends he grew up with in Cambridge, Williams had been a folkie. But as a seventeen-year-old freshman at Swarthmore College he had been consumed by the debate between the folk and rock camps. There *was* something of substance in rock and roll, he decided. Who could match the cultural impact of the Beatles? Was there an artist in any other medium whose influence was as complete as the one the now electric Dylan was having on Williams and his friends? An aspiring writer, Paul saw those issues as something deserving of real critical commentary, and he knew they weren't addressed by teen-oriented rock fanzines and pinup magazines like *16* or *Tigerbeat*. During the Christmas break of '65, Williams had commandeered a friend's mimeograph machine to print four hundred copies of a five-page rock and roll magazine he dubbed *Crawdaddy!*, for the Crawdaddy Club in London, where the Rolling Stones and the Yardbirds had gotten their start. Feeling his way, Williams spent most of the magazine reviewing singles, imitating trade magazines like *Billboard* and *Cash Box,* and trying to predict which records would become hits. But he took special care to send copies of the magazine to important record companies, and, in return, several of them sent him records. Williams knew he was on to something when a review of Simon and Garfunkel's *Sounds of Silence* produced a call from Paul Simon, who lauded him for publishing "the first serious thing that's been written about what we're doing." When Bob Dylan came to Philadelphia for two concerts just as Williams was putting out the second issue, the young publisher sent a few copies of his magazine to the theater, asking for tickets and an interview. To Williams's surprise, Dylan called his dormitory and invited him to hang out backstage. When the Blues Project came down from New York to play at Swarthmore a few weeks later, the band's keyboardist, Al Kooper, told Williams, "I heard all about you from Bob Dylan."

Paul worked up an edition to hawk at the 1966 Newport Folk Festival that led with an enthusiastic review of Dylan's new electric LP, *Blonde on Blonde,* making it clear where he stood in the now raging battle between folk and rock that had all but destroyed the festival the preceding summer. In addition to selling all the copies, Williams landed his first piece of record company advertising from Jac

Holzman and Elektra Records. Now more confident that he could keep *Crawdaddy!* going, he made the rounds of Boston's magazine stands, coffeehouses, record shops, and student hangouts, looking for places to sell his publication. He made a special point of stopping at Briggs & Briggs.

Sure, Landau said, Williams could leave a stack of his homemade twenty-five-cent music magazines on the counter. But he had an idea that could *really* help *Crawdaddy!* "I can do better than this stuff," Landau said. "Why don't you give me something to do?" Williams, who was now convinced of the viability of *Crawdaddy!* but still unsure what a "serious" rock and roll magazine should be, was more than happy to have the razor-sharp Landau on board.

"When I started people would say to me, 'How can you write about rock and roll?' " Williams recalls. "Taking it seriously, wanting others to take it seriously, the idea was 'Here's something that a whole lot of people have in common, that they're really passionate about. By talking about what we have in common, we really form a link here.' That was the crusade."

Landau debuted in *Crawdaddy!* #5, published in September of '66, with reviews of albums by several well-known bands, including the Byrds, the Young Rascals, and Mitch Ryder and the Detroit Wheels. But, more significantly, Landau used his new platform to promote his favorite local band, a Boston quartet named Barry and the Remains.

Despite appearing as the opening act on the Beatles' final American tour, the band never succeeded outside of New England. Yet the Remains were a huge influence on other Boston bands, and lead guitarist Barry Tashian a role model for many aspiring local musicians including Landau. The Remains mixed original songs—most of which emulated the current crop of British Invasion bands—with a healthy dose of blues covers, Chuck Berry songs, and party staples like "Louie Louie" and "Walkin' the Dog." But what set the band apart was its attitude. "There were a lot of other bands around Boston," says Tashian, "but they were the older-style groups that all dressed alike. They were very straight, more traditional show bands." The Remains were also louder than other bands—*much* louder. Those differences made the Remains Boston's first "underground" rock band, and a huge influence on the local groups who followed.

Tashian was an outstanding musician who had found remarkable early success. By the time he was in the eighth grade, he had appeared on *American Bandstand* as part of a group called the Ramblers, and he later cut an album with his high school band, the Schemers. But Tashian's parents were against him turning professional, and he enrolled at Boston University in a vain attempt to think about doing something else. He wasn't distracted for long.

At the end of his freshman year, Barry and a roommate took a school-sponsored charter flight to London and went looking for a little adventure. "We had a car and just drove all over Europe," Tashian recalls. "Mostly looking for girls." Tashian's most lasting impression, however, was provided by a band in London. Stoned, Tashian wandered into a club in Earl's Court, where an unlikely group of musicians were playing electric blues. "The drummer was from South Africa, the singer was Algerian, and the lead guitarist was a Londoner," he recalls. "I can't even remember their name. But they were playing 'Got My Mojo Working,' stuff like that. Maybe the fact that I was high had something to do with it, but I realized I'd never *heard* it this way before. When I got back from Europe, I said, 'Hey, I want to start a band.' "

That fall, along with bassist Vern Miller and drummer Chip Damiani, Billy Briggs, a friend and piano player from Westport, Connecticut, joined Tashian at BU and formed Barry and the Remains. Rehearsing in the cellar of their dormitory, the group began playing parties before settling into a regular Wednesday-night gig at the Rathskeller, a previously mothballed cellar in Kenmore Square. The response was immediate. "We were filling it up every time we played," says Tashian.

He dropped out of school, and the band cut a single, "Why Do I Cry," on a local label, that rose to number three in the Boston pop market. With help from a high school friend of Tashian's at Boston University, Don Law, the group landed a recording contract with Columbia's sister label, Epic Records. Law's father, Don Law, Sr., was an influential producer at Columbia who had not only recorded blues legend Robert Johnson and such seminal country performers as Flatt and Scruggs, Gene Autry, and Marty Robbins, but had been instrumental in making Columbia the first major label with its own recording studio on Nashville's Music Row. When his son told him there was a rock and roll band worth hearing up at school, the executive dispatched a young staff producer to Boston to hear and sign the

Remains. Don Law, Jr., also introduced them to a booking agent, John Sdoucos, who had tried unsuccessfully to rent Symphony Hall for jazz and folk concerts. He had found such stiff resistance from the city's established venues that even Joan Baez—her Boston roots and *Time* cover notwithstanding—was unacceptable to the hall's staid directors. As Sdoucos recalled, the chief objection was that Baez liked to take her sandals off when she played. " 'We can't have her—she's got dirty feet!' " Sdoucos recalls being told. "There was always a little hook as to why they didn't want to do something."

Sdoucos was looking for other outlets when he learned about the large cultural-activities budgets of the area's colleges. "The schools had *tremendous* budgets," he recalls. "The University of Massachusetts had eighty to one hundred grand. I said, 'Hey, can we do groups like the Coasters, the Drifters, Hank Ballard and the Midnighters?' "

It was on one of Sdoucos's subsequent college packages at Brandeis University in 1964 that Landau first saw—and flipped for—Barry and the Remains. "The Remains just did the jukebox records, but they did them so good that you couldn't believe it," he said. "They would do the Rolling Stones better than the Stones." After seeing them, Landau abandoned his attempts to play at the coffeehouse hootenanny nights, bought an electric guitar, and started his own rock band. Dubbing the group Jellyroll,* he drafted his college roommate as manager. And, emulating the Remains, he tracked down Sdoucos.

On a Saturday afternoon in January, Landau ventured over to a club in Somerville where the Remains were rehearsing. When the group took a break Jon played some recently cut Jellyroll demos for Sdoucos. After listening to Jellyroll's version of Chuck Berry's "You Can't Catch Me," Tashian began to demonstrate a few possible improvements—and the rest of the Remains soon launched into an impromptu version of the song that wiped out Jellyroll's demo. "All four of them went through what was by far the best version of the song I'd ever heard," admitted Landau. Sdoucos had his doubts about Jellyroll, but he was impressed by Landau's intensity.

The news of the Remains' impending recording date for Epic also caught Landau's attention, as did Don Law's role in arranging it. Impressed with Law's obvious power to make rock and roll dreams

*A salacious slang expression lifted off old blues recordings.

come true, Jon struck up a friendship with him. The relationship was a natural. "Don was never a young guy," says a writer who knew both men. "Nor was Jon." Let others herald a new Aquarian Age or some other hippie hash dream, Law and Landau had their eyes on something else.

"They both had an ambition to be successful in the music business, and they accepted it on its own terms," says Robert Somma, who wrote for *Crawdaddy!* "And you could smell it on them. Don was a no-nonsense guy, and his ambitions were quite broad. Jon was exactly the same. He had vast musical knowledge, but he was indifferent to it other than insofar as it could assist him in advancing in the commercial side of the business—and there were *not* a lot of guys around like that. They knew what they wanted, they understood the scene, they were familiar with business, they were adept at it. And to their credit, they were very much no bullshit. Jon would tell you in a second. He had a mercenary streak in him even then, and he was not ashamed of it."

Landau wasn't the only aspiring rock and roller drawn to Sdoucos and Law by their association with the Remains. They represented several other local groups, including the Hallucinations, a rock and blues band composed of art students from the Boston Museum School. Landau and his friend, Hallucinations' singer Peter Blankfield, not only shared a passion for rock and roll but also had similar upbringings and interests in the quickening civil rights movement. If anything, Blankfield's musical tastes were even more omnivorous than Landau's: his baptism into live rock and roll came via disc jockey Alan Freed's Bronx Paradise Theater shows, and with a convert's fervor he sought out every preacher of his new church, whether it was Elvis Presley, Bo Diddley, Bobby Darin, Frankie Lymon, or the street-corner doo-wop of groups like Nolan Strong and the Diablos. Nor did he stop with rock or rhythm and blues: Birdland, the jazz club off Times Square, maintained a roped-off "milk bar" for underage listeners, where Peter heard Dinah Washington, Cannonball Adderley, and Art Blakey and the Jazz Messengers. In the Village he discovered numerous folk clubs and Charles Mingus and Thelonious Monk alternating at the Five Spot.

It was while listening to folksinger Cynthia Gooding's Sunday show on WBAI, "Folk Singer's Choice," that Peter first heard Bob Dylan perform. "Bobby played 'Bo Diddley' and this song and that song," he recalled. "Talking about how he's a drifter and been working in the circus. When the show was over, I called the station and said, 'Gee, this guy was great.' Well, why don't we put you on the phone with him? So Dylan says, 'Yeah, man, I'm living over on Eighth Street. You know where Nedick's is?' Yeah! And that fucking day I was down there knocking on the door to see this guy that I thought was really cool."

Like thousands of others Blankfield became convinced that Dylan had the answers he was looking for. If only he could find the right way to ask the questions. "One time he was sitting at O. Henry's steak house reading the newspaper," Peter says. "I'm walking down the street and I see him and he sees me coming and tries to hide behind the newspaper because he knows I'm the kid who's gonna ask him a million questions. This is very embarrassing, but I was trying to ask him very high philosophical questions. Life and meaningful things. Looking back, I can see what a real pain in the ass I must have been. And Dylan is saying to me, 'Y'see that lamppost over there? How do you know it's over there? Man, you don't know *nuthin'*. You don't know *shit* about nuthin'. How am I supposed to tell you if you don't know nuthin'? Whaddaya comin' to me for?' "

If Blankfield was one of the first to discover that his new idol was more misanthrope than messiah, hearing Dylan nonetheless made the young painter question the direction he'd chosen. "One night at the Gaslight Dylan came in and said, 'Hey, man, I just wrote this song,' " Peter recalls. "And he put out these pieces of looseleaf paper ripped out of a spiral notebook. And he starts singing 'Oh, where have you been my blue-eyed son . . .'* And man, if I thought my mind was blown then! This was the first time I'd ever heard a song like that. He finished singing it, and no one could say anything. The length of it, the episodic sense of it. Every line kept building and bursting. The images! I was a real dedicated painter, but somehow music was starting to take hold."

When he heard a group of painters playing rock and blues one night at a party, he was finally forced to make a choice. "I was smashed, and I got up to this microphone to sing—or attempt to— and man, something just got hooked," Peter says. "The next day these guys had a rehearsal, and I came. And from that moment on, I never painted. It became so obsessive I had to leave the Museum School."

---

*The opening line to "A Hard Rain's A-Gonna Fall."

The Hallucinations got their first gig playing a homecoming at Windham College in Vermont. "We knew three songs," admits Blank-field, who was now calling himself Peter Wolf. "We played the longest, 'What'd I Say,' but people danced and, hey, we pulled it off. And we got paid. *PAID!* Three hundred and fifty dollars! And that was like—holy motherfucker!—to just play!"

Still, the Hallucinations were a young group with only a stumbling knowledge of what they should be doing to sound good. Like Landau, Wolf looked to the Remains as a musical model. When Barry Tashian first heard Peter's band, the advice he offered was even more humbling than the demonstration he and the Remains had given Landau.

"Barry played me the Otis Redding record 'Pain in My Heart,' and he said, 'Pete, listen to this—did you hear that thing at the beginning going dum-dum-doom-dum? That's a bass guitar. You need one of those for your band. I recommend getting rid of the tambourine player and getting one of these guys.' I said, 'Oh yeah? Bass guitar? We need one of those? Okay.' We just didn't know."

●

IN THE END, JELLYROLL PROVED A FALSE START FOR LANDAU. BEING IN A band required an ability to cede control that he just didn't have. When Don Law later sent Jellyroll's demos to his father and arranged a Columbia audition for Landau, Jon discovered to his horror that he didn't have the confidence to go through with it. Instead, he gave his attention completely to writing about music.

When Landau debuted in *Crawdaddy!* it was immediately apparent that his knowledge of music, combined with his intelligence and ambition, could forge a singular critical voice that set him apart. Almost from the first, Landau was able to express himself in print with the same forcefulness and brio that tended to overwhelm peers in conversation. Landau could be pedantic, melodramatic, or just plain awkward as a stylist, but his critical judgments were usually correct. Unlike many of the other *Crawdaddy!* contributors, he wasn't just preaching the gospel of the World According to Rock and Roll. As a rule, Landau never brought an overtly political slant to his writing about rock music, seeking to illuminate the meaning of the music rather than embroider it. Over time he would even come to argue that it was a mistake for rock to view itself as an art form.

Instead, he sought to develop a consistent critical aesthetic. His arguments regarding the merits or shortcomings of a particular band or record were based on logic and specific musical examples rather than dogma or emotion, although a positive review always transmitted the tremendous passion he felt for music. And because of his intelligence and self-assurance, it didn't matter whether he really knew as much about music as he claimed: Landau always *sounded* as if he did.

If Landau was cocky, he was shocked nonetheless the day Williams told him that several *Crawdaddy!* writers in New York had been thrown out of the Cafe Au Go Go because of a negative review that Landau had written of the Blues Project, the club's house band. Jon was a history sophomore in Boston who wrote about music once a month, yet his work was obviously being read in other places and having an effect on more and more people with each issue.

One of the people who was following Landau's writing with particular interest was Jann Wenner, a student at the University of California at Berkeley. An aspiring journalist, Wenner, in concert with his mentor, the highly respected *San Francisco Chronicle* pop and jazz critic Ralph J. Gleason, was starting a rock magazine to be called *Rolling Stone*. While he shared Williams's belief that rock and roll was worthy of serious coverage, he wasn't particularly impressed with the writing in *Crawdaddy!*—with one exception.

"There was all this kind of arcane stuff there," Wenner says dismissively. "Literary or cultural expositions. Jon was not the culture hound, but Jon knew what the music was. He was the first person who could write and also play and therefore understood the dynamics and mechanics of the music. I was trying to evolve writers and critics, and most of them came from literary, social, and cultural interests and didn't know how to write about the music as such. Jon was the first one who did."

Wenner sent Landau a letter, outlining his plans for the magazine and including a dummy of the first issue.

Landau was impressed by two things about Wenner and his project. Unlike Paul Williams, Wenner was prepared to run his magazine like a business. And he was willing to *pay* for pieces. "I got the flash that he was serious," said Landau. "I was being treated professionally."

Rolling Stone #1, published November 9, 1967, debuted with a cover story on John Lennon by Wenner. But inside, its music section was anchored by Landau's in-depth and largely unfavorable review of Jimi Hendrix's *Are You Experienced?*

Far more conservative than most other rock critics, Landau would come to evince two responses to psychedelia: indifference or hostility. His major criticism, that much of what the bands did that was "psychedelic" was musically superfluous, was in perfect harmony with the bottom-line approach Landau took in his dealings with others. And while his assessment of the music was generally borne out by time, his failure to hear beyond the flash and bombast of Hendrix and take the measure of his true originality would prove one of Landau's real critical gaffes.

Around *Rolling Stone,* Landau's antipathy toward psychedelic music and the excesses of the evolving counterculture that in San Francisco were so closely intertwined could raise hackles, including Wenner's. But their differences in tastes were of little practical consequence. Both Wenner and Landau were primarily concerned with business and success. It would be eighteen months before the two young men actually met, but they talked constantly and carried on an extensive correspondence regarding music, the business, and how the magazine should develop.

Between the covers of *Rolling Stone,* Landau continued to champion the music he loved. He wrote, as he had in *Crawdaddy!,* of two of his favorite rock groups, the Byrds and the Rolling Stones, and such high-octane soul singers as Wilson Pickett and Sam and Dave. And if the incident surrounding his review of the Blues Project for *Crawdaddy!* had given Landau his first proof that people far beyond his sphere were actually reading and responding to what he was writing, he was still unprepared for the kind of readership he had gained with *Rolling Stone.* He was in his dorm room at Brandeis one afternoon when the telephone rang.

"Jon Landau?" the woman on the other end asked. "Would you please hold for Jerry Wexler?"

Jerry Wexler! The vice president of Atlantic Records? Wexler was a legend—Jon had been seeing his name on the backs of records since he was ten years old. He had produced many of the greatest r&b and soul artists: Joe Turner, Ray Charles, T-Bone Walker, the Drifters, Solomon Burke, Wilson Pickett, Aretha Franklin. In fact, it was

Landau's glowing assessment of Franklin—and the recordings Wexler had made with her—in *Rolling Stone* #5 that prompted the call.

"Who are you?" Wexler asked as soon as he came on the line. "This article—the perceptions! Tremendous. Amazing."

Thrilled and stunned, Landau listened as Wexler said he was going to have a collection of Atlantic recordings pulled and sent to the writer. And if he ever had any questions for an article, Jon should feel free just to pick up the phone and call. Then Wexler, who had himself been a writer for *Billboard* before joining Atlantic, offered up the pièce de résistance.

"I'm really calling," he said, "because we're trying to decide between two songs for Aretha's next single. I want to play them for you over the phone and get your reaction."

Oh, man! Landau knew Wexler's request was part real, part seduction, and part Wexler's pleasure in seeing his own work as a producer praised in print. Still, even if Wexler and Atlantic had something to gain by currying his favor, the offer of assistance and a relationship was quite real. Landau already knew he wasn't going to make it as a musician—that was pretty obvious. What wasn't obvious was where writing about music could take him. If Wexler's phone call was any indication, pretty far.

2

THE
TEA PARTY

Few of the people hanging around Cambridge's evolving music scene in the mid-sixties had Jon Landau's ability to consider its potential as a business. Indeed, not many in the hothouse atmosphere of the time could bring themselves to think of music in such a cool, clear light.

Landau's rock and roll compatriot Paul Williams had no interest in following his intellectual crusade into the commercial realm. After moving *Crawdaddy!* to New York in 1968, he disassociated himself from the publication. The music was gaining widespread attention, not just from *Rolling Stone* but in the mainstream press as well, and he no longer felt the same call to a mission. Instead, he plunged headlong into the more spiritual and esoteric waters of the counterculture. He joined the Lyman Family, a commune in Boston's impoverished Fort Hill section.

Its founder and leader, Mel Lyman, was a banjo player and a member of the Kweskin Jug Band.* He had taken part in Richard Alpert and Timothy Leary's early LSD experiments at Harvard, and part of his

---

*Bandleader Jim Kweskin was also a member of the commune.

program was to administer large doses of the hallucinogen to members of the Family. In short order, the situation grew dangerously strident—Williams eventually fled the commune in the dead of night, fearing for his life. However, the Family also had a number of projects that addressed Boston's hip music community, including a brief-lived coffeehouse in a former synagogue on Berkeley Street, the Moondial. The site of a few music performances, the Moondial was primarily intended as a venue for avant-garde films, especially those by Jonas Mekas, Andy Warhol, and other members of the experimental Film-makers' Cinémathèque, whom Lyman had met in New York. To help get the project going, one of the Family members, Jesse Benton, the daughter of painter Thomas Hart Benton, turned to a thirty-two-year-old lawyer from Kansas City, Missouri, named Ray Riepen. Although an unlikely candidate to represent a charismatic drug cult, his chance association with the Lyman Family would have a far more profound and unexpected impact: he was about to become the first businessman to recognize that Boston's burgeoning rock underground represented both a major cultural shift and a new commercial market.

●

A CORPORATE LAWYER, RIEPEN HAD HANDLED CIVIL TRIALS FOR THE KANSAS City attorney's office before pursuing a master's degree at Harvard Law School. He had picked up a few clients around Boston and had helped Benton obtain a divorce. Riepen found her latest call intriguing. "She says, 'Would you help these guys out? They're gonna get a Ford grant, but they don't have any money right now,'" recalls Riepen. "I thought, 'My God, Andy Warhol—I've heard of him!' I didn't know anything about show business, but I thought it would be fun."

Riepen went to see the Moondial's landlord, and when he discovered that someone else was interested in renting the building and turning it into a dance hall, he urged his clients to let him sign a lease. But the grant money hadn't come through yet. "Being a bad lawyer, I put up my own money to sign this damn lease," says Riepen. "What did I know?" The following week he learned the Ford Foundation wasn't going to fund the project and went into a panic. "I'm a student at Harvard Law and I've got a five-thousand-square-foot synagogue in the South End."

Recalling his conversation with the landlord, Riepen decided that converting the synagogue into a ballroom wasn't a bad idea. A few months earlier he had gone to the Balloon Farm, a New York dance club, and, though hardly a rock aficionado, he was a voracious reader and well aware of the cultural changes taking place both in Boston and around the country. By 1967 it was obvious that Club 47, although still the standard-bearer among the Boston coffeehouses, was the wrong venue for the increasingly popular electric bands. Aside from its close association with acoustic folk artists, the club was simply too small and couldn't afford the acts. "My taste in music did not really go beyond 1815—I didn't like the later quartets of Beethoven," he quips. "But I was not living under a rock—I had seen the Beatles in Hamburg. And I did understand as well as anyone that acid, and at least pot, had hit the middle class. I didn't want a career in show business, but I thought, 'God, you've got eighty-three colleges and 240,000 students and the radio stations are playing Top 40 and pretending Joni James is the way to go. And with the arguable exception of Berkeley, this is the hippest town in America!' "

Riepen was aware that a successful group of New York club owners had already tried and failed to obtain the necessary permits to open in Boston. "They were told by everybody that there was no way to get this done because of the police," he recalls. "They were not going to open anything for rock and roll—that meant dope." With his background in Kansas City politics, Riepen knew that Boston's vast political and patronage machine would have to be stoked, and he was able to maneuver the project through the city's byzantine licensing maze.

"I talked about 'the young people' like I didn't know what was going on," he says, "and I was going to give some 'dances' on the weekends. I schmoozed these guys. You can't do that to the mayor's licensing board. But I was not trying to get construction permits, I was not trying to build some fancy place. I was not trying to take money out of anybody's pocket because I didn't have any money."

Riepen renamed the club the Boston Tea Party, a double entendre that was both a call to revolt against the commercialism of Top 40 music and a sly reference to marijuana.* He offered music on the weekends

---

*Riepen, who had seen Charlie Parker perform in the bars of Kansas City and described himself as a "desperately hip Midwesterner," knew "tea" was old hipster slang for marijuana.

with local bands, one of which was Peter Wolf's group, the Hallucinations, which rehearsed in the synagogue during the week.

He tentatively booked a few out-of-town bands, including the Velvet Underground, which became a regular attraction. Riepen, constantly worried about shakedowns and police pressure, hired Steve Nelson, a lawyer with a ponytail and a master's degree from the Kennedy School of Government, to book and manage the hall. "I knew Boston was incredibly corrupt," says Riepen. "And I was getting my share of people coming around. I thought, 'Well, if they raid us, the manager on-site is a lawyer.'" But the club just wasn't clicking. Acts came on a catch-as-catch-can basis, and Riepen was paying too much for them. He had even called the two leading San Francisco rock promoters, Bill Graham and Chet Helms, searching for any West Cost band that might be coming east. "We were getting Lothar and the Hand People, the Peanut Butter Conspiracy, all these fabulously hot acts," Riepen says sarcastically.

All that changed in early 1968 when Riepen met two men. One was Don Law, the young promoter who had worked with the Remains, the Hallucinations, and Jellyroll. The other was a struggling booking agent from New York named Frank Barsalona.

STUBBY, NERVOUS, AND SELF-EFFACING, FRANK BARSALONA DIDN'T LOOK like a man who would build a rock and roll empire. He had grown up on Staten Island and landed a job in the mail room of the GAC talent agency. When a job booking rock acts opened in the agency's talent department in the early sixties, Barsalona begged for it even though it wasn't what he'd envisioned for himself. "That wasn't the glamour part of the agency business," he says. "Motion pictures, television were the hip places to be. In those days rock was this bastardized part of show business that was going to be over in a couple of years. There was no future, there was no talent."

Barsalona soon discovered that it was easy to sign rock acts, hard to book them, and impossible to sustain their careers. Most of the established promoters GAC worked with were indifferent to rock and roll, and Barsalona found that most of them didn't know the music, didn't like the acts, and rarely attended their own shows—and if they did, they were likely to keep wads of cotton in their ears. Since GAC and the other agencies had little faith in the longevity of rock performers themselves, they took any bookings they could get. A large percentage of Barsalona's early dates came from fleecing amateurs who wanted to put on rock and roll shows.

"Essentially, they were young people who would come up with a certain amount of money and want to be in the rock business," Barsalona says. "If I got the call from a new kid who had some bread and wanted a show, I would sell him whatever I could sell him—for however much money I could get. And then if there was any money left, I would call my buddy at William Morris or Associated Booking: 'I got a live one—here's who you should call.' And they would do the same for me."

Barsalona became convinced that the agencies themselves were the biggest impediment to the careers of rock and rollers. "Everybody thought, 'These people are lucky to have a hit record—they'll probably have a follow-up and then they're history.' And basically that's how everybody felt. Every once in a while you'd have a Bobby Darin or a Connie Francis—but they were always looking to get out of that market. There was no respect for the rock and roll people. I realized we were part of the problem."

When Barsalona was fired by GAC in 1964, he formed a new agency, Premier, specifically to handle rock and roll acts. His initial clients included such American groups as Mitch Ryder and the Detroit Wheels, Little Anthony and the Imperials, Del Shannon, and several girl groups that included the Ronettes, the Chiffons, and the Shangri-Las. With the continuing impact of the British Invasion, Premier also needed to sign English acts. The agency's first British clients— Freddie and the Dreamers, Wayne Fontana and the Mindbenders, and Herman's Hermits—were hardly the kind of groups to inspire thoughts of long-term careers, but Herman's Hermits went on to score eleven Top 10 singles over a two-and-a-half-year run and helped establish Premier as the agency of choice among British managers.

It was Dick Friedberg, a partner whom Barsalona liked to ridicule as "a wiseass without substance," who signed Premier's breakthrough act, the Who. When Barsalona finally saw the band at their dress rehearsal for a Murray the K show, he knew they were incredible. Unlike Premier's previous pop acts from Britain, the Who was a band that demanded to be seen and heard, and their intelligence and musician-ship were indicative of the increasing sophistication and scope of rock.

Nowhere were these new developments more obvious than with the rapidly evolving "San Francisco Sound." As in the east, the Bay Area's underground rock scene had its roots in folk music. Many of the area's most influential rock musicians like Jerry Garcia of the Grateful Dead and Paul Kantner and Jorma Kaukonen of the Jefferson Airplane had started out playing folk and bluegrass. And if the groundbreaking work of Dylan, the Byrds, and the Paul Butterfield Blues Band had shown them the way to go electric, LSD turned up the volume. The Grateful Dead frequently functioned as the house band at Ken Kesey's famous "acid test" parties, and, before long, San Francisco's public rock dances were offering approximations of the acid tests, featuring ex-perimental lights and sounds to manipulate perception. By the spring of '66, there were at least two public dances, heavily influenced by pot and acid and conspicuously outrageous, being staged in San Fran-cisco each weekend.

In the Bay Area, business was a dirty word to virtually everyone in-volved in the music scene except Bill Graham, who ran the Fillmore Auditorium. Brian Rohan, the attorney for many of San Francisco's most important music figures, including Graham and the Grateful Dead, had no entertainment experience. He got the nod because he had represented writer and LSD proponent Ken Kesey on an acid bust—which meant Rohan was hip and trustworthy.

"It never really sorted out as a business," recalls Rohan, who blames the intensity of the drug scene. "Chet Helms was really the hippest guy and the one who started the scene. Chet would book an act at the Avalon Ballroom, and Graham would hear about it. Chet would sleep in on Monday morning, and by the time he woke up to call and con-firm the booking, Graham would have waked up at seven in the morn-ing and called the agents in New York.

"This was not a business town," adds Rohan. "With Kesey we had 'tank meetings.' A tank meeting is where you get a tank of nitrous oxide and everybody passes the hose around and talks. So if there's ten guys there, you're passed out twenty percent of the time. So everybody gets eighty percent of what's going on—but nobody gets the same eighty percent. And everybody thinks they know everything, and every-body knows *nothing*. Each person has a completely different point of view when the meeting's over. And these were not bullshit sessions, these were serious business meetings. But everything was done on the tank. Because when you were on the tank, sometimes you saw God, and God would tell you the answers. When you pass out on nitrous oxide, your ears come back before your eyes. So you think you've reached a new state of consciousness because you can hear people talking but *you can't see anything*."

The San Francisco mind-set was a mix of LSD and the old folk ethos: the bands thought of themselves as serious psychedelic artists, motivated by something more than money or the pursuit of fame. Of course, whenever it was time to do business, they got taken to the cleaners. "In San Francisco it's 'We are right, you are wrong, we took acid, you did not, we know everything, you know nothing,' " says Rohan. "They'd argue for hours about ridiculous things—nothing!—and then give up their balls. It was like clowns. A bunch of happy-go-lucky, bumbling kids with a lot of talent that did the best they could. It was not a shrewd, analytical thing."

Barsalona represented the Beau Brummels but none of the more significant San Francisco acts. Rather, most of Premier's artists had come to him through a series of arrangements with a handful of Britain's most aggressive young music executives. Aside from Kit Lambert and Chris Stamp, managers of the Who, Barsalona sought out Chris Blackwell of Island Records, Denny Cordell of Regal Zonophone, and Chris Wright and Terry Ellis of Chrysalis, and Premier was soon representing Procol Harum, Spencer Davis, Traffic, Savoy Brown, Joe Cocker, Spooky Tooth, and Ten Years After. Barsalona's reliance on foreign talent would prove fortuitous since the British bands were far more willing to treat rock and roll like a business, perhaps because it afforded working-class kids one of the few ready opportunities to overcome England's more rigid class system. While American rockers hardly had an exclusive lock on drug use, the work ethic of the British bands was, in general, decidedly different from that of their San Francisco counterparts. Both the bands and their handlers were hungry for success in a way that few American bands of the period were.

"When the West Coast acts came through there was an attitude," recalls Don Law. "You had to deal with a lot of bullshit. Egos, a heavier drug scene. They couldn't get things together. One show would be just dog shit and the next one would be great. English bands? Straight ahead. They were consistently better focused and prepared to play that market. There was an energy and intelligence that wasn't there from the West Coast bands. It was the musicians: 'I don't have a shot unless I do this. This is my opportunity to make it.' The first time Jeff Beck played [in Boston] he had Rod Stewart and Ronnie Wood. And he was chewing them out! 'You wankers! We've *gotta* play this thing better than we're playing it—these people came to hear that record . . .' *Really* chewing them out. You'd never hear that from a West Coast band."

With the rise of the San Francisco ballrooms, Barsalona recognized an appropriate venue for his bands. And if a national network of similar dance halls could be established, it would solve his biggest problem: finding enough work to justify an American tour. Prior to signing with Premier, Ten Years After had been booked by the William Morris Agency. Their first U.S. tour, in 1968, was a disaster.

"Bill Graham had written to us and said, 'If you're ever in America, please play the Fillmore West,' " recalls drummer Ric Lee. "My ex-wife put up a thousand pounds, and Chris Wright got some money from a publishing company somewhere—and on about two thousand pounds we came over on an eight-week tour. Out of the eight weeks we played six dates. It was a bunch of bullshit!"

Boston, with its huge student population, could be a key market, and it was an obvious starting point for a British band touring America. But Barsalona didn't have a Boston venue. With nothing to lose, Frank drove up and began making the rounds. He quickly found the Boston Tea Party. And while Barsalona didn't really know what to make of Ray Riepen, he knew the old synagogue, with a capacity of 750, was ideal for his acts. He immediately pitched Riepen and Steve Nelson. "Basically, all they were doing were local bands," recalls Barsalona. "I said, 'Look, you don't have to do local. This room is perfect. I have these acts from England. This music is just beginning.' " Riepen didn't require much convincing. For $1,250, Premier booked Procol Harum into the Tea Party for three nights.

Barsalona's arrival promised to solve Riepen's talent problems. But the hall was being run in a slipshod manner, and he soon made changes. Steve Nelson was out as manager of the Tea Party. His replacement was Don Law.

Riepen and Law were a unique and formidable pair. Both were exceptionally bright and hungry for success, but virtual opposites in temperament and talent. As a conceptualizer, Ray time and again would demonstrate the rare and extremely valuable ability to see the possibilities inherent in an unfolding situation before others could, regardless of whether it was business, politics, or culture in general. Says Harper Barnes, a fraternity brother of Riepen's at the University of Kansas who later worked for him, "His genius is seeing things that other people can't see or seeing them before anyone else. He was *brilliant* about figuring things out."

Law, while far from plodding, was extraordinarily disciplined. If Riepen delighted in being the first one to divine the big picture, Law had the patience to fill in its shades and shadows—something Ray could not do. Riepen's disinterest in mastering even the most rudimentary details of day-to-day life was legend. "When I met Ray he was sleeping on the floor of an apartment in Cambridge," recalls Joe Rogers, who worked for Riepen. "He had stacks and stacks of books but didn't even have a mattress." Indeed, just having an apartment was an accomplishment for Riepen. He frequently lived in his car until a friend or employee took him in—either because he was broke or couldn't be bothered to pay the rent. There were times when he ran several companies without an office. Employees would be summoned to meetings in his car. "His office was a Lincoln Continental," recalls Rogers. "And the dirty laundry was in the trunk."

With the help of Barsalona, who wanted to see Boston with all its students blossom as a market, Law was able to get the Tea Party strong acts and timely bookings. "They didn't know what the hell they were doing," Law says of Riepen in the ballroom's pre-Barsalona days. "Not that anybody did. He'd collect the receipts, sell some tickets, do some local things, and keep it going. But he was behind the curve. They were doing some known acts, but the guarantees* were too high. He wasn't really breaking any new stuff. It just wasn't happening." Once the club did start happening, however, it quickly gained its own momentum. And Riepen was able to see that his hunch was right.

"Christ, it was naturally an overwhelming success," Riepen says. "You had 250,000 white kids smoking a doobie for the first time in the history of man, and they thought this was fabulous. I could've had two

*The amount of money guaranteed up front to an act.

zithers down there as long as I had an overhead projector and a strobe light. They didn't care; they didn't know! It all sounds perfect if you've got five hundred mikes* under your belt."

Just *how* out of it the audience was became obvious to Law one night when the Tea Party caught fire—and nobody noticed.

"We had terrific fears of fire because it was an old, dry building," he says. "Obviously, people smoked; there was an area upstairs where they could go out and sit over the floor.

"One night Van Morrison was onstage and singing 'Up the Ladder.' I was on the floor, and I looked up and there were flames shooting out of the ceiling near the fan. So myself and the maintenance guy bounded upstairs. We're shooting fire extinguishers down this hole where the audience is. Van Morrison had the presence of mind to keep singing like nothing was happening—which was great, because people would have freaked. Somebody on the floor told me later that as all these flames and fire extinguishers and water were coming down, people were going ' *"Up the Ladder"—far out light show . . .*' "

●

JON LANDAU, LIKE HIS FRIEND DON LAW, WAS ALSO PROVING UNUSUALLY level-headed and dependable. As a critic for *Rolling Stone,* he was a welcome guest at the Tea Party. But even Ray Riepen, who shared Landau's ability to perceive business opportunities in the emerging culture before they became clear to others, was a little spooked by him. Riepen delighted in adventure, and his style as a businessman was to follow his gut instinct and deal with the consequences later. In that regard, Landau was his absolute opposite. "Jon never said or did anything in his life that wasn't planned out," says Riepen. "He was an extremely careful guy, extremely ambitious. Totally preoccupied with not making any mistakes and sensing the drift of things before he committed. He was the most careful guy I met in Boston about his own image. Very reserved, didn't have much of a sense of humor. For a young fellow, he always took himself very seriously."

After his initial miscue with the Jimi Hendrix review in the first issue of *Rolling Stone,* Landau had quickly righted himself. If his writing remained stiff, the reasoning behind his critical assessments grew more

---

*Five hundred micrograms of LSD.

and more impressive. He was still a passionate fan and much better when writing about music that he cared for. His tastes were more pop-oriented than his contemporaries', but with increasing frequency he was the rock critic weighing in with reviews that were on target, and beyond a continuing enthusiasm there was little to invite comparisons with Landau's earliest, sputtering work in *Crawdaddy!* His intelligence and increased confidence, combined with *Rolling Stone*'s rapidly growing stature, quickly made him the most influential and powerful rock reviewer in the country. Like Law, he remained fully aware of all that passed for hip, but both men were more excited by the commercial possibilities being suggested by the scene. "Jon always had his eye on the main chance," says Harper Barnes, who was both a friend and editor to Landau.

If Law rolled his eyes at how oblivious the blasted patrons at the Tea Party could be to a little thing like a fire, Landau positively cringed when confronted with the culture of hipness. His antipathy toward most of the San Francisco bands, who were the most conspicuous in their attachment to the counterculture, continued unabated. Barnes, who liked the Grateful Dead, was finally able to convince Landau to come with him to see the group.

"He said, 'Okay, Harper, take me. What is this all about?' " Barnes recalls. Jon was not swayed by the experience. If anything, he was horrified by what he heard. "Landau was just appalled that anybody would want to listen to that stuff because it was so sloppy and affected," Barnes says. In print, Landau slammed the Dead hard while praising the frankly commercial and decidedly unhip pop group Three Dog Night.

Nor did he see anything in the youth culture's much-advertised commitment to love and understanding. While attending a free concert by John Hammond, Jr., Edgar Winter's White Trash, and Emerson, Lake and Palmer, Landau watched with growing resentment as several people in the crowd drifted onto the stage. Their refusal to return to the audience severely curtailed the show. The concert was *free*, for God's sake! What more could these people possibly want? Landau cheered lustily as the police led away one particularly obnoxious couple—a reaction that was tantamount to counterculture treason. "I was glad to see them go," he later wrote. "And I swear to God I hope whoever they are, they never come back."

He took the opportunity to learn about the business. Having the Tea Party was a godsend: most of the new British bands played there before going on to New York, and his friendship with Don Law, as well as his growing stature as the critic who mattered, led to a relationship with Barsalona.

"I used to go down to cover the shows, and afterwards, Frank, Don, and I would wind up backstage or over at Ken's restaurant, discussing the performance," Landau recalled. "Actually, I'd mainly listen while Frank talked about everything, including the set list, lighting, sound, stage, clothes, and audience response. For someone like me, these get-togethers were the equivalent of a seminar in basic show business."

Landau's relationship with such powerful business types was viewed dimly by many of his peers at Brandeis. Jon was competitive and not averse to self-promotion: he liked to refer to himself as "the king of rock and roll."* There was a perception that he was hustling at a time when nobody else was and that he was very interested in making money—which he was. But he was also extraordinarily sophisticated. Unlike most of his contemporaries, Landau could see that the explosive music scene was being translated into a business that simply had not existed before. It wasn't just a couple of dozen folkies plunking down fifty cents for a cup of coffee at Club 47 anymore but thousands of kids shelling out $3.50 at the Tea Party each weekend. The ballrooms, the rapidly growing record labels, the magazines—all suggested possibilities that he found far more captivating than those suggested by a couple of joints and the *I Ching*. Indeed, Landau—unlike most other rock critics—had gone way beyond considering music from the standpoint of a devoted fan. His approach became less and less concerned with aesthetic judgments and more focused on the professional decisions that went into making records. He became keenly aware of recording techniques, producers, arrangements, and other variables.

Going to a concert or even just listening to a record with Landau was an active experience. "He was never a laid-back, vague person," recalls a former acquaintance. "He was very systematic. He would listen to a record or go hear a concert and sit there and think, 'They should

---

*There was a bit of jostling for this kind of adolescent bragging right: New York writer Robert Christgau took the title "the dean of American rock critics."

do this song first; they should never open with that song.' He had a critical faculty whenever he approached the music in any capacity; he was always at work. And he enjoyed that. It was liberating to him in a way that just nothing else was."

During his first year with *Rolling Stone,* Landau produced three important critical pieces—an unfavorable review of the highly popular English trio Cream, an essay on rock as art, and the exposure of an attempt to sell several bands from Boston, the "Bosstown sound," as a sham.

The Bosstown sound was an early and crude attempt by MGM Records to package the underground rock scene. MGM, which had failed to sign any San Francisco band of note, sought to create its own East Coast version by putting a lot of money behind a handful of Boston bands. If Landau didn't like the vast majority of the music coming out of Northern California—and he disliked it enough to be having fierce arguments with Wenner over *Rolling Stone*'s unstinting critical support for anything by Bay Area bands like the Grateful Dead—he at least recognized that it was a legitimate, homegrown scene. No one would be able to charge Landau with the kind of hometown favoritism he found so distasteful in the San Francisco–based Wenner. In a front-page story for *Rolling Stone,* Landau killed the Bosstown sound in its corporate cradle.

"The question is not *whether* there is a hype," he wrote of the MGM campaign, "but whether there is anything lying *beneath* the hype." The answer, said Landau, was no. The bands in question—Ultimate Spinach, Orpheus, the Beacon Street Union, and Eden's Children (which was signed to ABC Records)—were, respectively, "pretentious," "good schlock," "inept," and "boring," all tied together with the thinnest marketing ploy. He slammed the industry for hurting the city's developing music scene with the fabrication, adding that other and better Boston bands not associated with the marketing campaign—he mentioned his friend Pete Wolf's group, the Hallucinations—would be hurt by the hype.

As a reviewer, Landau was rapidly developing his ability to pinpoint precise problems with a performer or a recording. That set him apart from his more expansive contemporaries like Paul Williams, Greil Marcus, and Richard Meltzer, who frequently seemed obsessed with elevating rock by placing it in a broad social context or emphasizing its philosophical and mythmaking capabilities. Landau had no such agenda—his work was aimed at deciding whether a recording or show was good or bad. And when he laid someone out, it was with a thundering blow.

"It is hard to tell whether such a performance is the product of indifference or lack of sensitivity or both," he wrote of a performance at the 1968 Newport Folk Festival by Joan Baez—an artist he professed to admire. "Whatever its causes, it is necessary to state that singing a country song with a southern accent doesn't make one a country singer and saying 'Amen' after a gospel number doesn't make one the new Marion Williams. Style-hopping is unbecoming to a performer not equipped to do justice to the diverse traditions present in folk music. As a politician, Joan Baez may get my vote, but as a musician I fault her for the same thing she is so quick to fault others: she doesn't seem to care." He went on to savage a performance by San Francisco's Big Brother and the Holding Company, featuring Janis Joplin.

Landau's sharp negative criticism of Cream, at the time the leading English rock band, had a very real consequence. Guitarist Eric Clapton later cited it as a reason the band broke up. The trio played with an unusually high level of musicianship, but Landau—while lauding their abilities—took them to task for the bombast of their live shows, which he characterized as interminable displays of empty virtuosity. Clapton, who was more accustomed to being lauded as a rock guitar god, received a particularly cold shower. He was completely unoriginal, wrote Landau, "a master of the blues clichés of all the post–World War II blues guitarists . . . a virtuoso at performing other people's ideas."

Landau's most revealing and personal piece of the period, however, was an essay entitled "Rock & Art," which appeared in the July 20, 1968, issue of *Rolling Stone*. In it, Landau wrestled with the music's growing sophistication and, in stark contrast to the eagerness with which most other rock critics transferred the folk ethos to the new music, rejected the notion that rock was an art form. And while he tried to frame the essay as a response to some of the more grandiose claims being made for the music, he was also wrestling with his own problems regarding what he saw as the baggage that the changing times inflicted on the music.

Landau took the classic conservative position of a gatekeeper. The appeal of the early rock and roll of the fifties, he wrote, was that it was simple, unpretentious, and frankly commercial. Early rock stars like Elvis Presley, Little Richard, and Chuck Berry didn't aspire to create serious art, they were entertainers whose songs were built around the straightforward themes of adolescence: cars, balling, dances, school. The core attitudes of early rock and of formal art were antithetical. Rock and roll had begun as a form of commercial entertainment and it should stay that way. But now, he lamented:

> More and more people expect of rock what they used to expect of philosophy, literature, films, and visual art. Others expect of rock what they used to get out of drugs. And in my opinion, rock cannot withstand that kind of burden because it forces onto rock qualities which are the negation of what rock was all about in the first place.

Landau held out the limp hope that rock could ignore the changing world around it and rediscover its earlier voice. He despaired of rock's ability to produce a significant number of intelligent artists:

> There is nothing wrong with being serious if you keep it all in perspective and if you have the artistic ability to be serious. Most rock and roll musicians are banal, amateurish and insipidly stupid when they try to express their philosophy of life in the context of popular music.

Landau's stance was remarkably conservative. While qualifying the essay, he all but disallowed the possibility of a Bob Dylan. Indeed, he offered no recognition of the impact Dylan was having when, at the very least, Dylan had proven that the music could "withstand that kind of burden."

In his days with his band, Jellyroll, Landau had included songs by the Beach Boys in the group's repertoire. Like Brian Wilson, who had managed to write classic surfing songs for the Beach Boys without ever actually knowing how to surf, Landau saw rock as the purest expression of a romanticized vision of American adolescence. Balling? Dancing? Cars? Jon Landau was most comfortable staying at home and writing for long stretches of time. He imagined the world outside himself as it existed in the records he loved best, the records of his youth.

It was a vision of rock—and the America it represented—that would direct his work and the work of others in the years to come.

●

WHILE JON LANDAU REJECTED THE NEW UNDERGROUND CULTURE, RAY Riepen embraced it, nurturing a vision of himself as part of a new generation of socially and politically aware capitalists. "I knew that there was a real sea change even before Vietnam got heavy," he says. "We believed in 'sixty-six that maybe smart people were going to get control of things—not just guys who were 'b'iness' men. We were naive, but that's what we thought: guys who were smart and had taste would get control."

Looking for further business opportunities, Riepen took another cue from San Francisco, this time from a disc jockey named Tom "Big Daddy" Donahue. A savvy veteran of Top 40 rock radio who had peddled his influence as a well-known rock jock, running a small record company and publishing his own radio tip sheet (which allowed him to solicit record companies for advertising), he had read the writing on the wall for the teen culture of the fifties that had formed the basis for Top 40 and quit his job in 1965. In early 1967 he convinced the owner of KMPX, an FM station broadcasting foreign-language programming, to let him do a show featuring the underground rock records that Top 40 never played. By August, KMPX was broadcasting rock full-time. Donahue treated the music with a seriousness normally reserved for classical recordings. There were no jingles, disc jockeys didn't talk over records, and Donahue even took the clock out of the studio to ensure there were no time-and-weather announcements. The station was an instant hit in San Francisco, and within four months Donahue was programming a second FM station in Pasadena.

Riepen believed a similar station couldn't miss in Boston. But although capable of a static-free stereo signal, the influence of FM stations was minuscule in comparison to AM. Few people had FM radios at home, let alone in their cars, and Riepen quickly discovered that it was a net-loss industry—" a dollar-a-holler deal," as he saw it. "Most of the FM stations were owned by AM stations, and if you bought AM time they'd *give* you the FM time," says Riepen. "It was a tragic industry."

During the forties, when FM's future was cloudy, the Federal Communications Commission had encouraged AM stations to begin sister FM operations by allowing simulcasts of AM broadcasts on the FM band—and then pretty much forgotten about it. But in 1964, when an overcrowded AM band forced a freeze on the issuing of new licenses, the FCC reversed itself and decreed that all FM stations in cities with populations greater than 100,000 had to give at least half of their airtime to original FM programming. Many broadcasters resisted, and it took three years for the new rules to go into effect. But beginning in 1967, a lot of FM stations were looking for cheap programming.

Riepen pulled the Dun & Bradstreet reports on Boston-area broadcasters and went looking for the biggest loser he could find. WBCN, with a powerful fifty-thousand-watt signal, was the flagship station of a small northeastern network of classical stations in Chapter 11. Strapped for money, the station was selling time to outsiders, and its best source of income was early-morning religious programming. Riepen was able to convince WBCN's shareholders to let him purchase seven hours of daily airtime to program rock records from 10 P.M. to 5 A.M.

While WBCN was desperate enough to sell Riepen time, few industry professionals would take him seriously. He pitched his plan to play tracks from rock albums at a broadcasters' convention in Washington, D.C., and came up empty. "I said, 'You guys are fucking nuts,'" says Riepen. "'You've got *stereo*. I'm gonna play these album cuts, and I'm not gonna have a lot of commercials or allow jingles or talk-overs. I'm gonna play the records like they were classical music.' And they told me I was crazy."

Undeterred, Ray made the rounds of the student-run stations at Harvard, Emerson, Tufts, and M.I.T., collecting a staff of disc jockeys that included folk enthusiasts Tom Hadges and Steve Magnell as well as blues aficionado Joe Rogers. At 10 P.M. on March 15, 1968, at WBCN's Newberry Street studio, the twenty-two-year-old Rogers—using the on-air name Mississippi Harold Wilson—dropped a needle on a Country Joe and the Fish record, switched on the microphone, and announced the opening volley in "the American Revolution."

If the shareholders of WBCN were eager to take Ray Riepen's

money, they weren't particularly keen on having his scruffy, dope-smoking amateur disc jockeys in their station every night. There was intense animosity between the professional daytime staff (one secretary had decorated the office with pictures of Barry Goldwater) and Riepen's crew. "We were the people who snuck in there at night," recalls Rogers. "Until the letters started coming in."

Riepen's DJs had nonchalantly suggested that listeners get in touch with the station, and the response was both immediate and heavy. The format was a hit. But even more important was the reaction from Boston merchants. Record stores were reporting dramatically improved sales on rock albums that were being played only on WBCN. Sandal makers, clothing boutiques, sandwich shops, record and stereo stores, and concert promoters quickly became steady advertisers.

Although Riepen had installed a small studio backstage at the Tea Party to alleviate friction with the station's management—a setup that also paid a fortuitous double dividend for Ray since it made the Tea Party synonymous with WBCN's late-night broadcasts—the board of WBCN quickly changed its tune when the members saw the response. They struck a two-pronged deal that gave Riepen twenty-four-hour control over station programming and allowed him to purchase 220,000 shares in the station, making him WBCN's largest single shareholder. He was now responsible for the station's debt, but he was confident that his American Revolution couldn't miss. "I was dumb," he says. "But I was so sure that I said okay."

Riepen's radio adventures required money, and he was using the Tea Party for his cash cow—a situation that didn't cheer Law. And if he was confident about his prospects, he had no aversion to laying off a little of the action. Pete Wolf was among those Riepen canvassed. "If you've got ten thousand dollars you can come in and be a part owner," Riepen told Wolf on the eve of the WBCN deal. The proposition left the singer scratching his head: "Ray, what are you, crazy? *Ten thousand bucks?* I ain't got ten dollars."

If Wolf was unable to avail himself of a financial stake in WBCN, he would still play a key role in its success. Peter Blankfield was reborn again, this time as the Woofa Goofa, WBCN's jive-talking late-night disc jockey.

"The rest of us were just stumbling college guys who paused a lot and didn't know what to say but loved the music," says Joe Rogers.

"But Peter Wolf had the most developed, most interesting, most amazing radio show on the air."

As the Woofa Goofa, Wolf was the ringleader of a cast of characters. Some, like Freddie Lewis, Charlie "the Master Blaster" Daniels, Little Walter, and Dr. Demento,* were real; others, like the Kid from Alabama or Little Angel, were imaginary. Wolf and his crew specialized in hip patter—often trying to top each other's insults in a friendly contest known as "doing the dozens"—that, while a staple of African-American radio throughout the country, was new to Boston.

The Tea Party and WBCN proved a potent combination. The Jeff Beck Group was one of the first beneficiaries of Riepen's burgeoning underground empire. "Frank Barsalona started to experiment," Wolf says. " 'They're here, they're not doing anything—let's bring them in on a Thursday and see if it will fly.' We got a tape of the group, and WBCN would just play it and say, 'This group is coming and opening on Thursday.' And Thursday there were like sixty people there. By Friday there were lines around the block. The power of what was happening was totally focused, and this was a thing that WBCN had created: its listeners, the street thing, the buzz. The word got around, and it was just packed on Friday."

Although Riepen's vision was becoming more and more obvious, a lot of people still needed to be convinced. WBCN was a programming sensation—but advertising income remained slim. Because the station wouldn't condescend to canned advertising or to produce in-house ads with jingles, it was locked out of most ad agency buys. And that was where the money was. But Riepen firmly believed the station's credibility would win a large audience and ultimately overcome all obstacles.

"I turned down ugly commercials," says Riepen. "If they were designed for kids, we wouldn't let it on. We don't want that ugly shit on our station. The agencies were trying to figure out what this was. Of course, the more we did this, the more famous we became. And it turned out to be a fabulous success."

Women's Wear Daily sent photographers to Boston to shoot what was being worn at the Tea Party. Consumer brands, including shoe

---

*A name later used and popularized by another disc jockey, who specialized in playing novelty records.

companies and wine importers, started to sniff around, looking for advice from Riepen on selling to "the kids." "We understood what was going on and had done it in a way that was not pandering," he says. "We were trying to figure out something that wasn't trash."

Some of the overtures were unintentionally humorous. The National Tea Council, a trade group promoting the beverage, apparently missed either the irony or the drug reference in the Boston Tea Party's name. "A couple of guys from an ad agency and a production company came up and did a bunch of stuff," says Riepen. "They had a Miss Tea, you dig? A girl from Ceylon. They tried to get ahold of this 'tea' deal for the council."

Riepen's success also brought imitators, although most found that winning the market was a lot more difficult than Riepen's eccentric corn-pone schtick made it look. " 'BCN was always in jeopardy," says Rogers. "Shortly after it started, some Boston affiliate of GE was going to switch over to playing FM rock and roll. It was on for a couple of weeks and went away."

Riepen's sweetest triumph, however—and the one in which he proved not just his flair for corporate gamesmanship but his real genius for packaging the underground—was against a club named the Crosstown Bus. A well-financed start-up aimed at knocking off the Tea Party, the rival club spent lavishly on preopening advertising and debuted with one of the hottest bands in the country, the Doors. Riepen couldn't possibly come up with a band that was a better draw. Instead, he called in a favor. The Tea Party had provided a steady gig for Andy Warhol's musical protégés in the Velvet Underground despite the fact that they didn't draw well. Now Riepen wanted something in return. "Listen," Riepen told Warhol, "I'm playing the Velvets, and they're deader than a doornail. I want you to come up here and shoot a movie. I don't care if you've got any film in the camera, but bring Nico and Ultraviolet and all the rest of those cripples and get up here."

While the Crosstown Bus blitzed Boston with ads for the Doors, Riepen mounted his counteroffensive. The Tea Party distributed fliers around Cambridge that featured a simple, irresistibly hip come-on: YOU BE ANDY WARHOL'S NEXT MOVIE.

"We had the lights out, the cameras out, and we had lines down the street," remembers Law. "I don't even know who the band was—

nobody. And the Doors did just okay." It was a moment of triumph for Riepen, one he would recall with supreme satisfaction: "There was a line of women from Dedham in Pucci dresses three blocks long standing in the rain trying to get in Andy Warhol's next movie."

The Crosstown Bus didn't make it.

3

PURELY
PRAGMATIC
BUSINESS

RAY RIEPEN WASN'T THE ONLY BUSINESSMAN TO SUSPECT THAT THE rock underground signaled a major cultural shift and a wealth of new commercial possibilities. On St. Patrick's Day 1967, two executives from Warner Bros. Records, Stan Cornyn and his boss, vice president Joe Smith, traveled to Fugazi Hall in San Francisco's North Beach for a concert and party marking the release of the first album by the label's newest signing, the Grateful Dead.

The Dead weren't like any other performers on the label's roster, and the band certainly didn't throw the kind of parties the executives were used to attending for Sammy Davis, Jr., or Bob Newhart back at the home office in Burbank. While the band played, Cornyn, the label's director of creative services, checked out the crowd. He was particularly baffled by the sight of a woman sitting on the floor and swaying to the music, her head bobbing up and down in the smoke emanating from an old metal laundry tub filled with dry ice. But he was just as unsettled by the way he and Smith stood out: both were wearing the dark-blue Warner Bros. blazers company policy dictated. Custom-made by Carroll & Company of Beverly Hills with a "WR" emblazoned over the breast pocket, the jackets were meant to convey the company's class; instead, they made Cornyn and Smith as conspicuous as a pair of English butlers in a bikers' bar. But Cornyn knew that after nearly ten years as an undercapitalized record industry also-ran, Warner Bros. and its sister label, Reprise, were ready to try anything—and the new rock scene was both readily available and cheap.

When the band took a break, the two uniformed record executives strode to the microphone. Smith, a former Top 40 disc jockey whose convivial, wisecracking patter had made him a natural and visible spokesman for the company, was going to present the Dead with a copy of their new record.

"I just want to say what an honor it is," Smith said as he looked earnestly at the band, "for Warner Brothers Records to be able to introduce the Grateful Dead and its music to the world."

The executives shook hands with the band members, who were eyeing the official Warner blazers skeptically. After a long look, guitarist Jerry Garcia took the microphone.

"I just want to say what an honor it is," he said, "for the Grateful Dead to introduce Warner Brothers Records to the world."

The launch of the Dead's album marked the end of the blue blazers and announced a new corporate culture at Warner Bros. Records. Driven to underground rock by financial desperation, the company would do far more than figure out how to deal with the music. As one of the first mainstream record companies to embrace the new rock scene, the profits from Warners' record operation would far outstrip those of its film studio by the early seventies and become the company's cash cow. Warner Bros. Records would successfully absorb and package the seemingly antithetical counterculture—and do it well enough to convert the music into the financial engine for what would become America's largest media conglomerate.

WARNER BROS.' ROAD TO ROCK HAD BEEN A LONG AND RELUCTANT JOURney. One of the last Hollywood studios to enter the record business, the company had instead licensed its film music for release as sound-track albums to the likes of Columbia, RCA Victor, and MGM records. But by the late fifties, Jack Warner had finally tired of seeing Warner Bros. product make money for his competitors. It just didn't make any sense—the studio owned one of the country's largest music publishing operations. But Warner's disdain for the record business ran deep and was rooted in a disastrous experience with Brunswick Records in the thirties.

With the end of silent pictures, the studio had quickly and stunningly emerged as a major music publisher in order to obtain music for its films at a cheap price. In 1928, Warner Bros. cobbled together several existing independent publishers, including M. Witmark & Sons, Remick Music Corp., Harms Inc., and partial interest in New World Music Corp. Among the songs owned by the powerful new Warner firm, Music Publishers Holding Company (MPHC), were standards by Jerome Kern and George and Ira Gershwin. The studio soon discovered the music publishing company provided a second benefit: it generated a sizable profit—as much as $2 million a year.

With so much money obviously to be made in music, MPHC in 1930 acquired Brunswick, a popular record label whose broad catalog embraced recordings by Al Jolson, Duke Ellington, Red Nichols, and such top "race" and blues performers as Leroy Carr, Tampa Red, and Memphis Minnie. The studio further bolstered its roster by signing Bing Crosby. Its timing, however, proved terrible. The Depression all but destroyed the record business, and industry sales plummeted from 104 million records in 1927 to just 6 million in 1932. Brunswick was unloaded to Columbia Records.

The reversal left Warner Bros. executives stunned and bitter, none more so than Herman Starr, the Warner corporate director who had headed up Brunswick. Although running MPHC by 1939, he retained an abiding distaste for the record business, and few in the company ever questioned him. Once the bookkeeper for the Warner family, he was rumored to have taken a tax rap for Harry Warner, and his power within the company was formidable. From his perch at MPHC, Starr remained adamantly opposed to any further Warner Bros. record business involvement for decades. But his influence was dealt a substantial blow in 1956 when Harry and Albert Warner sold out their interest in the studio. Jack Warner remained, joined by Charles Allen, the head of the investment bank Charles Allen and Company, Serge Semenenko of the First National Bank of Boston, and investor David Baird as board members. It was Semenenko, one of the few bankers of the period with a strong professional interest in the entertainment business, who began to push Jack Warner on the issue of a record company.

The record industry had grown dramatically in the years following World War II. In 1945, record sales totaled $109 million; in 1958, they topped the $500 million mark. While the industry's success owed more than a little to the postwar boom and the growth of America's consumer culture, record companies did their part by introducing new and popular configurations. In 1948, Columbia debuted Dr. Peter Goldmark's 33$\frac{1}{3}$ long-playing (LP) album, and in 1949 RCA offered the 45 rpm single. It was foolish, Semenenko said, for the studio simply to make deals for other record companies to release its sound tracks. For the cost of less than one motion picture, Warner Bros. could start its own record company—and possibly reap a whole new income stream that could continue indefinitely. Additionally, a record company would be another way for Warner Bros. to use its contract actors.

In 1956, Warner Bros. agreed to buy Los Angeles's Imperial Records. The label, whose roster boasted Fats Domino and Ricky Nelson, was in trouble with the IRS and could be had for $2 million. The deal ultimately fell apart, but by deciding to tender an offer, Warner Bros. passed a psychological barrier: If it was willing to buy in, why not start its own record company? To build it, the studio hired Jim Conkling, the former president of Columbia Records. But while Conkling was an able administrator and capable of anticipating many of the problems that would face the new record company, he was hardly an artistic visionary. That was a problem because the label would have to start without a catalog of proven artists and find a way to compete. Conkling's own tastes were decidedly mainstream. He was married to one of the singing King Sisters, and that pretty much summed up his musical horizons.

Warner Bros. debuted in September of 1958 with a clutch of stereo albums meant to capture the upscale end of the mainstream market. The music was breathtakingly bland, even by the standards of the time. Along with an album by actress Connie Stevens—who played Cricket on the Warner Bros. television series *Hawaiian Eye*—they included *Dragnet* actor Jack Webb (a friend of Conkling's) reciting the lyrics to love songs in front of an orchestra; a rerecording of the sound-track score from the 1943 film *For Whom the Bell Tolls;* a double album of Dixieland jazz by clarinetist Matty Matlock and his Paducah Patrol; a "sophisticated" vocal octet named the Smart Set; *Sousa in Stereo,* arranged and conducted by Henry Mancini; and *Music for People with $3.98, Plus Tax, if Any* by Ira Ironstrings—a *nom du disque* for guitarist Alvino Rey, who was both Conkling's brother-in-law and under contract to Capitol Records. The albums were all commercial failures.

When Warner Bros. finally did score its first hit record in the spring of '59 it was, ironically, with a single aimed at the teen market, although hardly rock and roll. "Kookie, Kookie (Lend Me Your Comb)" by actor Edd Byrnes was a novelty record based on the character Kookie—a Hollywood parking lot attendant and pickup artist—that Byrnes played on the Warner Bros. television series *77 Sunset Strip*. Although a teen heartthrob, Byrnes was not a recording artist: Irving Taylor, the song's author, stood on one side of Byrnes during the session whispering the phrasing in his ear while producer Karl Engeman stood on the other side and snapped his fingers to give Byrnes the beat. Connie Stevens, whom the label hoped to develop into their own Doris Day, was pressed into service to handle the song's chorus.

Although "Kookie" reached number four on the *Billboard* chart, Stevens was not rewarded for her role in the record's success. Rather, Warner Bros., which had a lock on her career, treated her with arrogant contempt. A $300-a-week contract player on *Hawaiian Eye*, Stevens's deal with the record division provided the standard 5 percent royalty rate. But her participation on "Kookie" was seen by the label as a favor to Byrnes, and Stevens agreed to a reduced royalty of 1 percent in return for not having her name appear on the record. But when "Kookie" was released, Stevens discovered her name prominently displayed on the label, and, to add final injury to the insult, she was charged a share of the recording costs against her 1 percent royalty. The following year, when Stevens scored her own hit with "Sixteen Reasons," she was again hamstrung by Warners, this time by corporate politics. Because the song wasn't published by Warner's MPHC, the company wouldn't allow her to sing it on *Hawaiian Eye*, even though she had to perform a song on the show every week. The company also prevented her from singing it on *The Ed Sullivan Show*, which, aside from providing exposure for the record, would have earned Stevens $5,000.

Television tie-ins continued to provide Warner Bros. Records with its few hits, but the label was floundering. By 1960, the record operation was in the hole for $3 million, and the only thing preventing the outright liquidation of the company was that it would mean the additional loss of $2 million in outstanding receivables and inventory. A restructuring forced Conkling to report to Starr, who still despised the record business. After rejecting a proposal from Conkling that he and several other record company employees be allowed to purchase the operation, Starr agreed to keep it going for a few more months in return for deep cuts. Firings reduced the staff from one hundred to thirty, and Conkling, who had been paid $1,000 a week, took a voluntary cut to $500.

Desperate for any kind of hit, Conkling stooped to signing rock and roll acts, a move generally deemed to be beneath the dignity of a major label. Warner's first rock signing, Bill Haley, proved hopelessly past his prime and never got a record on the charts during his stay on the label. The second, the Everly Brothers, though only nominally rock oriented, was a good deal more successful. From 1957 through 1960, the Everlys had several big hits for Cadence Records on both the pop and country charts, including "Bye Bye Love," "Wake Up Little Susie," and "All I Have to Do Is Dream." Their presence on the Warner Bros. roster would go a long way toward dispelling industry speculation that the label was about to fold, essential if the company wanted to collect its outstanding debts. With his back to the wall, Starr did something out of character: he approved a mammoth contract that guaranteed the Everly Brothers $525,000 against an escalating royalty rate that topped out at 7 percent. Warner Bros. was literally betting the future of the record company on the duo.

The bet panned out. "Cathy's Clown," the first Everly Brothers single for Warner Bros., went to number one on the *Billboard* chart in April of 1960 and stayed there for five weeks, giving the company its much-needed credibility. Three months later, Warner Bros. enjoyed an even greater score when a cheaply made comedy album by an unknown, *The Button-Down Mind of Bob Newhart,* topped the album chart for fourteen weeks. The album would remain on the charts for over two years.*

---

*The sales and chart figures on Bob Newhart are a striking demonstration of just how much record industry economics have changed since the early sixties. According to Warner Bros., *The Button-Down Mind of Bob Newhart* sold 630,000 copies during its two-year chart run. Today, albums by established rock acts routinely have advance orders that are greater than that, and those kinds of sales figures do not guarantee a run at the top of the charts. Depending on the performer's past sales record and contract, 630,000 albums could be considered a failure. The Newhart album also had a list price of $3.98; the average compact disc has a current list price of $16.98.

However successful, those hits did not have a noticeable impact on the creative direction of Warner Bros. Records. The Everly Brothers were soon lost to a hitch in the marines, and, if anything, Newhart's success (the record "broke" in the Midwest) argued for sticking to the mainstream. Starr had cut back the number of albums, but not far enough to prevent the release of *Never Heard Gershwin with Bongos* or *Songs the Kids Brought Home from Camp* by John Raitt. The company continued to think in terms of concept and niche recordings, and one Warner memo suggested a collection of American folksongs featuring "a Warners contract artist who is a rugged outdoors type and can sing a little." Another memo, noting that Louis Armstrong was available, suggested signing him and recording an album of Italian songs with "Volare" as the lead.

In the fall of '61, Conkling retired and selected as his successor Mike Maitland, a Capitol executive. The company Maitland inherited was no longer in danger of being shuttered, but it was far from flush. Joe Smith, who had joined Warner Records as head of promotion in October, was shocked to discover just how badly things were going. "Warner Brothers was a great name, but a shitty company," he recalls. "We had a Christmas party downstairs. We bought two bottles of New York State champagne and stood around—twenty-seven people huddled together. Obviously, there were no bonuses, gifts, or anything. Maitland turned to me and said, 'Say something funny.' "

The following year offered more hope. The folk music boom was in full swing, and Warner Bros., while not interested in folksingers per se, capitalized on the trend with the overtly commercial folk trio Peter, Paul and Mary and another comedian, Allan Sherman, whose album *My Son, the Folk Singer* sold over one million copies. The record company ended fiscal 1962 in the black.

The positive balance didn't last long, though. In September of 1963, Jack Warner purchased Frank Sinatra's Reprise Records for $1.5 million and a one-third interest in the combined record company. The deal did not signal some new appreciation of the record business by the mogul; Reprise—even with Sinatra on its roster—was a loser. Warner bought the label as part of a broader deal to acquire Sinatra's services as an actor.

It seemed like a sound move. In 1960 the studio had grossed $10 million with *Ocean's Eleven,* a Las Vegas caper film featuring Sinatra and several of his "rat pack" buddies that cost $4 million to make. Even if Reprise continued to lose money, it was a cheap enough way of acquiring Sinatra's good will and services—and a potential gold mine for Warner Bros.

The deal did prove a gold mine. But not because Jack Warner bought Frank Sinatra. Along with a catalog of outdated, overvalued recordings and a pile of debts, the purchase of Reprise included the services of Morris "Mo" Ostin, a former bookkeeper and the head of Reprise who, by the end of the sixties, would prove the architect of Warner Records' success as a rock label. His ultimate value to Warner Bros. would dwarf Sinatra's.

OSTIN HAD LANDED IN THE RECORD BUSINESS BY CHANCE. HE GRADUATED from UCLA in 1950 with a degree in economics and bounced around from job to job while attending law school at night. In 1954 he stumbled into a career when he took a $100-a-week job as controller— although the job wasn't much more than a glorified bookkeeper—at Verve Records, the label owned by jazz impresario Norman Granz. Granz's younger brother, Irving, had been Ostin's neighbor, and Mo had sold programs for Norman at several of his Jazz at the Philharmonic concerts.

A leading jazz label whose roster included Charlie Parker, Dizzy Gillespie, Lester Young, Count Basie, Oscar Peterson, Louis Armstrong, Roy Eldridge, and Ella Fitzgerald, Verve was nonetheless in constant financial trouble and often for sale. In 1957, Ostin approached Mickey Rudin, a leading Hollywood attorney whose clients included Frank Sinatra, to represent Verve. The label was badly in need of legal advice. Verve had recently scored its first pop hit with Ricky Nelson's "A Teenager's Romance," only to have Nelson disaffirm the contract because he was a minor and then sign with Imperial. Now Granz wanted to sell—could Rudin find a buyer?

The attorney didn't have to look far. Capitol Records had angered Sinatra by refusing to start a personal label for him or up his royalty rate above the standard 5 percent, but Rudin had been able to negotiate a nonexclusive deal that allowed him to record an outside album for every one he delivered to Capitol. Sinatra, who entertained the notion of being the leading artist on his own label, was definitely interested in buying Verve, whose strong jazz roster appealed to him.

Granz's asking price had been $1 million—a figure that doubled when MGM Records in New York put in a bid. Rudin now had a problem; he was representing both Verve and Sinatra, but Sinatra—by far the more important client—was livid because he believed Granz was welshing on a deal to sell to him. In a move worthy of a contortionist, Rudin managed to conclude a deal on behalf of Granz with MGM for far more than Sinatra was going to pay and to placate the singer by suggesting they wait until the end of the MGM/Verve negotiations and then hire the key people away from Verve and start a new label. It was a shrewd and cutthroat strategy that made both of Rudin's clients happy at the expense of MGM.

Ostin, who had worked closely on the sale with Rudin, was asked to head the new Sinatra imprint, Reprise. Although the job was strictly administrative and accounting, Ostin was seen by the industry as an unusual and obscure choice—a sentiment even he was forced to second. "It was an idiotic move," Ostin admits. "I absolutely was not qualified to do the job."

If he didn't do much to distinguish himself during Reprise's first couple of years, Ostin could at least take comfort in having had nothing to do with picking the label's roster. Like Warner Bros., Reprise was not in the rock and roll business, as this was music Sinatra was vehemently and publicly opposed to. The Reprise roster was a mix of Sinatra's Las Vegas cronies like Sammy Davis, Jr., and Dean Martin, plus Jo Stafford, Rosemary Clooney, Dennis Day, the McGuire Sisters, and Dinah Shore—all well past their commercial peaks. Early Reprise albums like *The Ol' Calliope Man Visits a German Hofbrau, Sing Along in Greek, The X-15 & Other Sounds of Missiles, Rockets, Jets,* and Lou Monte's *Great Italian-American Hits* had nothing on Warner Bros. when it came to dreck.

Soon a series of pressures brought Rudin to Jack Warner's door with a record label to sell him. Reprise quickly became embroiled in a bitter fight with Capitol Records as the two labels matched each other's Sinatra releases, dulling sales on both ends, a situation that hurt Reprise far more since Sinatra's sales were the company's lifeblood. Sinatra was also pouring money into a casino he owned, and he was in no position to continue to underwrite a label that showed little sign of

becoming self-sufficient. Once again, Rudin proved himself a deft ne-
gotiator. As he proposed the sale, Warner Bros. could obtain Sinatra's
services as an actor if it would pay $2 million for Reprise. He suggested
that the company immediately depreciate the purchase, thereby getting $900,000 back in a tax credit. Sinatra would also pay $500,000
back to Warner Bros. for a one-third share in the combined record operation, so the studio was paying only $600,000 for Reprise. The deal
had a different cast when Rudin explained it to Sinatra: he was selling
two thirds of a company not making money for $1.5 million and a one-
third interest in a profitable company.

As far as the people at Warner Records were concerned, it was a
shotgun wedding. Maitland and his senior executives at Warner Bros.,
having only recently pulled into the black, were upset at being thrust
back into the hole by Reprise. Yet they had no choice. Ben Kalmenson, a studio director and close aide to Jack Warner, summoned the
Warner Records board of directors to a meeting in New York on the
eve of the purchase and made it clear that the studio would brook no
dissension over the plan to use the record operation to get Sinatra for
its films.

"Before there is any discussion, I just want you to know that this is
a deal that we're going into," Kalmenson said. "We feel we can make
some good money out of this picture deal. As part of the deal we're
going to acquire the record company, and, in turn, we will allow
Frank to buy a one-third interest. All of this is acceptable to Jack
Warner. In fact, Jack wants the deal and I want the deal. I expect each
of you to vote in favor of the deal. Are there any questions?" There
were none. Over at Reprise, Ostin and his staff were working fever-
ishly to help Rudin complete a deal that could very likely put them
out of work.

Indeed, Starr wanted to dump Ostin, but Ostin hung on, in part because he was viewed as Sinatra's man and in part because he knew far
more about Reprise than anyone else. It wasn't a congenial atmosphere. "I got the feeling that what they wanted to do was to pick my
brain for however long they needed me and then dispose of me," said
Ostin.

Even after the merger, both Warner and Reprise remained indifferent to changing tastes, and rock signings were a rarity. At the height of
the British Invasion, the Kinks, signed to Reprise via a licensing deal

with their English distributor, Pye Records, was the only successful band the labels signed out of the U.K. Canadian folksinger Gordon Lightfoot was signed by Warners and dropped after just one single.

Such continuing conservatism was endemic in the record industry. The prevailing attitude of many veteran record executives toward rock was summed up in the oft-repeated condescension "It smells, but it sells," and the idea they cherished was to make a record that smelled a little less but still sold. Over at Capitol, executives at first refused to re-lease singles by the Beatles, who were signed to the company's English parent label, EMI.

The mainstream record companies—including the struggling Warner/Reprise—preferred pop records that could be palmed off as rock and roll. Petula Clark had been a successful pop singer in England for a decade when Warner Bros. licensed her single "Downtown" in the fall of 1964. The following year the record won the Grammy Award for Best Rock & Roll Recording—an outrageous misnomer. Clark's Grammy had more to do with what was going on in the American music industry than it did with what kind of performer she was. Who cared if her style was straight out of the English music halls? Clark was young, her records were up-tempo, and—not to be overlooked in those days of Beatlemania—she was *English.*

Yet as the Beatles, the Rolling Stones, and other British bands racked up hit after hit, it became increasingly apparent that the music so many record executives loathed was not going away. And as the American folk-rock scene gave birth to a new rock underground there were changes much closer to home than London or Liverpool that Warner Bros. could continue to ignore only at its peril. Indeed, several of the company's competitors were already combing the rock and folk clubs in California and setting up shop in Warner Bros.' backyard.

●

LOS ANGELES WAS LITTLE MORE THAN A DISTANT PROVINCE FOR THE record industry when Paul Rothchild made his first West Coast trip in 1964 to scout talent at UCLA's Folk Festival for Elektra Records. But he was immediately struck by how closely the amateur scene paralleled what was going on back home in Boston. "There was an active folk movement, and I found a couple of very interesting artists," he said.

"None of them onstage, all sitting around campus singing." Excited by what he heard, he quickly signed two acts.

As in Boston, the professional facilities were few and far between, and with the exception of Capitol, the big record companies were back east in New York. Prior to joining Warner Bros. Records, Joe Smith had found little going on in the business when he left a job as a Boston disc jockey in 1960 to move to Los Angeles and work as a salesman for a local record distributor. "This was an outpost," Smith recalls. "All the promotion guys representing East Coast companies knew that after three o'clock we could take off. Nobody was gonna call you. It was sleepy time down south."

The two major folk clubs in Los Angeles were the Troubadour on Santa Monica Boulevard and the Ash Grove on Melrose, and, as in Boston, that meant no rock and roll. For that, there were only a few options. One was Gazzarri's on La Cienega Boulevard. Lou Adler, the producer of the surf duo Jan and Dean, wandered into the club one night in 1963 and heard guitarist Johnny Rivers playing with just a drummer. "There was this strange feeling in there," Adler said. "Something was happening. It was like an adult Dick Clark show. Nobody had been dancing in California. At Gazzarri's they were dancing." To try and capture that strange feeling, Adler hired a remote-recording truck and cut Rivers live at the club. When owner Bill Gazzarri sued to stop release of the album, Adler helped Rivers land another gig at a new and more cooperative club, the Whisky-a-Go-Go, where they recorded Rivers's *Whisky-a-Go-Go* album. By May of 1964, Rivers's cover of the Chuck Berry song "Memphis" had reached number two on the *Billboard* Hot 100 singles chart.

The record's success instantly put the Whisky and the Sunset Strip's handful of music clubs on the map, but it was a former folkie who brought the Strip's rock scene into full flower in late '65. Jim McGuinn (who would soon change his name to Roger McGuinn)—the same guitarist who'd been booed for playing Beatles songs in New York folk clubs—had moved to Los Angeles and formed a new folk-rock band called the Byrds. This time his choice of material, electric versions of folk songs by Pete Seeger and Bob Dylan, was on target. After eight months of playing to empty chairs at Ciro's, an old Hollywood nightclub a few blocks from the Whisky, the group scored two number one Columbia singles, "Turn! Turn! Turn!" and "Mr. Tambourine

Man," and Ciro's immediately became the hottest club in Hollywood. Kids from all over Los Angeles's ever-enlarging suburban sprawl flocked into Hollywood, creating a circuslike atmosphere on Sunset. Right behind them came the record executives. If the prescient Lou Adler could still be found hanging out on the Strip, well, now he had a lot of company.

One of Adler's new competitors was Billy James, a publicist at Columbia Records' small Los Angeles office. In the year and a half since he'd come out west, he'd handled press for many of the label's biggest artists, such as Doris Day, Patti Page, Percy Faith, Ray Conniff, and Andy Williams. Like Rothchild, James was nearing thirty and was an avid folk and jazz fan. The Byrds were folk musicians who had made a transition to rock, and James—an early advocate of Bob Dylan following the singer's signing by Columbia in 1961—found it an easy transition to make.

Aside from his legitimate love for the new music and his excitement about what was happening in Los Angeles, James discovered that being associated with the music gave his career a new cachet. With the exception of Dylan—whom Columbia A&R man John Hammond had rightly recognized as an artist of tremendous importance—the large label's pop roster lagged behind the times. James worked hard to promote the Byrds, both within the company and to the media, and when the band broke his own star rose. He was particularly valuable to Columbia because he had the right business attitude: he was decidedly unimpressed by the attendant spirit of rebellion that was beginning to be felt on the Strip.

"I didn't believe the dream of the sixties," says James. "I had ten years on a lot of the people. The fact that kids could be dancing in a nightclub to music that had lyrics about a Welsh mining disaster was wonderful; the fact that meaning had been injected into a pop, essentially trivial medium thrilled me. All those notions were quite wonderful—but meaningless unless they were converted into hit records. That was my job, and I cared about my job."

Building on his success with the Byrds, James convinced Columbia to create a new position for him as the company's first head of artist development. The job's description was a bit fuzzy—the general idea was that Columbia should take a more active role in developing the careers of its performers.

We acquire artists, James had argued, and that's equivalent to the research effort of other industries. But while we've got the "r," there's no
"d" to go with it—we leave the development of our artists to their
agents and managers. Why? We give them cash advances and have a financial stake in their careers, so we're in the development business
whether we like it or not.

Columbia president Goddard Lieberson ultimately had to weigh the
merits of James's argument, and he opted to give him a shot. One day
in the autumn of '65 James was surprised to learn that Lieberson
was in Los Angeles and wanted him to meet him at Igor Stravinsky's
house in the Hollywood Hills. Lieberson asked the delighted and flabbergasted James if he would take him to Sunset Strip and show him
what was going on in Hollywood.

Like many of his coworkers, James almost worshiped Lieberson, a
dapper patrician under whose leadership Columbia became as classy
a record company as its president. He had personally supervised
dozens of Broadway cast recordings, including *South Pacific, My Fair
Lady, The Sound of Music,* and *Camelot.* His wide-ranging interests in
drama, history, and literature had led him to record a broad spectrum
of nonmusical works by Shakespeare, George Bernard Shaw, Bertolt
Brecht, Robert Lowell, Eugene O'Neill, and Samuel Beckett as well as
a series of lavish book-and-record sets on such topics as the Civil War,
the Mormon pioneers, and the Irish Uprising.

James and Lieberson started at Barney's Beanery on West Santa
Monica Boulevard, a popular bar for musicians, painters, and out-of-
work actors, and then strolled the length of the Strip, where literally
thousands of kids were hanging out. But despite Lieberson's willingness to be introduced to the new scene, the record company just
didn't get it, and James lost his powerful advocate when Lieberson was
soon kicked upstairs. "New York was expressing concern about me because they weren't exactly sure what I was doing," James says. "What
I was doing was combing the clubs. And there was incomprehension
regarding what was going on out on the street." James tried and failed
to get Columbia to sign singer/songwriter Tim Buckley, comedian
Lenny Bruce, Frank Zappa's Mothers of Invention, San Francisco's
Jefferson Airplane, and a sixteen-year-old singer/songwriter from
Orange County, Jackson Browne. Even James's victories were failures:
the Rising Sons, an influential Sunset Strip rock and blues band

featuring guitarists Taj Mahal and Ry Cooder, was signed, but their album wasn't released;* a quartet from Venice, California, the Doors, was given a six-month option that lapsed without any recording.

When Elektra asked James to open a West Coast office for them in the fall of 1966, he jumped at the chance and encouraged the Doors to accept Paul Rothchild's offer to sign and produce them. If staid Columbia wasn't ready to take the burgeoning Los Angeles music scene seriously, hungry Elektra certainly was. Rothchild, who had prodded the folk label into electric music with the Paul Butterfield Blues Band, viewed the Hollywood clubs as proof that Los Angeles was the new Mecca for hipness. He felt the same excitement on the Strip that he had on Bleecker and MacDougal streets in Greenwich Village and in the coffeehouses of Harvard Square. But prescient as he was, he never imagined that the Doors would make him a millionaire or that the embryonic folk-rock movement he had helped to identify would move quickly into the mainstream and give rise to a new global business. Unlike most of the music executives who would come after him, Rothchild had followed the music to Los Angeles because he was a believer.

"The stories started filtering back east," Rothchild remembered. " 'There's a freedom out there; it's the west.' 'The record companies are starting to sign, and there are places to play.' 'Marijuana is ten dollars a kilo out of Mexico—we're paying five dollars a lid in New York City.' 'People are mellow and laid-back, there's none of the uptight bullshit.' 'It's warm 365 days a year—your boots don't get all salty and fucked up.' It sounds like what Woody Guthrie's been talking about since day one: the Garden of Eden. And we got out there and found out it was true.

"And as each day goes by, the dress gets weirder, the friendships get deeper, and the streets get more packed. People meet each other at parties, in the parks, everybody's carrying an instrument, and groups form out of serendipity. It's like the break on a pool table: four million balls kissing each other."

AFTER YEARS OF SIDESTEPPING ROCK MUSIC, IT WAS NOW IMPOSSIBLE FOR THE executives at Warner/Reprise in Burbank to ignore what was happen-

*The Rising Sons recordings were finally put out nearly thirty years later.

ing just over the hills in Hollywood. "It was becoming quite clear that those acts who had paid our living were over," says Stan Cornyn. Sinatra, whose own sales had become hit or miss, was finally persuaded to loosen up the labels' policy toward rock acts. "I felt strongly that in order for us to compete and build a company it was necessary for us to be contemporary," says Ostin. "Purely pragmatic business."

Reprise A&R man Jimmy Bowen was given the green light to find rock talents. He quickly turned up two, right there in Los Angeles. One was Jack Nitzsche, an arranger, songwriter, and producer who had worked with Phil Spector and the Rolling Stones. Nitzsche offered Ostin new insights into the rock scene. "Mo Ostin and I were really close," Nitzsche said. "A week didn't go by where we didn't go to lunch. It was real warm, personal; it wasn't business. He'd ask me, 'What's marijuana like?' He'd ask me, 'What's cocaine like?' He'd ask me all kinds of things—he was an accountant. He didn't know, and he didn't pretend to. But he sure tried to learn, and did."

Nitzsche had also cowritten the song "Needles And Pins," a hit for both Jackie DeShannon and the Searchers, and he introduced Bowen to the song's coauthor, his friend Sonny Bono. When Bowen learned that Bono and his teenaged girlfriend, Cherilyn Sarkasian LaPier, were trying to make it as a singing duo named Caesar and Cleo, he got the nod from Ostin to sign them as well. But Bowen wasn't the only entertainment executive interested in the singers. Through Nitzsche, Bono had also met a pair of eager young show business hustlers, Charlie Greene and Brian Stone. "Greene and Stone wore dollar signs on gold chains around their necks," recalls John Hartmann, who booked some of their acts while an agent at the William Morris Agency. "That's how obvious they were. And they signed up everything that moved and wound up owning huge publishing [rights] on a lot of acts." They were about to sell Mo Ostin the same act twice.

Like Warner Bros., Greene and Stone's interest in rock was recent. Initially a starstruck bookkeeper, Brian Stone liked to tag along whenever his childhood friend, Charlie Greene, ferried performers around Manhattan nightclubs in his job as a low-level press agent for the PR powerhouse of Rogers, Cowan, and Jacobs. "We became very close with Bobby Darin, Sammy Davis, Keely Smith, and Louis Prima," says Stone. "I thought I wanted to be an accountant. I was an idiot." The duo worked briefly as publicists for bandleader Lionel Hampton, but a taste for the high life produced a mountain of debts and forced a hasty departure from New York for greener pastures.

Hitchhiking to Los Angeles in 1960, they arrived dead broke. Walking around Studio City one Sunday afternoon, Greene and Stone passed the Revue Studios lot on Lankershim. Curiosity—strictly professional, of course—got the better of them. They jumped the wall and had a good look around. They noticed the rows and rows of bungalows used for dressing rooms and offices. The door to one was ajar, so they went inside—and discovered the best scam in Los Angeles. "It had a couch which opened into a bed and had a shower and a telephone," says Stone. "So we just stayed there. Nobody came around checking."

The next morning brought the moment of truth. They didn't relish the idea of being thrown out or arrested. Instead, they decided to try taking charge. "We just pulled our normal, pushy New York shit: first thing we did was call the guards at the front gate. 'This is Mr. Stone in Room one-sixty. We wanted to make sure there's a permanent pass left for our staff. This is Greene, Stone Associates.' And that was that. From then on, our names were at the front gate, along with a bunch of other people who never existed."

Emboldened, they requisitioned a typewriter from the prop department and ordered a sign for the front door from the art department. They were soon conducting business on the dressing room telephone, writing letters on Revue stationery, bribing the mail-room boy, and charging meals at the studio commissary. "We used to sign the check and leave," says Stone. "I have no idea who picked up these checks; we'd just sign them. At the end of each week, they'd come around with a clipboard and say, 'Did you authorize these phone calls?' Pages and pages of calls. We'd initial it, and they'd disappear. It was one of those places where nobody dared question anything." Even better, they were able to solicit work as press agents from the actors on the lot. The arrangement finally unraveled when the partners overreached: they pitched Alan Miller, the head of Revue.

"Most of the studios had their own internal publicity departments," recalls Stone. "Revue didn't. Each show had its own press agents, indies. We decided that because we knew so many people, we wanted to pitch for the whole studio." Miller listened politely, but eventually had them thrown off the lot.

Unfazed by the setback, the duo parlayed their client list into a full-service PR business and moved into music by recording rock and roll versions of standards like "That Old Black Magic" and "Yes Sir, That's My Baby" with one of their clients, Billy Daniels. Jack Nitzsche was hired as the arranger. "Jack was the very first human being I ever saw with long hair," says Stone. "I couldn't believe it—he had hair over his *ears*." As an arranger for Phil Spector, who specialized in over-the-top, two-and-a-half-minute masterpieces like the Ronettes' "Be My Baby" and the Righteous Brothers' "You've Lost That Lovin' Feelin'," Nitzsche had developed a flair for bombast, and he hired about twenty background singers to work on a Daniels session. Bono and his girl-friend were two of them.

Impressed, Greene and Stone invited them back to their office and proposed becoming their managers, producers, and music publishers. "How can we make a deal?" Bono asked. "We already have a record about to come out." Stone assured them there would be no problem. "Don't worry," he said. "We know Mo, let us handle it." The deal was struck, including a rich 25 percent management fee.

A few weeks later, Greene and Stone organized a session for one of Sonny's new songs, "Baby Don't Go." Tape in hand, they called Ostin and said they wanted him to hear a new act named Sonny and Cher. "I listened and said, 'This is great,' " the executive recalls. "When I found out I'd been hoodwinked, I was pissed off at those guys." Worse, he'd agreed to a better royalty rate for Sonny and Cher than he had for the same act as Caesar and Cleo. Stone maintains that he and Greene never made the duo's identity a secret and that they simply convinced Ostin to release both records simultaneously—arguing that having two records by the same act under different names gave the label two shots—but he doesn't dispute that Ostin felt he'd been had. "Sonny didn't want to screw Mo," Stone says. "But I think Mo was a little pissed off that we'd made a record. He sent us a contract that was a one-record deal. We were very surprised."

All the chicanery appeared academic when "Baby Don't Go" stiffed everywhere except Los Angeles. Ostin, still angry, also released the duo from their original contract as Caesar and Cleo when Bono wouldn't drop Greene and Stone. Sonny and Cher were shopped to Imperial Records, where executive Bob Skaff passed on the duo but signed Cher as a solo artist. The deal left her free to record for someone else as half of Sonny and Cher. Atlantic Records president Ahmet Ertegun wanted to be that someone else, but Greene and Stone were skeptical because Atlantic was a rhythm and blues label; its only bona fide white star had been Bobby Darin. Still, Ertegun was able to sway Greene and Stone.

Ironically, Atlantic had no trouble breaking Sonny and Cher. Their second single for the label, released in July of 1965, was "I Got You Babe." It went to number one and stayed there for three weeks, selling over one million copies—Atlantic's biggest hit to date.

At Imperial Records Bob Skaff had wanted Cher to record "I Got You Babe," but his consolation prize wasn't too shabby. Taking note of the Byrds' success with "Mr. Tambourine Man," Cher recorded another Dylan cover the band performed nightly at Ciro's, "All I Really Want to Do." The Byrds' publicist, Derek Taylor, accused Sonny and Cher of ripping off the band, and Columbia responded by releasing the group's version of "All I Really Want to Do" the same day that Cher's single hit the streets. But despite the success of "Mr. Tambourine Man," Cher's version did far better, reaching number fifteen on the *Billboard* chart in the summer of 1965. The Byrds had to settle for number forty, an outcome that reportedly disappointed Dylan as much as it did the Byrds.

During the summer and fall of 1965, Sonny and Cher were the hottest act in the record business, with four Top 20 singles. They might have been crass knockoff artists, but their success was genuine and it would provide Greene and Stone with an entry to the emerging underground rock scene by attracting a young rock band whose originality was beyond dispute, Buffalo Springfield.

4

RIOT
ON THE
SUNSET STRIP

"ISN'T THAT YOUR FRIEND NEIL?"

Barry Friedman nudged Stephen Stills and pointed at the old black Pontiac hearse caught in traffic on the other side of Sunset Boulevard.

Neil? The first and last time Stills had seen Neil Young had been in 1965 in Fort William, Ontario, over a year ago. And how the hell would Friedman know? His only knowledge of Young came from hearing Stills talk about the young Canadian songwriter whenever the conversation turned to putting together his dream band. Still, the wagon carried a set of Ontario plates and there were definitely two longhairs in the front seat. This was worth a closer look.

Stills and Richie Furay left Friedman in the car and ran across Sunset. It *was* Neil! Later, over joints, Stills told him he was going to start a band—the best band in Los Angeles. He had been living with Dick Davis, a former folk musician who had introduced him and Furay to Barry Friedman, one of Los Angeles's hipper young record producers. Friedman had signed Stills and Furay to a personal management contract.

Friedman was one of the few people on Sunset Strip with real roots in the Los Angeles music scene. He had been a publicist for the

Troubadour and then Cinnamon Cinder, a teen club in Studio City owned by disc jockey Bob Eubanks.* Eubanks hosted his own dance party show on local television, which Friedman produced. Barry put the bands on live rather than have them lip-synch to their records—an unusual arrangement, especially for a small show.

"The first thing we noticed with live music was that it sounded like shit on television," he says. "None of these old farts who were doing the sound knew what it was supposed to sound like. So I ended up down in the sound booth pointing and saying 'No, no, those things over there are drums. See that guy over there? Turn that mike on so you can hear what he's doing.' Real simple stuff like that. But the bands liked it. They'd never sounded so good on television before."

As a result, groups asked Friedman to accompany them into the recording studio and act as an interpreter with the staff engineers employed by the record companies. "These old guys at the Columbia studio didn't know what to do," says Friedman. "I knew what it was supposed to sound like, so I got to tell the guy that what he was doing was stupid and that, yes, it's all right for these people to smoke a joint in the studio."

Friedman saw that the Beatles' success had created a seller's market for rock and roll bands. "At that point anything you went in the studio and recorded, there was some record company who would buy it within twenty-four to forty-eight hours." Having sold Columbia a recording of a piano being destroyed with sledgehammers, he knew he wouldn't have any trouble finding a deal for Stills's new band. "I said to [Stills], 'If you could have any band, who would these people be? Every one of them should be as good as you are.' " Stills told Friedman about Young.

Like Stills, Young had made up his mind to be a musician while in his early teens. His father, Scott, was a popular sports columnist for Toronto's *Globe & Mail,* and his mother, Rassy, was a regular on *Twenty Questions,* a TV quiz show in Winnipeg, where she and Neil lived after the Youngs divorced in 1960.

A scrappy kid plagued by health troubles, he survived a bout of childhood polio during the epidemic that swept Canada in the summer of 1951. Young was also color-blind and, by the time he was in his late

*Eubanks later became nationally known for *The Newlywed Game.*

teens, suffered from epileptic seizures. A loner, he was completely focused on music. At thirteen he had broken up his first band, the Jades, when the other guitarist missed a rehearsal because of school hockey practice.

By sixteen, Young was leading a Winnipeg quartet named the Squires, and he dropped out of high school the following year. The Squires had to cover a lot of territory, sometimes traveling as far as Churchill, eight hundred miles to the north. To make the trips, Young purchased a 1948 Buick hearse. It was cheap, great for equipment, and allowed him to make a dramatic entrance. "I loved the hearse," Young recalled. "Six people could be getting high in the front and back and nobody would be able to see in because of the curtains. And the tray— the tray was dynamite. You open the side door and the tray whips right out onto the sidewalk. What could be cooler than that? Pull up to a gig and just wheel out all your stuff on the tray."

The Squires' repertoire had grown to include many Young originals. Their set lists also included weird rock versions of folk standards like "She'll Be Comin' 'Round the Mountain" and "Clementine." "I wrote all new melodies," said Young. "We changed them totally with rock and roll arrangements." Young was now singing, despite the fact that his voice was shrill and brought cries from the audience to "stick to instrumentals." Even his mother had to admit that his singing was in "an interesting key."

In June of '65, the Squires decided to take a shot at the big time: Toronto. But despite landing a manager, they quickly fell apart after failing an audition for a record producer. A folk scene was blossoming in the city's Yorkville section, where Young worked briefly as a solo performer before hooking up with bassist Bruce Palmer and future funk star Rick James (then known as Ricky James Matthews) in a band called the Mynah Birds. The group cut an album for Detroit's Motown label that was never released and came to an abrupt end when James, who was AWOL from the navy, was arrested.

Bereft of new prospects, Young began to look south. "I knew my only chance to be heard was in the States," he said. In late February of '66, he and Palmer—along with a couple of friends to share expenses— climbed into the hearse and snuck across the border without work permits. Things had to be better in California.

"I was happy to see fucking *anybody* I knew," said Young. "And it seemed very logical that we form a band." Furay and Young had met when Young had made a brief trip to New York—Furay even remembered an original song Young had taught him then, "Nowadays Clancy Can't Even Sing." Stills and Young would play the lead guitar parts, Furay would sing and play rhythm, Bruce was the bassist. Within the week the band picked up drummer Dewey Martin from the Dillards, an electric bluegrass band that had toured with the Byrds. Even the group's name—Buffalo Springfield—presented itself: it was the brand name on a steamroller parked near Friedman's house.

The band rehearsed over the next few days, and Friedman went to work. He called Ed Tickner, who co-managed the Byrds, and arranged for Buffalo Springfield to open the group's upcoming five-date tour. He also called Paul Rothchild at Elektra. Convinced that Buffalo Springfield was a potentially important band and deserved to be treated seriously, Friedman knew the label's emphasis on quality performers and growing interest in the new Los Angeles rock scene made it the perfect home for the band. Indeed, Elektra founder Jac Holzman was eager to sign them, and it looked like a lock. But Friedman had failed to take an accurate read of his musicians, particularly Stills and Young. Yes, they considered themselves topical artists. But they also craved the stardom of the Byrds. It was an oversight that Dick Davis, whom the musicians had promised an equal share in the group, did not make. Instead of seconding Friedman's choice of Elektra, Davis introduced Buffalo Springfield to Charlie Greene and Brian Stone.

"They wanted the trappings, the associations of success," Davis says of the band. "Because success meant exposure. Greene and Stone were unabashed, and they exerted a powerful influence. The hype of success: *if you're not successful yet, we'll just lie about it and you will be.* They pretty well enchanted the group."

Davis's overtures couldn't have come at a better time. The overly generous 25 percent commission Greene and Stone were taking had led Sonny and Cher to dump them. "We saw [Buffalo Springfield] and said, 'We want to sign you guys for everything,' " recalls Stone. "And we did."

As with Sonny and Cher, "everything" meant music publishing, record production, and management—albeit this time for the standard 15 percent. In return, they advanced Buffalo Springfield $5,000, an amount that seemed like a fortune to the band. Most of the money went toward renting cars and buying new instruments.

Friedman was livid. Buffalo Springfield—the band he had fed and housed—and his pal Dick Davis had betrayed him. For money! "I pushed for Elektra because I felt their music deserved some kind of ethic behind it, that they weren't money-grubbing like Brian," says Friedman. "I was believing in all this peace and love shit. Unfortunately, they chose what they chose. They were young guys who wanted immediate success. Promise them a Maserati, they'll follow you anywhere." As he recalls it, he was simply strong-armed out of the picture. "Charlie took me to New York and got me outrageously stoned and drove me around in limousines and wouldn't let me eat," he says. "We had to get hot dogs from vendors through the window until I signed a release and let them go."

RECORD COMPANY INTEREST IN BUFFALO SPRINGFIELD WAS STRONG. AT Elektra, Holzman was still eager to sign the band. And at Warner Bros., Mo Ostin's twenty-three-year-old protégé, A&R man Lenny Waronker, son of Liberty Records cofounder Simon Waronker, was also high on the group.

While urging the label to sign Buffalo Springfield, he had been made the point man for a group of bands the label acquired when it purchased Autumn Records for $10,000 from Tom Donahue, the KMPX disc jockey whose groundbreaking "underground" format had inspired Ray Riepen at WBCN. Begun in 1964 by Donahue and two other disc jockeys, Bobby Mitchell and Sylvester Stewart (later known as Sly Stone), Autumn had scored a couple of hits before running into financial trouble. Waronker was tapped to produce three of its acts— the Beau Brummels, the Mojo Men, and the Tikis. To work with him, he called in two pianists, his childhood friend Randy Newman and Leon Russell, and another friend, pianist and arranger Van Dyke Parks. This was the beginning of a creative circle that, with Ostin's blessing, grew up around Waronker at Warner/Reprise and quickly became key to the company's success with rock.

Without a lot of money to lure acts, Ostin hit on the idea of creating and empowering a diverse team of in-house rock producers. "My father's attitude was always to be an A-and-R-driven company," says Michael Ostin. "He took the model from early Hollywood when MGM was *the* premiere company because of Irving Thalberg. It was

Thalberg's theory that if you tied up all the best directors, writers, and stars in Hollywood, you were going to make the best movies. My father saw that, and it was very clear to him that even though you couldn't do it on that level, still, you would contract artists and if you had the record *makers*—the record producers were analogous to the directors of films—you would be making the best records and ultimately the best artistry. And that would be a drawing card."

Ostin's faith in Waronker's taste was so great that he was willing to overlook his prior experience with Greene and Stone to get Buffalo Springfield. "Lenny wanted them very, very badly," he says. "He and I really were in hot pursuit. I was angry with Brian and Charlie. But to get an act—I even invited them to my house for dinner."

Instead, Greene and Stone phoned Atlantic. Label president Ahmet Ertegun, who had signed Sonny and Cher, was vacationing in Acapulco, so they made their pitch to Jerry Wexler. Although he disdained rock and roll, Wexler certainly wasn't going to ignore a tip from the managers who had given Atlantic its biggest pop act. "In those days we followed good leads," he says. "Ahmet went up there and signed them." Frustrated, Waronker consoled himself by having the Mojo Men cut a version of one of Buffalo Springfield's songs, "Sit Down, I Think I Love You."

Just weeks after forming, Buffalo Springfield was playing exciting gigs at the Whisky, and Atlantic was eager to record them. But their work in the studio went far less smoothly. "Their songs were sensational, they were great players, they were just a great group," says Stone. "But it's a far cry from a great group [to] a hit record. Back then you made singles, and you made them to be hits. If not, you were out of business."

The band quickly discovered the downside of its deal with Greene and Stone. The managers did know their way around the music business, but it was increasingly obvious that they knew a good deal less about making rock and roll records than advertised. Unhappy with the results, the musicians telephoned their managers the day after completing *Buffalo Springfield* and begged them to scrap the album and start over. Stone refused, and Ertegun sided with him.

When *Buffalo Springfield* flopped, the band blamed the managers. And without a hit record, Greene and Stone had no idea how to build the band as a concert attraction. "It was just pathetic," admits Stone.

"We'd go to some dates, and eleven people would show up. The guys were depressed." Says Dick Davis: "Nobody wanted to put them on the club circuit or put them out opening for another band. It seemed like everybody was trying to save the Buffalo for a big break, for a big shot at stardom and money. The group was starving."

Just as problematic were the seizures and blackouts Young was having. John Hartmann, one of the band's agents, saw the group in San Diego and watched with incomprehension as Young suffered a seizure onstage. "I said, 'Charlie, is this part of the act?' " Hartmann recalls. "I looked at his face and it was white. He said, 'No. This is not good.' " Out in the parking lot Hartmann found Young laid out over the back of a Corvette. "This nurse had her hand down his throat, keeping him from swallowing his tongue."

Young had suffered seizures before his arrival in Los Angeles, yet Davis saw a direct relationship between the pressures of the band and the recent onset of symptoms. "Neil's first attack came within a month of meeting Stephen Stills," he says. "As far as I know, his last came shortly after he left the band for good."

Young was given a battery of tests at UCLA and diagnosed with epilepsy. He was treated with Valium and Dilantin, yet the episodes remained fairly common. He frequently blacked out after working himself into a frenzy during his solo in the set closer, "Mr. Soul." "It happened at Ondine's [in New York], it happened at the Troubadour, it happened at the Whisky, at the Music Circus in Covina," says Davis, who would kill the lights and pull Young offstage.

When not performing, Young exploited his condition. "Sometimes we'd just be sitting at the Beef and Beer having a sandwich," recalls Davis, "and Neil would be interested in a girl and all of a sudden pass out. Then she would take him home and take care of him." Such obvious benefits left Stills skeptical, and in the absence of commercial success the friction between them grew. "Neil got very dizzy, said he got headaches," recalls Stone. "And Stephen said go fuck yourself."

Buffalo Springfield was on the verge of breaking up, a victim of internal squabbles and primitive management. But the Sunset Strip scene, which had brought them together, would provide the band one more opportunity.

IN THE SUMMER OF 1966, BUFFALO SPRINGFIELD SETTLED IN FOR AN EX-tended run at the Whisky. The scene on the Strip was drawing more and more kids into Hollywood every night. Laurel Canyon, the twist-ing artery connecting Ventura Boulevard and the suburban valley to Sunset with the nightly carnival of Hollywood, had become the music and drug capital of Los Angeles, the holy hills of the hip. The bunga-lows perched precariously on Lookout Mountain, Wonderland Av-enue, Ridpath Drive, and a handful of other dusty Canyon roads became a de facto rock and roll colony. Everyone involved in the scene who could afford to lived above Sunset in the Canyon, while those still trying to make it lived at the bottom of the hill, coming up to party in the neighborhood that the *Los Angeles Free Press*, the city's leading un-derground newspaper, had dubbed the "freak sanctuary." Recalls Barry Friedman, "There were actors and musicians and writers, and we all just kind of walked in and out of each other's houses. And the music that was coming out of the houses—it was everyone you ever wanted to hear."

Despite the great vibes, the unforeseen crowds of kids ushered in a new set of conflicts on Sunset. When several traditional-nightclub own-ers switched to operating licensed teen clubs in an effort to cash in on the scene (and some, like the Whisky, lowered their age of admission to eighteen), growing traffic problems and the constant presence of thousands of teenagers drew complaints from merchants, and the Sun-set Strip Chamber of Commerce urged the police to intervene. In Hollywood, where law enforcement was handled by both the Los An-geles Police Department and the county sheriff, this led to two primary courses of action: permits and licenses for teen clubs dried up, and a 10 P.M. county curfew for anyone under eighteen was zealously enforced.

The curfew law had been framed as a deterrent to public loitering and was not meant to prevent minors from being out or attending any show or activity. But charges soon began to circulate that police were using it indiscriminately to drive kids off the Strip, routinely handcuff-ing fourteen- and fifteen-year-olds. Leaflets urging a November 12 protest of "police mistreatment of youth on Sunset Blvd." succeeded in drawing a crowd variously estimated at between one thousand and three thousand to the front of Pandora's Box, on the eastern end of the Strip. The protest stopped traffic. A city bus caught in the middle of the congestion was forced to discharge its passengers when demonstrators climbed onto the roof. A window was broken in a nearby liquor store, and a few fistfights between kids and servicemen were also reported.

Despite the protest's limited scope, the local newspapers made a meal out of what they dubbed the riot on Sunset Strip. LONG HAIR NIGHTMARE blared the headline in the *Los Angeles Herald Examiner*. An editorial in the November 15 *Los Angeles Times* closed its eyes to the indiscriminate use of the curfew law, declaring that there were "no deep-rooted sociological or economic causes for the weekend rioting. Irresponsibility was simply fanned into complete disregard for the rules and standards."

The *Los Angeles Free Press* took exactly the opposite position. After labeling the editorial page writers at the *Times* "stupid old men" exhibiting "intellectual panic at events that are beyond your understanding," the weekly provided solid, firsthand reporting of the continuing demonstrations. While openly sympathetic to the protestors, the *Free Press*, and particularly reporter Brian Carr and publisher Art Kunkin, proved nowhere near as one-sided and sensational in its coverage as the mainstream news media. While blaming the police for waiting too long to make demonstrators stay on the sidewalk, Carr also chided the protest's organizers for not providing adequate leadership. A non-bylined piece—purportedly by an unnamed twenty-six-year-old teacher—detailed mass arrests and brutal police treatment of citizens who just happened to be walking on the Strip. But the paper also let police spokesmen print statements in their entirety (an offer the L.A.P.D. took advantage of and that the more strident sheriff's office declined), interviewed club owners, sought to identify leaders within the protest, and ultimately wrapped the disaffection of kids on the Strip in the mantle of the peace and civil rights movements:

> The long hairs are asking, with some justification: why should hair length, a beard or sandals be any more a true test of a man than skin color? They point out that, more often than not, it is not they but the conventionally dressed youth or adult who abandons social courtesies in the night club atmosphere of the Strip and bothers other people. They say that they have as much right to eat in a restaurant, go to a movie or walk in the street as a Negro. They argue that

their defiance of some social conventions does not mean that they are either imbeciles or criminals, that it takes intelligence on their part to make a choice that is different from that of the majority. And those under eighteen say: "Shortly we'll be asked to fight in the dark jungles of Vietnam. Why shouldn't we be allowed to visit the area of our choice in Los Angeles after ten P.M.?"

Like the *Los Angeles Free Press*, Greene and Stone were aghast at the spectacle of the police running kids off the Strip, although their objections were far less ideological. Sunset Strip was ground zero for the local music scene, and shutting it down would be a disaster for Buffalo Springfield. They quickly joined with several other music executives to form an ad hoc committee to rally industry support.*

Though performing in San Francisco the week of the protest, Buffalo Springfield was all too familiar with the way the police often dealt with longhairs. Greene, Stone, and Neil Young had each been arrested a few weeks earlier on the flimsiest of pretexts. The incident began when Dick Davis, coming out of the Whisky one afternoon, was stopped by an officer from the sheriff's department.

"The guy says, 'I want to talk to you,' " says Davis. "I was at a parking meter two cars up. Completely innocent, I said, 'Just a minute.' I wanted to put money in my meter because I realized I was going to get a ticket. So I ran up and put the money in and came back. And by that time he'd gotten out of the car and run up to me. I was stunned. He grabbed me and slammed me up against the parking meter and kicked my feet. Just wild, he was crazy."

Others, including Young, came out of the Whisky to see what was going on. The deputies took identification on Davis, Young, and several others and ran their names for outstanding warrants. When an unpaid traffic ticket turned up on Young, he was arrested.

When Greene and Stone showed up at the station on San Vicente to bail Young out, Greene was promptly arrested for his own outstanding traffic tickets. "They put Charlie in a cell," says Stone. "I said, 'Just a minute. I'm bailing them out.' And they said, 'Let us see *your* ID.' "

*The group, the Community Action for Facts and Freedom Committee (CAFF), was chaired by Byrds co-manager Jim Dickson and also included the Byrds' publicist, Derek Taylor, the group's Gene Clark, music executives and Strip regulars Michael Vossi and David Anderle, Woolworth heir Lance Reventlow, disc jockey Elliot Mintz, Fifth Estate coffeehouse owner Al Mitchell, and the Whisky's Elmer Valentine.

Stone, of course, had his own outstanding traffic warrants. "I knew if they got my ID I was dead. I said, 'I'm not giving you my ID. I haven't committed any crime—I'm just bailing someone out. Here's the money, please let them out.' I was talking very politely, but these guys were so pissed. I feared them worse than anything. They said, 'Okay, you're under arrest.' " Attorney Lee Phillips eventually came to bail everyone out. But the police were slow to release Young.

"They weren't letting go of Neil," says Davis. "We couldn't figure out what they were keeping him for. Finally, they let him out, and he had been beaten. They had taken him into a cell and really given him a rough time. It left Neil pretty shaken for a long, long time."*

Despite missing the "riot," Buffalo Springfield still managed to come up with the record, "For What It's Worth," which chronicled events in Hollywood and became the new anthem for the crowds on Sunset Strip. Returning to Los Angeles from San Francisco the following week, Stills had dropped by a party at the Topanga Canyon ranch of Terry Sachem, who worked with the Beach Boys. Among the guests were guitarist Danny Whitten, his friend Will Hinds, and singer Robin Lane, who was briefly Neil Young's live-in girlfriend.

"We were all sitting in front of the fire," says Lane, "tripping on acid. Stephen picked up his guitar and started playing this little riff—and he started singing: 'Something is happening here; what it is ain't exactly clear.' And he'd write it down. 'Stop, hey, what's that sound.' And he just wrote this song right there in front of everybody."

"We ran into the studio the next day," says Stone, who saw the record's success as vindication of his production abilities. "We over-dubbed some hand claps, but it's a very simple record. The little guitar line that runs through the record is played by Neil . . . We miked the foot drum, and, really, the record is just that. No more."

Delighted with the results, the managers called Ertegun in New York and played the recording over the phone. "Fabulous!" he enthused. "I love it. Who are they?"

Having already learned the downside of selling the same act twice, Greene and Stone assured Ertegun that he already had the band under

---

*According to Stone, he and his partner later sued the sheriff's department over the arrest and won a settlement. Their attorney in this episode, Lee Phillips, is a leading Los Angeles entertainment attorney, whose later clients have included David Geffen and Jon Landau.

contract, and Atlantic agreed to rush-release the single (although Erte-gun first tried, unsuccessfully, to get Stills to drop a verse—"There's a man with a gun over there/telling me I've got to beware"—that referred to the police). It was an immediate hit, especially in Los Angeles, where Greene and Stone had enough juice to get prerelease copies played by disc jockeys. "I swear," says Lane, "it wasn't two days after the party that I turned on the radio and there it was. That was Charlie Greene and Brian Stone. They must've done something right."

With a hit single on their hands after several misses, Atlantic re-pressed the group's debut album, adding "For What It's Worth." As a single, the song reached number seven. But the song's success wasn't enough to ensure the future of Buffalo Springfield. The problem wasn't talent; if anything, there was an overabundance of talent. The downside of Friedman's original pitch to Stills—that the band should only include musicians who were as good as he was—had become ap-parent. "Nobody wanted that band like Stephen did," says Davis, "and that's why he was the acknowledged leader." Stills was more than a little proprietary about that role, and Young's position was proving too nebulous for his talents. He and Stills were both ambitious, but they were getting in each other's way. Robin Lane recalls an enraged Stills bursting into the bungalow she briefly shared with Young in Laurel Canyon. "Neil didn't want to go to some rehearsal or session," she says. "And Stephen was *so* pissed off. He picked up my guitar and was going to smash it over Neil's head. *'You're ruining my career! You're ruining my career!'* "

Although they were initially united, first by ambition and then by a dissatisfaction with the way their debut album, *Buffalo Springfield*, sounded, the band quickly became a collection of individuals pursu-ing their own interests. "Everything we recorded, each guy would listen," Stone says. "And Bruce would say, 'Y'know, I think I need a little more bass.' Oh, okay. We flipped the bass. And Dewey would say, 'Foot,* I need a little more foot.' And then Stephen would say, 'I don't hear my little lick in there.' Each guy would want his part a little more, a little more, a little more—and push everything up until we're back to Bruce saying, 'I can't hear my bass anymore.' It was re-ally difficult."

*The bass drum, played with a foot pedal.

As Buffalo Springfield moved inexorably toward its disintegration, Warner/Reprise was solidifying as a powerful home for underground rock. Under Mo Ostin's direction, the company's executives now took to the streets in search of new talent the way Paul Rothchild, Billy James, and Lou Adler had. They quickly found it, but not in the clubs of nearby Hollywood.

In 1966, Warner Bros. Pictures bought the rights to a book based on the beatnik scene in San Francisco's North Beach district and approached Stan Cornyn about going there to research and write the screenplay. He jumped at the opportunity and opted to begin his research at City Lights, the bookstore that served as a gathering point for literary Beats. But he quickly sensed that something was superseding the North Beach scene. "I saw these strange posters," he recalls, "that were interesting and largely illegible." Venturing over to one of the Haight Street dances advertised by the posters, Cornyn stumbled onto the nascent psychedelic scene. He had no idea what to make of it.

"I wore a Nehru shirt to fit in and was scared shitless," he says. "I saw things I had never seen before. *Light shows.* It was experimental art, black lights and strobes set inside television sets. It didn't have a name yet—to me at least."

When Cornyn returned to Los Angeles, he told Ostin and Joe Smith what was going on up north. Like Columbia's Goddard Lieberson, Ostin was keen to have a firsthand look at the developing scene and weigh its commercial potential. A few weeks later, he and Cornyn took their wives to San Francisco. "We stayed at the Fairmont," says Cornyn, "but walked Haight-Ashbury." They were put off by roach clips, but they saw an opening for a record company without a lot of money. "Mo and Joe had nothing to lose by signing acts," says Cornyn. "Acts were fairly cheap, and they knew they didn't want to compete with the established labels. So they scrounged around and took risks. Not because they necessarily had an artistic philosophy, but because it was what you could get. And then if you have the attitude right, you hope maybe you'll sell a few by word of mouth in San Francisco. Then by word of mouth you sell a few in Boston. And it starts. All you can do is blow on the tinder."

Joe Smith wanted to sign anything in the Bay Area that smelled even vaguely like a rock band. "Joe was frustrated by a budgetary constraint because he thought he could fly up to San Francisco and sign twenty or forty acts for five thousand dollars apiece and have the whole thing," says Cornyn. Instead, Mike Maitland approved just enough money for Reprise and Warner Bros. to each sign one psychedelic band. Ostin and Reprise made a bad choice, picking a Los Angeles group, the Electric Prunes. Smith and Warner Bros. signed the Grateful Dead.

Again, Tom Donahue provided the entrée, dragging Smith and his wife to hear the Dead in all their psychedelic trappings at the Avalon Ballroom. They weren't like any group he'd ever seen before, but Smith could at least appreciate that the Grateful Dead were a real rock and roll band. "Tom," he told Donahue as they stood in the wings of the Avalon stage, "I don't think Jack Warner will ever understand this." Replied Donahue, "I don't know if I understand it myself, but you've got to sign them because this is where it's going."

Dealing with the Grateful Dead and San Francisco's psychedelic consciousness proved a cultural and financial turning point for the company. The Dead were a band, but they aspired to more. Yet what that "more" entailed was almost indefinable. They were, of course, closely associated with the drug culture. Aside from being the house band for the acid tests, the group was bankrolled by LSD chemist Stanley Owsley—not the kind of "partner" Warner Bros. was used to having. The musicians also lived and conducted business communally. Smith, who was used to shuttling back and forth between Los Angeles and Las Vegas to schmooze Frank Sinatra and Don Rickles, would have to make a major adjustment, and he wasn't the type to go native. "How could I hang out with the Dead?" he was still asking himself twenty-five years later. "With their wives and kids and the house on Ashbury Street? Jesus, it was Fellini time." Still, if Warner Bros. wanted to get a piece of this—whatever *this* was—he was going to have to make the relationship work. He was pleasantly surprised to discover that the Dead were far from ignorant and that he shared some common ground. "All of the Grateful Dead went to college," says Smith, a Yale graduate. "Of course, when they started gassing up with acid it was a little difficult to talk to them."

The Dead's solution to that small problem was to urge Smith to trip with them, a suggestion he never warmed to. Indeed, he worried that the band—who slipped the similarly recalcitrant promoter Bill Graham a hit of acid when he wasn't expecting it—was going to "dose" him. "They always told Tom Donahue that they were gonna get me," Smith fretted. "I didn't see the necessity for it myself."

Talking business with the Dead could be difficult. The group's extended family participated in business discussions, and Smith— expecting to talk to the band's managers—could find himself in a meeting with fifty or sixty people. And while the Dead had some unorthodox requests, such as a budget for handing out nuts and fruit to concert audiences, success was not anathema to their agenda. Wanting Smith to take LSD during the negotiating sessions did not preclude Grateful Dead managers Rock Scully and Danny Rifkin from trying to get as much money out of him as possible.

When the band came down to Burbank with the tapes and artwork for a double live album, label executives were aghast at the title the group had selected, *Skull Fuck*. The Dead had control over all aesthetic decisions from recording to cover art. But Smith—who reminded the band that they were $120,000 in the hole to the label and weren't going to see any royalties until Warner Bros. was repaid—found them remarkably pragmatic when the subject was their career.

" 'This is what you want to call it?' " Cornyn recalls Smith asking when the executives and musicians sat down in a Warners conference room. " 'Yep. *Skull Fuck*.' He said, 'I think you should understand— and we will make a survey for you—that if you call it this you probably will not be in Sears.' And then he named all the other obvious places where the record would not be sold. He did not take the position that Warner Brothers Records wouldn't put this out. *They* pulled back because it hurt the pocketbook. Joe played that beautifully."

Despite the fact that those early albums didn't sell well, the Grateful Dead proved a priceless asset for Warner/Reprise. They were authentic American bohemians, the acid-munching standard-bearers of the underground. The Dead challenged convention—and now, by inference, Warner Bros. did as well. "They were really the springboard," said Bob Krasnow, who then headed Warners' short-lived black music label, Loma. "People said, 'Wow, if they'll sign the Grateful Dead, they must be going in the right direction.' "

"We became the notorious place to be if you were a record act," says Cornyn. "We were daring in our signings and appeared to be daring in our exploitation of signings. We would do anything."

San Francisco wasn't the only place Ostin and Joe Smith went searching for rock bargains. "Mo and Joe—but especially Mo—would get *Music Week*, the British record journal," recalls Cornyn. "Wetting their index fingers and moving from page to page looking for 'stuff.' Mo found a new act, just on the English charts, and called up on a lark. 'Is it available for the U.S.?' 'Yes, it is.' Without knowing too much we signed this Experience act. Didn't know much about it but brought it over. Had an awful-looking cover. Just awful."

Ostin had unwittingly landed one of rock's creative giants. Even when he saw the Jimi Hendrix Experience perform the following year at the Monterey Pop Festival, Ostin was far from impressed. He found Hendrix's performance, which included squirting lighter fluid on his guitar and setting it afire, an embarrassment. Recalls Ostin, "I was thinking 'Jesus, does he have to showboat?' "

If Ostin didn't know what to make of Hendrix, he wasn't alone— neither did most rock critics. Jon Landau turned up his nose at *Are You Experienced?* in the first issue of *Rolling Stone,* and Robert Christgau in his coverage of the Monterey festival for *Esquire* termed the guitarist "terrible." Appalled by his stage antics, Christgau termed Hendrix "a psychedelic Uncle Tom" and was more impressed with sidemen Noel Redding and Mitch Mitchell. Still, if it was difficult to recognize Hendrix's originality on first exposure, he would soon become a potent seller for Reprise—cause enough for executives to label him a genius. "One gets over one's embarrassment," observes Cornyn.

Aside from providing Ostin with his first glimpse of Hendrix, the Monterey Pop Festival also led him to hire executive Andy Wickham, who would play a key role in Warners' transformation into a successful rock label. A young assistant to one of the festival's organizers, Lou Adler, Wickham, like Warner Bros., had detoured into rock. A commercial artist working for Grey Advertising in London in the early sixties, he began to suspect that there was a more interesting and lucrative way to make a living when his friend, graphic designer Charlie Watts, became the drummer for the Rolling Stones. Wickham soon followed him into rock and roll and moved to California to work for Adler.

Initially excited by America's promising music scene, Wickham began to take a somewhat dimmer view of the evolving pop culture when he struck up a friendship with Phil Ochs. The protest singer, who remained committed to folk music's political/activist tradition, had little use for the increasingly commercial underground scene, which he viewed as hypocritical.

Wickham's new outlook led to a falling-out with Adler. Asked to write the festival's program notes, Wickham obliged with a vehement indictment of the show and its participants, charging that any claims to being social crusaders were a sham and that the artists and the festival's promoters were motivated solely by commerce and greed. The essay was never printed, but he was proved at least partly right: the Monterey Pop Festival wound up serving primarily as a commercial showcase for the record companies. Executives flocked there, and the price for bona fide underground San Francisco bands skyrocketed. The previous year, RCA had signed the Jefferson Airplane for $25,000; around the time of the festival, Capitol picked up two acts, the Steve Miller Blues Band and the Quicksilver Messenger Service, for guarantees of $40,000 apiece. Then, in the wake of an impressive performance at Monterey, CBS Records paid Janis Joplin and her band, Big Brother and the Holding Company, an astounding $250,000. Clive Davis, who was now running CBS Records, was giving his competitors notice that the industry leader now believed in the commercial legitimacy of the new music and wasn't averse to using its deeper pockets to get the best talent.

Warner/Reprise couldn't afford to practice Davis's brand of checkbook A&R. Instead, Ostin made just one acquisition at Monterey. He hired the now unemployed Andy Wickham as house hippie, the company's official emissary to the underground. If Joe Smith wasn't going to mingle with the acts, it was becoming pretty obvious that it wouldn't hurt business if somebody did.

Although Wickham kept an office at Burbank, was paid $200 a week, and given his own secretary, his real work was to be part of the Laurel Canyon cognoscenti, keeping one hand on the pulse of the underground and pointing potential signings toward the label with the other. Among those Wickham had a role in bringing to Warner/Reprise were Eric Andersen, Jethro Tull, and Van Morrison. During his first week at the company, Wickham urged Ostin to sign Joni Mitchell. Just twenty-three, the Canadian folk singer had come to Wickham's attention when Tom Rush and the duo Ian and Sylvia recorded her song "The Circle Game." After hearing a tape of a club performance and being told that Mitchell looked like a blond Joan Baez, Ostin quickly gave his approval.

With the roster beginning to reflect the changing market, Warner/ Reprise undertook an important campaign to carve a hipper corporate identity with its newfound young audience. The emergence of rock and underground publications provided the labels with an appropriate outlet for print ads; indeed, record companies became one of the most important sources of advertising revenues at *Crawdaddy!* and *Rolling Stone,* and Jim Fouratt, an executive at Columbia Records in New York, went so far as to brag that he was responsible for funding the underground press. Unfortunately, the ads Columbia ran were often an embarrassment and looked exactly like what they were—an ill-conceived attempt by a major corporation to pretend it was part of the counterculture.

"If you won't listen to your parents, the Man or the Establishment . . . Why should you listen to us?" asked a Columbia Records ad in the November 9, 1968, issue of *Rolling Stone*—suggesting that Columbia, owned by CBS, wasn't part of the Establishment. The following month a photograph of seven men lounging around a jail cell ran under the legend *"But the Man Can't Bust Our Music."* "The Establishment's against adventure," began the copy for the ad, which, inexplicably, was for classical albums. But Columbia reached a stomach-turning low in counterculture pandering in the December 21 issue with an ad slugged *"Know Who Your Friends Are."* Aside from the obvious inference that the people at Columbia Records are your friends, the ad showed a half-dozen young people—including a Native American wearing a headdress—passing a joint. "And look and see and touch and be together," ran the copy alongside pictures of eight covers for recently released albums. "Then listen. We do."

Fortunately for Warner Bros., Cornyn, now writing the company's ads, was young enough to appreciate the music and just a little too old to be on the "us" side of the us-and-them equation. His offbeat, self-deprecating print ads for Warner/Reprise—which were far smarter than any other record company's—either deflated his labels' hype or acknowledged that Warners was a seeker of lucre and that any hippie truths being purveyed were just the by-product of happenstance. Cornyn was comfortable enough with the company and the talent of its artists not to put them on a pedestal. Where the autohype of other labels produced a self-important stream of interchangeable promotions for unfailingly brilliant artists who, when they failed, were replaced by new brilliant artists, Warner/Reprise made its pitch like a bemused huckster on a psychedelic midway.

Cornyn's early ads for the Grateful Dead and the Fugs lampooned traditional teen magazine giveaways. For the Dead, it was a fictitious "Pigpen look-a-like contest" built around the group's legendary toxic keyboardist, Ron "Pigpen" McKernan. For the Fugs, which included noted New York poets Ed Sanders and Tuli Kupferberg, there was the "Win a Fug dream date competition."*

Not all of Warner/Reprise's new artists liked being treated so glibly. When ads appeared bemoaning the fact that the company couldn't sell albums by Randy Newman and Van Dyke Parks and attempted to either give them away or sell them for a penny, Parks accused Cornyn of ruining his career. Another ad, meant to convey that Joni Mitchell had yet to achieve any real market penetration, was slugged *"Joni Mitchell Is 90% Virgin."* When Mitchell's manager called to say it had reduced her to tears, Cornyn pulled the ad. "Mo stopped by my office and casually said, 'You might think twice about some of those,' " he recalls.

It was a potent reminder that the record company's new signings— Joni Mitchell, Jimi Hendrix, Randy Newman, Van Dyke Parks, and the Grateful Dead—all took themselves quite seriously. The ascendancy of a more ambitious pop culture had created pop *artists,* who, although they might still crave the luxury of being pop stars, demanded control of their work, image, and careers.

It was uncharted territory, but Warner/Reprise was willing to take the gamble. Financing—and waiting for—an album by the Grateful Dead was an unnerving experience. Unhappy with their first album for Warner Bros., the group spent nearly two years and over $100,000 working on an album they could never seem to finish.

"Sinatra used to make records for twenty-two thousand dollars in three nights," says Joe Smith. "Frank didn't know how to turn on the tape recorder. But everything changed. These people were using all the technology. They were very demanding about how they were positioned,

---

*One of the entries Cornyn received read: "Dear Sirs (or whoever you are): I would like to go out with Tuli because I would like him to fuck me. Barbara. P.S. Even if I don't win I would like it."

packaged, and sold. They wrote these songs, and the records meant a lot more to them than Dean Martin's records ever meant to him. He could hear one of his records and say, 'When did we do that?' "

NEIL YOUNG TOOK HIS MUSIC SERIOUSLY. THROUGHOUT THE ASSOCIATION with Greene and Stone, he had been eager to learn as much as he could about making records—whenever they cut another performer, he would be there watching and learning. It didn't take him long to recognize that arranger Jack Nitzsche was the real production talent, and the two started collaborating on a series of recordings that included "Broken Arrow" and "Expecting to Fly," which ended up on Buffalo Springfield albums. But aside from developing his music, he was looking for a better way to make it as a rock star. Young told Nitzsche he wanted "lots of money and star fame" and suggested that the best way to get it would be by combining the lyric approach of Bob Dylan with the music of the Rolling Stones. Nitzsche encouraged Young to quit Buffalo Springfield, and the rocker began an on-again, off-again cycle of involvement with the band.

"Everyone thought of the group as the strongest unit for success," says Davis. "And Neil didn't. In the end, of course, he's right. Nobody expects groups to stay together except the group and the fans. The managers, the professionals—they know those groups aren't going to stay together. Jack knew. But we didn't."

Atlantic, however, tried to keep the band going. If unable to really break the group, the label at least recognized that it was important—both musically and in establishing Atlantic's attractiveness to other rock acts. With dissension and continuing unhappiness ripping the group apart, Ahmet Ertegun personally produced their second album and even persuaded Greene and Stone to release them from their management and production contracts. But the personal animosities and inability to achieve more than fleeting commercial success had already taken too much of a toll. Buffalo Springfield was now a group in name only, their third album largely a collection of independently recorded tracks, delivered by their authors as finished masters. By the time the group appeared at the Monterey Pop Festival, Young was gone for good. In a harbinger of things to come, he was replaced at the festival by David Crosby of the Byrds.

Nitzsche was convinced that Warner Bros. was the place for any rocker who took himself seriously. "Warner Brothers was making music for adults rather than children," he said. He brought Young to see Ostin, and a Reprise solo contract with a $15,000 advance was quickly arranged. Neil Young was betting his future on the company that was betting on rock. But if the industry and the musicians were now looking west to Warner/Reprise to see how the new music should be recorded and promoted, they had to look east to New York to see how careers should be managed. The old-line show business hustle of Greene and Stone hadn't worked for an artistically ambitious group like Buffalo Springfield. A different outlook was essential. Bob Dylan's manager, Albert Grossman, had a different outlook.

5

CUMULUS
NIMBUS

Tucked off a bend in a winding road in the hills above Cannes, Moulin de Mougins looks like hundreds of other French country inns with its old stone foundation and pebbled parking lot. But looks can be deceiving. To gourmands worldwide, chef Roger Verge and his restaurant are not chef and inn but priest and temple. On a winter's night in the last week of January 1986, a small group of believers gather in a private room to dine on one of Verge's renowned meals and sit shivah for the soul of Albert B. Grossman. All are wealthy men in their fifties: Seymour Stein, whose Warner Bros.–owned Sire Records is home to Madonna, Talking Heads, and the Ramones; Shep Gordon and George Greif, who manage Alice Cooper and Barry White respectively; and David Braun, the former president of PolyGram Records.

Bob Krasnow leads the memorial service. Now the chairman of Elektra Records, he met Grossman in the early seventies when his adventurous little label, Blue Thumb Records, was about to go bust. He remembers how Grossman—then still the most powerful artist manager in the record business—didn't give him the money to save Blue Thumb but got him so stoned that it took him seven hours to drive the ninety miles to Manhattan from Grossman's house in Woodstock. "Albert was the first guy with designer grass," Krasnow remembers with a nostalgic sigh. "I was whacked out of my mind."

It was the start of a long friendship, one that had ended just a few days earlier when Grossman died quietly of a heart attack on the overnight flight from New York to London. He was just fifty-nine, but most people thought Albert Grossman was much older. He had *always* looked older, even as a young man, with his resonant voice, strange affectations, and prematurely gray hair. "The first impression I had of him was that he was an old man," says Suze Rotolo, who met Grossman in Greenwich Village in 1962 when he was floating in and out of Gerde's Folk City and the Gaslight like a great gray cloud, trying to become the manager of Rotolo's young boyfriend, Bobby Dylan. "He was probably, what, thirty? But he was an adult."

Grossman did become Dylan's manager. And Janis Joplin's manager as well. He created and guided Peter, Paul and Mary, and among his other clients he counted the Band, Richie Havens, the Electric Flag, Gordon Lightfoot, the Paul Butterfield Blues Band, Ian and Sylvia, Todd Rundgren, Odetta—a stable of talent that made him more powerful than the record company presidents he, by turns, negotiated with, bullied, and taught.

Grossman knew what to do with his power. He was a builder: he built houses, restaurants, theaters, recording studios, power stations; he even built his own town in Upstate New York. He owned nightclubs in Chicago and New York and was a partner with Bill Graham in the Fillmore East. But along with that, he fashioned something far more intangible, impressive, and lasting. He built artists. And he built the rock and roll business.

Walking around the table at Moulin de Mougins, Krasnow offered a final benediction and personal remembrance of Grossman to each man. When he came to David Braun, he paused.

Braun, more than anyone in the room, owed his start in the record business to Grossman, who had hired him as his attorney in 1962. Two weeks after their first meeting, Grossman came by Braun's office with a withdrawn young man who took a seat off in the corner. "Dave," Grossman said in his oversized baritone, "I want you to meet the next Frank Sinatra." It was about the last Braun saw of his new client, Bob Dylan. But that was all right because suddenly Braun found himself deliriously busy—courtesy of Albert Grossman. "He brought in Odetta, Gordon Lightfoot, Ian and Sylvia," Braun says. "I was like the king of the folkies."

Over the next seven years, Braun would help Grossman negotiate deals that redefined the pop record business: Recording contracts that paid huge sums but—more important—gave Grossman's clients unheard-of control of their careers and work. New, artist-owned music publishing companies and production firms. Lucrative performance fees. Like no one else before him, Grossman recognized the untapped leverage at his fingertips, the simple and insurmountable advantage he had over the record companies and others when he came to the negotiating table: "If the bird ain't happy, the bird don't sing." The financial power of the performer—especially a singular performer like Bob Dylan or Janis Joplin—was just one of Albert's lessons, and it wasn't lost on David Braun. When it ultimately came time for him to choose between Grossman and Dylan, it was a no-brainer.

Braun waited tensely in the rich silence of Moulin de Mougins for Krasnow to pass sentence on him. "Albert loved you, too," he finally said. "Even though you betrayed him."

Damning Braun was, if not wrong, not quite right: somehow, regardless of the intentions, betrayal was never far from Albert Grossman.

●

ALBERT GROSSMAN WAS THE CHICAGO-BORN SON OF RUSSIAN JEWISH IMmigrants. Earning a degree in economics from Roosevelt College, he took a job as a public housing administrator at the Deerborne Homes on the South Side. After work, he liked to hang around a club called the Offbeat Room, and it was there that Grossman befriended folksinger Bob Gibson in 1955.

"Al was a real stoic kind of guy," remembers Gibson with a laugh. "You never knew what the hell he was thinking." Still, Grossman confided that he wanted out of the housing authority. With Gibson's encouragement, Grossman and Les Brown—a college friend who would later become the television critic for *The New York Times*— opened the Gate of Horn in 1957, a small club two blocks off the main strip of nightclubs on Rush Street. Grossman also began to manage Gibson.

"At that time there were the people who did it according to Hoyle with the agency deals and the management deals, and then there were the rebels," recalls Gibson. "I was definitely one of the rebels. Al said, 'You people have to be protected.' Albert was the first of the guys to see there were people trying to make statements with what we were doing. And they had to interface with some real business types. He was going to put the music back in the music business."

San Francisco folksinger Odetta became Grossman's second client after he brought her to Chicago for an appearance at the Gate of Horn. He began spending less and less time at the club, devoting more of his energy to promoting his artists. He often traveled on the road with them, taking the measure of the scene, the talent, and the business in other cities.

Paul Rothchild met Grossman at a New York party in 1958. "There was a whole bunch of gospel people there," he remembers. "I had been following the gospel world for years, but I'd never been able to hang out with them after a show. These were hard-drinkin', hard-smokin', sucky-fucky, dirty-talkin', crazy-livin' people, and it blew my mind. And who was at the center? Not Albert Grossman, *Al* Grossman. This was before the incarnation of Albert Grossman. This was Al Grossman, young hustler from Chicago. That was my first sighting of him, and it was impressive."

Promoter George Wein met him at about the same time, when he booked Odetta into his Boston club, Storyville. "We got to hang out every night when he was there with Odetta," says Wein. "He was brilliant and knew the folk field." As the promoter for the Newport Jazz Festival, Wein was encouraged by the reaction to an afternoon program of folk music at the 1958 festival and began planning an entire folk fest for the following year. He hired Grossman as the producer.

Along with Detroit jazz promoter Ed Sarkesian, Wein and Grossman also formed Production and Management Associates (PAMA) as a partnership. Wein urged Grossman to come to New York, and Grossman began looking for someone to buy his stake in the Gate of Horn. He quickly found Allan Ribback, a graduate student at Indiana State University with an earnest love for the music and a small inheritance.

Says Ribback, "Albert offered me a job as a co-manager. I think it was mainly because he wanted to borrow five thousand dollars . . . He had a kind of charisma. He was quiet, but very intelligent and always seemed to know more than he said. He could deal with people and get them to do things for him."

Ribback bought a one-third interest in the club for $5,000. But he soon realized he didn't want to be in business with Grossman—"I felt he was a bit of a crook"—and he asked to buy him out. The more Ribback wanted out, the higher the price rose, until he agreed to pay Grossman $20,000 for the final one-third interest. "He was happy to sell his share for more than it was worth," says Ribback, still smarting more than thirty years later.

Even a pro like Wein was discovering that it was difficult to be in business with Grossman. "Albert was a strong one-way street," says Wein. "He was a brilliant man and a good man in his way, but a tough son of a bitch."

Wein shared his Central Park West office with Grossman, and Grossman even lived with him and his wife when he first came to New York. But he quickly found Grossman's approach, both to life and business, completely alien. "I'd come home at two or three in the morning and he'd be sitting there smoking pot with somebody," he recalls. "Not exactly my wife's lifestyle. He owed a lot of money, and people would call him and come by. Al could not stand to talk to people he owed money to, so he kept dodging them. They'd call at three o'clock in the morning, four o'clock, trying to get him in. He wouldn't talk to them. And my wife would answer the goddamn phone. She was ready to kill him."

Still, Wein was unwilling to consider that Grossman might actually stiff him. In 1960, he borrowed $15,000 to keep the three PAMA partners alive, but Grossman refused to pay his share of the loan. Even years later he continued to refuse Wein's entreaties.

While willing to take advantage of a business associate, Grossman was serious about protecting and providing for his clients. He demanded that his folksingers be treated with the respect due *artists*—a concept that was unusual in the pop music business to say the least. "Albert was the first guy to insist his artists be treated like artists," says Jim Rooney, who managed Club 47 in Cambridge. "And if they weren't, he wouldn't work with you. A lot of people took him to task for that."

Grossman tended to look down on agents, most of whom viewed

folk performers only as nightclub acts. He had something far broader in mind. "Albert took folk music out of nightclubs and put it into concerts," says David Braun, adding that Grossman was careful to refer to his clients' *concerts* rather than their *performances*. "So you had 'an artist' appearing at 'a concert.' It always struck me as funny. I considered an artist to be Isaac Stern. And here were these folksingers. Clive Davis said that as soon as they began being called artists instead of performers the fees went up."

Grossman's commercial flair was a prickly subject in the earnest world of folk music. By and large, commercially successful folk acts like the Kingston Trio were viewed as crass pop acts by the faithful. But Grossman's clients were legitimate folksingers by any standard. That he wanted to see them succeed in the commercial sphere did not sit well with many. Although he was the original producer for the Newport Folk Festival, the festival's board of directors, with the exception of his own client, Peter Yarrow, would later have nothing to do with him. "Albert Grossman was a no-no to the board," says Wein. "He was so commercially involved, they didn't want him associated with it."

Nor did his aggressive pursuit of commercial success appeal to every folksinger he worked with. Joan Baez flirted with having Grossman as her manager, but when he urged her to sign with powerhouse Columbia Records, she opted instead for the small, folk-oriented Vanguard label. Baez eventually selected manager Manny Greenhill, a more accepted fixture in the folk world.

But others, equally committed to the folk tradition, were willing to put themselves in Grossman's hands. Peter Yarrow found him confrontational but bracingly honest: "He was very intuitive. Very gutsy, very street. He was also brilliant. A genius, in my opinion. But he immediately established his dominance in our relationship, which was always there. There was an edge to Albert which put me in awe of him. Not because of his brilliance, but because of the magnetism and the energy and the aggressiveness of his persona."

That aggressiveness was based in large measure on Grossman's faith in his own aesthetic judgments. He believed deeply in his own taste, particularly in his ability to differentiate between what was authentic and what was not. And once Grossman deemed that a performance, or a person, fell on the wrong side of that line, he freed himself of all constraints of taste and tactics.

"A nonauthentic piece of creativity to him was not just to be ignored or discarded," says Yarrow, "it was *bullshit*. Now this is principally about entertainment, but it is also in terms of being—*people* to be disdained. And his emphasis was so powerful because the difference between something that was bullshit and something that was brilliance was to other people just a shade of gray. But to him it was absolute black and white."

Grossman managed Yarrow for a year before he approached him with an idea. Would Peter consider being part of a folk trio? As Grossman described it, the group would also include a strong female performer and another male singer who would also be a comedian. Nothing about the group, Grossman promised, would diminish Peter as an artist. "Albert was very, very sure of himself—that this was a great thing to do," he recalled. "In me, he found a willing partner who sensed what he was reaching for."

Peter, Paul and Mary—with Paul Stookey and Mary Travers teaming up with Yarrow—proved a potent combination, both artistically and commercially. Grossman quickly received offers for the trio from both Atlantic and Warner Bros. Records and was so confident the group would be a hit that he even considered starting his own record company for them. He ultimately selected the fledgling Warner Bros.—but not before leaving Atlantic Records vice president Jerry Wexler in the lurch.

"Grossman brought me Peter, Paul and Mary, and they did a live demo of 'Where Have All the Flowers Gone,' " says Wexler. "I was totally knocked out. I made a deal for a single with an option for an album. I was too cautious, but it was set, the contract was drawn. The day of the session, I get a call: 'Mary has laryngitis.' "

Grossman had found a better deal. Artie Mogull, an executive at Warners' music publishing division, Witmark Music, had introduced him to Herman Starr, the dictatorial head of Warners' music operation, and a publishing and recording contract with a princely $30,000 advance was arranged. "Of course, the record hit big, and Albert and I were both heroes," says Mogull, who later went to work for Grossman.

On the heels of their success, Mogull and Grossman cooked up another deal: anytime Grossman brought Witmark one of his clients for music publishing, Grossman would personally get 50 percent of Witmark's share of the publisher's income. It was a particularly sweet inducement. Grossman was already getting a 25 percent commission from his artists, a steep fee that he liked to brag he was more than worth.

"He used to always say he charged his artists much more than most managers did," says Krasnow. "I said, 'Well, how come your rates are so high?' He said, 'Because every time you talk to me you're ten percent smarter than before. So I just add that ten percent on to what all the dummies charge for nothing.' "

Grossman's arrogance was justified. His innovations, such as the insistence that Peter, Paul and Mary retain all creative control of the recording and packaging of their music, were well ahead of the curve. Those demands would become standard for rockers by the end of the decade, but they were revolutionary in 1962. "They would take as long as they wanted to record their album," Warner Bros. executive Stan Cornyn says of Peter, Paul and Mary. "Deliver it when it was finished and mastered to their satisfaction. Ignoring entirely any schedules we had for its manufacture. And they would deliver artwork for the front and back. This was unheard of. Unheard of!" Yet the trio's commercial and artistic success had proven Grossman right.

Grossman's greatest achievement, however, was creating a commercial environment in which his clients could make a lot of money but preserve their integrity. This facet of Grossman would prove particularly appealing to Bob Dylan, who harbored ambitions that were at odds with the puritanical ethos of many in the folk movement. Grossman had no difficulty recognizing Dylan's authenticity—or his commercial potential. Already heralded as the prodigy of the Village folk scene by *New York Times* critic Robert Shelton and signed to Columbia Records by John Hammond, Dylan was a whale in the folk music pond. And for all the artistic pronouncements, making money was not an unimportant issue to him.

One of Grossman's first moves as Dylan's new manager was to strike fear into the heart of Columbia Records by threatening to have Dylan's contract vacated because the singer had signed it without parental consent while he was still a minor. The gambit didn't work, but it signaled the start of a rocky relationship between Grossman and Hammond, whom the manager did not think was a far-sighted enough producer for Dylan, as well as the arrival of a strong advocate for an act that was becoming more and more valuable to the label.

One of the primary ways that Grossman raised Dylan's value and visibility was through the use of his song catalog. At Hammond's suggestion, Dylan had signed a music publishing deal with Leeds/Duchess Music for a meager advance of $1,000. Once Grossman had Dylan in hand, Mogull pulled off one of the great steals of all time when he bought Dylan out of his Leeds/Duchess contract simply by re-paying the advance and then signed him to Witmark for $5,000. In the summer of 1963, Peter, Paul and Mary's recording of Dylan's "Blowin' in the Wind" went to number two on the *Billboard* pop singles chart. The Dylan-penned follow-up, "Don't Think Twice, It's All Right," also reached the Top 10.

"Peter, Paul and Mary really cracked through when they started singing a couple of Dylan tunes," says Paul Rothchild. "Simultane-ously, Albert broke two acts at the same time. No, he broke three acts: Peter, Paul and Mary, Bob Dylan, and Albert Grossman. All of a sud-den, he was a commercial commodity, a bankable event."

ON JUNE 1, 1965, DRUMMER BOBBY GREGG'S OPENING SNARE-DRUM BEAT on Bob Dylan's "Like a Rolling Stone" resounded like a rifle shot from radios across the country and announced a musical revolution. In the three years leading up to that moment, Dylan's songs had already re-defined the lyric parameters of popular music, demonstrating better than any others that the seemingly simple folk idiom could express the most sophisticated and ambiguous emotions. But this was some-thing else—this was a rock record. It was not a two-minute-and-thirteen-second rock and roll single like those made by Chuck Berry or Little Richard or the Beach Boys or even the Beatles. It wasn't about dancing or driving or teenage love lost and found. This was an elec-tric epic, simple in its music but remarkably complex and ambitious in its scope. Its length, subject matter, and performance were totally at odds with what constituted a hit single. "Like a Rolling Stone" erased every rule of pop music.

First, it clocked in at a gargantuan six minutes and nine seconds, easily twice as long as a single was supposed to be. It was also lyrically daunting, defying all attempts to fix its precise meaning yet arresting in its coupling of a childish malevolence with a sense of pain and dis-illusionment far more adult than anything normally heard in a pop song. And then there was Dylan's vocal: a thin, scratchy, nasal whine. It was the voice not of a pop star but of a bitter truth.

"Like a Rolling Stone" became a huge hit and did more than any other record of its era to direct rock music away from the constraints of the single format. Rock music, it was now apparent, was capable of far more than almost anyone had imagined. Albert Grossman was right: his client was an artist.

The fact that Dylan was creating work that was far more than pop product was the ultimate vindication of the rules of creative control that Grossman had laid down for the labels beginning with Peter, Paul and Mary. Up until then, the record companies had owned the artists and, in the vast majority of cases, told them what to do and how to make records. Once it became apparent that the record companies needed his clients to deliver hits—and not the other way around—Grossman was able to seize his leverage and gain better and better deals.

By the mid-sixties, Grossman had settled his Albert B. Grossman Management (ABGM) into offices at the corner of East Fifty-fifth Street between Madison and Park avenues in Manhattan. It was a big operation. There were offices for a parade of ever-changing partners and associates, who invariably departed in a blizzard of bad feelings and lawsuits. There was an in-house booking operation to sidestep paying agency commissions for many of the more successful acts. There were music publishing companies like Fourth Floor Music, Dylan's Dwarf Music, and the Band's Canaan Music. There was a press liaison, Myra Friedman, road managers including John Cooke, Jonathan Taplin, and Dylan's friend Bobby Neuwirth. There were business managers, both in-house and outside, and an army of bookkeepers and secretaries. Other Grossman clients like producers John Simon and Elliot Mazer were also on hand to work with ABGM's artists.

On the strength of Bob Dylan and Peter, Paul and Mary, Grossman had attracted a client roster of unparalleled creativity. That, in turn, gave Albert carte blanche with virtually any record executive, including Clive Davis and Mo Ostin, the powerful heads of CBS and Warner Bros. Records. ABGM was the crossroads of the emerging rock record business.

"The guy had unbelievable connections," says singer Nick Gravenites. " 'What record company do you want to be on?' Jesus, he'd pick up the phone and the president of that company would be there. And it wasn't a question of whether there was a deal or not, the question immediately was 'What *was* the deal?' It was real clout." Says Mike Friedman, who, as a Grossman management associate brought Todd Rundgren to ABGM, "It was essentially a business of children and outcasts when I came into it. It was such a primitive business; nobody really knew how to do it. The rules were being created, and he was just making it up as he went along."

"The thing that I recollect is how everyone came to him, looked up to him," recalls booking agent Dan Weiner. "He was *the* unique manager of the time. Bill Graham was often up at the office. The managers of the Grateful Dead and the other San Francisco bands came to hang with Albert. Everybody looked to him to find out how it should be done."

Grossman's relationship with Dylan was the key. It was a partnership of visionaries. While Dylan created songs whose content, form, and imagery challenged the limits of pop music, Grossman set about to extend the boundaries of the business. "Albert was the first guy I ever knew who was willing to renegotiate in the middle of a contract," says film producer Jonathan Taplin, who was a road manager for Dylan and the Band. "Certainly there was a love-hate relationship between record company presidents and Albert, but there was also a great deal of respect. Because ultimately Albert would make an argument that was real: the way artists had been treated up until then was not very fair. Starting with Peter, Paul and Mary, then Bob, then Janis, he upped the ante. Around sixty-seven, he had so much leverage that he pretty much controlled everybody that was important in the folk-rock area."

"Everybody was at the mercy of the labels, and the only reason Albert was able to write the book was that he had everybody," recalls Mike Friedman. "If they wanted a deal on Paul Butterfield, they had to deal on the next one that he was bringing."

Making a deal with Albert Grossman was far from an easy thing to do. Despite his intelligence, Albert could be awkward, and he was definitely not a conversationalist. "He was quite inarticulate, actually," says graphic artist Milton Glaser, who designed album covers and posters for Peter, Paul and Mary and Bob Dylan. "He was a cultivated guy and knew a lot about a lot of things. But you never felt that he was at ease with himself. If you had even a quiet conversation, there was a point at which Albert would absolutely run out of things to say." Grossman was able to turn his uneasiness to his own advantage in business dealings. "He could wait anyone out," says Krasnow. "He could just take command of a room and make everybody kind of come to him. I was convinced he was ninety percent Chinese. He would wait for a wall to fall on him."

"He'd enter into some kind of business discussion and say five words," recalls Gravenites. "And the other person would talk, and Albert would say nothing. He'd pick at his tooth with his little finger. Then there'd be silence, and the other person would start talking again, revising the deal. Without Albert saying anything!"

"It was incredible to watch," says Mike Friedman. "He would come in with a piece of paper and say what he wanted, and these guys didn't know how to talk to him because you *couldn't* really talk to him. He'd look vaguely at the ceiling and say things like 'Well . . . maybe we oughta be looking around a little bit . . .' It was hard to fight with him—unless he was mad at you about something. And then he'd blow you away. But if he was negotiating with you, it was almost passive-aggressive behavior: he tells you what he wants, and whatever you want you never get. It wasn't a negotiation. But you just couldn't get enough of it."

Filmmaker D. A. Pennebaker captured Grossman working with an agent to negotiate stiff concert fees for Dylan in the 1967 documentary *Don't Look Back*. Outside the frame, Pennebaker had a chance to observe Grossman at work when the two convinced Janus Films to distribute the feature. The moviemaker found it a chilling experience.

"I couldn't believe what went down in that room," says Pennebaker. "It was as if it was the other way around, as if they wanted something from him. He just destroyed them. It wasn't good-natured at all, but on the other hand, it wasn't mean. It was like he was looking at their underpants or something, it really had a strange feeling. And it scared me a little bit—I'm hoping he's on my side all the time."

To Jerry Wexler, Grossman was a fraud—and a condescending one at that. "He had people buffaloed," he says. "He would talk in tongues. He had a habit of going on and on and not saying anything. And cryptically he'd look at you. The suggestion was that if you're a cogent-enough person, you'll understand what I'm getting at. If you don't dig me, you're some kind of insensate asshole."

Along with his pregnant silences, Grossman showcased a whole catalog of affectations and mannerisms. The most unusual was the way he smoked a cigarette. Placing it between his pinkie and fourth finger, Grossman would make a fist and draw the smoke through his hand. It was a ritual that seemed to have no basis in tobacco smoking, although it was suggestive of the way hashish is smoked through a chillum, a kind of straight-stem pipe. Grossman's habits made for interesting theater and served to keep people off balance. "Whoever would be negotiating with him would be mesmerized and going 'Yeah yeah yeah,' agreeing to his points and looking at his cigarette," says Vinny Fusco, who worked for Grossman throughout much of the sixties and seventies.

"I came up with a nickname for him that stuck," says Gravenites. "Cumulus nimbus. We called him the Cloud. You could see it—it's huge, gray, and august—but when you went up to touch it, it wasn't there."

Grossman's office was also set up to provide him with the upper hand. "It was the most intimidating experience in the world to come into this guy's office," says Mike Friedman. "It was so Albert. Dark? It was a cave. There was a mahogany desk and a Tiffany lamp with like a twenty-watt bulb. Files piled so high on the desk you couldn't see Albert behind them and a visitor's chair so low that when a guest sat in it, he couldn't see Albert anyhow. I used to call it 'the sucker chair.' And Albert had a voice like the voice of God coming from the walls. People were looking around, barely able to concentrate on what they were doing. You couldn't see anything! His house was the same way."

Friedman was at a meeting in Grossman's home near Woodstock when Bob Krasnow and his partner, Tommy LiPuma, came looking to raise money to save Blue Thumb Records.

"They flew in from California on the red-eye, and I picked them up at the airport at like five o'clock in the morning and drove all the way up to Woodstock," says Friedman.

Along with getting stoned, Grossman spent the whole day showing his guests all the buildings and tracts of land he had acquired around Woodstock and in the nearby town of Bearsville. As daylight faded, so did his visitors. He ushered his exhausted guests into a room lit only by a candle, where LiPuma searched in vain for a light switch. Says Friedman, "They had reams of paper and files and proposals, and they couldn't stay awake, they couldn't see their papers. We could have just as easily been in the kitchen with the lights on. Instead it was this little dark, dank room with a candle, and it was the most humiliating experience I have ever seen anybody go through. And then it was over. The deal never happened, and I have a feeling it was never supposed to happen. But Albert wanted to see the deal."

The only person who was as indecipherable as Grossman was Dylan—and their closeness and similarities led to a great deal of speculation within both the music business and the folk community about who had invented whom. The reality was that they were unusually well-matched soul mates.

"They were kindred spirits," says Suze Rotolo. "Albert never denied who he was, but he had that way of observing and not being forthcoming. Bob never gave a straight answer. He couldn't at that time. He was creating his own legend and his own fiction of himself. It's not that one copied the other. They got along because they both were observers and very smart and could, in very few words, figure things out. I think they were genuinely attracted to each other for that similar way of looking at the world."

While working on *Don't Look Back* and its unreleased follow-up, *Eat the Document*, D. A. Pennebaker also observed the unusual Dylan/Grossman rapport. "In a way, he was a moneyman, and Dylan was very interested in money," says Pennebaker. "*Very* interested in money. But Albert was different from most moneymen. When we went to England and we were hanging out with the Beatles, we never saw Epstein [Brian Epstein, the Beatles' manager]. They had nothing to do with him. He was like some outsider, and they always made slighting references to him. But Albert hung out with us all the time. Dylan really liked that—he was kind of a father."

Grossman was a seeker in his own way, attempting to identify and respond to what he perceived as authentic. Although they would later have differences, he never doubted that Dylan was a truly great artist, and his client's impact on his personal life was enormous. While the growth of the record industry over the next decade would be built on the co-opting of the underground hip culture—or, perhaps, on its willful surrender—Grossman was one of the few businessmen to embrace the culture. Record executives who knew him were stunned when he went native.

"Grossman used to wear a five-button suit," recalls Joe Smith, at the time vice president of Warner Bros. Records. "Tie, neat. One time Peter, Paul and Mary were playing the Hollywood Bowl, and he brought out this guy to hang with him. I had to baby-sit him—Bob Dylan. So I took him around the Warner Bros. lot to the soundstages, took him home to dinner one night. He had long hair; he was strange. But he was going on tour, and Grossman was going with him. I said, 'You watch Grossman shake him up—he'll come back looking like he's okay.' Grossman came back looking like fucking Benjamin Franklin! Hair down to here, wire-rim glasses, never wore a tie after that."

His transformation was far more than cosmetic. In later years, ponytails would become an accepted look for entertainment executives, but when Grossman took to tying his hair back with a hunk of telephone wire it was a statement fraught with real consequences, a public repudiation of mainstream values and politics. The country was deeply divided over the Vietnam War and the drug culture, and his appearance frequently provoked a strong reaction, perhaps because he looked even older than he was.

"There were people who hated him," says Mike Friedman. "A woman came up to us in a restaurant one night—it was Robbie Robertson, Gordon Lightfoot, John Simon, Albert, and me. And this woman starts screaming 'The Star-Spangled Banner' in Albert's face at the top of her lungs. That was the kind of shit that happened all the time. Walk down Park Avenue and people would be yelling—at *him*. Nobody was yelling at Robbie. He was the event and really precipitated a reaction on a visceral level that none of the other people did."

"Albert would've been an entirely different person had not Bob Dylan come along," says Vinny Fusco. "He's a businessman with short curly hair, an economist. You could look at Albert's passport pictures: there was B.D. and A.D.—Before Dylan and After Dylan. Bob Dylan made Albert over."

DYLAN'S IMPACT ON THE WIDER WORLD WAS ALSO PERVASIVE. HE WAS almost unquestionably the most influential artist of his generation.

Grossman did a great deal to shield Dylan from the incessant and often irrational expectations of his fans, and there were also the ceaseless professional demands that he was, of course, a master of defusing.

"Albert understood the role of the manager was to supply the link to the commercial world so these artists would not have to deal with it," says David Braun. "With Dylan, of course, he reached the apogee. Because Dylan didn't want to deal with anyone. And Albert was extremely protective of Bob—more so than of the others."

The insularity that Dylan demanded and that Grossman so masterfully provided—along with the belief that anyone he deemed inauthentic was not entitled to polite behavior—gave birth to a perverse culture of personality that surrounded both the manager and his artists, delineated by an effete hipness and exclusivity.

"This whole thing was based on us and them," says Mike Friedman. "Hip people versus lame people. That's what it was all about. You can talk about Albert being cynical and eccentric and Dylan being a tortured artist, but it's the rock and roll business, man. You can put it in any context you want artistically, but it was having a great time and doing whatever you wanted to do and getting away with it because you were so hip. Y'know, Tommy James and the Shondells never had the same kind of fun because they weren't hip."

"That scene around Dylan was strange," says actor Peter Coyote. At the time, Coyote was a member of the Diggers, a theatrical-political troupe from San Francisco that gained fame throughout Haight-Ashbury for giving out free food and clothes and espoused a philosophy described as "assuming freedom." "Free because it's yours" was the Digger credo. Coyote and the other Diggers, especially his friend Emmett Grogan, were afforded a warm welcome by Grossman, who allowed them to use the ABGM offices for various projects, including rallying American support for the French student strikes of 1968. They lived largely by their ability to network and broker deals between the underground and the straight world and were delighted to have him as a patron.

"We made a lot of shit happen," says Coyote, "but the truth of it was we were always broke. So when you got somebody like Albert opening up his house to you, and giving you a car and serving you the best organic gourmet food and the best grass and hash and acid and introducing you to gorgeous women—y'know, it was great. And we paid for that by what we taught. Because that was the only commodity we had to trade. So Albert got to sit front-row-center at the wildest show in the world. This porcine, psychedelic Ben Franklin. And he knew if anything went down, Emmett and I were there in front of him like a couple of dog soldiers. So he could play."

Grossman provided a luxurious stop on the underground railroad, but Coyote still found the scene distasteful. "Bobby Neuwirth and Dylan and that crew were mean," he says. "Cold. There was this thing that revolved around Albert as the manager of *Janis* and *Dylan* and the hippest of the hip. There was a meanness, an edgy kind of competition. People had to be on their toes. You got the feeling of ins and outs; when you were on top it was fine, but you could lose status quickly and suddenly be excluded. We had entrée because we were the hippest of the hip, too, but we were just there for a look. We were sort of impervious to it because we didn't give a shit if we were in it or not. Of course, that makes you cool enough that they want you in it. But it was like weasels driving intruders away."

Neuwirth had an expression for outsiders who were looking to latch on at the office or in the scene: they were trying to get their "hip card punched." "I never forgot that expression," says Mike Friedman. "Because in a way that was a lot of what it was about and why people go into the music business. Because it's fun and it's hip. They don't talk about art and poetry. It's about getting laid and being cool and privileged. It was America's royalty in a sense. There was a real sense of 'us'—you either get it or you don't get it. If you got it you were okay, and if you didn't get it you weren't okay."

Grossman was a master gamesman, and Dylan learned his lessons well. Mike Friedman had been working with Grossman for about six months and had yet to meet Dylan when Grossman, snowed in in Woodstock, called one morning and asked him to take Dylan to screen a movie, *Tell Me That You Love Me, Junie Moon,* at the East Side town house of director Otto Preminger. Preminger hoped to get a Dylan composition for the sound track, so a rough cut of the film had been flown in from California for the songwriter to see.

At Preminger's home, a butler escorted them into a tiny elevator and up to the top floor of the town house, where Dylan and Friedman were ushered into a screening room. "Instead of having the room prepared, Preminger had it arranged so all the tricks would go off once we were there," Friedman says. "He had a coffee table in front of him. The top rolls back and there's a bunch of buttons. He pushes one and a shade comes down; pushes another and the lights start to dim; pushes another and a picture behind us slides to the side revealing a projector."

For his final flourish, the imposing, bald German director pushed one more button.

"Roll 'em!" he called.

"I looked at Dylan, and his eyes were rolling back in his head," Friedman says. "It was not a good movie. Not even close. And being the rough cut, it was almost unbearable."

When the film finally ended, Preminger took his guests downstairs and seated them at a table. A chef in full toque arrived with menus, and the three men ordered lunch.

To break the silence that hung over the table, Friedman offered that he had just seen Preminger on a television talk show criticizing several new films as too violent. How, Friedman asked, did Preminger justify the scene in *Junie Moon* where a man blinded Liza Minnelli's character by throwing battery acid in her face?

Preminger stared incredulously at Friedman.

"That is not violent!" he said. Dylan leaned across the table toward the director. "It's pretty violent, Otto." Preminger slammed his hand on the table. "Do you want to do the music for the movie or not?" he demanded.

Dumbfounded at how abruptly the meeting had disintegrated, Friedman prepared to leave. "That's the end of the meeting, right?" he thought, wondering where in the neighborhood he should take Dylan for lunch.

But Dylan seemed unfazed. "Y'know, Otto," he said. "That's a pretty good movie. I'm not really sure. I'd like to see it again."

"What?" asked Preminger, who had already sent the print by courier to Kennedy Airport. "What do you mean?"

"Yeah," said Dylan. "I'd like to see it again tonight, Otto. And I'd like to bring my wife, and we'd like to have dinner." He paused a moment and then added: "And we'd like it if you weren't here."

"What?"

"We'd like to be alone to see the movie. We'd like it if you weren't around."

"I *live* here!" cried Preminger. "This is my *house*!"

"I know," said Dylan, "but it's really important, you know, for us to see it this way."

Preminger, desperate to have Dylan for the film's sound track, was on the hook.

"Stop the plane!" he yelled to an assistant.

The chef was also summoned back from the kitchen, and Dylan ordered steaks and wine for the evening.

"Now, Otto," Dylan said as lunch was finally served. "We'd like to come at about seven o'clock. So . . . don't be here."

The rest of the meal went off without incident. But when Friedman and Dylan finally left, Friedman couldn't contain himself. "Would you mind telling me what that was about?" he asked as soon as they were on the sidewalk. "How could you *bear* to sit through that movie again?"

Dylan frowned. "I ain't gonna watch that movie again," he said. "I just wanted Sara to see the house because we're fixing up our own place in the Village and it's got some good ideas."

Days later, when Preminger called Grossman to see if Dylan would allow him to use an instrumental track like "Nashville Skyline Rag" under the film's opening credits, the manager lowered the boom.

"Albert screamed at him," says Friedman. "How all he was interested in was getting the credit on the screen. How he was exploiting Dylan and didn't understand Dylan as a songwriter since this was the only thing Dylan ever wrote that didn't have words."

Dylan and Grossman would also prove unable to keep these hip cons out of their own relationship. One particularly valuable game revolved around an Andy Warhol lithograph.

Warhol had been trying to convince Dylan to appear in one of his films, and in 1965 Dylan consented to a brief screen test. Not enamored of Warhol, he asked for something in return for his time and cooperation. Although he appeared to be irked by the request, Warhol—perhaps looking to gain cooperation on a film in the future—grudgingly obliged. Dylan and Bobby Neuwirth left the Factory with a Warhol lithograph, which they lashed to the roof of their car.

Dylan later told Grossman about the lithograph, adding derisively that he really didn't want it. Grossman perked up: he'd take it. After mulling it over, Dylan said he'd be willing to trade the picture for the sofa Grossman had in his office. The deal was struck. The print, a multiple image of Elvis Presley that became known as *Double Elvis*, would be assessed at the time of Grossman's death twenty-one years later at between $250,000 and $400,000. How much loose change Dylan may have found between the cushions of the couch has never been ascertained.

The relationship cut both ways, and it cut deeply. Guests at the Grossmans' wedding in 1967 in Woodstock couldn't help but notice when the bride, Sally, disappeared with Dylan. Left to entertain his guests alone, Grossman sat and chewed his thumbs for three hours.

WOODSTOCK, NEW YORK'S HISTORY AS AN ARTIST'S RETREAT CAN BE TRACED back to the turn of the century, but Albert Grossman and Bob Dylan put the town on the map of popular American culture. Milton Glaser had urged Grossman to buy a house in nearby Bearsville in 1963. "We were living in Woodstock, and a big, fabulous house came up for sale for fifty thousand dollars," recalls Glaser. "We didn't know anybody who had fifty thousand dollars except for Albert."

Dylan was the first of his clients to follow Grossman upstate, living for several months in his house before buying a place nearby. Although the move to Woodstock was always couched as a way of keeping Dylan at arm's length from the music business and his fans, there were also rumors that Dylan needed to be pulled out of New York City because he had developed an alcohol and amphetamine problem.

"I was always led to believe that Albert got him out of New York and moved him up there because he was in trouble," says Mike Friedman. Adds Peter Yarrow: "When Albert and Bobby were on the outs years later, he said to me that he believed that it was not just a question of saying whether Bobby would or would not have been able to be Bobby—to be who he was, protected and allowed to perform as he was—but it's possible that even Bobby's life would've been in jeopardy."

The speculation over Dylan's physical stability only intensified on July 29, 1966, when radio stations broadcast a news bulletin that he had been severely injured in a motorcycle crash in Woodstock. Just how serious the accident actually was remained a mystery. Subsequent reports that Dylan had broken his neck were an exaggeration, as perhaps was Dylan's own account to journalist Robert Shelton, in which he said he was thrown over the handlebars of his bike. Another journalist who was close to Dylan and Grossman, Al Aronowitz, was in a car following Dylan, who was taking the motorcycle to a repair shop. Aronowitz recalls Dylan's spill as a minor mishap.*

The incident, regardless of its seriousness, precipitated an even deeper withdrawal by Dylan. Ironically, it also gave the town of Woodstock greater notoriety. The town became a mecca for musicians like the Band, Paul Butterfield, Van Morrison, Tim Hardin, and Geoff and Maria Muldaur—most of whom were managed by Grossman. And more and more kids came to the Catskill community looking to check out the scene.

Just how much cachet the town's name had became obvious when a group of young entrepreneurs selected it as the site for a rock festival in the summer of 1969. When the town denied them the permits and forced a move to White Lake, New York, it was still called the Woodstock Music and Arts Festival. Twenty-five years later, during the Band's induction into the Rock and Roll Hall of Fame at New York's Waldorf-Astoria, the group's Robbie Robertson noted, "If it hadn't been for Albert, we'd probably be known as the Poughkeepsie Generation."

While Dylan did not perform at Woodstock, August 19, 1969, the last day of the festival had a separate significance for him and Grossman: their seven-year management agreement expired. They continued to work together even without a contract, but the strains in their business relationship were becoming more pronounced. Dylan, who frequently worried about being cheated, had come to view his manager with skepticism. The problem was twofold. First, the services that Grossman could offer Dylan in building his career were largely complete. Second, Grossman was getting an unusually large commission.

---

*Others around Dylan have also cast doubt on the veracity of Dylan's accident. During the course of a dinner the author had in Bearsville with Sally Grossman and photographer Barry Feinstein—a former husband of Mary Travers and a close friend of Grossman's—Sally described how she had been interviewed by an English journalist who had written an article on Woodstock that included a map identifying local points of historic interest, including the site of the accident. Upon hearing this, Feinstein snorted. "Yeah?" he asked. *"Where?"*

He had purchased Dylan's management contract from Roy Silver in 1962 for $5,000. At a time when many managers received a 15 percent commission, Silver's contract called for him to receive 20 percent of Dylan's earnings. Grossman upped the figure to 25 percent. Based on what he'd done for Dylan, it was hard to argue that he wasn't worth the money. But what was left to be done?

"The ultimate destiny of the manager who breaks the act is to get blown off," says Vinny Fusco. "It's almost irrevocable. Unless the artist is going to continue to grow and needs a grower, now anyone can do the job for a lot less money. Get a fucking bookkeeper."

That is, in fact, almost what Dylan did. Naomi Saltzman, who worked as an administrator for Grossman and had functioned as a personal assistant for Dylan and his wife, graduated from gofer to business manager.

One of the factors leading to the breakup was a bill for furniture. On a trip to England, Dylan and Grossman had purchased antiques, and, afterward, the bill for Grossman's purchases, $1,100, came to Dylan's production company, Ashes & Sand. Whether Grossman had intentionally sent his portion of the bill to Dylan remains unclear. But according to several people who worked at ABGM, Dylan viewed it as an example of Grossman's guile.

The fact that Dylan was no longer being managed by Grossman did not spell a simple ending to their relationship. In the mid-sixties, Grossman had set up music publishing companies for several of his artists, an innovation that assured they would retain control over some of their most important assets. It also made his clients significantly more money since they would now receive the publisher's income on their own compositions as well as the songwriter's fees. (Larger, established music publishers were paid a percentage to administer the artist-owned companies.) In 1966, when Dylan's publishing agreement with Witmark expired, he and Grossman—with Artie Mogull's assistance—formed Dwarf Music. Instead of a 25 percent management commission on Dylan's publishing income, Grossman received 50 percent of the publisher's share. This kind of arrangement would soon become standard. In terms of income, the 50 percent publisher's share was roughly analogous to receiving a 25 percent commission: the client was receiving 100 percent of songwriter royalties and 50 percent of publisher's royalties, i.e., 75 percent of all music publishing income. But being part of an artist-owned company provided a manager with something in addition to income: equity. Grossman was more than a representative and adviser to Dylan. He was a partner.

A split between the two was now more complicated than an expired management contract. In 1970, they reached a settlement that, aside from formally terminating the management agreement, recognized Grossman's continuing rights in Dwarf Music. But since Dylan had grown suspicious of Grossman's handling of his finances, his new representatives would now keep the books.

There were, it turned out, reasons to be suspicious. There was nothing as obvious as theft, but Grossman's willingness to use his leverage in dealings with outsiders was also evident in his relationships with his own clients. His 50 percent share of Witmark's early publishing deal with Dylan—a backdoor arrangement that the artist may not have even known about—netted him over $3 million. Also questionable was the way Grossman and Artie Mogull had used the leverage of Dylan and Dwarf Music to enrich several music publishing companies in which Dylan did not have a stake.

At the time that Dwarf was established for Dylan, Mogull and Grossman also started two other publishing companies of their own, Callie Music and Albet Music. Named for Mogull's daughters, they were established to publish the songs of other performers. Attorney David Braun, who was representing both Dylan and Grossman at the time, was given a 7.5 percent stake in the two companies.

A few months later, Mogull negotiated a subpublishing deal with B. Feldman, a British publisher interested in representing Dylan's Dwarf catalog in the U.K. Surprisingly, the deal Mogull struck did not pay Dwarf a cash advance. However, Callie and Albet—which had no copyrights or songwriter contracts—received a $10,000 advance from the British firm. And when Mogull and Grossman later ran into money problems with the two companies, they solved them by selling Dylan a 15 percent stake for $15,000.

Dylan's break with Grossman presented a problem for David Braun. Which client was he going to stay with? When he picked Dylan, he lamely told Grossman that it would be harder for the artist to find another lawyer. Grossman, despite good-naturedly commenting that he thought it was the right move, didn't buy it. "We shook hands, embraced," remembers Braun. "I don't think I was at the *door* when it was all over the streets that I had fucked Albert Grossman, the man who gave me Bob Dylan. It was *all* over."

Dylan and Grossman continued to fight over the settlement. At one point Dylan claimed that his ten-year songwriting agreement with Dwarf was too long. At the end of one particularly long and fruitless day of discussion, Grossman came up with a novel suggestion for a settlement. In the elevator with Dylan and the lawyers for both sides, Grossman reached into his pocket and took out a quarter.

"Bob," he said. "You think you're right; I think I'm right. Why don't we just flip for it? If I win, the contract goes to term. If you win, the deal's over now."

Bob Gordon, a Grossman attorney, remembers that Dylan looked stunned by the offer. His attorneys immediately yelled for Dylan to ignore the offer. The deal eventually went its full term.

Dylan, however, showed just what a good student he'd been once the roles were reversed. After he took over the administration of Dwarf, Grossman proved unable to get satisfactory accountings. In 1981, he sued Dylan, alleging, among other things, that he was owed more than $500,000 in commissions on record royalties as well as other income on publishing. The suit, which outlived Grossman, was settled with his estate in the fall of 1987. Dylan, the voice and conscience of a generation—the man who once sang "Money doesn't talk, it swears"—ponied up $2 million.

THE SPLIT WITH DYLAN WAS THE FIRST INDICATION THAT THE JOB WAS TAKing its toll on Grossman and that he was losing his enthusiasm for management. There were other clients he still cared deeply about, like Peter Yarrow, Mike Bloomfield, Paul Butterfield, Robbie Robertson, and Janis Joplin, but he would soon prove incapable of responding to the serious crises many of them were having. Everywhere around him, it seemed, the heroin needle dug in. His first wife, Betty Spencer, had been a junkie. Peter's younger brother had died of an overdose. Michael Bloomfield, a bright Jewish kid from Chicago, like Grossman, who loved the blues, was a junkie. Butterfield was a bad alcoholic. Joplin was both an alcoholic and a junkie.

Even without these nightmares, each client required a tremendous amount of care and pampering, which made Grossman feel more like a wet nurse than a rock manager. In 1968, Dylan made Grossman write to Clive Davis, the head of CBS Records, to ask for a free set of backyard toys from CBS's Creative Playthings division for his children. The Paupers, a band managed by ABGM, had to be told that the money MGM Records had advanced them for a promotional tour was not to be spent on eating shrimp cocktails for breakfast every morning. The Electric Flag, an exciting horn band fronted by Bloomfield, was robbed by drug dealers in Detroit, who took Bloomfield's money, drummer Buddy Miles's clothes, and saxophonist Herbie Rich's wig. Vinny Fusco had to send them money to get home and meet them at the airport. Grossman was running out of patience.

"Albert always said he wanted to be the architect, not the janitor," says Yarrow. "When you conceive of a building, then you let it go and let it be a building. He didn't want to take care of the janitorial work. And those were his words."

He tried to preach self-sufficiency and planning to his clients. Many of them didn't want to hear it. "He once said, 'If you listen to me, by the time you're forty you'll be able to retire. All you have to do is listen to me,' " says Barry Goldberg, keyboardist with the Electric Flag. "He cared about Michael [Bloomfield] because of his talent and intellect. And the Electric Flag could've gone on for a long time if everyone had listened to him. But everyone was too young and wild. No one had learned the rock and roll lesson yet—that if you just went along with the moves, in a few years you could control your own fate. It was totally because of drugs and craziness that it became too much."

The weight of caring for his clients began to tell on Grossman. He had to force Paul Butterfield to accept a record deal with a $250,000 advance—extremely generous considering Butterfield's slim sales. But according to Nick Gravenites, Grossman didn't want Butterfield to share the advance with his band. "The band was bitching and moaning, saying they wanted their piece of the action," he says. "And Albert just said no, forget it. If you're gonna do that I'm not gonna get you the deal. It wound up [with] screaming, crying, tears. But finally Albert prevailed. He'd be willing to put a quarter of a million bucks in Paul Butterfield's pocket, but he wasn't gonna pass it around. 'Your manager, your clout got you this kind of money. Keep it!' Though it was good business, I think it helped bring Butterfield down. He went along with it in the end, but I believe he never forgot that."

To Gravenites, who considered himself "small potatoes" among Grossman's clients, it was proof that the manager cared more for some of his artists than he did for others. And while that was true, some saw a different motive in Grossman's advice to Butterfield. "Albert knew that Butterfield was his ward for the rest of his life," says Mike Friedman. "There was never gonna be a time when Butter wasn't broke and he wasn't going to have to support him, which happened. This was probably his way to get somebody else's money to do that. And I know he cared for Paul a lot."

By the early seventies Grossman had stopped going to his Manhattan office completely. The clients who wanted his time and attention could come to him. Many of them, like Butterfield, Todd Rundgren, and the members of the Band, did, and a room in Grossman's house was reserved for Joplin. A small, terminally hip, and incestuous universe—with Albert Grossman as the sun—coalesced in Bearsville. "Man, it was a real small town," says Mike Friedman. "Everybody was doing everybody. It was awful."

Grossman believed he could make the entire music business, like his clients, come to him. He formed his own record company, Bearsville, built a recording studio, and asked Jim Rooney, who had run Club 47 in Cambridge, if he'd like to oversee it. Rooney arrived to discover that the roof wasn't even on the building yet. But Grossman had plenty for him to do. He wanted to open a restaurant, the Bear, in another building he owned on Route 212. Could Rooney draw a floor plan for the liquor board? Absorbed with his own ever-shrinking world, Albert's insularity, which he had once parlayed so brilliantly into a mystique for his artists, was now more than an affectation. It was real, and it was a liability.

"One of the problems with Albert was that he was too hip," says Taplin. "With Dylan he had perfected this strategy that the best thing to do was not communicate. Stay away from the press. *Music from Big Pink* is the apotheosis of that theory: don't be known, be mysterious, and you'll be big. But the Band never could get out of that 'too hip' thing and never had the great success they probably could have if they'd been a little more willing to make some compromises with the music business. There was never an attempt by anyone to try and make a record that could be played on the radio. Nobody would ever say, 'Y'know, if you'd just get one record on FM radio, you might sell ten times as many records.' Which is usually the kind of news that a manager is supposed to give. But Albert would never have thought of doing that."

The Band, and Robbie Robertson in particular, had done an incredible job of walking the line that divided Dylan and his former manager. For several years they continued to work and socialize with Dylan while still being managed by Grossman. But by the mid-seventies, they had left the Bearsville orbit and followed Dylan out to Malibu. There, Dylan and Robertson succumbed to the earnest courting of another manager who had long admired Grossman for his power and artists, David Geffen.

Although Albert could console himself with the $625,000 the Band had to pay him to get out of its management contract, the split hurt. He had still harbored hopes of one day having Dylan and the Band on Bearsville Records, and now Geffen—whom he detested—had them for his label, Asylum. "And then," says Fusco, "Robbie said in *Rolling Stone* that he went with David because he's *there*, he's hip. Well, that hurt Albert a lot."

The loss of the Band, his last great act, signaled the end of Albert Grossman as a serious player in the music business. But he had already been devastated by the death of Janis Joplin in October 1970. Remembers Yarrow, "His energy and spirit were severely damaged when Janis died. As if he'd lost his alter ego. He adored Janis."

Others were less charitable in their assessment of what he had done for Joplin. Myra Friedman, Joplin's publicist and biographer, had been frustrated in repeated attempts to get Grossman to urge Joplin into a treatment program. "He didn't want to confront things," she says. "He either had a philosophical resistance to doing it or perhaps he felt inadequate. I know there were other artists who were in some trouble, and this is particularly upsetting since Albert hated heroin. He really did love Janis, but he babied her. He failed to take real command of the drug situation and Janis's personal behavior."

"At the end, he wasn't preoccupied with anybody's well-being but his own, that's for sure," says Bob Krasnow. "Albert was clearly interested in his own pleasures."

"He was the baron of Bearsville," says Michael Lang, one of the producers of the Woodstock Festival. And he could be regal in his generosity. Richard Manuel, the Band's troubled pianist, returned to Woodstock from Malibu after the group split from Grossman and found his former manager willing to help him through detox. When Manuel's house had no fuel, Grossman filled the oil tanks. Shortly after Grossman's death, Manuel hanged himself.

Peter Coyote also saw a streak of sentimentality in Grossman. When Peter's father, Morris Cohan, died, his debts forced Peter's mother into bankruptcy.

"My dad went to MIT when he was fifteen," says Coyote. "And one of the ways he won the respect of the older guys was that he was a phenomenal billiards player. So was his father. We had my grandfather's custom-made pool and billiards tables in the house. They were beautiful. So when I was shopping around trying to sell stuff, I thought of Albert.

"One of the things I was trying to do was save my farm, which was my dad's favorite place on earth. As soon as it would snow he would go up there and sleep on the lawn. I wanted to bury him there under a hickory tree because my old man really was a hickory tree. He was a totally tough, homicidal person. It was a big failure in my life that I was not able to pull it off and save it. Anyway, I guess I mentioned this to Albert."

Years later, when a hickory tree near the studio was struck by lightning, Grossman remembered Coyote's unfulfilled wish for his father. Three beams were cut from the trunk and hung over the billiards table. "At least some part of him is buried under a hickory tree," Grossman told Coyote.

Yet the baron could still be capricious and cruel. When keyboard player Barry Goldberg telephoned his ex-manager and said he wanted to introduce him to his fiancé, the couple were invited upstate to the house. Arriving by bus in a snowstorm, they spent a congenial evening in the kitchen, eating hors d'oeuvres and talking. At midnight, Grossman rose, stretched, and turned to his guests.

"Where are you staying tonight?" he asked.

Goldberg was speechless. "What do you mean?" he finally asked. "I'm here, my bags are here. It's midnight."

Albert shook his head. "You're a big boy now," he said. "You're on your own."

Barry could feel himself shrinking in front of his fiancée. "I don't believe you're doing this," he said.

"Well," replied Grossman, "you better get on the phone because the cats just had kittens in the only guest room and we can't disturb them."

Goldberg called Paul Butterfield, with whom he'd played regularly in Chicago years before. To his horror, Butterfield—his soul brother!—also turned him down. "Sorry," said Butterfield, "but our dog just had puppies."

Goldberg could feel a rising tide of nausea in his stomach. *Woodstock*—where every animal's got a bedroom! Finally, Grossman suggested he call Jim Rooney.

"I barely knew the man!" recalls Goldberg. "Yet Albert would have thrown us out into the cold, I swear to God. And Jim said, 'Okay, come on over. He didn't even *know* me. I woke up the next morning and was so upset and embarrassed that I threw up. We got on the bus and went back to New York. That was my last confrontation with Albert. The next time I saw him was at Michael Bloomfield's funeral."

Soon, friends and clients would be gathering for Grossman's funeral. When he died on his flight to London, it was Krasnow who signed for the body and arranged for him to be shipped home to Woodstock. Back in Bearsville, behind the restaurants and theater he had built, Grossman's private contractor Paul Cypert took his Cat bulldozer out one more time and dug the grave. It was, of course, a completely illegal burial. At the memorial service, Robbie Robertson and Peter Yarrow delivered the eulogies. Bob Dylan, who was still being sued by the Grossman estate, didn't show.

"I kind of lost interest in Bob Dylan after that," says Krasnow. "I thought, 'You get beyond these problems.' "

To others, Dylan's absence at any of the memorial services for Grossman was immaterial. Peter Coyote, for one, believed he had heard Dylan eulogize Grossman with chilling accuracy years before in the song "Stuck Inside of Mobile with the Memphis Blues Again."

"You know how Albert smoked a cigarette—between the pinkie and fourth finger?" asks Coyote. "One day I'm in Albert's office, he's sitting there, and Dylan is playing on the loudspeaker:

Mona tried to tell me
To stay away from the train line.
She said that all the railroad men
Just drink up your blood like wine.
And I said 'oh I didn't know that'
But then again there's only one I've met
And he just smoked my eyelids
And punched my cigarette.

"And Albert's sitting there with this cigarette out of his fist! All of a sudden it popped to me how literal and precise Dylan was: The train-men are like the railroad robber barons—drinking up your blood like wine; smoking your eyelids is tricking you; and punching your ciga-rette. And there he was! Albert was framed up against these huge loud-speakers, and Dylan was calling it down."

6

The Man
from the
William Morris Agency
(King David)

Two innovations made Albert Grossman the first modern rock manager: he recognized the artistic credibility and impact of his clients, and he translated it into creative freedom and financial power. His great business lesson—appreciate, empower, and follow the artist—was a direct result of his real affinity for the music and the underground culture. Because he knew his clients were artists of consequence, he didn't interfere in their creative decisions, and that made him different from the old-line managers like Charlie Greene and Brian Stone who had proceeded him. As with Ray Riepen in Boston, who saw himself in the vanguard of a new, socially aware capitalism, Grossman sympathized with the changes going on around him. He was at least as interested in ideas and an obsessive search for authenticity as he was in money. Like Dylan, he saw that most people didn't make those distinctions, and he held them in contempt. Ironically, when he proved the commercial value of his mantra—*Believe in the artist*—it was embraced by the very businesspeople he looked down on. None would make more of the business opportunities suggested by Grossman's lesson than an extraordinary young man whose single-minded focus wasn't on exploring and empowering the underground but simply success—a hungry talent agent Grossman had worked with and whom he ultimately came to detest, David Geffen.

"David expanded the Machiavellian book from Albert Grossman to the next chapter," said producer Paul Rothchild, who conducted business with both men. "He made out of very little a whole lot. And in the process, he taught the industry a different set of lessons. Talk about art of the deal—he's inventive, he's creative, and he plays hardball with a smaller, harder ball than anyone else. He is absolutely brilliant at what he does. Albert did not like David. And I think it was because he saw a kinship there. When you see yourself in your children, that is a bad day."

Both men shared similar working-class Jewish backgrounds. But their careers were driven by strikingly different interests. Unlike Grossman, whose love for folk music led to his involvement with the emerging business, David Geffen's aspirations revolved around power and glamour. Even as a teenager he dreamed of being a Hollywood mogul.

Born in 1943, he had been raised in Brooklyn's blue-collar Borough Park, the second of two sons. When David was seventeen, his father, Abraham, died. An intellectual who preferred reading books in French or Spanish to business, the elder Geffen apparently left the world without making a positive impression on his younger son, who faulted his father for not providing him with a better and more affluent life. Neither did he inherit his father's scholastic bent. While his older brother, Mitchell, attended UCLA Law School, David just managed to scrape through New Utrecht High School with a sixty-six average.

If Geffen dismissed his father as a dreamer, he certainly did not lack for his own dreams. As a child, his fantasies revolved around the movies and the theater, and he devoured all the gossip he could find about the entertainment world in Hedda Hopper's and Walter Winchell's newspaper columns. Although his brother liked to say he was a wealth of worthless information, David divided Saturdays and Sundays between the two movie theaters nearest his family's apartment, the Loews on Forty-sixth Street and New Utrecht Avenue and the Loews in Borough Park. When not watching the double feature, his eyes would drift up to the ceiling murals that depicted a night sky far more vast than the Brooklyn flatlands.

To Geffen, the neighborhood theaters were palaces. But they were just an intimation of what waited across the river in Manhattan. On his first trip to Radio City Music Hall, he strolled down the aisle of the great Deco theater, imagining himself on his way to the stage to accept an Academy Award. And there were the Broadway shows, first with his parents and later on his own, when he would save up $2.90 for a second-balcony seat to *Gypsy* or *My Fair Lady.* "I could see for myself there was a better life," Geffen said. "I wanted it."

As a teenager, he discovered *Hollywood Rajah,* a biography of the feared studio boss Louis B. Mayer by film critic Bosley Crowther. But while Mayer became his idol, it was David's mother who would prove the most important and lasting influence in his life. In later years the associates and employees who marveled at her son's extraordinary focus and hunger for success would dub her "The Explanation."

Batya Volovskaya was a self-made businesswoman and the family breadwinner. A Russian immigrant, she had worked as a seamstress during the Depression. She started her own business making brassieres and corsets in the family's three-room Brooklyn apartment and later opened her own shop nearby on Thirteenth Avenue, Chic Corsetry by Geffen. Life for David revolved around the shop, where his mother would cook the family's meals between waiting on customers.

Batya, who called her son "King David," dispensed a unique blend of business advice to her son. The first ingredient was a large measure of an immigrant's faith that he could rise or fall based on his own willingness to work hard and believe in himself. "You've got to put blinders on and run your own race," she would tell him. The second part was an ongoing, daily lesson in the fine art of the *handl* (bargaining) as Batya and her customers bickered over prices.

Geffen was particularly taken with his mother's ability to define the limits of a transaction, even on something as mundane as ladies' undergarments. He liked to recall how she once misquoted a price to a customer's advantage but was able to build an escape hatch by insisting that the price was only good if the item was purchased at that moment. The woman left the shop to do some comparison shopping and returned to discover that Batya wouldn't give her the original price. "My mother taught me how not to get hustled," said Geffen.

Despite Batya's instinct for her son's business talents, Geffen followed high school with a couple of stabs at college. He lasted one semester at the University of Texas before flunking out and then went on to Los Angeles to stay with his brother, Mitchell, at UCLA. He landed a small part as a high school student in a 1961 film called *The Explosive Generation* and, after seeing the results on the big screen, had his nose fixed. Mitchell chided him into giving college another shot by summoning the harshest invective in the family lexicon: "you're going to be a failure just like your father." He lasted another semester, this time at Brooklyn College.

His early attempts at work were equally unsuccessful. Fired after a brief stint as an usher at CBS, he landed a second low-level job at the network but was fired from that as well. But not, he would tell people, for lack of trying but because he was too aggressive. Now twenty-one, Geffen was growing increasingly desperate. He couldn't stay in school, and even though he wasn't afraid of hard work, he couldn't seem to hold a job. Still, he harbored hopes of making it in show business. Fortunately, he was about to land a job at the William Morris Agency, where hungry young men could make their show business dreams come true.

Launched from a two-room office on Fourteenth Street in 1898 as an agency for vaudevillians, William Morris was the world's largest and most profitable talent agency in 1964, the year Geffen walked in off the street and filled in a job application form. Billing itself as "the agency of the show world," it had grown from vaudeville to forty departments, including motion pictures, television, theater, music, literature, public appearances, recording, concerts, and merchandising. There were 150 agents representing actors, writers, directors, producers, and production companies. In television alone, where the agency generated 60 percent of its commissions, William Morris was easily number one, representing twenty-seven weekly hours of network programming. Its closest competitor, Ashley Famous Talent Agency, represented just 8.5 hours a week.

The prior year had been a very good one indeed for the agency. The U.S. Justice Department had determined that MCA, William Morris's long-standing rival, was violating antitrust laws by acting as both a television and motion picture producer and talent agency. When the government forced MCA to choose between them, it stuck with production—and William Morris's most formidable competitor vanished.

If a clear field could be expected to encourage complacency among the agents at William Morris, its corporate culture all but made that impossible. Agency founder Bill Morris was a man Batya Geffen would have admired, an immigrant and former office boy who crafted his own success. For thirty-four years he presided over an agency whose clients included Charlie Chaplin, Will Rogers, and Al Jolson, and company lore had it that Mr. Morris died of a heart attack playing pinochle at the Friars Club following a heated argument with a Loews executive over a contract for Eddie Cantor.

Training to be an agent at William Morris meant enduring a unique and rigorous process, a cross between executive boot camp and brainwashing. "We all think alike," bragged one agent the year Geffen joined the training program.

Although prospective agents were not required to have college degrees, Geffen opted to say he had spent the last four years as a theater arts major at UCLA rather than recount his true academic career and failed tenures at CBS. He was hired.

Geffen, who likes to say that one of the great business lessons his mother taught him was "to tell the truth," would later go out of his way to make this story, as well as the sister tale of its consequences, part of his personal legend. As Geffen would recount, he soon discovered that while William Morris was willing to hire nongraduates, it did check trainees' résumés. Fearing he would be fired, Geffen made sure he was the first one in the mail room every morning in order to intercept the return letter from the school.

Geffen had little trouble squaring his actions with his mother's lessons. "It was either give William Morris what they wanted or give up my dream," he said when asked about the contradiction. "It has nothing to do with what my mother taught me. I just don't believe in taking no for an answer."

Just what the admonishment to "tell the truth" really meant to Geffen is hard to determine, especially since he is the sole source of the story on lying his way into the William Morris Agency, though unscrupulous behavior within the ultracompetitive world of talent agents is not necessarily something one hides. Sandy Gallin, a close friend of Geffen's who trained during the same period at another agency, GAC, liked to advertise that he got out of that firm's mail room by convincing an agent's secretary to quit—and then securing the job for himself (the story was even included in an official PR bio that Gallin employed years later when he became a successful manager).

At various times, the UCLA transcript story has had different twists, although in some cases it is difficult to tell whether the embellishments are Geffen's or the reporters'. When the story appeared in a 1975 *Esquire* profile, it included a trip to a printer, where David had the UCLA letterhead reproduced and forged a reply; by 1982, the version appearing in *The New York Times* was more modest, saying Geffen had "steamed it open and, with a little sleight of hand, changed the reply from no to yes." Sometimes the articles said a college degree was a requirement, which it wasn't, and other times Geffen portrayed himself as simply worried that he needed an extra edge. In 1988, he told an interviewer that he had felt impelled to lie on his application to William Morris after he had truthfully filled out an application at the Ashley Famous Agency and been rejected. But in another 1988 piece, *Time* reported that Geffen blamed William Morris for his actions for—in the magazine's words—"requiring that credential for a low-level job."*

If these actions showed him being clever or somehow avoiding something unpleasant, Geffen was not loath to admit to things that clearly fell outside the boundaries of telling the truth. He bragged that he had used his "wits and instinct" as a teenager for such mundanities as signing his own bad report cards—and for such weightier actions as lying to stay out of the wartime army.

Irving Azoff, a former employee of Geffen's who has been by turns friendly and feuding with him for the last twenty-five years, says Geffen believes he is telling the truth even when he isn't. "He, in his mind, creates and believes things, and they become facts regardless of what happened," he says. "But I actually believe he convinces himself that that's the way things go down."

Working at William Morris was an invitation for Geffen to unbridle his desire. Behind the facade of a genteel hierarchy and tradition, the agency taught its trainees that there were tremendous financial rewards in the entertainment business for anyone willing to do whatever it took to adhere to one simple rule: win.

The trainee program was an intense and thorough indoctrination. A

---

*Geffen was never afraid to change a story radically in public. In the mid-seventies he said that Atlantic Records founder Ahmet Ertegun had loaned him $50,000 to help him in his early days as a manager and that Ertegun had never allowed him to repay the debt. He repeated the tale over the years until 1982, when he abruptly disavowed the story, telling *The Washington Post* that he "made it up" to make Ertegun look good. For his part, Ertegun insisted that the story was true and that he did bankroll Geffen.

stint in the mail room was just the first phase, and it could last from five to fifteen months. During that period, the trainee was a mere plebe, handling personal errands for the agents. But being in the mail room also provided an opportunity to see and read everything that came in and out of the office. Memos, opened letters, telexes, contracts, scripts—a trainee was expected to read them all and learn. Geffen's close friend Barry Diller, who created the Fox television network and later headed the home-shopping channel QVC, credited his education in the entertainment business to sitting in the William Morris mail room and reading through a row of file cabinets filled with client contracts.

William Morris trainees invariably developed an attitude—many liked to compare the program to a rarefied, Harvard-like education in the entertainment business. And they came to view the industry and the agent's role in it as almost primordial.

"The music industry was invented thousands of years ago when guys were pounding on logs in caves and guys took chickens at the door," muses former William Morris agent John Hartmann. "That's where the first artist and manager got together. Somebody had to count the chickens while the guy was playing. So they go to the agent and say, 'Get those guys in the next valley to come over with *their* chickens.' That's the core of the business: people come and give chickens. Everybody else is ancillary, all the lawyers and Indian chiefs and record executives and stuff. It's an old thing. It's not computers."

Surrounded by established, successful agents, Geffen emulated the William Morris style, spending his first agency bonus on ten tailored suits. Years later, much would be made of his hectic schedule, which might include more than one hundred telephone calls, a personal routine involving daily hour-long workouts, and strict adherence to the Pritikin diet. Yet Geffen's routine and interests—including his penchant for collecting art and stated preference for Mozart—were an almost perfect copy of top William Morris agent Sam Weisbord's regimen, which was reported in a magazine profile on the agency in 1964, the year Geffen joined the training program:

> He is a driving, dedicated dynamo, completely devoted to his profession—which in his case is almost a "calling." Weisbord is an extremely capable organizer. Despite a hectic schedule, Weisbord, up

at 6 A.M. each day, finds time for a one-hour workout at the gym and weekend hikes in the sand. He avoids high cholesterol foods, otherwise adheres to a Spartan-like regimen he feels necessary to maintain the physical well-being to carry on his work. Weisbord's nonwork activities are not all physical; he possesses a much-talked-about art collection as well as a classical record collection.

The ladder out of the mail room was usually through the secretarial pool, and if trainees didn't know how to type and take shorthand they learned it on their own time. The first assignment was often as a "floater secretary," filling in when other secretaries were absent. After several months of moving between departments, a trainee could ask to be assigned as an assistant to a particular agent or department, with the expectation that he would eventually become a junior agent in that area. Aside from giving an overview of the agency's activities, this was also an exercise in corporate Darwinism. "You took a few weeks to survey your surroundings, and then you picked the weak link," producer and manager Bernie Brillstein said in recalling his 1955 rise out of the mail room. "You watched whose assistant was getting promoted or fired so you could kiss the agent's ass."

The education then began in earnest. Assistants were given complete access to negotiations and the structuring of deals, including listening in on telephone calls. After a year, a talented assistant could rise to junior agent. Along with "college credentials," Geffen's application for William Morris included an imaginary period as an assistant on *The Danny Kaye Show*. Geffen became an assistant in television, the agency's most important department, selling comedy writers to shows.

But looking around, David could see that others were already achieving the kind of success he hungered for. He was particularly impressed by the young head of the music department, Jerry Brandt. Like Geffen, Brandt was an up-from-the-streets Brooklynite. He'd originally been tossed out of the training program for holding up a television department meeting for an hour and a half while he smoked marijuana in Central Park with the renewal contracts for *The $64,000 Question*. "I didn't know they were all waiting," he says. "I got fired on the spot."

Undaunted, he went to GAC, where he found a mentor in Roz Ross, the music agent who dragged William Morris's rival into the rock and roll business in the early sixties. "She was the first to see it," recalls Brandt. "At that point if you booked rock and roll acts, you were threatened to be fired. She defied that: 'Fire me!' she said. I thought, 'That's my horse.' "

Ross showed Brandt how to cobble together enough dates to build tours for some of GAC's early rock clients like Del Shannon and the Dovells by looking at ads in out-of-town newspapers. "She made me see who was playing bands in Ohio, and we'd call them up and build a circuit," he says. Where there were no music promoters, they called wrestling promoters. "Hey, if you can promote wrestling, you can promote rock and roll," says Brandt, "because all you're doing is putting asses in the seats. Back then, you brought in the fucking amps and there you are."

One of Ross's biggest clients was *American Bandstand* star Dick Clark, whose Caravan of Stars package tour was a steady moneymaker that helped define the early rock concert market. The Clark show could sell fifteen thousand seats in some markets—a tremendous showing—and helped establish promoters and a circuit.

Ross, with Brandt in tow, left GAC for William Morris. This time he made the most of it, convincing Nat Lefkowitz, the manager of Morris's East Coast office, to have the agency represent the Rolling Stones.

An accountant and attorney, Lefkowitz's interest in rock and roll was strictly bottom line, and Brandt won him over by claiming the English band could command an unheard-of $25,000 a night. But Lefkowitz was the exception. "Everyone else, except the guys in legit [the theatrical department] hated it," says Brandt. The Stones proved as good as Brandt's word, though, and he became head of the six-man music department. Geffen, who didn't miss much that went on in the agency, noticed that Brandt was doing very well. "He kept seeing me coming in and out of limousines all day," says Brandt. "I said, '*Schmuck!* What does Norman Jewison need you for? Stay with people your own age. Go in the music business. Then *you'll* ride in limousines.' " It was the best advice David Geffen ever got.

Switching to the music department, Geffen eagerly went to school on Brandt, who was impressed by his drive and extraordinary focus. "He stood in my office day in and day out," Brandt recalls. "Just absorbing." It didn't take long to see that Geffen, even by the cutthroat standards of William Morris trainees, was a standout. "I looked at him and saw it in his eyes," says Brandt. "This guy wants more than I can give somebody."

Geffen was always on the lookout for a score. Steve Leber, who would eventually follow Brandt as head of the music department, remembers Geffen buying shares in Cameo Parkway Records—a company co-owned by Allen Klein, the business manager for the Rolling Stones—and urging him to get in. "He said, 'You should buy this stock,' " says Leber. "It was the first time David ever made any significant money. He made about sixty thousand dollars, and in those days it was a fucking fortune."*

Geffen's ambition and acuity became legend, even by agency standards. He was credited with the ability to read documents upside down on the desks of other agents. While still a trainee, he had gotten into trouble for being overly aggressive and only a tearful appeal to Nat Lefkowitz's wife, Sally, saved his job. Says Leber, "When I first saw David snooping around—reading all the memos, opening up everybody's mail, staying very late, making phone calls to the guys in California, doing all the smart things—I knew David Geffen was going to make it."

Making contacts and negotiating contracts were only part of what William Morris taught its agents. As Albert Grossman could attest, being able to handle the considerable egos of the clients was a skill of at least equal importance. Pampering, hand holding, and the sublimation of one's own ego could be a full-time job. "I did the Stones tours in the sixties," recalls Leber. "I had to be with Mick Jagger all the time and kiss his ass. 'What's hurting you, Mick? Who are we gonna fuck over this week?' " But it was all in a day's work, and Geffen learned the William Morris lesson: a star is a star.

Happenstance and hunger had landed him, a young man whose personal tastes hewed closer to Broadway than to the Brill Building, in the rock and roll business just as the music was about to roar into the mainstream. As a junior agent, he never got near the agency's big rock acts like the Rolling Stones or Elvis Presley, but he was the New York

---

*Geffen, while allowing that Leber "probably is right," has only the vaguest recollection of buying Cameo Parkway stock and couldn't remember whether he had actually made $60,000. "People remind me of things I don't remember all the time," he said. Cameo Parkway, which shot up seventy points over a month on rumors that Klein was going to fold the Stones' music publishing company into the Philadelphia record label's otherwise slim assets, eventually collapsed. Trading in the company's stock was suspended by the Securities and Exchange Commission, and it was de-listed by the American Stock Exchange.

contact for Buffalo Springfield. He would later become the agent for several of Albert Grossman's acts, including Peter, Paul and Mary and Janis Joplin. Working with Grossman's clients helped him make another leap. But the agency, with its disdain for the budding rock business, was behind the curve. Grossman was building the most lucrative and powerful management firm in the business. Suddenly Geffen, who had switched to the music department only because it looked like a fast career track, found he had a deep love and admiration—à la Grossman—for these artists. And if it was difficult to measure Geffen's sincerity against the depth of his own self-interest, one thing was certain. He could really turn on the love light. "David is a very seductive person," a close associate would later say. "When he talks to an artist, he always makes them feel as if they are at the center of the universe. It may all be an act, but it's a hard act to follow." It was through Grossman's associate Artie Mogull that Geffen met the client he used to inaugurate the next phase of his career, Laura Nyro.

Nyro, who resembled a chunky Morticia Addams, was both unusually talented and just plain unusual. Dressed in black with her long hair reaching down to her thighs, Nyro wore purple lipstick and used Christmas-tree ornaments as earrings. "She was weird," says Mogull, who became her first manager when she was just eighteen. "No two ways about it." He was supervising Bob Dylan's Dwarf Music for Grossman when he stumbled upon Nyro in the spring of 1966. "I bought a secondhand piano for the office," Mogull recalls, "and Dylan came to the office and says, 'The piano is out of tune.' So I go to the Yellow Pages and hire a tuner. The guy comes the next day and starts tuning my piano. Tells me his daughter writes songs. I say, 'Listen, do me a fucking favor: just tune the piano.' *Everybody* writes songs. But the guy just wouldn't give up. So to get rid of him I said, 'Tell her she can come up tomorrow and play me some songs.' "

The next day Nyro came to the office, and Mogull was stunned. "The first song she plays me goes, 'I was born from love and my poor mother worked the mines/I was raised on the good book Jesus 'til I read between the lines.' That was it—I signed her for everything."

Not to Dylan's company, of course. Mogull, as Stone and Greene had done with Buffalo Springfield, signed Nyro for management, production, and publishing and got her a recording deal with Verve Records. Her first album, *More Than a New Discovery,* failed to attract much attention. Nyro's debut at 1967's Monterey Pop Festival, however, earned her more notoriety than she wanted. Wearing a grotesque black dress with just one sleeve and a single gossamer angel wing, Nyro performed an ill-conceived, soul-revue-inspired club act with female backup singers and an unrehearsed band. Even the between-song patter proved wildly out of synch with the psychedelic tenor of the festival.

"Hello, all you guys out there," cooed one of Nyro's backup singers.

"There's chicks out there, too," said Laura. "Don't forget about them."

"That's right, Laura. Well, hello, guys and chicks."

Nyro bombed, her show passing into pop infamy. Even *The New York Times,* which otherwise heralded her as a songwriting talent comparable to Leonard Bernstein and George Gershwin, reported that the phrase "almost as bad as Laura Nyro" had become the definitive put-down for an inept performance. "They laughed her off the stage," says Leber. "I was standing right there. She was crying, screaming, yelling. She couldn't believe it—she was the worst performer in the world."

Mogull, an industry sharpie with a quick tongue, was not the type to help her deal with the rejection. Quite the opposite. He was enraged that Nyro had embarrassed them in front of an audience that included many of the music industry's most important executives.

"She had never performed publicly before," Mogull recalls. "She wanted to 'surprise' me. And she surprised me. When she came off the stage, she said, 'How did you like it?' I said, '*How did I like it?* It reminded me of when I was a kid: my father took me to the circus and three elephants came out and did a dance to music.' She discharged me that day." But regardless of what Nyro said, he still had her under contract.

Geffen heard about Nyro after her Monterey debacle from the Association's producer, Bones Howe, and Steve Binder, television director for *The Steve Allen Comedy Hour.* Binder wanted to book her on the program, while Howe was eager to cut some of her songs with a group he was recording, the Fifth Dimension. After they played Geffen one of Nyro's songs, "Wedding Bell Blues," he called Mogull and said he wanted to represent her.

"[Mogull] put her down terribly, but I had to meet her," Geffen told Joe Smith. "So he took me over to her apartment on Eighth

Avenue. She lived at 888 Eighth Avenue in this one-room apartment filled with cats. It was a nightmare, but she and I became instant best friends."*

Mogull, while mystified by the mutual attraction, readily agreed to Geffen becoming her agent. Like Mogull, Geffen could hear how talented she was. But unlike Mogull, he would tell her. "Geffen loved this girl," recalls Leber. "He knew what to do with her."

Geffen left William Morris in 1968 to become a music agent at Ashley Famous. But he frankly and publicly admitted that his commitment to Nyro was unique. "The others are business," he told a reporter for the *Los Angeles Herald Examiner*. "Laura is a passion."

In fact, on both a personal and professional level, Geffen became infatuated with Nyro. "I wanted her to be the biggest star in the world," he said. "I don't know whether that was *her* ambition, but it was *my* ambition." He spoke often of his love for her and even told associates he wanted to marry her. Still, she could be hypersensitive and did not hesitate to remind him who the star was.

Passion and sensitivity notwithstanding, Geffen's competitiveness and desire for success also fostered a vicious streak that interfered with his otherwise consummate abilities as a hand holder. A *koch leffer* (pot stirrer), he couldn't resist taking shots at Mogull in public and humiliated Nyro when he told a reporter that her former manager referred to her as "that fat freak." Still, he was proving an extraordinary advocate for his client.

In the fall of 1968, Nyro, at Geffen's urging, hired his lawyer and sued to break Mogull's hold on her. The attorneys argued that Nyro had been under twenty-one and her contracts with Mogull, producer Milt Okun, MGM (which owned Verve Records), and Mogull's publishing company were invalid. Since the contracts had not been affirmed—as they were required to be for a minor—the court agreed that the production, recording, and management contracts were invalid. But it upheld Mogull's publishing contract on a technicality: the transference of rights in the publishing deal included the boilerplate phrase

---

*Once again, there are two stories and Geffen is the source for both. In the early seventies he told *Life* reporter Maggie Paley that his first meeting with Nyro took place at William Morris: "Her manager brought her to my office, and there she appeared . . . long hair, black clothes, purple nail polish. She sat down in a chair, and I was speechless. But we had a kind of vibration for each other."

"I hereby sell, assign and transfer," and the judge ruled that a minor under twenty-one but over eighteen is liable for a sale in New York.

Geffen succeeded Mogull as Nyro's manager. And, with the formation of a new company, Tuna Fish Music, also succeeded him as her publisher for new compositions. As part of the arrangement, one Grossman had pioneered, Geffen and Nyro were partners. The idea was to reserve ownership for the songwriter by creating a private publishing company set up by the manager and administered for a percentage by a larger, established publishing company. With music publishing royalties and fees split between the author and the publisher, a 50 percent share of the publishing company meant Nyro was actually receiving 75 percent of the publishing money received: 100 percent of the writer's share and 50 percent of the publisher's share. The other 50 percent went to Geffen.

Nyro's work as a songwriter had attracted some attention while she was still with Mogull—Peter, Paul and Mary had recorded one of her songs—but under Geffen's guidance, she rapidly evolved into one of the most successful songwriters in pop music. He gave Bones Howe first crack at Nyro's new songs, and he selected "Stoned Soul Picnic" for the Fifth Dimension. On the heels of the record becoming a big summer hit in 1968, a broad range of artists including Frank Sinatra, Barbra Streisand, Three Dog Night, Blood, Sweat and Tears, and Harry Nilsson were soon interpreting Nyro's music.

With the court decision freeing Nyro from Verve Records, Geffen urged Columbia Records president Clive Davis—who had witnessed the public assassination at Monterey—to give her another listen. Although initially skeptical, Davis ultimately signed Nyro after an audition in a conference room in the company's Fifty-second Street offices. Her first Columbia album, *Eli and the Thirteenth Confession*, proved a high critical success. By the release of her next album, *New York Tendaberry*, in the fall of 1969, Nyro was a recording star in her own right.

Geffen clearly had the patience and skill Mogull lacked to build Nyro, both in her own eyes and in the eyes of the public. Though coyly shy onstage, Nyro wanted to be popular, and, with Geffen's prodding and protection, she began making tentative forays into performing again, playing small solo shows that spotlighted her songs and personality and gradually rebuilt her confidence. "I kept her incommunicado for two years," Geffen said, "because I knew that if she performed before there was an audience for her, she would be hurt." By Thanksgiving of 1969, Geffen's strategy had paid off handsomely: a pair of Carnegie Hall concerts were sellouts. It was an extraordinary turnaround for a performer whose career had been left for dead on the stage of the Monterey Pop Festival. But approaching Davis proved Geffen's smartest move. After years of spurning rock music, Columbia was now paying top-of-the-market prices for young talent. And if William Morris taught its agents anything, it was how to get the money. Now, with Nyro firmly established, Geffen was going to get as much of it as he could for both of them. It was a chance to make a big score—the kind of chance he might never get at an agency like William Morris, where longevity and loyalty were rewarded over innovation and achievement.

Indeed, William Morris operated as a closed corporation. Shares were parceled out to key agents and executives by the board of directors. If an agent left the company or died, his stock could only be resold to the agency at whatever price it wanted to pay. When Stan Kamen, who had spent thirty-five years with the agency and risen to head of the motion picture department and a seat on the board, died in 1986, he owned 23,000 shares of William Morris's common stock, approximately 7 percent of the company's outstanding shares. Despite the fact that the agency's annual revenues were fast approaching $60 million, Kamen's shares were repurchased for $1.2 million, a figure *Forbes* magazine estimated was just half the value of Kamen's stake in William Morris's real estate holdings alone.

Even in 1964, when Geffen joined William Morris, such false corporate paternalism—even with the potential for $50,000 bonuses—was driving much of the best talent out of the agency. "I decided I was getting all the love I could handle at home," quipped an agent who left for a better-paying studio job.

Looking at his coworkers, Geffen could see that while it was the best place to learn the business, there was no guarantee that the board of directors would pay you what you were worth. Jerry Brandt, after failing to convince client Allen Klein to take him in as a partner, had found his ticket out with his own rock club, the Electric Circus. Harvey Kresky, who had been Sonny and Cher's agent, took over their management from Greene and Stone. Those who stayed, especially in the music department, often became increasingly bitter and frustrated.

Leber, still in his twenties when he became head of the department, quickly discovered what Brandt had come to take for granted: the agency was badly behind the times when it came to the burgeoning underground rock scene. Worse, the board was largely indifferent and unwilling to take these hippies seriously. Television was their god. "They never respected the music department," says Leber. "If I wanted a new stereo system, I had to beg." He was also shocked by what he heard at the board of directors' meetings. "I have Class A stock in the company and I'm doing great, but I'm listening to them discussing guys' careers who are forty and fifty years old and they're going to fire them. I say to myself, 'I gotta get out of here. This is death row.'"

Geffen correctly came to take a cynical view of loyalty William Morris–style. Abe Lastfogel, the agency's president, had been the ultimate company man. Childless and homeless except for hotel suites within walking distance of the Morris offices in New York and Los Angeles, he liked to say the agency and its clients were his family. He was a good deal more straightforward in his private conversations with Geffen. "I once asked him to what he attributed the intense loyalty of his men," Geffen said. "'Loyalty is something you pay for,' he told me."

Obviously, he hadn't paid David Geffen enough. Nor did his new boss, Ted Ashley, with whom Geffen was soon butting heads. After less than a year, he quit Ashley Famous to become Laura Nyro's full-time manager.

When Davis signed Nyro to Columbia, her career was in bad shape. Now she was a star. When it came time to negotiate her contract renewal, Geffen had a lot of leverage, and he could expect to secure her a lucrative deal. In a creative twist, Geffen and Davis piggybacked the new long-term extension of her recording contract onto the sale of Tuna Fish Music to CBS's own music publishing arm, April-Blackwood, for 75,000 shares of CBS stock. Before he could complete the deal, however, he had some maneuvering to do. Mogull still had some of Nyro's songs and a continuing claim to be her publisher. Geffen, who had done his best to malign Mogull, now offered him $470,000 for the songs he held and to give up any claim on Nyro's later material. Mogull thought he'd died and gone to heaven—or at

least to wherever it is that music business hustlers go. He quickly
agreed, marveling at how he'd won a final great victory in his battle
with Geffen. Only later did Mogull learn that Geffen and Nyro were
working on a deal with Columbia worth millions. "He still outsmarted
me," says Mogull.

On the surface, the Columbia deal looked like a blockbuster: CBS
stock had been trading at around forty dollars a share, making the
arrangement worth $3 million. But as the deal dragged on for months
without closing, the price of a share dropped to twenty-five dollars,
and Geffen requested—and received—an adjustment. But if Davis was
willing to make Geffen whole, David was loath to reciprocate. When
CBS's stock rebounded sharply, rising to forty-eight dollars a share,
Davis, saying he was under pressure from his corporate people, asked
for an adjustment of his own to bring the price back in line with what
it was originally worth. Geffen was unimpressed—and unwilling to
make the adjustment. The deal sat unsigned.

Davis wasn't the only person having a problem with Geffen and the
deal's structure. Richard Barovick, whom David had recommended to
Laura when she was suing Mogull, had continued to represent both of
them, but he now suggested one of them should hire a separate attorney. "While they were acting and working together, I saw no conflict,"
said Barovick. "When a sale was involved, I did." Geffen's response
was to quit Barovick altogether. "He didn't find it a palatable situation," the attorney says. "He was a good guy and a good client and had
referred a lot of business to me, including Blood, Sweat and Tears. In
his head, it was inconceivable that a guy he had referred business to,
a guy he was friends with, wouldn't help him."

Although Barovick is quick to add that he doesn't believe Geffen
was suggesting he do something unethical, the attorney had given
good advice, especially since the deal Geffen had negotiated for Nyro
was extraordinarily beneficial to himself. Normally, a recording contract extension for a hot star like Nyro involves a guarantee, that is, a
large cash advance and an agreed-upon number of albums for which
the performer is guaranteed a certain amount each time. Nyro's deal
had no guarantee. Instead, it was structured as a purchase by Tuna
Fish Music with a long-term extension of Laura's recording contract
included as part of the purchase price.

Selling the publishing company got Nyro what appeared to be a big score, although Davis would later defend the deal by claiming he had acquired assets through it. But as co-owner of Tuna Fish, Geffen received 50 percent of the money. If the deal was structured as a simple contract extension, his share as Nyro's manager would have been a standard commission, normally 15 percent.

It was a unique deal with impressive numbers, and it proved a lot about David Geffen. He was a hard worker who knew the business, but he brought a lot more to the table than ambition. The William Morris Agency's corporate boot camp had taught Geffen the hard facts of the business, how talent must be wedded to money to craft a career. But it was his own particular genius that led him to apply those lessons to a breed of performers who appeared at odds with the traditional entertainment industry. He could recognize and nurture artists, he could kill for his clients and himself, and—when Laura Nyro's new deal was finally signed—it made him a millionaire at twenty-seven.

Most important, David Geffen had discovered his professional salvation in rock. Driven by dreams of being a mogul, he would expand the roles he'd played as Laura Nyro's advocate and exploiter to carve out a unique and powerful position as the go-between for a generation of new artists and the business emerging in their wake.

7

CHIEFS AND
INDIANS

BY THE END OF THE SIXTIES, COLUMBIA, ATLANTIC, ELEKTRA, AND Warner Bros. had all been recast as rock labels, yet the cultural gap between the underground and the business remained. Even as rock's broad commercial appeal was fully realized, the folk ethos—that the music, not the money, was the important thing—remained paramount for an artist's credibility. "An artist never got involved with his business," recalls singer Peter Wolf. "It was sacrilegious. Because you weren't a businessman, you were an artist. You were a musician. The idea of talking about demographics and sales points—it was ludicrous. You didn't, morally, even involve yourself with that. That was like equal to saying you were promilitary. You just didn't deal with it."

Into that gap stepped David Geffen, whose success with Laura Nyro was proof that he could help an artist cash in without making it seem that he or she had sold out. He had revived her career, made himself a small fortune, and succeeded Albert Grossman as the artist representative with a sure feel for business. But it was a significant leap from Grossman, a folk fan who shared many of his client's bohemian tendencies and could be counted on to treat the record companies with contempt, to Geffen, a workaholic who didn't take drugs and viewed the labels as a partner. He was a businessman and smart enough to know a good thing when he saw it. "Geffen was an opportunist," says Joe Smith. "Very quick and smart. Laura Nyro: he became her friend. It was easy to become these people's friends . . . they recognized that they needed someone to represent them who could count, negotiate."

With an eye to the business, Geffen had parlayed the great William Morris Agency lesson—know where to get the money—into a successful, ongoing relationship with Clive Davis. Aside from the Nyro deal, Geffen had tipped Davis to several moneymaking acts, including Chicago and Mac Davis, and the label chief was both grateful and likely to listen to him again. To find the proper talent, however, Geffen would have to turn his other eye to the street, and he accomplished that by using another William Morris tradition, taking on a protégé. Much as Jerry Brandt, the former head of the music department at William Morris, had extended a hand to David and shown him the true and largely untapped value of the emerging rock and roll business, Geffen had in turn taken Elliot Rabinowitz, a young agency trainee, under his wing.

It was hardly a relationship of equals and never would be, even when Rabinowitz later became Geffen's partner. But Geffen's young protégé had something to give him in return for his business tutelage: he was in touch with the music. Like Geffen, he was an up-from-the-streets New Yorker longing for a career in show business. But as early as 1965, Rabinowitz had managed a group named Robert's Rules of Order. (Although he wasn't in the band, he was clearly its driving force. "Roberts" became Rabinowitz's chosen show business name, which he legally adopted in 1967.) Geffen's and Roberts's similar backgrounds and age made for a natural affinity, and Geffen—already a junior agent—soon took to tutoring him on the virtues of showing up at six-thirty in the morning to read everybody's mail.

Compared with Geffen's, Roberts's tenure as an agent was brief. In early 1967, while prowling the Greenwich Village clubs in search of talent, he heard Joni Mitchell, whom Neil Young had befriended three years earlier in Winnipeg. The twenty-three-year-old had found her voice as a songwriter, and Roberts was excited both by her singing and what he rightly perceived as a surfeit of superior songs. "She was a jumble of creative clutter with a guitar case full of napkins, road maps, and scraps of paper all covered with lyrics," he later recalled. Roberts quit his job at William Morris to manage Mitchell. She was scuffling along on fifteen-dollar-a-night gigs at New York's Cafe Au Go-Go when Andy Wickham at Warner/Reprise Records tracked her down and offered her a recording contract. Roberts enlisted his friend and mentor, Geffen, as her agent.

While Roberts flew to Los Angeles to meet with Wickham and Mo Ostin, Mitchell went on the road for a string of club dates. In Coconut Grove, Florida, she met David Crosby of the Byrds. Renowned for both his generosity toward good musicians and an affection for attractive women, he became an immediate Mitchell supporter and offered to produce her debut album. He also became Roberts's second client. His support of Mitchell was important in two ways: Crosby introduced her and her manager to the Laurel Canyon cognoscenti, and his presence in the studio allowed Mitchell the freedom to make the record she wanted without any overt interference from Reprise.

Settling into Hollywood's Sunset Studios to record *Song to a Seagull* while Buffalo Springfield was there working on what would prove to be their final album, Mitchell eagerly introduced Roberts and Crosby to Neil Young. The band had just gotten free of Greene and Stone, and Elliot wasted no time making a pitch to manage them, promising to arrange an appearance at the upcoming Rome Pop Festival. They hired Roberts—and ditched him just as quickly two weeks later when the Rome show was canceled. A few weeks later, when Young quit the band for good, he asked Roberts to manage him as a solo artist.

Unlike Charlie Greene and Brian Stone, Roberts harbored no creative ambitions as a record producer to interfere with Young's. He had absorbed the William Morris lesson: "be aggressive for the client, but in no way compete." Competition was something Young would never stand for in any event, and Roberts—who possessed a sharp, disarming wit—never let it become an issue. "Neil is a king," says Harlan Goodman, who worked with Roberts and Young, "and Elliot is a jester."

Young had already developed a clear sense of his own professional ambitions as well as the knowledge of how to achieve them. But he still needed a sympathetic business representative. "Neil needs somebody to front him," says Will Hinds, who worked with Young and several other artists managed by Roberts. "Not to manage him, to front him. Someone who will viciously go out and get done what he needs done. Elliot will do that. Elliot is absolutely honest for his artists. [But] he'll steal from a record company, from an agent, to see that his artists come out on top."

"Elliot has many strengths," says John Hartmann, a former management associate. "His instincts are terrific. He has the ability to get a great overview of what it is, of what careers are. And he has no rules. Zero. Whatever it takes, Elliot will do."

Young was not an easy client to keep happy. "You're dealing with a true eccentric," observed Warner Bros. Records' Mo Ostin. "And a guy who is totally his own person. Completely unpredictable—which is part of the greatness. Always willing to take risks, always willing to do something that would be viewed as maybe even dangerous. Never following trends. Whenever you'd think he'd go right, he'd make a left on you. If you believe in the artist, if you believe in his talent, if you believe he speaks the truth, then you have to be supportive of him. And to try to force him to go in a particular direction to follow his last record that was successful would have in some ways destroyed him . . . You have to encourage the artists to do whatever they think is right."

Over time, Roberts would prove the perfect manager for Young: a good friend, a great front man, and a goading business presence who nevertheless knew not to push his client too far. "Elliot did an incredible job of managing Neil," concludes Harlan Goodman. "And Neil did an incredible job of managing Elliot."

Unlike Geffen, Roberts would hang out with his rock star clients, smoking dope, playing cards, or chasing women. He was also willing to suffer humiliation and danger as a price of admission. In 1967 Roberts spent four terrifying days in jail after a cop observed him and Crosby smoking pot in Crosby's van in front of the Whisky-a-Go-Go, pulled them over, and discovered a kilo of grass and a loaded gun in the back of the van, none of which Roberts had known were there. But Roberts's bonhomie also masked a fierce determination, one that had been drilled into his head in no small part by Young. The rocker had briefly fired Roberts early in their relationship for killing time on a driving range before a show instead of staying in his hotel room in case Neil wanted to reach him.

"Elliot could kill, and he knows it," says Hinds. "He'd sit down and get high with you, but if Joni was onstage and you were fucking with her sound, he was on you, willing to literally knock you out if you didn't change it. I don't think he ever fucked up a career. I've watched the guy sit there and get so fucking high nobody else could *walk*—and then run business. There had to be something in him doing it from a gut level. This guy never carried a briefcase in his life, and he's walking around with fifteen careers in his pocket. He works from instinct and soul and not from brain."

Signed to Reprise by Ostin, Young released his first solo album, *Neil Young,* in early 1969. Plagued by sound and technical problems, the majority of the collection, with the exception of one song, "The Loner," was marked by self-consciously obscure lyrics. The record was not well received, and Young quickly changed direction, developing a more direct and raw rock sound. But to put it over, he would need something he didn't have on *Neil Young*: a band.

During the waning days of Buffalo Springfield, Neil had sat in at the Whisky with a local group named the Rockets. A ragged outfit, they were better known for selling pot than for their music. "I don't remember them ever working," says singer Robin Lane, who was friendly with group guitarist Danny Whitten. "They were definitely the first garage band I ever knew. They smoked pot and sold it and jammed."

Neil recruited Whitten, along with Rockets drummer Ralph Molina and bassist Billy Talbot, as his new rhythm section and rechristened them Crazy Horse. Together they cut *Everybody Knows This Is Nowhere,* a straightforward rock album that was recorded in just two weeks and released a scant four months after *Neil Young*. Musically, it was an about-face from its predecessor. Tracks like "Cinnamon Girl," "Down By the River," and "Cowgirl in the Sand" became underground radio hits and effectively launched Young as one of rock's premier singer/songwriters.

While Young and Mitchell were clearly on the ascendancy, the future of Robert's other client, David Crosby, was somewhat murkier. The ex-Byrd, fearing his boat was going to be repossessed, had approached Elektra producer Paul Rothchild about making a record. Crosby, Rothchild, and Stephen Stills spent several afternoons in the pool at John Sebastian's house in Laurel Canyon, trying to plot their next move. "Sebastian had blown up the Lovin' Spoonful for their internal problems," says Rothchild. "We're all wondering what to do. All these guys were out of deals and didn't know whether to shit or go blind."

The answer, obviously, was to form a new group. Working up a few songs by Stills, the trio rehearsed informally and invited Graham Nash of the British group the Hollies to join them. Recording two songs as demos at Los Angeles's Record Plant, Rothchild took the tapes back to New York and played them for Jac Holzman at Elektra. Holzman was eager to acquire the group, but every member had signed recording contracts with their former bands that included options on later work. And while it was unlikely that CBS Records was particularly concerned with keeping Graham Nash, who had been signed to Epic as part of the Hollies, or Crosby, whom Columbia viewed as a troublemaker within the Byrds, Ahmet Ertegun at Atlantic had remained a big booster of Stills even after Buffalo Springfield fell apart. "Everyone in the A and R department at Elektra is shitting their pants, it's the best thing they've heard in their *lives*," says Rothchild. "Jac said, 'I'll pay anything, I must have them.' I said, 'You can't. I have to play them for Ahmet.' "

As Rothchild recalls, Ertegun was as impressed as Holzman: "In the middle of the first song, Ahmet takes out the checkbook and says, 'Fill in the number. I don't care—whatever it is doesn't matter.' "

Sebastian opted to pursue a solo career, but the others were ecstatic and joined Rothchild in New York. As Crosby's manager, Roberts was eager to see the band signed and working. But sorting out the recording contracts each musician had signed as members of earlier groups appeared to be a problem since only Stills was signed to Atlantic. Roberts turned to David Geffen for help.

Geffen's first impulse was to make a deal with Clive Davis at CBS Records, and he went to see Jerry Wexler determined to get Stephen Stills's release. It was a bad move. Wexler, who didn't like agents in general and Geffen in particular, had a temper that bordered on the irrational, especially when he thought someone was trying to shuck him or his company. He gave Geffen a deluxe reaming and threw him out of Atlantic's offices.

Ertegun was horrified. He wanted Crosby, Stills and Nash, and he hadn't failed to notice that Geffen was steering moneymaking acts to Columbia. Ertegun took a special delight in any opportunity to best Davis, who, in contrast to Atlantic's frugality, had built CBS Records' rock roster with a free-wheeling checkbook.

"Ahmet really played [Clive]," says Bob Rolontz, then the head of publicity for Atlantic. "Anytime Ahmet would get an act that wasn't quite right, he would spread the word that it was a great act and Clive Davis would be there with dollars in his hand." Atlantic later succeeded in dumping Delaney and Bonnie on Columbia via this strategy, selling their contract to Davis for $600,000 when Atlantic became convinced Delaney Bramlett's drug habit was uncontrollable and that the band would never make it. "Six hundred thousand dollars," Wexler would later marvel. "Think about it: pure profit. How many albums do you have to sell to clear six hundred thousand dollars? It's more creative than making records!"

Wexler could throw fits and view Geffen as beneath contempt if he wanted to, but Ertegun was taking a longer view. "Ahmet stole Geffen away from Clive Davis," says Rolontz.

The day after Wexler had given Geffen the bum's rush, Ertegun rolled out the red carpet. Geffen was appropriately flattered: "He was the most charming person I'd ever met in my life. He just sucked me right in. Because of Ahmet, as soon as I got Crosby, Stills and Nash free of all their other contracts, I signed them to Atlantic Records."

The William Morris Agency had taught Geffen to find financial sources, but Ertegun's attraction was more than simply money—Clive Davis was an easier touch. Ertegun's gentility, sophistication, and power were a mesmerizing combination. "When I first met him, if there was any excuse to call him up I would," Geffen remembered. "He would always pick up my phone call. It made me feel very important."

"I think David Geffen really wanted to be Ahmet Ertegun," says Ned Doheny. A guitarist and songwriter later managed by Geffen and Roberts, Doheny was a scion of the Los Angeles family who gave their name to Doheny Drive. "I've known Ahmet all my life," says Doheny. "He knew my parents, so I knew him as a child. David really longed for that legitimacy and sense of culture—which he never had and never will. Because Ahmet is a horse of a different color, a man from another time and another country."

It was the beginning of an intense mentor/protégé relationship. Ertegun, with one hand on the purse strings and the other extended in friendship, was a revelation to the young agent.

That Ertegun could so captivate Geffen was no surprise. One of the most successful and creative executives in the music business, Ertegun was also the most worldly. The son of a Turkish ambassador, Ertegun combined a courtly, continental demeanor with a passion for African-American culture. In 1947, Ertegun's hobby became his avocation when he borrowed $10,000 from his family dentist and, in partnership with Herb Abramson, a talent scout for National Records, launched Atlantic as a black music, or "race," label. It was a portion of the market that the major record companies like Columbia and RCA-Victor had largely ceded to small independents. The success of Atlantic's rhythm and blues performers helped lay the foundation for rock and roll. By the mid-fifties, the music was beginning to cross over to the white audience, which constituted an increasingly large portion of Atlantic's record buyers. "Our distributors would call us and say, 'Hey, we're getting calls from white jukeboxes, one-stops, and even some white radio stations,' " says Wexler, who joined Atlantic as a partner in 1953. "A station like WLAC [an r&b outlet in Nashville, Tennessee] would be broadcasting into twenty-two states, non-directional, clear signal. Transistor radios had just come in. And Southern kids at the beach, suddenly in addition to Patti Page and Perry Como, they're hearing Fats Domino and LaVern Baker. That's what did it—Southern kids at the beach. At all levels of Southern society there was exposure to black music, whether or not it was conscious, apprehended, and digested. But it was all around and the breakthrough came when the transistor radio came in."

It was a natural jump from making black records that white listeners were buying to signing white performers to make black-influenced records for the white audience. "That *is* the history of rock and roll," says Wexler. After blowing an opportunity to sign Elvis Presley, Atlantic made its first real foray into the white pop market in 1958 with Bobby Darin. Ertegun never looked back. Atlantic went from being a niche label to a major international record company. And Ertegun was unique among American record men. While Clive Davis and Joe Smith put on love beads and donned Nehru jackets to mingle with the counterculture, Ertegun never had to. Like no one else, he was as at home in the White House as in a roadhouse. Record producer Joe Boyd ran into him entertaining guitarist Eric Clapton one night at a London club and, in the course of their conversation, discovered that

Ahmet was in the middle of a three-day trip that had begun in Paris at the opening of a Picasso show at the Pompidou Centre, as the guest of Georges and Madame Pompidou, continued on to London for the meeting with Clapton, and would conclude with an overnight flight to Cleveland, where he was to meet with an influential disc jockey.

The timing of Geffen's relationship with Ertegun would prove particularly fortuitous. In June of 1969, just months after the signing of Crosby, Stills and Nash, Atlantic's parent company, Warner–Seven Arts, was sold. The sale created Warner Communications, Inc., one of the most successful American multimedia companies of the next twenty years. Under WCI, Ertegun's power would increase subtantially and provide a rare opportunity for his young protégé.

It was the second change of ownership for Atlantic in as many years. After more than two decades as an independently owned label, Atlantic had been acquired by Warner–Seven Arts in 1968. The company was a weird amalgam: Seven Arts, owned by Elliot Hyman, had been a small New York company specializing in syndicating old movies and cartoons to television when it stunned the film world in November of 1966 by purchasing Jack Warner's controlling interest in Warner Bros. for $32 million. "It was as if the *Pasadena News* bought *The New York Times*," said Warner Bros. Records executive Joe Smith. "As ludicrous as that."

The film studio that Hyman purchased was not in good shape. But Seven Arts' arrival coincided with the commercial boom of the rock underground, and Warner/Reprise Records was on the verge of becoming a big moneymaker. Hyman's investment banker, Alan Hirschfield of Charles Allen and Company, urged him to expand Warner–Seven Arts' record holdings and arranged for Hyman to meet Jerry Wexler and Ertegun and his brother Nesuhi. In 1968, using profits from the Warner/Reprise record labels, Hyman purchased Atlantic for $17.5 million.

It seemed like a lot of money. Just a few years earlier, Atlantic had nearly been sold to ABC's Paramount Records for $1 million. But it wasn't quite enough to quell all of Ertegun's misgivings. Aside from having scant regard for Hyman, Atlantic's former owners, who had stayed on to run the label, soon concluded that the record company had been worth much more—perhaps double. And when Steve Ross and his Kinney National Services, Inc., materialized the following year with an offer to purchase Warner–Seven Arts from Hyman for $400 million, Ertegun's worst fears were confirmed. "When Steve Ross first bought the company my brother and I were ready to leave and do something else," says Ertegun. That was very bad news for Ross, who had almost no experience in the entertainment industry and knew nothing about the record business. Prior to acquiring the Ashley Famous Talent Agency from Ted Ashley two years earlier, he had been an undertaker.

Ross had married into Riverside Memorial Chapels, a family-owned chain of New York funeral parlors. But he had resourcefully built an auto rental business by leasing out his father-in-law's fleet of limousines at night when they weren't being used for funerals. After merging the rental business with Kinney, a parking lot operator, Ross folded in the funeral homes and a brother-in-law's office cleaning business to form a small conglomerate and took the company public in 1962. Five years later he set out to remake Kinney as an entertainment company.

With Ted Ashley as his adviser, Ross began shopping for a movie studio. The duo soon focused on Warner–Seven Arts, but made an unsettling discovery. Consultant Manny Gerard, a security analyst specializing in the entertainment business, laid Warners' money-losing studio bare. "You realize," he told Ross and Ashley at a meeting in the spring of 1968, "that this is a record company. Essentially, all the earnings come from the record business."

The plan was for Ashley to take over the day-to-day running of the studio and get the picture company back on its feet. In the meantime, the record operation would have to carry the ball. Strong management would be essential, and Ertegun was both a key record executive and a large Warner-Seven Arts shareholder. It was Ashley's job to convince Ertegun that Ross was someone he should be in business with. "I called Ahmet one day and suggested he stop by and meet Steve Ross at his office," recalls Ashley.

Ertegun demurred. Ashley suspected the record man believed he should be the one buying the company, not Ross. He also got the distinct impression that Ertegun couldn't see himself working for someone who'd been in the funeral business and run parking lots. On top of that, there were rumors that Kinney was mobbed up. Caesar Kimmel, Kinney's executive vice president and the original owner of Kinney's parking lot business, was the son of Emmanuel Kimmel, a well-known New Jersey gambler. A few years earlier, Ross and Kinney had become enmeshed in a gambling case brought by the New York district attorney after the elder Kimmel arranged for Kinney limos and parking lots to be used to shuttle gamblers from New York to New Jersey for a crap game. Throughout the investigation, Caesar Kimmel had steadfastly maintained that his company had nothing to do with running the gambling operation, and no charges were ever filed against its executives. But in the wake of the Warner–Seven Arts deal, Kinney found itself once again under a microscope.

"I've lived with this over the years," Caesar Kimmel complained to *Forbes* magazine. "The charges that we are run by the Mafia. It just isn't true. We don't wear shoulder holsters. We've never been under the influence of any underworld group."

Taken together, Ross's background and Kinney's unsavory reputation formed a formidable obstacle as Ashley wooed Ertegun. But if there was one thing the former agent knew, it was how to sell a client. "I told him Steve was a remarkable guy," he recalls. "I'd sold him my business when I could've sold it to six other guys, so obviously I thought Steve was a man with something special." Ultimately, he arranged a sit-down between Ertegun and Ross. "Finally, I said, 'Look, Ahmet—this is going to happen. Let's not get stuck here; come on over to my office, we'll meet at my place.' I never said 'neutral ground,' but it finessed the question. Ahmet recognized what I said was fundamentally true: we were going to wind up owning Atlantic Records, so let's start making a bed instead of rumpling it."

The meeting went surprisingly well. As Ross was fond of relating, he had cribbed for the sit-down by talking to the teenage son of a friend. When, over dinner at New York's 21, Ertegun sought to show the Kinney chief how little he knew about the record business by bringing up the recently signed supergroup Blind Faith, Ross trumped him by noting who was in the band and that they had sold out Madison Square Garden before they had even released a record. More important, however, was Ross's willingness to let his record executives run their labels without day-to-day interference and to compensate them handsomely with stock options and big bonuses. In the latter respect, Ross was a revelation to the people at Warner Bros. It had been a standing joke in Burbank that Jack Warner believed profit sharing was a communist plot.

Over time, Ertegun and Atlantic flourished under Ross. And the two men found a good deal of common ground. When they wanted you, it wasn't a business proposition. It was a romance.

"Everybody wants to be Ahmet, even Phil Spector," says Brian Stone, the former manager of Buffalo Springfield. "Half the people think he does nothing. Jerry [Wexler] was always beefing: 'Ahmet does not do day-to-day work. He comes in at one o'clock in the afternoon.' I'd ask Ahmet what the hell everyone was so pissed off about and he'd say, 'Let me tell you something: they *say* that. But if I stop doing what I'm doing, there's no company. I'm the one who signed all the acts.' Which is the truth. He's the one who flies over and schmoozes with Mick Jagger. Ahmet's the one he loves and wants to talk to. Period. And his double is Steve Ross. They're real class. And they give that genuinely to people who are the lowest scum on the earth, me included. Just become part of them and they'll be happy to take you to the finest place in the world and sit you at the table and give you all the respect in the world. And treat you like they mean it."

CROSBY, STILLS AND NASH WERE DELIGHTED TO HAVE AN AGGRESSIVE AD-vocate like David Geffen handling their contract negotiation. As far as David Crosby was concerned, Geffen was an obvious shark—but he was *his* shark.

Such cynicism had its rewards, but it wasn't risk free. Several years later, when John Hartmann took over management of Crosby, Stills and Nash, he quickly came to the conclusion that Geffen hadn't always put the band's interests ahead of his own.

"I read Crosby, Stills and Nash's existing contract with Atlantic Records," Hartmann recalls. "And then I went back and read the original contract. And I discovered there were only two principal changes from one to the other. One was that Geffen had his commission written in to pay direct. And the other was that Atlantic got more product. There was no increase of money to the act and no increase of royalty to the act." Hartmann says he used the discovery to pry a new contract for the band out of Ertegun.

One thing Geffen did do for the band during those early ne-gotiations was ease out Paul Rothchild, who had worked with the group from its inception. Rothchild was thunderstruck. "Geffen was managing nobody," he says. "Nobody! He was a low-life agent! Ahmet says he's gonna sign them, they've got the basics of a deal. There's no Geffen in sight. Rothchild's gonna produce. Modest points. But because of what I've done for the band, I'm going to get a five percent managerial piece, a little override for putting the thing together and selling it. Geffen listens to the tape, the cash registers go off madly in his mind. He says, 'What the fuck do you need Rothchild for? He's taught you how to do the sound. Produce yourselves. Forget the management thing— you don't have to give him his five percent.' I get cut out."

For Rothchild, who had been personally responsible for leading Elektra Records along the creative path of the sixties from Tom Rush to the Paul Butterfield Blues Band to the Doors, all of whom he signed and produced, it was a bitter moment that profoundly altered his perception of the relationship between the artists and the business. "This was the beginning of the end of the love groove in American music," he says. "To me, that's the moment. When David Geffen enters the California waters as a manager. The sharks have entered the lagoon. And the entire vibe changes. It used to be 'Let's make music, money is a by-product.' Then it becomes 'Let's make money, music is a by-product.' "

Artistically, Crosby, Stills and Nash were the clear-cut successors to Buffalo Springfield. But where the earlier group had foundered commercially, the new group's self-titled debut album was an immediate success. Released in 1969, *Crosby, Stills and Nash* sold two million copies that year and became an FM radio staple, spawning a legion of imitators. The stardom that had eluded the group's members in each of their previous bands now came to them exponentially. Before the group played its first concert it was one of the most successful acts in the world.

Why was Crosby, Stills and Nash such a big hit while Buffalo Springfield never achieved the success it deserved? As far as David Geffen was concerned, the answer was simple: he did it. Unlike Roberts, who steadfastly remained behind the scenes, Geffen was eager to talk to the press and expand, literally, upon his role in the group's success. A fawning *Newsweek* profile of Geffen credited the success of the group—which soon added Neil Young—to Geffen's genius. According to the magazine, which quoted only Geffen and appeared to rely solely upon him for its information, the story behind

the band's success was that the agent had taken "four washed-up musicians out of three failed bands and made them CSNY, selling their
act for $10,000 a night before anyone had heard them or seen them
perform in public."

When it came to personal publicity, Geffen pulled no punches.
"This is one of the few places in show business where an executive like
me can be a star, too," he crowed to a writer from *Time*. Even Ertegun,
his new hero and mentor, wasn't spared Geffen's need to grab the
limelight. When *New York* sent writer Andrew Tobias to profile the Atlantic chieftain, he found Geffen following everywhere in Ertegun's
wake like a dinghy after a yacht. Geffen repeatedly collared the writer,
urging him to drop the Ertegun angle and write about him instead.

For all his hunger and brilliance, Geffen remained a little rough
around the edges. Stopping for lunch with Ertegun at a Schrafft's—a
chain of Manhattan restaurants particularly popular with little old
ladies—Geffen suggested to his companion that it would be really
great to yell "Fuck!" at the top of their lungs. And, although already a
millionaire, Geffen was still so insular that during his first trip to the
Riviera with Ertegun he asked the elder record man if there were any
recording studios in France. "France is like Brooklyn," Ertegun
replied with pithy condescension. "They have everything."

While Geffen's attitude toward artists ranged from open disdain to
awe and affection, he undeniably had a gut instinct for their talent.
And he had a genius for facilitating it. "He had total faith in their abilities," says producer Bones Howe, whom Geffen briefly managed. "He
had a description—he said these people are 'significant artists.' The
significant artist is an artist who creates their own music, records it,
and produces it. As opposed to pop artists, who use other people's
work and it's all fabricated. These people create and craft themselves.
And he was fascinated with that process. And was smart enough to
know that his best contribution was to make the ground ready and fer-
tilize it and then step away."

Geffen had become a vice president at Creative Management (now
ICM) in Los Angeles in 1969 and could not legally be a personal
manager while acting as an agent regardless of the type of guidance
he dispensed to performers like Laura Nyro or Crosby, Stills, Nash
and Young. Conversely, under California law, only agents can
directly obtain work for performers. In actuality, Geffen's close

relationship with his clients meant that he frequently functioned like a manager, even if his protégé, Elliot Roberts, legally managed the artists. But after Crosby, Stills, Nash and Young became bona fide, bankable stars, Geffen told Roberts he was tired of being an agent and wanted to become Elliot's partner. Roberts, not surprisingly, balked at the prospect of having to share the management commission on a group of established, highly lucrative performers. But Geffen was insistent. "Don't be stupid," he told Roberts, "I'll make you more money than you've made alone."

Roberts capitulated fully. In the new firm, the Geffen-Roberts Company, Geffen got top billing, and for a very good reason: he owned 75 percent of it.

The clients believed Geffen-Roberts was an unbeatable team. Roberts was the nice one—"a cat who is like us," David Crosby told *Rolling Stone*—but still tough enough to get the job done. And if for some reason he ever came up short, Geffen operated as the doomsday weapon.

"You just naturally do get to love the cat," Crosby said of Roberts. "Unless you gotta write a contract with him. In which case you may just not ever want to speak to him again. He's armed robbery in a business deal. And if he doesn't rob you blind, we'll send Dave Geffen over; he'll take your whole company. And sell it while you're out to lunch."

●

AS DAVID GEFFEN WAS RELENTLESSLY MAKING HIMSELF INTO ONE OF ROCK'S most powerful managers, his mentor, Ahmet Ertegun, was consolidating his own position at the newly formed Warner Communications, Inc.

The record operation Steve Ross and Kinney purchased was, as advertised, the real moneymaking division at Warner–Seven Arts. But senior management at Warner/Reprise was embittered by the fact that their profits had been used to buy Atlantic and make its executives significant shareholders in Warner–Seven Arts. Between them, the Erteguns and Wexler held 66,000 shares of the company's common stock, while the Warner/Reprise executives were simply employees. The relationship between Atlantic's chiefs—Ahmet and Nesuhi Ertegun and Jerry Wexler—and Mike Maitland, the top executive at Warner/ Reprise, was particularly poor. Maitland believed that as vice president of the music division he should have the final word over all record operations, Atlantic included. Ahmet Ertegun did not agree.

Regardless of Maitland's ambitions, it was obvious where the real power within the record division lay even before Ross and Kinney acquired the company. Following Warner–Seven Arts' purchase of Atlantic, Ertegun and Wexler played a key role in solidifying the future power base of Joe Smith and Mo Ostin, the top executives under Maitland at Warner Bros. and Reprise respectively.

Both Smith and Ostin had been seeking new contracts, which Maitland had put off negotiating. When Wexler, now a major stockholder in the corporation, got wind of the unsigned deals, he and Ertegun urged Elliot Hyman, the head of Warner–Seven Arts, to make sure Maitland put them under contract. The reason, ostensibly, was that Warner–Seven Arts ran the risk of losing two valuable executives to other labels. "I knew that MGM was on a scouting trip and so were other companies," said Wexler.

Left unsaid was the fact that such an intervention would make Maitland look bad. The record division head had wanted to combine many of Atlantic's back-office functions such as accounting and distribution with those existing departments at Warner/Reprise, a move that would have increased his power at the expense of Ertegun and Wexler. Instead, Maitland now found himself on the defensive.

While waiting at Kennedy Airport with his wife for a flight to Greece, Maitland was paged over the loudspeaker. Picking up the phone, he discovered an enraged Hyman, who told him he could not leave the country until he had new contracts signed with Ostin and Smith. The contracts—which solidified the power and prestige of Maitland's two ranking assistants—were closed within twenty-four hours.

"I think Ahmet was concerned about Mike ultimately becoming more powerful than Ahmet," Mo Ostin would later say. "Ahmet, in his manipulative fashion, said and convinced Hyman—and subsequently Ross and Ashley—that the real strength of the record company was not Mike Maitland, but Joe and Mo."

Once Kinney entered the picture, Ertegun became an open devotee of the two executives, especially Ostin. And with Ross relying heavily on Ashley to take control of the disastrous Warner Bros. Films, Ertegun made the most of Ross's dependence upon him at the record division.

Weeks after the Kinney buyout, Ertegun gave a stunning demonstration of his continuing antipathy toward Maitland by blatantly ignoring an agreement Atlantic had just made with Warner/Reprise.

In the summer of 1969, Atlantic agreed to help Warner Bros. Records in its efforts to establish labels overseas by having its product handled in Australia by an about-to-be-launched Warners label. But when Warner Bros. Records executive Phil Rose arrived in Australia to set up the operation, he discovered that Atlantic had signed a new, four-year licensing deal with another label just the week before. Maitland complained bitterly to Ashley, but to no avail. "Ahmet wasn't listening to Ted Ashley too much at that time," said Rose. "He had rapport with Steve Ross in New York."

As he had done with Hyman, Ertegun was again urging Ross and Ashley to extend Ostin's and Smith's contracts. Ross did not need much convincing. All he knew about the record operation was that it generated most of the profits for his company, and as he had demonstrated in his wooing of Ertegun, he was eager to keep the people who could best run those operations. Ostin, while aware that his star was very much on the rise, had two years remaining on his contract and was in no hurry to sign away his choices. "I had no real interest in leaving Warners," he later recalled, "but MGM and ABC had offered me the presidency of their companies, and I wanted to keep my options open. So I never signed the contract, which led to Maitland's undoing."

In January of 1970, Ertegun went to an Atlantic sales meeting in Palm Springs and met Ostin afterward in Los Angeles. When Ostin still balked at signing a new contract, Ertegun suggested that he was going to take over the record operation and intimated that Maitland's days with the company were numbered. "He really tried to do a sales job on me," said Ostin. "It was like he was selling an artist."

Ostin worried that he would be viewed within the company as having stabbed Maitland in the back. Ultimately, his attorney, Werner Wolfen, convinced him that Maitland's fate was sealed regardless of whether he took the job or not. Wolfen's advice to his client proved both sage and succinct: "Don't be a schmuck."

That Sunday, January 25, Ashley went to Maitland's house and told him he was out. Though surprised, Maitland accepted the news without overt rancor, declining a proffered job at the film studio. A week later, Ostin was named president of Warner Bros. Records; Smith, executive vice president.

"The impression I got was [that] in their estimation I was the stronger of the two," Ostin observed. "I think Ahmet made the choice. Ahmet made the evaluation of the two guys who he felt had the greatest value to the company, and he just said, 'This one is number one, and this one is number two.' I certainly don't think Ted Ashley made the decision, nobody at Kinney did, so it had to be Ahmet."

Among the Warner and Atlantic employees, there was a clear perception that Ertegun had "gotten" Maitland. And although Smith made a point of telling people there had never been a vendetta, privately Ostin told employees that Ertegun "wanted to emasculate Mike."

Regardless of the corporate posturing, the relationship between Warner/Reprise and Atlantic was now remarkably smooth. There remained little doubt within Kinney as to who had the hammer at the record operation. "Ahmet ended up moving Joe Smith, Mo Ostin, and five or six other good guys up to the top of their record companies and throwing out the bums," says Bob Rolontz. "Remember, Ahmet is a talent scout. He can walk into a dump, pick out the kid who's playing trumpet, and say, 'He's a star—I'm gonna sign him now.' He also can walk in and see six guys who are marketing guys and say, 'This is a good marketing guy, get him.' His feeling for talent was at all levels. There's no question about it: Ahmet goes out to the coast, they have this meeting, and it ends up there ain't no Maitland in the company anymore. Gone. Ahmet is the chief, chief, chief. Ahmet had this wonderfully summarial title—Chief of the World."

ON THE HEELS OF ATLANTIC'S SUCCESS WITH CROSBY, STILLS, NASH AND Young, Geffen urged Ertegun to sign another act he managed, Jackson Browne.

Although just twenty-two, Browne had been around the music business for quite some time. He had met Billy James, then the house hippie at Columbia Records, when he was sixteen and playing coffeehouses in Orange County. James was unable to interest the label in Browne but succeeded in getting him a recording contract at Elektra. While Browne never released a record there, Elektra also signed him for music publishing, and one of the record company's other artists, Tom Rush, recorded two of Browne's songs, "These Days" and "Colors of the Sun."

If Browne was unknown to the general public, the Rush recordings established him as something of a prodigy among the growing clique of young Southern California songwriters. James marveled at how a teenager could write a song like "These Days," a mature, brooding, even despairing composition. But with the exception of the Rush covers, Jackson's two-year stint with Elektra Records was a washout. In 1967, when his manager/protector Billy James left Elektra, the label dropped him. He got a second shot the following year when Barry Friedman, the original manager of Buffalo Springfield, decided he wanted to produce Browne for Elektra.

Friedman took him and guitarist Ned Doheny to the Paxton Recording Ranch, Elektra's studio on an isolated stretch of the Feather River in Northern California's remote Plumas National Forest. A former hotel, the ranch had also seen service as an alcohol rehabilitation center and a whorehouse before Friedman convinced Elektra head Jac Holzman that the blossoming West Coast rock scene could benefit from the kind of back-to-the-woods environment Albert Grossman was building at the Bearsville studio near Woodstock. There were just too many distractions in Los Angeles, Friedman argued, and Browne and Doheny—who were whiling away their days getting stoned and skinny-dipping with teenage girls in Paul Rothchild's swimming pool—were just the kind of artists who needed to get out of town. But the ranch proved a disaster. Getting there entailed two plane trips and a jeep ride, and women were a rarity. "There was a lot of sharing going on," says Friedman. Worse, Friedman was no administrator and Holzman pulled the plug on the Paxton Ranch after just eight months while dropping Browne for the second time.

Still, Browne's talents as a songwriter had won him the admiration of several other performers, including David Crosby, who sang his praises to *Rolling Stone*. "[He's] a stunner," said Crosby. "He's got songs that'll make your hair stand on end." He urged Browne to send a demo to Geffen.

Geffen did exactly what most people in the entertainment industry do with unsolicited material from unknown performers: he threw it out without a listen. As luck would have it, his secretary noticed Browne's 8 X 10 glossy in the garbage and fished out the recording.

"You know that record and that picture and that letter you threw out?" she asked him the next day.

"You go through my garbage?" asked Geffen.

"Well, he was so cute that I took it home. And he's very good. Listen to the record."

Geffen did and was particularly taken with one song, "Jamaica Say You Will." Contacting Browne, Geffen told him that he "wanted to look after him."

The largely unknown singer and songwriter proved to be a hard sell. Geffen sent Browne on the road as an opening act for Laura Nyro and arranged cozy auditions around the pool at his Los Angeles home for Clive Davis and Ahmet Ertegun, but he couldn't get him a deal. Ertegun's unwillingness to sign him led to sharp words between the Chief of the World and his hungry number one brave.

"I'm telling you, this guy is good," Geffen told Ertegun. "I'm the guy who brought you Crosby, Stills and Nash. I'm doing you a favor."

Ertegun wanted no favors. Despite Geffen's assurance that Atlantic would "make millions" with Browne, Ertegun instead suggested that Geffen start his own record company. "Then we can all have millions," Ertegun snidely retorted.

Geffen took Ertegun's response as a challenge. "I thought, 'Fuck him. I will start a record company,' " he recalled.

Despite the caustic one-upmanship of their exchange, the notion of Geffen starting his own label wasn't unique. Throughout Atlantic's early years, Wexler and Ertegun had made numerous deals with outsiders to bring them under the Atlantic umbrella—and onto the company's corporate ledger.

"One thing that I encouraged early on was for entrepreneurs to bring in artists or finished masters and we'd give them a label," explains Wexler. "Anybody could have a label, even little guys. Who gives a shit what the logo is? What it's all about is billing."

One of Atlantic's sharpest deals in the sixties was to distribute the Memphis-based soul label, Stax. Aside from providing Atlantic and its independent distributors with a steady stream of hit records, the deal's fine print ultimately gave Atlantic ownership of any of Stax's master recordings made during the term of the agreement, an incredibly bad deal for Stax, whose naive owners literally gave away the store. With the rise of the underground rock scene, Atlantic had pursued a similar strategy. Ertegun forged distribution agreements with British rock start-ups like Island, Virgin, and RSO records, and Wexler agreed to have Atlantic bankroll Phil Walden's Capricorn Records.

Ertegun was at the height of his influence with the new Kinney management, and financing for Geffen's label was a lock. "It came up at a board meeting, and I didn't even know it was on the agenda," says Ted Ashley. Support for giving Geffen his own label proved strong. "I said, 'Look, I'd like to offer a short dissertation on this guy.' As did one or two other people who knew of him. David had many advocates."

Perhaps Ertegun had simply grown tired of Geffen's constant attentions—he wasn't averse to belittling his protégé in public—and might have been giving Geffen enough rope to hang himself. But unlike the deal for Crosby, Stills and Nash, the new label, which Geffen dubbed Asylum, was real proof of Geffen's power and reputation. Regardless of the competition and tension between him and Ertegun, it was Geffen, not Browne, the Warners board was betting on. The only person at the company who believed in Jackson Browne was David Geffen.

Browne, who had already experienced more than his share of false starts, was appropriately grateful. "Some people would never get on record at all if it weren't for the more ambitious people with an eye on careers and managing people's lives," Browne told journalist Cameron Crowe. "David Geffen helped me get into the studio and helped me get a perspective on it. He also, of course, is somebody who's involved with careers and albums as vehicles to fame. Fame being the result, not the by-product."

Browne's assessment of Geffen, while a good deal more flattering than Rothchild's conclusion that "the sharks have entered the lagoon," was essentially the same. The ascendancy of Geffen, who was frankly interested in the traditional show business prizes of money and stardom, was an indication that the record business had caught up with and surpassed the music. Warner Bros. Records had embraced the emerging rock scene because it had few options—and been the beneficiary of incredibly fortunate timing. Geffen, with his appreciation for the commercial potential of "significant artists," was smart enough to make his own luck. Asylum Records would capitalize on an emerging group of singer/songwriters and, unlike previous projects like the Paxton Ranch, provide the structure to transform them from amateurs into professionals.

If anything at all proved lucky in Geffen's decision to start Asylum, it was having Jackson Browne as his first artist. Browne was about to open Geffen's eyes and ears to a big, lucrative new world. "David grabbed this L.A. sound," says Irving Azoff, a former Geffen-Roberts employee. "He's not an A and R guy, but he's got a gut way of figuring it out and he's a brilliant businessman. He didn't go out in the clubs and find it—he signed one guy, Jackson Browne. And Jackson Browne just led everyone else into his office. One right after the other."

8

Brothers and Sisters,
I Give You
a Testimonial:
The MC5

J ON LANDAU DID NOT ASPIRE TO DREAMS OF HOLLYWOOD GLORY, YET, like David Geffen, he had an outsized desire to succeed and recognized that rock could provide his professional path. The similarities between them were instructive of how the business and the music were moving toward each other. Geffen, who had come to the business without any interest in rock music, had seized upon it as his best opening. Landau, who loved the music with a passion but wasn't cut out to be a musician, had found a home in the increasingly successful rock press. From his new perch, Landau, like Geffen, had instantly appreciated the business opportunities, spying a role for anyone smart enough to negotiate the ever-shrinking gulf between the industry and the art. In the coming years, the gap between their starting points would shrink until virtually meaningless and the two would recognize in each other a kindred soul.

But at the moment, they were still worlds apart. Geffen was the nascent industry's acknowledged up-and-comer, while Landau was about to get his first real shot at the business. On the spring day in 1969 that his Brandeis classmates were gathering for commencement exercises, Jon Landau was bound for Ann Arbor, Michigan, to pro-

duce an album by the group the MC5 for his friend and mentor Jerry
Wexler of Atlantic Records. A group of kids from Detroit, the MC5
had become the focus of the local underground scene through an alliance with John Sinclair, the poet, marijuana activist, and founder of
the youth-oriented White Panther Party, who was their manager. In
many ways, Michigan's underground rock scene paralleled what was
going on in Landau's hometown. But around Detroit, the MC5 were
more than a rock band—they were the standard-bearers for the White
Panthers and the coming revolution.

It was a revolution that Jon Landau had no interest in, but he had
argued successfully to Wexler that the MC5 could be a commercial
success. While many of the band's fans were drawn by the promise of
adventure implicit in the White Panther Party's seductively subversive
credo—"rock and roll, dope and fucking in the streets"—Landau was
drawn by the raw energy and excitement of the band's live performances as well as their commercial potential. That was what *he* wanted
to transfer onto record. As far as he could see, the band's political bent
was hopelessly naive and served only to distract them from the business of making music. Indeed, the space for overtly political, radical
performers was shrinking as the business grew. Unlike the MC5, Landau embraced the fact that making music was a business. Although
each of the emerging commercial rock enterprises with which it was
affiliated—be it Warner Bros. Records, the Boston Tea Party, or
Rolling Stone—owed much of their success and impetus to what had
begun as an underground culture, they were proving vastly different
from the small specialty labels, coffeehouses, or literate magazines
that were part and parcel of the earlier and smaller folk movement.
The new rock music had a mass appeal that folk never had, and the
companies it spawned rapidly came to reflect that wide audience. The
MC5's roots were fed by the same underground spring, but their politics didn't fit the developing landscape of the new rock business.

Their first label, Elektra Records, hadn't shied away from icono-
clasts or activist performers like Phil Ochs when it was a small folk
company. Now, however, it was riding rock into the commercial mainstream, and the MC5 fell outside those parameters. The band's militancy had hurt them with not only their label, but the increasingly
powerful national network of concert promoters that Frank Barsalona
at his Premier Talent Agency had put in place. In Boston, Landau's

friend Don Law had banned them from the Boston Tea Party; in New York, the MC5 had run afoul of promoter Bill Graham, which meant the band couldn't play the most important rock venues in either New York or San Francisco. As much as getting their music down on tape, Jon Landau's job was to make the band commercially acceptable.

"Jerry truly believed in Jon Landau," says publicist Danny Fields, who had also urged Wexler to sign the band. "Jon convinced Jerry that the band got a raw deal at Elektra, that they were musically to be heard and potentially a hit-making and successful group. And that we would obliterate all this political baggage which came with them." Jon Landau had his work cut out for him.

●

WAYNE KRAMER DIDN'T GO TO COLLEGE. HE'D GROWN UP "DOWNRIVER" IN Lincoln Park, Michigan. It could have been Wyandotte or River Rouge or Allen Park or Melvindale. Each was downriver from Rouge, the Ford Motor Company's main plant.

In 1958, when Kramer was ten years old, the Motor City's economy was firing on all eight cylinders: Ford had a 31 percent share of the American car market, and Rouge was one of the largest industrial complexes in the world, boasting its own steelworks and 32,000 auto-workers. The downriver towns were all blue-collar, home to a massive concentration of mechanics, line workers, and other skilled laborers. Still, in the vast, carefully graduated socioeconomic strata of suburban Detroit they ranked close to the bottom. No foremen or engineer who could afford to live a rung up the suburban ladder in a tonier town like Taylor would ever be caught downriver.

Kramer's father and mother split up when he was a kid, and his mother began seeing a man who played guitar. The music he made with his buddies was the most important development in Kramer's life. "Every few months his pals would come over and they would have electric guitars and violins and they would set up in the living room," he remembers. "Some of my most exciting memories of that period are waking up late in the evening and hearing a band playing in the living room. Rushing out—'Mom, can I stay up? Can I stay up?' Just awestruck at the sounds of these instruments. They'd play a set and then go into the kitchen and drink whiskey and I'd jump on some-body's electric guitar. It was just fabulous."

A drag-racing fanatic, Kramer had a weekend job out at the track selling ice cream just so he could watch the drags. Still, he had to admit that no matter how much ice cream he sold, he was never going to realize his dream of owning a hot rod. But an electric guitar—that was something else.

There were literally hundreds of bands around Detroit. "The auto plants were rollin', so parents had money to buy kids electric guitars," says Kramer. Among his friends in Lincoln Park, the vogue was for guitar instrumentals played by bands like the Ventures, Johnny and the Hurricanes, and the Frogmen. Then Kramer discovered Chuck Berry and Bo Diddley.

"I realized there was a difference between most of the white stuff and what the black musicians were doing," he recalls. "There were certain sounds that had more *drive* to them."

His mother watched with mixed emotions as her son began to dig deeper and deeper into music. She sat him down one day for a heart-to-heart talk. "My mother said, 'Wayne, you can do whatever you want with your life, I want you to pursue your own interests. But I have to warn you about this life of a musician. It is not an easy life. It's a rough life. You have to work at night and sleep in the day. There's always alcohol and drugs around. And Wayne, there's a lot of loose women.' I wasn't too sure before, but I was sold then."

By 1963, Kramer had his first band, a junior high school outfit named the Bounty Hunters in honor of Connie Kalitta's renowned dragster. He soon became friendly with Fred Smith, the bongo player in a rival band called the Vibratones, and began spending afternoons at Smith's house showing him guitar parts. They decided to take the best musicians from each group and form a new band.

The group, which kept the name Bounty Hunters, was having a rough time staying together—the drummer was charging other members for using his amplifier. Still, they were able to play teen dances. Hanging around the scene, Kramer met Bob Derminer, Lincoln Park's resident teenage beatnik. "He was two years older," says Kramer, "which was a big difference back then. He could *drive*. And he was into jazz." He was so into jazz that he now called himself Robin Tyner, in tribute to McCoy Tyner, the pianist in John Coltrane's quartet. And he wasn't interested in rock and roll. He was an intellectual.

Kramer was subsequently surprised late one Friday night when he ran across Tyner sitting in a White Castle parking lot. "It was about two in the morning," recalls Kramer. "He was drunk as a skunk, had let his hair grow out, and was playing the harmonica. I said, 'Yo— what's with that? I thought you didn't like all that rock and roll stuff.' He said, 'No, man. Have you heard about this band the Rolling Stones? They just changed the whole thing for me.' " Kramer asked Tyner if he wanted to be involved with the Bounty Hunters.

While Kramer and Smith each thought of it as *his* band, it was clear that Tyner, with his interest in jazz and a rebellious intellect, wanted to take things in a more unconventional direction. And he sure wasn't going to be in any band named for a drag racer. He became lead vocalist and suggested they change their name to the MC5, short for the Motor City Five. That would be kind of cool, more like a serial number than a name. Starting in 1964, they played private parties or school dances and after a while latched on to Detroit's teen-center circuit.

"Every little community in downriver—and, later we discovered, all over Detroit—had a teen center," says Kramer. "Like a gymnasium that they used somewhere on Friday night for dances. And these were our gigs. Usually there'd be a couple of other bands and you got to hear who was doing what. I used to come home from school and get the phone book out and call every municipality, trying to book my band. And you could get paid—fifty, sixty dollars for the band! It was exciting. And there were girls! The potential was unlimited."

Despite the local dominance of Berry Gordy's Motown label, with its remarkable superstar roster that included the Supremes, the Temptations, and the Four Tops, the MC5 had their ears elsewhere. Part of the formula was a rambunctious need to play louder than anyone else. But even more than that, Smith and Kramer heard something powerful and foreboding in the most basic rock and rhythm and blues.

"The Motown stuff was a little tame for me," says Kramer. "Chuck Berry, he was more dangerous. We had a great rhythm section, and we started working on this concept of drive—the music had this forward power. I think it came from that kind of adrenaline you have when you're sixteen or seventeen, when your hormones are pumping so fast that you're almost insane. There was this *sound* that gave us what we needed. We weren't getting it from Bobby Vinton and the music on the radio. We weren't getting it from what parents and teachers were telling us. But we were getting what we needed from this certain kind of music that we started to call high-energy music."

And then there was James Brown. When the 1965 concert documentary *The T.A.M.I. Show* came to a theater in Detroit, Kramer was there seven nights in a row. The film featured Chuck Berry, the Beach Boys, Jan and Dean, the Supremes, Smokey Robinson and the Miracles, Marvin Gaye, and the Rolling Stones, but it was the blistering performance of James Brown that mesmerized Kramer. Brown stalked the stage like a man beyond reason and control. Indeed, his act was built around the notion that Brown *couldn't* stop singing. As his band, the JBs, vamped on "Please, Please, Please," Brown would be draped in a king's robes and led from the stage by his backup singers, the Famous Flames, only to wrest himself from their grasp, fling the robe from his shoulders, and come running back onstage time after time, each reprise more dramatic and desperate than the one before. By the end, Brown would be on his knees, sweating, trembling, pounding the stage, screaming for release from the unspeakable tortures of his soul. Wayne Kramer sat in the dark Detroit movie theater and knew he had seen God.

"Our show was based on the dynamic of James's show. It was going to start at ten-and-a-half and go up from there," says Kramer. "On a bad night we were going to be great—and on a good night we were going to be unbelievable." The Five didn't play for their audiences, they incited and assaulted them. And along with James Brown's pyrotechnics, there was Tyner's interest in avant-garde jazz, which was leading the MC5 to experiment with free-form music, creating musical interludes without meter or key.

Kramer finished high school in 1966 and moved out of his mother's house in Lincoln Park that fall—the day after she told him he'd have to get a job and help pay the bills if he wanted to stay—and moved in with a woman in the downtown Detroit neighborhood of Warren Forest. His band mates were already living in the same area, adjacent to the Wayne State campus of the University of Michigan in what was then known as the beatnik neighborhood. The scene's cultural home was the Artists Workshop, a bohemian performance and rehearsal space. Its founder, John Sinclair, and his wife, Leni, lived in the apartment upstairs.

A poet and jazz critic, Sinclair grew up in Flint, where his mother was an English teacher and his father worked the line for Buick. He wrote his master's thesis at Wayne State on William Burroughs, but his interest in the Beats and their rejection of a mainstream lifestyle was more than academic. As a kid he hung around black barbershops and pool halls, and he developed a passion for avant-garde jazz. Though white, he felt an affinity with the emerging black nationalist philosophies of Malcolm X and Elijah Muhammad. Sinclair was a true "hippie" in the word's original meaning.* "I spent two or three years being part of a black community up in Flint because that was the only place where there were people like me," Sinclair says. "Like the person I wanted to be. There weren't any white people like that."

The Workshop's membership was modest—there were about twenty artists and primary supporters and perhaps an additional one hundred people who came to the Workshop's readings and concerts. But Sinclair wasn't looking for converts. "We didn't really *want* an audience. We were looking for a place for ourselves and people like us. Even when we'd do flyers, we'd only give 'em to certain people. Couldn't give 'em to the squares—we didn't want them to come."

Sinclair was an equally adamant proselytizer for marijuana, which he referred to as "the sacrament." Along with actively lobbying to have it legalized, Sinclair was well known around Wayne State as the person to see if you wanted a couple of joints. Before he had set up the Workshop, he had been arrested once for possession and had received a $400 fine and two years probation.

By the summer of 1965, the Workshop and its shows were drawing successively bigger crowds, and they soon began to attract police attention. In August 1965, Sinclair gladly obliged a visitor who said he was looking to get his hands on some marijuana. The visitor, an undercover narcotics officer, promptly arrested Sinclair, and in February of '66 he began serving a six-month stretch in the Detroit House of Correction.

Just before Sinclair's incarceration, Rob Tyner had discovered the Workshop and come down with a classic case of teenage hero worship. "I'd gone there a couple of times and got literally blown back," Tyner recalled. "The very foundation of everything I understood was

---

*"Hippie" was an African-American slang expression in the forties for a white person who wanted to be part of the black scene because it was "hip."

shaken by the intensity of John Sinclair himself in the flesh and the people he associated with."

The Workshop was also a good fit for the MC5. "We'd played a couple of jobs for beatniks before, and we loved to play for them," says Kramer. "Unlike the suburban kids, they didn't care what you played. You could play anything you wanted as long as it had a good beat and they could dance their asses off."

Sinclair began to take on the aura of a political prisoner and leader in exile. When he was released in August, the Workshop threw an all-day music and poetry fest to mark his homecoming.

One thing Sinclair had not been expecting at his party was a teenage rock band from downriver. But the Five were looking to hook into the Workshop: they needed a place to rehearse. And they believed Sinclair could help the band. Says Kramer, "We had a serious streak of felonious thinking. We considered ourselves the young hustlers, young scam artists. Our thinking was 'Look, this hippie thing is going to be big. It's going to be *big*. If we get all the hippies to like us, we'll get over.' So how do we get all the hippies to like us? We get the king of the hippies to be our manager. That's John. It's really crass and manipulative and small-minded, but that was the way we looked at it."

Sinclair, however, wasn't interested in hearing the MC5, let alone managing them. And he was unaware of the first flowerings of hippie culture, which had coincided with his six-month jail term. "It seemed like when I got out everything was different," says Sinclair. "Back then six months could seem like ten years. These kids started coming around from the suburbs. You had the civil rights movement, the war, the little tendrils of protest that got bigger and bigger. So many things were happening, and there was so much activity. Those kids wanted to get out of the suburbs—it was negative propulsion."

The first meeting of Sinclair and the MC5 did not augur good things: Sinclair, high on freedom (at the very least) and surrounded by his friends and family, ignored the band and their request to play. By the time the MC5 finally got to plug in, he and Leni had gone upstairs to bed. "We had waited all day to play for him, and then at two in the morning they finish with all the fucking poetry," recalls Kramer. "We had these huge amps, Vox Super Beatle one-hundred-watt tube amps, and we *cranked* the shit up." Halfway into the band's third song, Leni came downstairs and pulled the plug. It wasn't until

Sinclair was reintroduced to Tyner months later that the relationship really clicked.

The Sinclairs had moved to an apartment across the hall from the office of Detroit's underground paper, *The Fifth Estate,* the brainchild of Harvey Oshinsky, who had discovered underground newspapers via the *Los Angeles Free Press.* Sinclair was already writing a local jazz dispatch for *Down Beat,* and he expanded it for *The Fifth Estate,* including local psychedelia and poetry and renaming it "The Coat-Puller." Also working on the paper was a friend of Tyner's, artist Gary Grimshaw. The Sinclairs struck up a friendship with him, Tyner, and Frank Bach, another musician who was writing a rock and roll column for the paper.

Sinclair decided he had underestimated both rock and roll and the MC5. "You could see that something big was happening," he says. "Rock and roll was growing and it was going to include jazz and it was going to include blues and all the interesting things from the past." He was also impressed by the group's ambition. "They were really exciting. It wasn't very well shaped, but bursting with energy and the idea of taking it somewhere else. They called themselves 'avant-rock,' which was intriguing to me as an avant-gardist. Their self-concept was well beyond being a pop group, although they wanted to be a pop group, too. Tyner was an intellectual, a rock and roll intellectual. The other guys figured they were freeing their minds and their asses would follow. But they aspired to make music of import. Like John Coltrane."

Tyner and Sinclair became fast friends, and the MC5 moved their equipment into the Artists Workshop. Within a few months they landed what would prove to be the best gig in Detroit, when Russ Gibb wandered into one of their rehearsals.

A high school teacher–cum–biker, Gibb visited San Francisco in the summer of '66 and attended a dance at the Avalon Ballroom. Inspired as Ray Riepen had been in Boston, Gibb came home to Detroit in 1967 and rented the Grande (pronounced "Grand-ee") Ballroom, an old, Moorish-style hall on Detroit's west side, and developed it into a San Francisco–style rock venue. It quickly became a stop on the developing underground circuit being nurtured by Premier.

Gibb wanted to hire a house band, and when he asked Jerry Goodwin, a Detroit disc jockey, if he knew of any good bands who played their own music, Goodwin sent Gibb down to the Artists Workshop. For $125 a week, the MC5 became the house band at the Grande.

Although they had all the swagger and ego any rock band would ever need, the MC5 stumbled onto original music almost by accident. When they were slated to appear on a local show headlined by the Rolling Stones, the Five faced an unusual dilemma: their repertoire included a lot of Stones songs, and they obviously couldn't play them if the Stones were also on the bill. "We had to dump 'em and learn new material," says Kramer.

Lack of management was a big problem. The band could see that they needed someone with experience and a plan to take them to the next stage. But unlike the members of Buffalo Springfield, whose frank pursuit of stardom had made them eager to put their careers in the hands of well-connected music industry hustlers like Charlie Greene and Brian Stone, the MC5 held an earnest belief that they were "righteous" artists who should have nothing to do with showbiz. And unlike Dylan, who'd found a worthy coconspirator in Albert Grossman to help him reap the rewards of success without seeming to be in its thrall, the MC5 were simply too unruly and raw to be that calculating.

Sinclair was the obvious choice. Aside from his status as the city's number one poet/outlaw, he was their friend. The band was well within the Artists Workshop sphere and its blossoming drug culture, which was growing increasingly political as its disillusionment grew.

"There was starting to be a clearer division between the straight world and the hip world," says Kramer. "Friends from high school were going to Vietnam and coming back in body bags. And then there was the drug thing. We're all smoking reefer—and we can see this thing is not addictive, we're not knocking off Seven-Elevens in order to keep smoking joints. So they lied to us about that. They lied to us about the war. They're lying to us about everything else."

The real sea change, however, was the introduction of hallucinogens like peyote and LSD. Sinclair had no trouble expanding his definition of "the sacrament." Under their influence the concept of the Artists Workshop, and subsequently the MC5, began to change into something a bit more radical, vaguely political, and decidedly communal. Sinclair, who had originally looked down his nose at rock and roll, now began to see the music, in concert with LSD, functioning as the twin pillars of a soon-to-emerge messianic age. "LSD," he wrote, "was the catalyst which transformed rock and roll from a music of simple rebellion to a *revolutionary* [italics Sinclair's] music with a program for living in the New Age of post-industrial, post-scarcity abundance which will come to flower with the final collapse of western civilization."

Sinclair was also taking notice of what was going on in other cities—particularly San Francisco—and giving it his own spin. After meeting Grateful Dead manager Rock Scully backstage at the Grande, Sinclair found himself wondering why he couldn't carve a role for himself in the burgeoning business of the underground. "I saw that he was a cat like me and manager of a band with a record on Warner Brothers and a national tour," says Sinclair. "That was my epiphany—how a weirdo like me could function in a business aspect."

He was also thinking on a grander scale. The Workshop, in keeping with the changing times, evolved and became Trans-Love Express, an artists' commune. And although Trans-Love also included the people who supplied the light show and operated a head shop at the Grande as well as a handful of artisans and other musicians, its economic and artistic center was the MC5.

Trans-Love was the archetypical, drug-fueled rock and roll commune. Says Sinclair: "You went out and got as much money as you could and paid as many bills as you could, bought as much food as you could, and tried to keep things going until you took over the world. We were assured of ultimate success by massive doses of LSD."

If Sinclair's business plan was suspect, his talents as a rock and roll propagandist (a term he favored over "publicist") were first-rate. The growing success of the Grande was certainly helping to establish the MC5, but Sinclair was doing a good deal to stoke their growing reputation as Detroit's revolutionary/outlaw rock band. It was simple. Sinclair was both a columnist for the city's underground paper, and—because of his public advocacy of drug use—a police target. There was always plenty of trouble to go around, and Sinclair began to use his column to chronicle the "revolutionary guerrilla tactics" of the MC5. It wasn't long before Sinclair had transformed a series of relatively minor scrapes with the law into an ongoing war with the pigs, played out every other week in the pages of *The Fifth Estate*.

Sinclair's dispatches—and the Five's legend—really began to solidify with a May 31, 1968, gig at the Grosse Point Hideout. The club, one of a chain of Hideouts owned by rock manager Punch Andrews, drew a capacity crowd of four hundred kids that night, perhaps helped by a

Gary Grimshaw–produced handbill that showed the band, naked in front of a backward American flag, along with the legend "Break through American stasis with the MC5."

During an opening set, Sinclair and drummer Dennis Thompson had stepped outside to smoke a joint with a group of local kids when the club's security guards saw them and called the police. About to be arrested, Sinclair and Thompson got word to the band. Ron Levine, the group's roadie, took the microphone in front of the packed club and urged the crowd to surround the police outside if they wanted the show to go on. And although the police dragged Levine offstage and quickly closed the club's doors to prevent a confrontation in the parking lot, the manager was sufficiently shaken to have the police release Sinclair and Thompson. It was a triumphant MC5—and an equally jubilant audience—that rocked the Hideout that evening. When the exasperated club manager later shut off the electricity in a bid to end the frenzied show, the audience—led by guitarist Fred Smith—chanted "Power! Power! Power!" until the electricity was turned back on and the band allowed to finish.

The following weekend at the Grande, the Five wanted to celebrate their victory over the police state by burning an American flag during an opening set for the English blues-rock trio Cream. Gibb, however, warned the band that he would have them arrested. Instead, the show climaxed with Tyner ripping a plastic flag to shreds and then hoisting a 4 × 5-foot red banner inscribed with a marijuana leaf and the word FREEK. To put just the right finish on the spectacle, a member of the lighting crew walked onstage—naked—and settled cross-legged at the lip of the stage, where he chanted "Om" as the final chord of the band's ear-shattering performance faded into an electric hum.

The show put the Five in the doghouse with Gibb, but he continued to defend them from the Grande's landlord, who had wanted to have them barred from the hall for some time. At issue was the band's signature song, "Kick Out the Jams," with its opening rally cry, "Kick out the jams, motherfucker!"

The song actually had its roots in the band's gang-war attitude toward other groups. The Grande was *their* hall in *their* town, and any band getting onstage with them had better be ready to rumble. "Every week there'd be some new band coming into Detroit to play at the Grande," says Kramer. "And we would tear them new assholes. Ultimate

Spinach and the Beacon Street Union came in from Boston; in a way, I felt bad for 'em—they were nice, didn't play too loud, professional. And they got creamed. We used to yell at the other bands: 'Kick out the jams, motherfucker! Or get off the stage!' "

If the band's adventures seemed contrived or childish, there were also real confrontations involving real issues. In July of '68, Sinclair and Smith were beaten and arrested by police following a show the Five played at the Loft, a barn-turned-club in Leonard, Michigan. As Sinclair later reported the events, the band was owed money by the club's owner for previous shows and had agreed to appear as part of a deal to settle accounts. But the band—which was to be paid up front—still didn't get what it was owed and played an abbreviated set during which they urged the audience not to patronize a club that cheated musicians. The club's security officer called the county sheriff's department and said the band was inciting the crowd. Police in full riot gear responded and, when Sinclair refused to leave without the band's money, he was clubbed and maced. Smith, hearing Sinclair yelling, ran over and jumped on the police. The two spent the night in the county jail before being arraigned on charges of assaulting a police officer. Each had to post $2,500 bond.*

The steady gig at the Grande, along with their other adventures, strengthened the bond between the band members. "They were in the center of the hippest thing going on," says Sinclair. "It was right around June that the show just congealed. It took time and development, personal development, group development, and scene development." Their "high-energy" approach made them the most exciting live act on the local rock scene. And it earned them the highest accolade that Detroit kids had to offer: the MC5 were "killer."

Into that scene came two jive-talking hustlers with whom the MC5 and Sinclair formed a deep and immediate bond: J. C. Crawford and Panther White. Crawford and White were the high priests and sole parishioners of the Church of Zenta, whose only purpose appeared to be raising money for Crawford and White to live on. Crawford, as it turned out, was a drummer and an avid James Brown fan. Like the

*Charges against Smith were later dropped. Sinclair served a short term in the Oakland County Jail on assault charges. He was far more upset that sheriff's deputies held him down and forcibly gave him a haircut than he was by the time served.

Five, he had committed every note of Brown's *Live at the Apollo* to memory. And, of course, he could recite the album's famous "Star Time" introduction, in which Brown was touted as the eighth wonder of the world and the titles of his hit records rattled off like a king's list of conquered nations. Devising strategy with the help of "killer" tokes of marijuana, the group agreed that what the MC5 really needed was a master of ceremonies to open their shows—the MCs' MC. Crawford, of course, was the man. Within weeks, the leather-jacketed Crawford was opening the MC5's shows with a rabble-rousing setup, delivered in the persona of a fire-and-brimstone Southern preacher.

"Brothers and sisters," Crawford would shout. "I wanna see a sea of hands out there, let me see a sea of hands! I want everybody to kick up some noise, I wanna hear some revolution out there, brothers, I wanna hear a little revolution! Brothers and sisters, the time has come for each and every one of you to decide whether you are going to be the problem or whether you are going to be the solution! You must choose, brothers, you must choose. It takes five seconds—five seconds of decision, five seconds to realize your purpose here on the planet. It takes five seconds to realize that it's time to move, it's time to get down with it. Brothers, it's time to testify! And I want to know—are you ready to testify? Are you READY? I give you a testimonial: The MC5!"

That summer, Trans-Love sent the MC5, the Up, and a new band, the Psychedelic Stooges, to play at the protests planned for the Democratic Convention in Chicago. Norman Mailer gave the band its first positive notice in the straight press in his coverage of the convention for *Harper's*. But more important was the fact that Sinclair's *Fifth Estate* columns were being reprinted in other underground newspapers around the country. The Detroit newspaper was one of five original members of the Underground News Service (UNS), an organized, though ultimately unsuccessful, attempt to put together an alternative national news wire. The most influential and widely read paper served by the web was New York's *East Village Other* (or *EVO*), and Sinclair was delighted to discover that it was reprinting some of the MC5's exploits.

"Now *EVO* was *the* flagship of weirdness," says Sinclair. "This was a *huge* triumph—to be in *EVO* week after week—for me this is like the front page of *The New York Times*."

The band had scraped together $500 and cut a single on the local

A Square label. Sinclair, on a trip east to hustle up work for the band, took the record to *EVO* columnists Bob Rudnick and Dennis Frawley, who also hosted a weekly radio show, "Kokaine Kharma," on WFMU, Upsala College's station and one of the first underground college stations in the country. There, Sinclair met Danny Fields, who hosted a show at the station and also happened to be the "house hippie" for Elektra Records.

FIELDS'S ROLE AT ELEKTRA, LIKE ANDY WICKHAM'S AT WARNER BROS., WAS to bridge the gap between the labels and the new underground. A dropout of both Harvard Law School and New York University's graduate school, Fields had wound up editing a couple of short-lived teenybopper magazines, *Datebook* and *Hullabaloo,* in 1966. But Fields's tastes were far too hip for his readership. Instead of running pieces on pinup pop acts like Herman's Hermits, he filled the magazines with stories on Bob Dylan and the Velvet Underground and published the first American magazine interviews with Pete Townshend and Roger McGuinn. He was fired from *Datebook* after publishing an issue with a cover quote from John Lennon: "I don't know which will go first, rock and roll or Christianity."

Fields was trying his hand as an independent publicist when a friend in Los Angeles asked him to look after a new band that was coming to New York to play Ondine's. The performance by the group, the Doors, impressed Fields so much that he urged Elektra's president, Jac Holzman, to release the song "Light My Fire" as a single. The idea was ridiculous. The track was six minutes long, and no Top 40 radio station would play it. But eight months later, after disc jockeys convinced Elektra to release a shorter version, "Light My Fire" became a million-selling, number one single, the biggest hit in the label's history. The Doors' success transformed Elektra into a commercial rock label.

Holzman, seeing the future, offered Fields a job as director of publicity and artist relations. His real role, however, was to tell Holzman and the label what was going on in the underground. In that capacity, he would wield a lot of influence. Elektra had grown dramatically in the four years since Paul Rothchild joined the company, but it still had only twenty employees. If Fields had an idea for a record or heard an artist he thought the label should sign, he simply walked into Holzman's office and told him.

Fields liked the MC5 record and was so intrigued by Sinclair's war stories that he went to Detroit to see the band for himself. After catching them on a Saturday night and then seeing the Psychedelic Stooges at the Five's urging on Sunday, Fields—who was supposed to be at the Elektra office—called Holzman Monday morning from Ann Arbor. He didn't hesitate to lay it on thick.

"Jac," Fields said, "you may be upset that I'm not back in New York, but I just found you the two most incredible new bands in the United States. You've got to sign them both."

"Well," said Holzman, apparently unfazed, "what do they want?"

Fields put his hand over the mouthpiece just long enough to confer with Sinclair.

"Twenty thousand bucks."

"Okay," said Holzman. "Twenty thousand for the big one and five thousand for the little one. Shake hands on the deal, and come back to New York."

Wayne Kramer was twenty and all his dreams were coming true: "It was probably the happiest I'd ever been in my life. All my work was happening—it was better than I'd planned it. I couldn't have figured that it was gonna come out *that* good."

The MC5's deal with Elektra also provided Sinclair and the band with a national forum for their views, which, aside from the legalization of marijuana and LSD, now included calls for the end of the draft, the end of private ownership, the freeing of all prison inmates, and the end of money.

Within two months of signing with Elektra, Sinclair announced the formation of the White Panther Party, whose ten-point "program"—announced in *The Fifth Estate*—included all of the above points as well as full endorsement of the Black Panther Party platform. The White Panthers may have started as a stoned-out, dining room table riff (its manifesto listed each member of the MC5 as a "Minister of War" except for Tyner, who was "Minister of Culture"), but its officers—who also included Sinclair, White, Crawford, and a couple of other Trans-Love cronies—were obviously starting to take themselves seriously.

In Sinclair's columns, rock and roll—and specifically the rock and roll of the MC5—was now a tool for overthrowing "the white honkie culture that has been handed to us on a silver plastic platter and is meaningless to us. We *breathe* revolution," wrote Sinclair. "We are LSD-driven maniacs in the universe. We will do anything we can to drive people out of their heads and into their bodies. Rock and roll music is the spearhead of our attack because it's so effective and so much fun. We have developed organic high-energy guerrilla rock and roll bands who are infiltrating the popular culture and destroying millions of minds in the process. With our music and our economic genius we plunder the unsuspecting straight world for money and the means to carry out our program, and revolutionize its children at the same time."

Of course, Sinclair's revolutionary act of "plundering" was simply the radically correct way of excusing the MC5 for having accepted a big payday from the system they were railing against. This was the rub, and it would prove to be a continuing problem for the band. Couldn't they be revolutionaries *and* rock stars, too?

DANNY FIELDS HAD A SIMPLE PLAN FOR HELPING THE MC5 ACHIEVE STARdom. He called Richard Goldstein, the pop critic for *The Village Voice,* and Jon Landau, the chief music critic at *Rolling Stone,* and told them that Elektra had just signed "the best goddamn band in the world." In his view, gaining Landau's support was critical. "I'd say he [was] the single most influential person in America on the rock scene. I knew they were what he'd always been looking for: the definitive hardrock band."

Fields quickly flew Landau out to Detroit to see the band. Landau, who had never heard of the White Panthers or Sinclair, found them intimidating. "I never met anybody like Sinclair," he recalled. "When you shake hands with John Sinclair, you're shaking hands with somebody. He just had a presence." Visiting the White Panther headquarters on Hill Street in Ann Arbor was even more uncomfortable. "These people were just too far out," he said.

Still, when they went to hear the band that night, Landau didn't disappoint Fields. He had reservations about the group's musical abilities, but he was bowled over by their energy, which reminded him of his old Boston favorites, Barry and the Remains. Sitting in the hotel later that night with Fields, Landau began to critique the show, pointing out the band's strengths and weaknesses. "Stop right there, man," Fields said. "Write it all down and I'll pay you. Elektra will pay you. Write us a memo of your assessment of the band."

Landau was ecstatic at the prospect of being paid by a record company to tell it how to record one of its groups. He had already written a similar memo on singer/songwriter Tim Buckley for Elektra and had sent letters to Holzman seeking a job as a producer in 1967, right around the time he began writing for *Rolling Stone*.

Whatever conflicts existed between his roles as a critic and a consultant, Landau chose to ignore them. According to Fields, Landau was instrumental in getting Goldstein to write positive pieces about the band for both *The Village Voice* and *The New York Times*. At *Rolling Stone*, Landau's enthusiasm for the group resulted in a long, fawning article on the MC5 being promoted to a cover story, an incredible coup for Fields and the band considering that the group didn't even have an album out.

If Landau ever told anyone at *Rolling Stone* that Elektra was paying him as a consultant, it probably wouldn't have even mattered. Such standard journalistic distinctions seemed lost at the magazine, despite its growing influence. Publisher and editor in chief Jann Wenner had encouraged Atlantic Records to sign singer Boz Scaggs and was going to produce his label debut. The MC5 presented Landau with a good opportunity to network and get a foot into record production.

The band's album *Kick Out the Jams* was recorded live, an unorthodox move. Generally, bands would record three or four albums, building a repertoire and hoping to generate hits, before cutting a concert collection. But Elektra wanted to capture and capitalize on the band's explosive performances. To stoke the interest in the album, released in March of 1969, Elektra organized a short East Coast tour in December of '68. The idea was to establish the MC5 in three of the most important markets: Boston, Cleveland, and New York. It quickly became clear that the MC5 and Elektra Records had wildly divergent views on what was to be accomplished.

On December 15, the MC5 kicked off their tour at the Boston Tea Party. In the spirit of solidarity with other revolutionary enclaves, Sinclair and the band agreed to turn some of their time, and the microphone, over to a member of a New York anarchist cell known as the

Motherfuckers. Like Sinclair, the founders of the group had been poets. But the group had degenerated into violence, and by the late sixties the Motherfuckers had a very tough reputation, acting as Bobby Seale's bodyguards whenever the Black Panther leader came to New York. Ben Morea, one of the group's leaders, was facing assault charges in Boston for stabbing a serviceman, and the Motherfuckers said they wanted to use the MC5's show to publicize his case.

Once they got the spotlight, however, they told the crowd they were being ripped off by the Tea Party and launched into the then common cry that music should be "free." Don Law was less than amused. He banned the MC5 from the club. But perhaps even worse than being barred from the city's most important rock venue was the fact that Law was one of a tightly knit group of key rock promoters that, for all intents and purposes, had control of the national rock and roll touring circuit. The word was sure to go out on the MC5.

When the band got to their next gig, at New York's Fillmore East, the Motherfuckers were waiting for them. This time, the issue was free tickets. Bill Graham, the Fillmore's owner, in discussion with the Motherfuckers and other neighborhood groups, had previously agreed to turn the Fillmore over to the community on Wednesday nights for free events, and the MC5 made their New York debut without incident at one of these shows. But Graham was unhappy with the Wednesday-night arrangement. He said people—most notably the Motherfuckers—were abusing him and the theater by openly smoking dope and creating problems with the police.

On December 26, Elektra rented the Fillmore and sponsored a second free show by the MC5. Still angry at the Motherfuckers, Graham held back several hundred tickets that Elektra and the MC5 had intended to distribute. When the Motherfuckers began to collect outside the theater, Graham—who had a fiery temper and was not averse to using goon tactics himself—stood in the Fillmore doorway and refused to let them in. In the ensuing brawl between the crowd and Graham and his bouncers, Graham received a broken nose when he was hit in the face with a chain.*

Despite the Boston debacle and the further troubles in New York,

*Graham would later claim that it was Robin Tyner who hit him with the chain, although Tyner was almost certainly backstage at the time.

Sinclair and the Five sided with the Motherfuckers. "We heard about the fight as we were waiting to go on," says Sinclair. "I told them we weren't gonna go on unless they let them in. Brilliant move. The Elektra people were so mad at me, and reasonably enough. But I was saying 'We can't have this. It's a free concert, these people want to come in, let them in.' And finally they let them in. That was the last thing we ever had to do with Graham. We burned him down."

Getting on the wrong side of Graham was worse than crossing Don Law. As the top rock promoter in both New York and San Francisco, he effectively blackballed the band from both cities. When the band later toured the Bay Area, they were barred even from playing a San Francisco State University strike benefit held at the Fillmore.

By June their album had reached number thirty on the *Billboard* chart. But the obscenity issue that had plagued the band back in Michigan again reared its head. The song "Kick Out the Jams" had been released as their first single. After some debate, the band had agreed to cut a "clean" version—i.e., substituting "kick out the jams, brothers and sisters" for "kick out the jams, motherfucker"—to be promoted to radio and sold as a single while keeping the other version on their album. This was not enough, however, to placate Bill Gavin, a leading radio programming consultant who published a widely read weekly tip sheet. He urged programmers not to play even the "clean" version.

"As I see it," Gavin wrote, "stations who give airplay to the single risk public condemnation of encouraging sales of the album . . . I view today's radio as responsible for insuring its listeners against undue offense." His remarks appeared alongside an enthusiastic plug for a Red Skelton recording of the "Pledge of Allegiance."

Gavin's wasn't the only industry voice raised against the record. Several large retail accounts, including Sam Goody and Handleman, a "rack jobber" that supplied records to large department stores like Sears, refused to carry it. Holzman went to Detroit to try to convince the MC5 to let him release an alternative, "clean" version of the album. Unlike the Grateful Dead, who changed the title of their concert album from *Skull Fuck* to *Live/Dead* when Warner Bros. executives suggested stores would refuse to stock it, the band wasn't swayed.

Elektra went ahead and changed the album anyhow, something the group didn't discover until they were in California on a self-financed promotional tour. There they learned the local distributor had shipped his old stock back to Elektra in expectation of receiving the new version. Incensed at what they viewed as blatant censorship, fearful that their revolutionary fervor would be lampooned in the underground press, and upset that they had spent money to come to California only to find there weren't any albums to sell, the band lit into Holzman.

"The MC5 had a hemorrhage," admits Holzman, although he stands by his decision. "I didn't suppress their speech. Go talk on somebody else's corner, don't talk on mine. It's inconsistent with how I view my label."

Holzman would soon have his own hemorrhage. Back in Michigan, several record retailers had been busted on obscenity charges for selling *Kick Out the Jams*. Hudson's, Detroit's biggest downtown retailer, wouldn't stock the record. Their own hometown! The band took out an ad in *The Argus,* Ann Arbor's underground paper, that read, *"KICK OUT THE JAMS, MOTHERFUCKER! . . . and kick in the door if the store won't sell you the album . . . FUCK HUDSON'S!"* Along with the Trans-Love logo, the band signed Elektra's name to the ad and sent the label the bill.

According to Holzman, Hudson's parent company, Dayton Hudson, responded by sending back every album on Elektra and its sister label, Nonesuch, it had in its stores. The executive, despite a history of recording and supporting activists like Phil Ochs, had had enough. He telephoned Sinclair.

"John, what are you doing?" Holzman asked. "You cannot put our logo in an ad that we do not support."

"Well, Jac," said the White Panther leader, "you gotta support the revolution."

"I support your music," replied Holzman. "I don't support your revolution."

"Jac, I don't know what I'm gonna do."

"I know what *I'm* gonna do," said Holzman. "You've got a very successful record. I'm going to give you your contract back. Go record elsewhere. I don't want you recording for me anymore."

Fields berated Holzman as a hypocrite for not standing by the Five while defending the label's biggest moneymaker, Jim Morrison of the Doors, who had been arrested for supposedly exposing himself in concert. "It's all right for Morrison to take out his cock, but the MC5 can't take out their ad," he argued. Holzman fired Fields.

In some ways, Holzman was generous in kicking the MC5 off Elektra. *Kick Out the Jams* had been a Top 30 album and managed to sell over 100,000 copies, which made it a very good time for the band to look for another label. The day the MC5 were given their release, Fields urged Kramer to call Landau and see if the critic could get his friend Jerry Wexler at Atlantic to sign the band.

Landau was only too happy to make the call and act as the band's intermediary. "Look," he told Wexler, "I just got the word that the MC5 received an unconditional release from Elektra. Would you be interested in discussing it with them?" Landau also made it clear that he believed Wexler and Atlantic could succeed where Holzman and Elektra had failed.

Since the debut of *Rolling Stone,* Landau had vigorously pursued his friendship with Wexler. The critic sent a steady stream of letters containing advice on how Atlantic could stay abreast of the burgeoning underground rock scene. In return, Wexler tutored him in the dollars-and-cents realities of the business.

"You're putting out a lot of crap," Landau had once told Wexler derisively. "Iron Butterfly and all that shit."

"Jon," Wexler had replied, "we're a record company. We're in business to manufacture, record, distribute, sell 33 and 45 rpm records. Don't judge us by the crap, judge us by what we've done—you know what we've accomplished." "You know," Landau persisted, "you put out four bad records for every good one." "Maybe we put out ten," said Wexler. "But look at the good ones and see what's there." Landau did just that—and concluded that what was "there" constituted a large portion of his record collection.

The MC5 wasn't the first act Landau urged Wexler to sign. He had also championed Livingston Taylor, the younger brother of singer/songwriter James Taylor. Like James, Livingston had been a patient at McLean psychiatric hospital, and through an acquaintance who worked as a music therapist there, Landau was introduced to him in 1968. Greatly impressed, he first sent the eighteen-year-old Taylor to Elektra, but Holzman declined to sign him.

Landau, who wanted to produce Taylor, had pitched him to Wexler in early 1969 during a visit to the executive's Long Island home with

Phil Walden, the former manager of Otis Redding. Wexler, who deemed most rock music crap, passed. But as they were leaving Wexler's house, Walden offered to sign Taylor to Capricorn Records, the new rock label he was starting. Landau was surprised—didn't Phil want to hear him first? No, Walden assured him, an audition wasn't necessary. If Jon liked him that was good enough. In fact, Walden wasn't really interested in Taylor. He wanted Landau working at Capricorn.

Walden, like Wexler, had been sufficiently impressed by the young critic to take him under his wing, helping him with articles and teaching him the business. "He was an Otis Redding *fanatic*," Walden says of Landau. "He could talk about him for hours. We were like two old maids on the phone. He wanted to know every detail."

A few months before the visit to Wexler's house, when Landau was researching an article on Southern music for *Rolling Stone*, Walden served as his guide.* While visiting Walden at his office in Macon, Georgia, Landau accompanied him to Fame Studios in Muscle Shoals, Alabama, where several of Atlantic's most important artists like Aretha Franklin and Wilson Pickett recorded. And while Landau was eager to see where so many of his favorite records had been cut, Walden wanted him to meet a young white session guitarist working at Fame, Duane Allman.

Walden was starting Capricorn to get out of the r&b business and concentrate on the burgeoning white rock market. But although he knew enough to run a record label, he wasn't an expert on rock. In Landau, he recognized someone who was. The next morning, on the 6 A.M. mail plane flight from Muscle Shoals back to Georgia, Walden confided that he had an opportunity to buy Allman out of his contract with Fame Studios and was thinking about managing him. What did Jon think of the guitarist? Landau declared Allman fantastic. The Allman Brothers Band, which Duane formed with his brother, Gregg, became Capricorn's biggest act.

At Wexler's house, Walden's offer to sign Livingston Taylor and let Landau produce him had been an overture, an indication to Landau of the faith he had in his taste. Walden soon played the rest of his

---

*The piece never ran in *Rolling Stone* but provided the backbone for Landau's senior thesis at Brandeis.

hand, asking Landau to become the head of A&R for Capricorn. But just when Walden thought he had him sewn up, the chance to produce the MC5 for Atlantic came along. Landau blew off Walden and placed his bets on the bigger label and the established band. "He came down to Macon and found an apartment," recalls Walden. "And then Wexler gave him the MC5 to produce and convinced him that he'd be better off remaining north of the Mason-Dixon Line." Landau held on to the chance to produce Taylor for Capricorn, though.

After talking to Landau and Fields, Wexler signed the MC5 for $50,000, more than double what they had received from Elektra. The band members were ecstatic to have landed on their feet so lucratively. And they were hopeful that Landau's presence as producer would buy them some muscle in the rock press. To the band's amazement, *Kick Out the Jams* hadn't been a hit with underground critics, who had called them everything from poseurs to incompetent musicians. "It was gangster theoretics," says Sinclair, who figured Landau's status among other critics would produce a more sympathetic response: " 'Gee, Landau! This'll be great.' "

HUNGRY TO CARVE OUT A NICHE FOR HIMSELF IN THE RECORD BUSINESS, Landau was as eager as the band to see the new album succeed. But unlike the MC5, he believed the cool critical reception to *Kick Out the Jams* was deserved. "The Elektra album told the truth about the MC5," he said. "In a lot of ways it was an accurate report. It was an excellent technical recording of what they did those nights and it betrayed the fact that they were not organized."

Aside from the fact that the Elektra album had been only a moderate seller, its loose, scattershot improvisations were just the kind of performances that Landau regularly railed against as a critic. The liberation from the confines of the single format that Dylan's "Like a Rolling Stone" had so brilliantly announced for rock was, as far as Landau was concerned, more freedom than most performers had the talent to handle—and that included the MC5. As a producer, his job was to help artists articulate their vision, but he had strong opinions about how that should be accomplished.

Arriving in Ann Arbor, Jon discovered that a lot had changed since the Halloween recording of *Kick Out the Jams*. As a result of growing

friction between the band and other members of Trans-Love, particularly between the band's girlfriends and the other women in the commune, the MC5 had moved into their own farmhouse in nearby
Hamburg, Michigan.

Tensions were also developing between the band and Sinclair, who
was facing yet another drug trial. He had been part of a large bust of
fifty-six people in Detroit in '67 orchestrated to break up the Workshop scene, and all of his motions were just about exhausted. This
would be his third drug conviction, and he was looking at a long
prison term. His court costs seemed endless, and what would happen
to Trans-Love and his wife and children if he went to prison?

Fields and Landau were not interested in Sinclair's problems. Their
job was to transform the MC5 into a viable act for Atlantic. The politics of the White Panthers was a harmful distraction to the band's career. For all of the group's onstage rhetoric, neither Danny nor Jon
was convinced that the members of the MC5 really knew much about
politics or had any deep convictions about it. "Their manager taught
them to say all these things," said Fields condescendingly. "They
didn't believe all this stuff—they didn't even know what it *meant*.
They were the sons of auto assembly workers, people who screw on
windshield wipers."

Landau began to wonder out loud just how committed the MC5
were to a political agenda. "I'm picking up that they're unhappy," he
recalls. "I begin to get the feeling that they never were very political
. . . that John wielded a tremendous influence over them as a personality and not as a political teacher. Nobody in the MC5 has ever read
The Red Book or ever will."

Instead, Landau gave them permission simply to be rock and roll
stars: "It's hard for me to conceive of somebody being in a rock and
roll band whose goal's not to be a rock and roll star. That's the most
natural thing in the world regardless of what anyone says. And that's
what they wanted to be and the thing that most interested me about
them was I felt that that's what they were."

Of course, if that was now the goal, why would they want Sinclair to
be their manager? The issue became a major point of discussion between Landau and the band. Landau, who would later publicly brand
Sinclair "an amateurish manager," obviously had an opinion. But
he was very careful not to come on too strong. If there was a place he

wanted the band to wind up, it would be far better if he simply framed the discussion and they seemed to get there on their own. It didn't take long.

"They're beginning to ask what I think is a legitimate question," Landau recalls. " 'What is he doing for us? He is our manager, right? We require a professional manager. We are a professional rock and roll band. There are certain things that have to be done that are not being done.' I was involved in the discussions, naturally. The weight of my comments were, in general, that John was not functioning as their manager and that this had to be dealt with. I didn't propose what the solution was at this stage, but I simply offered that as an observation."

Bassist Michael Davis, however, remembers Landau actively pushing for a change. "We basically fired them at Landau's urging," he recalled. "He said, 'These people are dragging your ass down. You guys got something going, and you do it this way, we make a product that's correct. You gotta get rid of all these freeloaders.' Basically he said, 'Sinclair's fucking out of his mind, he's a fucking nut, and all these people around him are a bunch of parasites. Time to clean house.' The way it went down was fairly rude."

The band invited Sinclair out to their house but just couldn't bring themselves to put their cards on the table. It devolved into a typical MC5/John Sinclair/White Panther powwow where a lot of dope was smoked and nothing was accomplished. Afterward, Landau and the band agreed that a concrete proposal was needed. On the eve of Sinclair's court date they held another meeting and this time included David Newman, a music business accountant Landau and Fields had brought in. The band told Sinclair that they were unwilling to pay him 20 percent because they needed money to pay a new manager and a booking agent. Instead, they offered 15 percent of their concert earnings, 20 percent of any Elektra royalties, and nothing from the Atlantic payments, saying Sinclair had played no part in its procurement (Fields, however, got a 10 percent finder's fee of $5,000). When Sinclair resisted the proposal, the band offered to pay him 5 percent of all income instead.

"What do you think of all this?" Sinclair asked Landau. He was possibly on his way to prison, the band was deserting him, and he wondered what role Landau had played in this sudden change of heart.

"I think what's happening is that the band is recognizing that they are an individual entity," replied Landau. "As much as they sympathize with what you're doing, they recognize that they've got their own goals, their own desires, and that your relationship with them is based on your providing them with a service for which they're paying you. And what I think they're trying to tell you—which I agree with them about—is that they are reevaluating your contribution to this whole thing and they're saying 'This is how much it's worth.' "

Sinclair felt betrayed. Was that all it really was—a relationship based on providing the MC5 with a service for which they paid him? "It was traumatic," he says. "Newman looks in and just says, 'Man, these people are ripping you off. All this money is going to these people in Trans-Love and you don't even live there anymore.' This was a situation that had existed for maybe thirty days! For two and a half years we took care of them and they were working for $125 a night. The Trans-Love people they maligned so much were people who loved the band." He rejected both offers.

Sinclair's trial on possession of two joints came up on July 22, 1969. He was found guilty that day and sentenced to nine and a half years in prison. Appeal bond was denied, and he was immediately hustled off to begin serving his term. None of the MC5 came to visit him in prison. Except for one letter from Kramer trying to explain the band's position on the management fee, Sinclair never even heard from them.

"They left me there," says Sinclair. "I never got a penny, they didn't buy me a carton of cigarettes. My wife was pregnant, the phone got shut off, all of that. They never did anything to help." Beside himself with rage, Sinclair fired a letter back to Kramer. "You guys wanted to be bigger than the Beatles," he wrote, "and I wanted you to be bigger than Chairman Mao."

WITH SINCLAIR AND TRANS-LOVE OUT OF THE PICTURE, LANDAU FOCUSED on making a cleaned-up, stripped-down MC5 album. But as he and the band began recording at East Detroit's GM Studios, the producer made an unsettling discovery. Bassist Michael Davis and drummer Dennis Thompson couldn't play their parts. Says Kramer, "At one point he suggested bringing in [bassist] Jerry Jemmott. Anyway, we went around and around with it. Everyone learned his part note by note."

Landau's own lack of studio experience was also a factor. "Landau was really inflexible because he had never produced a record before so he was learning, too," says Davis, who wondered if he was up to handling the pressure. The end result, *Back in the USA*, was certainly tight but surprisingly sterile.

Where the band had ripped through *Kick Out the Jams* with a lusty bombast, they now applied a controlled energy. The biggest single factor accounting for the difference was Landau. Despite pledging that the record would be whatever they wanted it to be, *Back in the USA* was at least as much an expression of his aesthetic as the MC5's. As a critic he had eschewed the long, free-form style favored by the psychedelic bands that had characterized *Kick Out the Jams,* and ten of the new album's eleven songs were under three minutes. A champion of fifties rock, Landau had sandwiched the group's originals between covers of Little Richard's "Tutti Frutti" and the title track, a Chuck Berry standard. If the album was an attempt by the MC5 to distance themselves from the powerful influence of Sinclair in favor of their own musical identity, then it was a failure: they had traded Sinclair's values for Landau's.

Similarly, if Landau's mission was to create a new, commercially viable MC5, he, too, had failed. *Back in the USA* did not attract any new fans for the band and alienated many of their die-hard followers. *Big Fat,* an underground magazine that devoted a good deal of space to following Sinclair's drug case and subsequent imprisonment, buried the Five's new album with faint praise, terming *Back in the USA* "not a thoroughly bad album."

Sinclair, on hearing *Back in the USA,* believed that Landau had simply missed the point. "Landau liked the Five," he says, "until he got into the studio and started breaking down tracks and listening to them and said, 'Hey, these guys can't play.' Well, there was a Gestalt, a whole thing. Any one of them would have been a relatively mediocre talent. Together they were something different. They fit together and made something that was much bigger than the talent involved. And he cleaned up everything and made them sound like Booker T. and the MG's."

Back in the USA, though like the group's other albums destined to become a touchstone for the punk rock movement of the late seventies, was a commercial flop. It sold less than half as many copies as *Kick*

Out the Jams. Perhaps Landau saw the trouble coming. Despite repeated entreaties from the band for him to succeed Sinclair as their
manager, he demurred. "We pushed him and pushed him and pushed
him," says Kramer. "But he was determined to be a record producer."

Not, however, for another MC5 album. The next year Atlantic
paired the band with another young producer, Geoffrey Haslam, and
it proved an excellent match. Haslam knew how to make records; he
had been an engineer and was able to edit out the band's mistakes.
The musical problems that had dogged *Back in the USA* disappeared.

The result, *High Time,* proved to be the band's best album. An ambitious melding of high-energy rock and a dissonant modern jazz
style, it firmly touched all the artistic bases the band had ever laid
claims to. Unlike *Kick Out the Jams,* the playing was pointed, and the
musical goals achieved were far broader than those set on *Back in the
USA.* The MC5 had finally proven their chops.

No one cared anymore. Atlantic had lost interest in the MC5 and
offered only minimal marketing support for the new album. Worse,
several members had developed heroin habits and the group slowly
disintegrated; Tyner and Thompson eventually quit on the eve of a
European tour. Kramer returned the favor by walking offstage halfway
through a farewell show at the Grande on New Year's Eve. "I went to
Fred and said, 'Y'know, I can't stand any more,' " recalls Kramer.
"And that was the end of the MC5."

Now a full-blown junkie, Kramer led a few unsuccessful bands. Unable to handle the death of his dreams, he focused most of his attention on a new street life, which included selling guns and stolen
television sets. In 1974 Kramer sold a pound and a half of cocaine to
a DEA agent and landed in a federal prison in Lexington, Kentucky,
for four years. To his surprise, he was reunited there with MC5 bassist
Michael Davis, also serving time on a cocaine charge.

Sinclair's own post-MC5 journey was equally twisted and disappointing. While in prison, he had gained national prominence. An
editorial in *The Washington Post* railed against the inequity of giving
him nine years for the possession of two joints, but it was the New
Left—particularly well-known radicals Bobby Seale, Jerry Rubin, and
Dave Dellinger, as well as such prominent poets as Allen Ginsberg and
Ed Sanders—who transformed Sinclair's case into a leading liber-
tarian cause.

Rubin ultimately delivered what would prove to be the biggest guns in the White Panther arsenal: John Lennon and Yoko Ono. The ex-Beatle and his wife had moved to New York, where they attempted to immerse themselves in both the musical and political scene of the left. For the latter, they asked Rubin to act as a go-between, a role he was flattered to play. Rubin's interest in Sinclair's case led to the Lennons' decision to make a rare concert appearance in support of the White Panther leader.

On December 10, 1971, three days before the Michigan Supreme Court was slated to hear a motion to grant Sinclair an appeal bond in light of an imminent softening of the state's marijuana statutes, 15,000 people attended a rally and concert for him at Ann Arbor's Chrysler Arena headlined by the Lennons. Along with their fifteen-minute appearance, which included the debut of Lennon's "John Sinclair," the eight-hour rally also featured Phil Ochs, Stevie Wonder, Archie Shepp, and Bob Seger. For Sinclair, who broke down in tears while addressing the crowd by phone, it was a moment of both frustration and supreme triumph. Although his immediate future remained uncertain, marijuana had been largely decriminalized in the state owing in no small part to his case and the work of organizations he had helped found. The White Panther Party, which had started as a giggle around the dining room table in Ann Arbor, had actually accomplished something.

Four days later, Sinclair was released from Jackson State Prison and went to meet Lennon and Ono in New York. They agreed to help him organize "the Guitar Army," a grander, national forum for many of the views he had originally expressed with Trans-Love and the MC5, and they pledged to headline a month's tour and donate their fees to local causes. "It will be the regular scene but without the capitalism," said Lennon. It couldn't get any better than this. The most important rock star in the world was now Sinclair's patron. "It's nights like this," Sinclair told his wife as they were getting ready to leave the Lennons' apartment at The Dakota, "that make it clear why they wanted to keep me in the penitentiary."

That was as close as John Sinclair ever got to his dreams. The Guitar Army tour was soon put on hold as the Nixon administration stepped up efforts to have Lennon deported as an undesirable alien. Sinclair returned to Michigan, where he helped organize the critically acclaimed Ann Arbor Jazz and Blues Festival and continued to push his cultural program as a Detroit ombudsman. But he had lost his patron. And when the charged rhetoric of the era dissipated with the close of the Vietnam War and the end of the Nixon administration, he also lost his moment. Divorced from Leni, he moved in the late eighties to New Orleans, where that city's rich African-American music heritage could nurture a middle-aged Beat poet.

Like the members of the MC5, Sinclair nursed his share of resentments, and even Rob Tyner's death in 1992 didn't repair the rift. Over the years, Tyner had laid the collapse of the MC5 on Sinclair, portraying himself in interviews as a naive kid who had been used by him. It was a bitter pill. "Tyner got to where he'd just harp on how I dragged him into this," says Sinclair. "That was all bullshit, and it hurt me."

By contrast, he and Kramer were able to rekindle their kinship. "We reconciled after he did his time," says Sinclair. "He understood how I felt." One night on the telephone they chewed over the old, crazy times when the future seemed so clear.

"Well, John," Kramer said with a laugh, "next time the revolution comes—"

"Hey," replied Sinclair, cutting him off, "next time the revolution comes, I'm gonna duck."

9

CORONATIONS
AND BEHEADINGS

THE COMMERCIAL FAILURE OF *BACK IN THE USA* WAS THE BEGINNING of the end for the MC5, but not for Jon Landau. Unlike the band, he saw clearly that the power of the music and the broad, romantic appeal of the underground scene was being transformed into a marketable commodity by corporations and entrepreneurs whose goals—survival and wealth—had nothing to do with promoting a counterculture. Landau not only recognized this, he embraced it. "When you are making records," Landau declared in an essay that soft-pedaled his miscues as the MC5's producer, "you are also making business." In comparison to the chaos that surrounded the MC5, the lucrative concert scene Landau returned to in Boston and the power of WBCN could only confirm this view.

Record companies, which had been throwing advertising money at *Rolling Stone, Crawdaddy!*, and a wide assortment of smaller underground publications in their attempts to influence a new and potentially lucrative market, now turned their eyes and growing marketing muscle toward the new underground rock stations. In 1968, the same year that Ray Riepen launched "the American Revolution" on WBCN, Atlantic Records became the first label to hire a promotion man solely to cultivate airplay for their product on progressive FM stations.

Just how Atlantic should "work" their records to these new stations and their quasi-professional disc jockeys was something of a mystery. In both programming and mentality, the new FM stations were antithetical to their AM forebears, a reaction to the Top 40 format with its short playlist of hit singles and ceaseless commercials for teen-oriented products like pimple creams and colas. The traditional method of record promotion in that world was as subtle as the format: cash was king. The widespread practice of paying disc jockeys for airplay predated rock and roll radio, but it was at the center of the payola scandal that began in 1959 and the discrediting of AM rock radio, personified by the prosecution and public humiliation of pioneering rock disc jockey Alan Freed. The disc jockeys at WBCN and at dozens of other underground stations sprouting up around the country prided themselves on the fact that they were not professionals but idealists motivated by something other than money. They saw themselves as players in the broader political and social movements taking hold in the country.

"Everyone had already decided that whatever else they did with their life they did not, barring physical torture, want to go into their father's business," says James Isaacs, a Boston music critic and disc jockey. "They wanted to express themselves and have meaningful lives. At the same time you have a whole new form of musical expression cropping up. Performers as writers, not Tin Pan Alley. The event that catalyzed everyone, of course, was the war, and it was just another way to protest the war, to express yourself, to show that your generation was going to be the most talked about generation since Paris in the twenties."

Such sentiments resulted in radio programming that was amateurish and self-important but also outrageous and exciting. A Boston retailer and early advertiser on WBCN, Underground Camera, sued the station after disc jockey Charles Laquidara touted a sale on Honeywell cameras by telling listeners they could go to Underground if they wanted to buy a camera from a company killing babies in Cambodia. The suit was dropped after WBCN threatened to subpoena Honeywell executives.

WBCN's disc jockeys prided themselves on reaching out to the community through special programs that would make any professional radio manager cringe. Along with such quaint features as a missing dog and cat report, the station made its political leanings evident with *Lock Up,* a weekly request show for prisoners. As part of the program, anyone serving time within the station's broadcast reach could buy a radio from WBCN for two dollars.

"We imagined that this was solidarity with the people who were war protesters," says disc jockey Joe Rogers. "But we don't have any federal prisons around Boston. The people we were broadcasting to were the people who steal your car. But that's an idea that was lost on us. Anyone in prison was a friend of ours."

In an environment where disc jockeys liked to think of themselves as political and social activists, a record company promotion man with a jacket and tie and a grab bag of well-traveled jokes was not going to make it. Neither was the fifty-dollar handshake that had been a mainstay of AM promotion. The record companies needed a new and appropriate FM promotion man who, like their house hippies, could provide a bridge to the underground. Atlantic found one in Mario Medious.

He was one of a kind, and not because he was an African-American. Golden-tongued and unfailingly hip, Medious—or the Big M, as everyone called him—proved the perfect businessman for a group of people who loathed business. A former bookkeeper, Medious had spent several years handling the payroll checks for Atlantic before transforming himself into the company's high-stepping, trash-talking goodwill ambassador to the underground.

It was a formidable task. "These guys hated promotion men," Medious says. "Back then it wasn't about no payola with FM stations. These cats just weren't about it." Instead, he sought to fit in to the scene by creating a bigger-than-life persona that was equal parts street hustler and clown. "I'd walk into a station and act a complete fool," he says.

If Medious was a fool, he was a fool worthy of Shakespeare, speaking truths behind an outlandish disguise. Raised in Chicago, he was a blues fan who knew more about the roots of rock than most of the FM jocks. He wasn't afraid to ridicule a disc jockey for playing a bad record, even if it was on Atlantic. "I'd walk into a station and say, 'Man, what are you playing here? Take that shit off!' I'd be promoting a Led

Zeppelin record to these guys at the stations and they'd say, 'Oh, that's the greatest blues track ever recorded!' And I'd say, 'I don't know about that, man.' "

Medious was careful to promote only the Atlantic releases he thought were credible. "They would give you a priority list of records to work," he says. "And nine times out of ten I didn't pay any attention to it. I'd work the ones I liked or that had something I could identify with. I guess that honesty really helped me."

Perhaps just as important was an ever-present stash of marijuana, which helped ease the sell-job. "I would go to the radio stations and sit up and smoke pot with the cats for about an hour or so and listen to all the stuff they were playing," he says. "Then I'd pull out whatever records I had in my bag. That's how I picked up Peter Wolf at WBCN. He was into the blues. He was the first cat I knew who if I called off a tune, he knew who wrote it. Wiped me right out."

Mario's visits to WBCN could lead to havoc. Medious got one on-air disc jockey so stoned that he fell asleep on the toilet while the promotion man took over the show and played nothing but new Atlantic releases for two hours. But for Wolf and most of the jocks at the station, Medious was a welcome sight. They found the idea of payola abhorrent—taking money to play a record would be a disgustingly corrupt violation of the music and make them as low as an AM disc jockey—but letting Medious buy them a cheeseburger and get them stoned was well within the bounds of accepted behavior. "Mario was the first guy from a record company who could understand the habits of the culture," says Wolf.

Medious's outlandish personality seamlessly blended business and fun. Aside from free records, Medious also often carried other highly prized promotional items like T-shirts advertising Atlantic acts. While dispensing such goodies with a flair that was ostensibly countercultural, he also sported a set of values that was hardly an improvement over traditional promotional methods.

"While I was out there on the college campuses I was looking for all the fine chicks," he says. "I would give my T-shirts for unknown acts to the chicks with the biggest chests so that when they were walkin' down the street somebody's gonna be readin' that! Guys come over and say, 'Uh, well what's that?' 'Oh, that's a new band!' But he's only interested in what she has. A flat-chested chick ask me for a T-shirt, I'd say, 'No more, baby,' even if I had fifty more in my case! And all the guys would crack up; the disc jockeys loved me."*

Medious proved wildly successful, and, as early as the summer of 1968, his growing influence and that of other underground promotion men was becoming obvious. Profiling the emerging Los Angeles rock scene for *Rolling Stone,* Jerry Hopkins noted that "a new style of promotion man is being created—one who supplies caps and tabs of LSD rather than booze. But he's still a promotion man and that makes him twice as bad, nay, evil, when fooling around with LSD, a far cry from booze."

The widespread use of drugs within the new culture was an issue that record companies like Atlantic had little trouble with. On a trip to a radio station in Tucson, Arizona, Medious was able to score a pound of marijuana, which he later charged back to Atlantic. "For one hundred dollars I was getting people high all over America!" he says. "When I got back to New York they said, 'How much did it cost?' I said, 'Oh, it was about five hundred dollars.' "

Medious, whose job as Director of FM Promotion and Special Projects also included such responsibilities as traveling with touring bands, was expected to keep Atlantic's artists just as happy as the disc jockeys and journalists. That meant anything from taking keyboardist Brian Auger to hear American jazz musicians in black clubs in Philadelphia to keeping the members of Led Zeppelin stoned. When Atlantic had a difficult time getting Stephen Stills to sign a new contract, Medious said he was dispatched by Atlantic to California to give the rocker a pep talk "and maybe something for his nose." Stills re-signed with the label.

That incident notwithstanding, Medious was far more than a Dr. Feelgood. If Atlantic and other record companies were willing to sanction the use and distribution of drugs in order to achieve their commercial aims, the social use of drugs had as much to do with bonhomie and etiquette as it did with corporate cynicism. Bob Garcia, who filled a similar position at A&M Records, remembers the label providing disc jockeys with "anything from hash brownies to free meals to bottles of booze. It was nothing to go on the air with Tom Donahue or

---

*Sexism was pervasive at WBCN. The word "chicks" was used liberally on the air—until a group of women released a clutch of real chicks in the studio.

someone like that with everyone smoking dope in the studio," says Garcia. "All of the psychedelic part of it—whether it was marijuana or mescaline—was nothing more than asking someone for a root beer. It was almost expected. Obviously, a musician could probably do no wrong by playing live in the studio or acting as a guest DJ or having this particular disc jockey listen to the music under the influence of whatever it might be."

For their part, many of the disc jockeys, artists, and music journalists felt a camaraderie with Medious. "It really was Mario's personality," says former *Rolling Stone* writer Stu Werbin. "My memory is that people gave Mario drugs more than that Mario gave people drugs. You went to dinner with Mario because it was more fun to be with Mario than someone from another label. At *Rolling Stone* I was barraged by the PR and promotion people. And at that point it was personality that made them successful, not who you got drugs from."

Medious's wide orbit and impact inevitably led to a collaboration with Wolf and Landau. While sitting backstage at the Tea Party with Led Zeppelin, Medious heard another band playing a hot opening set of blues standards and old r&b hits. "I was in the dressing room and I heard them playing 'Serve You Right to Suffer,' a John Lee Hooker tune," says Medious. "And man, they were *killin'* it."

By the time he got to the stage to see who was playing, the band was off. But he saw Wolf, whom he recognized from the station, standing in the wings.

"Where are all the brothers from Chicago that just got done playing 'Serve You Right to Suffer'?" Mario asked.

"Yeah, man," Wolf said. "That was us."

Momentarily embarrassed—"I felt like a bucket of water then," he remembers with a laugh—Medious quickly recovered and asked Wolf what label his band was on.

"We ain't got no label," he said.

"Well, shit, man," said Medious. "If Jerry Wexler heard you guys he'd flip."

Medious took a tape of Wolf's new group, the J. Geils Band, back to New York for Wexler and his partner, Ahmet Ertegun. To his surprise, Medious found them less than enthusiastic about signing the band. "They played it and said, 'This ain't nuthin' but a blues band from Boston—this ain't gonna sell no records,' " he recalls. But Medious was adamant that the band had to be heard. "I was pissed," he says. "I argued with them until they figured they'd do it just to keep me satisfied." Of course, Wexler knew someone else in Boston he could ask about J. Geils. He called Landau, who was eager to help hook the band up with Atlantic. Along with providing a ringing endorsement of their talents, he quickly took an active role in helping the band get a deal and flew to New York with Wolf to negotiate with Wexler.

With coaching from Medious, they knew about how much cash to ask for: $25,000 per album plus an additional $25,000 in tour support. "That was a lot of money in those days," says Medious. However, the more subtle and potentially lucrative points of a record deal such as publishing revenues and label options were something Landau and Wolf were ignorant about.

With just Landau as their adviser—no attorney, manager, or agent—the J. Geils Band cut what proved to be a tough, long-term deal. Wolf, the die-hard r&b fanatic, had just one nonnegotiable point: Wexler wanted to put the band on Atco, the company's rock imprint, but Wolf made it clear that the band had to be on Atlantic because that was the label Ray Charles had been on. It was of no consequence to Wexler, but he seized on the issue as a negotiating ploy and made a big show of caving in. Delighted by their "victory," the band gladly agreed to what Wolf would one day view as onerous terms. "It was probably the same deal they gave to LaVern Baker in 1952," he later moaned. "We were ready to pay Atlantic to let us be on the label. And we did." Mentor or not, Wexler didn't let his friendship with Landau stand in the way of a tough contract. But Wexler gave him the nod to produce J. Geils.

It was an opportunity that neither Landau nor the band was ready to handle. Returning to GM Studios in Detroit, where Landau had produced *Back in the USA,* they began working on an album. But once again, Landau quickly found himself in over his head. His painstaking and plodding production style couldn't approximate the excitement of the group's live performances. After spending three days in the studio while Landau tried to get the sound of the kick drum he wanted, it was obvious that this producer/band matchup wasn't going to work. "The band felt [they] didn't need to be in the studio for six months," says Fred Lewis, then working as road manager for J. Geils. "It wasn't clicking." Discouraged, Landau quickly telephoned Wexler and begged out of the project. "He called me after two or three weeks and said, 'Hey, I can't hack it—I'm withdrawing,' " says Wexler. "So now I've got a band and no producer." Everyone agreed to cancel the rest of the sessions and postpone the album. It was a completely different story when the band returned to the studio a year later. With Seth Justman added on keyboards, producers Brad Shapiro and Dave Crawford cut all the tracks for *The J. Geils Band* in just three days.

When the record came out, Landau, now editor of the influential record review section at *Rolling Stone,* opted to write about the album himself rather than assign it an impartial reviewer. Not surprisingly, his review was a rave. He heaped praise on the band he had recommended to Jerry Wexler, comparing the unknown group favorably to the Rolling Stones and terming the LP "the best album I've heard in some time." He failed to alert readers to his friendship with Wolf, his role in bringing the band to Atlantic, or his aborted production of the album he was now reviewing. In truth, *The J. Geils Band* was a good album, good enough to be recommended by a disinterested critic without a personal and business relationship with the group. As a reviewer, Landau had had no qualms about slamming a performer like Joan Baez for a lack of credibility. But as an aspiring player within the developing business, he seemed disinterested in holding himself to the same standard.

WOLF AND THE OTHER MEMBERS OF THE J. GEILS BAND HAD NOTHING against success. And, like Landau, they did not ally themselves with any underground ideology. "We were not political," says Wolf. "We tried to put on a show, proving our conviction by the energy onstage. It was an active, rock and roll thing: when you saw Jerry Lee Lewis kick that piano stool across the stage, there was something about that energy that got you. And it was our job to get the audience crazy. It was that kind of sensibility and integrity—that traditional rock and roll roadhouse band that when you heard they were in town, you said, 'Man, those cats really cook. I'm gonna go down and see 'em.' "

The group's desire to be a show band was fortuitous. Although their album was being well received, it was apparent that playing the emerging ballroom circuit was the key to success. Wolf had observed the impact Frank Barsalona and his Premier Talent Agency had had on the success of Riepen's Tea Party and was eager to hire Barsalona as the band's agent. In the two years since Barsalona had come hat in hand to Boston begging for a venue, he had become the dominant booking agent in rock, succeeding brilliantly in his plan to knit together a national circuit of ballrooms and underground rock promoters. "There didn't seem to be a question in anyone's mind that Frank was the most powerful person in the industry," says Werbin, who was then covering the business for *Rolling Stone*. "There was no sense of anyone—be it Clive Davis or Ahmet Ertegun—being number one other than Frank."

Barsalona had become the true kingmaker of the underground. His roster of successful bands gave him the leverage to dictate opening acts to promoters and help make new stars. More than that, he could make or break a promoter. A friendly, cooperative promoter might reap a huge business advantage over competitors by not having to pay Premier a guarantee, the up-front portion of a band's fee that had to be paid weeks before the concert; conversely, someone who balked at Barsalona's packages or prices might wake up to discover a new, Barsalona-backed competitor in his city.

Howard Stein, a New York promoter, found himself by turns on the right and wrong end of Barsalona's shotgun. Despite being in New York, he was enlisted to promote Premier concerts in Minneapolis, Miami, Chicago, and Texas. "I was sort of a puppet promoter," he says. "My value for those people was putting on the shows that they wanted for the price they wanted and very often with the opening acts they wanted. You were very aware of what they wanted and when they wanted it." In return for being cooperative, Stein became the preferred promoter for Premier acts in Manhattan after Bill Graham closed the Fillmore East in June of 1971, a coronation that gave him a huge advantage over other area promoters like Ron Delsener because it provided Stein with a steady stream of acts to present. "I was the Barsalona baby," says Stein. "Delsener was out of the loop, completely out of it."

Still, Stein began to spit the bit as he realized that the growing power of Barsalona and the acts was making the relationship one-sided. "It was completely a seller's market," he says. "When I entered the business you could buy an act for a thousand dollars and gross twenty-five thousand. By the time I left, you could buy it for twenty-five thousand and gross a thousand. It was a complete reversal. The promoter was kept on the brink of paranoia; that's how you were used. 'Hey, Howard, I love you so much. I *hope* Ron Delsener doesn't get this show.' You were disposable. There was always some kid who'd inherited money who would do the show for nothing."

Stein's growing frustration led to a break with Barsalona. "The guy basically made me and ended me. Like a magician, he took me out of a hat and then made me disappear. Because I wasn't . . . with the program."

The J. Geils Band was eager to get with the program. They lobbied hard to have Premier as their agent, and Barsalona—in a display of his power—arranged for the band to play as an opening act at the Fillmore East so he wouldn't have to go to Boston to see them. Impressed, he eagerly offered to represent them and booked them for a second show at the Fillmore. Aside from keeping the band in front of the New York audience, Barsalona had an ulterior motive. J. Geils needed a manager, and he wanted his friend Dee "Little Angelo" Anthony to see them. Wolf, who had met Anthony at the Tea Party when Dee was touring with Traffic, loved the idea. "Dee Anthony! He was hotcakes," Wolf says.

A former road manager for Tony Bennett and Buddy Greco, Anthony was the kind of show-business hustler the folk-rock crowd would have had nothing to do with in the days of Club 47. But under the steady ministrations of Barsalona, the scene's commercial potential had come into focus and a creeping professionalism—with success as the goal—now impelled the bands. It wasn't just the promoters like Howard Stein who needed to be with the program but the artists as well. For them, Dee Anthony was the program.

Short, barrel-chested, and thickly built, the bearded Anthony looked more like a professional wrestler than a professional manager and spoke in the profanely colorful street language of the Bronx, where he'd grown up. Intimations that Anthony was mobbed up were rife, an impression encouraged by Anthony's friendship with Joe

Pagano, a reputed soldier in New York's Genovese crime family who had been identified by government informer Joe Valachi as a heroin smuggler and murderer. At a *Billboard* convention in Los Angeles, Anthony allegedly threatened A&M executive Bob Garcia in front of several dozen conventioneers, saying he would break Garcia's arm and kill him because he thought the executive was hiding one of his clients, Humble Pie guitarist Steve Marriott.

"Dee was feared," says Garcia, adding that such sentiments didn't prevent Anthony or Barsalona from being considered "members of the A&M family. We thought of him not just as a manager but as a friend and a consultant. But there was also the Dee school of lifetime contracts. The hints that if you didn't stick around you would wind up with your footprints in cement and all that blather." Still, British managers who were eager to have Premier as their American booking agent took note of Anthony's close friendship with Barsalona and invariably hired Anthony's firm, Bandana, as their U.S. associate. Anthony was soon the American manager for such British acts as the Troggs, Traffic, Savoy Brown, Jethro Tull, Ten Years After, and Spencer Davis. All were booked by Premier.

His more menacing aspects notwithstanding, Anthony relied on his previous work with traditional nightclub and concert acts to preach a professional approach to mounting a concert. He and Barsalona were a formidable team that could take a band, line up a national tour of the most important rock venues in the country, and inject a sense of mission.

"Their promises were very down to earth," says Humble Pie drummer Jerry Shirley. "They cut right to the quick: 'Okay, guys. We're gonna go ta woik. We're gonna woik and woik and woik. And when we're done woikin', we're gonna woik some more.' A conversation with Frank and Dee was, in the first place, hysterically entertaining. And in the second place, they feared no one. Absolutely no one. They were the little guys who had become big guys, and they demanded a tremendous amount of respect. The Premier philosophy was you throw it against the wall three hundred and sixty-five days a year and eventually you'll break America. That was their approach."

Anthony's bands had to learn how to work a crowd. "Dee had this Al Jolson theory of showbiz," says Wolf. "He would talk to me about working the spotlight: 'Jolson got down on his hands and knees—*you* get down on your hands and knees. Sit on the lip of the stage. Never, never, *never* walk into a crowd without applause—always have announcers.' "

Behind the scenes, Bob Garcia at A&M watched Anthony and Barsalona coach Humble Pie: "I remember Frank and Dee standing behind a stack of speakers showing Peter Frampton and Steve Marriott how to move. The band literally came here with no stage [presence]. And these guys showed them the basic steps."

"It was almost vaudevillian," recalls Shirley. " 'Respect the boards,' they'd tell you. I learned every show-business credo about working an audience and how to build dynamics onstage from Dee and Frank. When a new band came and played the Fillmore, Frank would literally sit in the fifth row and listen to the show. And then he would come back stage and say, 'Take this song and move it down the list to number three. Put this song as your opener. Take this song and develop it. Throw this song out.' Then Dee would go over the finer points, the literal moves: 'When you move center stage, that's good. When you just stand there, that's not good.' They were like football coaches."

Before each performance, Dee would gather his bands backstage for preshow pep talks, a habit that earned him the nickname "Little Angelo," a reference to Angelo Dundee, Muhammad Ali's corner man. "I wanna see ya leave a pint of blood on that stage," he would snarl. "No one leaves this group alive!" While the bands were performing, Anthony would be behind the amplifiers on his knees, the twenty-four-karat-gold coach's whistle he normally wore around his neck clenched between his teeth. "If you were flagging a little," recalls Shirley, "he'd blow this whistle. Right in the middle of the show! He'd intimidate you into picking it up a notch. And you'd do it."

THE INCREASING PROFESSIONALISM OF BOTH THE TOURING CIRCUIT AND the musicians was a natural development. The appeal of the music and the excitement of the small, local scenes—whether in Boston, San Francisco, Los Angeles, New York, or Detroit—simply exploded into the national consciousness. Ironically, the mass appeal and successful commercial exploitation of the hip culture would lead to the downfall of Ray Riepen, one of the first people to recognize the business opportunities it presented.

The Tea Party had actually managed to clear a profit of $16,000 in 1967, the first year it opened, and Riepen had withstood the Crosstown Bus's first challenge to his hegemony over the Boston rock scene. But by 1970 his club was in deep trouble. It wasn't a lack of interest that now threatened the Tea Party but its success. Bands and agents, seeing the growth of the national rock scene, were rapidly raising their prices, causing promoters like Howard Stein and Bill Graham to despair of the future of the business—at least as they knew it.

In a replay of the fate that had befallen Club 47 and the other Boston coffeehouses, the higher band fees were making the Tea Party, with its capacity of 750, untenable. To make matters worse, a new, larger competitor, the Ark, located in a garage behind Fenway Park's left-field wall, could handle 1,700. In an attempt to hold on, Riepen bought the controlling interest in the Ark when that club foundered, and he moved the Tea Party into the larger venue.

Riepen tried to combat the new club's losses with staff layoffs and an infusion of $50,000, but it wasn't enough. The sense of community and the word of mouth that had fueled the local scene when it was smaller had all but disappeared, steamrolled by the national success of the music. Established acts could attract bigger audiences and make more money by playing larger halls, while the sense of discovery that had fueled interest in new and developing bands during the early days of the Tea Party was no longer evident. "Kids just weren't interested anymore in listening to groups starting out," Riepen laments. "They wanted big, established names." In the last week of December 1970, the same week that Bill Graham shuttered the Fillmore West in San Francisco, the Tea Party simply failed to open, and *The Boston Globe* reported that the club had racked up losses of over $1 million.

Even after the Tea Party closed, Riepen expected to ride the wave of what he correctly perceived as a sea change in American culture and popular taste. Eight months before the club's failure, he purchased another underground property: a youth-oriented weekly newspaper.

Since the success of *Crawdaddy!*, both the music and the counterculture had proven fertile ground for publishers. After making a halfhearted attempt to buy into *Boston After Dark,* a weekly entertainment guide published by Steve Mindich, Riepen and a partner, Richard Missner, decided instead to buy into a small, student-oriented publication, *The Cambridge Phoenix,* and go head to head with *Boston After Dark.*

Although poorly run, the weekly had a promising staff, including photo editor Peter Simon, photographer Jeff Albertson, and writers Laura Shapiro, Joe Klein, Stephen Davis, and Stu Werbin. The struggling weekly welcomed Riepen's influence and Missner's money with open arms, announcing in an editorial that they were the saviors of the publication. "The staff retains editorial and esthetic autonomy," declared publisher Jeffrey Tarter and editor Joe Pilati, neither of whom lasted the year.

Riepen wanted a first-class publication and showed a real willingness to spend Missner's money. The paper was renamed *The Phoenix,* and the new owners pumped the circulation up to fifty thousand copies. Money was spent lavishly on the editorial side—or what was considered lavish in a world where two dollars was the typical payment for an album review. Riepen expanded the paper's page count and made two key hires to ensure the weekly's success: Harper Barnes, his old fraternity brother from the University of Kansas, was brought over from the *St. Louis Post-Dispatch* as managing editor. And Jon Landau became the paper's top music critic.

Though Riepen and Landau had vastly different styles, the owner firmly believed that Landau was the obvious choice for anchoring the publication's all-important music coverage. The newspaper's financial survival was tied to record and concert advertising, and Landau's presence gave its music section instant credibility with both readers and advertisers.

"Landau was always sort of in a different class from everybody else," says Bob Williams, who sold advertising for *The Phoenix.* "He was sickly but had great power of intellect and great personal power on a one-on-one. His copy, of course, his connections to the business, were in a league of their own."

Barnes was the editor, but he considered Landau the most important person on his staff. "He had so much prestige because of *Rolling Stone,*" says Barnes. "Landau was one of the few people in 1970— along with Bob Christgau—who had any credibility at all as far as rock. And he'd produced the MC5 record. Atlantic Records knew they couldn't tell him what to say, but because he was in the paper they would advertise. He was taken seriously."

The Phoenix quickly found itself locked in a bitter struggle with *Boston After Dark*. *The Phoenix* took a long view of the marketplace, expanding its editorial pages far beyond what its advertising base could reasonably be expected to support, and, under Barnes's editorial stewardship, it quickly raised its level of writing and reporting. The increased competition forced *Boston After Dark* to ratchet its coverage up a notch. Suddenly, Boston had two quality weeklies focusing on pop culture and politics.

Even more important to *The Phoenix*'s success, however, were Riepen's decisions to offer free personal classified ads and to sell the paper via long-haired street hawkers. The hawkers—who purchased copies of *The Phoenix* for five cents apiece and resold them for twenty-five cents—quickly became a fixture on the streets of Cambridge and downtown Boston and gave the paper a hip visibility. Although *Boston After Dark* eventually followed suit, it was too late. *The Phoenix* had gained the upper hand.

Once again, Riepen's instincts had proved dead-on. If the Tea Party was no longer feasible, the ultimate success of WBCN and *The Phoenix*—which were growing in size and influence with each month—seemed just a matter of time, and Riepen's future as a local power broker and wealthy businessman a lock.

That wasn't all he was interested in, though. To Riepen, his accomplishments were all the proof anyone needed to affirm his status as a cultural tastemaker and enlightened businessman and not one of the old-line "money-heads" he frequently derided. It was a distinction lost on many of his employees, in large measure because he was in a position of authority within a subculture that considered all authority suspect. But Riepen desperately craved acknowledgment of his vision. When it wasn't forthcoming, he goaded his employees mercilessly.

"Ray's basic problem," says former *Phoenix* photo editor Jeff Albertson, "is he's a guy with a one hundred seventy-five IQ walking around in a world of ninety-five IQs. He can't stand to have to reason with these people; he has no patience for the real world as it is. And because of that he offends people."

Even Harper Barnes found working with Riepen impossible. "Ray

Riepen is a classic American entrepreneur," he explained. "He is a genius at putting things together, at seeing things that other people can't see or seeing them before anyone else. But there should be a deal with Ray. He should be permitted to start anything he wants, and he should be forced at gunpoint to get out within six months. Because his problem is he keeps fucking with it."

The great tragedy was that Riepen did, in fact, have an abundance of taste and vision. He, and not the people at the Tea Party, WBCN, and *The Phoenix*—who were quickly growing to despise him—was the originator, and he was clearly excited by something more than making money. It was Riepen who had conceived of WBCN's format as "the American Revolution." It was Riepen the news junkie who insisted that WBCN subscribe to foreign news services so it could receive reporting on Vietnam from non-American sources. It was Ray Riepen's radio station that, in stark contrast to virtually every established news outlet in America, spurned the word "Vietcong" in favor of National Liberation Front because that was what the organization called itself. Although his FCC license—and his payday—hung in the balance, Riepen loved to portray WBCN as a bunch of outlaws and troublemakers. He bragged that the station's telephone system had crashed under the weight of all the taps various government agencies had placed on it. Unlike many of the other entrepreneurs who followed him into the underground, Riepen was a believer and he had an affinity and sympathy for the people spurring the political upheaval of the day. The case of Bo Burlingham was a striking example of the depth of that belief.

Through his friend Michael Ansara, who had headed the Harvard branch of Students for a Democratic Society (SDS), Burlingham had been introduced to some of the disc jockeys at WBCN. When a position as news director opened at the station, Bo applied. Burlingham impressed Riepen by suggesting WBCN could produce high-quality news reports that would include rock music and be aimed squarely at younger listeners. What Burlingham didn't tell Riepen was that he had briefly been a member of the radical Weathermen faction of SDS and that he'd been arrested for participating in the Days of Rage protests in Chicago. He had also been to Cuba in the summer of '69 as part of a delegation that included such well-known radicals as Bernadine Dohrn. But that was all in the past as far as Burlingham was concerned. When the Weathermen went underground in January of

1970, he quit the group. "I decided I didn't want to be a fugitive," says Burlingham. "I didn't want to be part of that." The Nixon administration's Justice Department, however, had other plans.

On his fourth day at WBCN, Burlingham saw a story about several of his former associates come over the Associated Press wire: FLASH! THIRTEEN WEATHERMEN INDICTED IN DETROIT.

"It comes up," recalls Burlingham, "and says, 'Attorney General John Mitchell announced today that thirteen leaders of the Weather underground have been indicted for conspiracy to violate the federal firearms and explosives act.' Okay—this is a pretty big one. So I keep reading. 'Bernie Dohrn, Mark Rudd, Bill Ayers . . .' Okay, I knew they were all underground."

The list of those indicted continued, first with several others Burlingham knew were also underground and then with a few that he was certain were not members of the underground. But he wasn't prepared for his shock when the last name on the list proved to be Robert Burlingham.

Gripped by fear, he tore the news flash off the Teletype and hurried into the next room and showed the wire report to disc jockey Charles Laquidara.

"Charles," said Burlingham, "take a look at this."

"Not now," said Laquidara.

"*Charles,* I think you better take a look at this."

Laquidara took the news report. "Oh, shit!" he said. "What are we going to do for a news director now?"

"Charles, I have to say that's not my foremost thought," said Burlingham.

Unsure where to turn, Burlingham got lucky when Michael Ansara showed up at the station and promised to help him find a lawyer. Riding around Boston on Ansara's motorcycle, they stopped to call Riepen. "I felt bad," recalled Burlingham. "He'd given me this chance and here, four days on the job, his news director is the subject of a federal indictment."

When Burlingham showed Riepen the news story, the owner's reaction was less than uplifting: "Shit! They're gonna throw the book at you! That Panther Twenty-one case in New York? That's nothing compared to this!" Yet Riepen called Burlingham's mother to recommend a lawyer.

The day after the indictment was handed up, Burlingham turned himself in, one of the few defendants in the case to do so. After posting a high bail and agreeing to check in with the U.S. Attorney's office every day, Burlingham went to see Riepen again.

"I got a little problem here, Bo," Riepen said, explaining that his status could effect the station's license. "I'd love to keep you on, but I've got my board of directors and the Federal Communications Commission to think about."

Burlingham knew he was in no position to argue—he was grateful that Riepen was still talking to him. And he was subsequently surprised when his boss offered him a new job as a writer at *The Phoenix.* "He was a real gentleman about the whole thing," says Burlingham, who gladly accepted the offer and began writing under his wife, Lisa's, name.

Riepen's support provided Burlingham with a career. It was also a side of Riepen that few of his employees ever acknowledged. They preferred to ignore his more subtle and prescient accomplishments in favor of branding him a crass exploiter. And although he had empowered the staffs at WBCN and *The Phoenix,* they quickly came to view him as the enemy.

Riepen's antagonistic behavior was in stark contrast to the pampering disc jockeys and journalists were getting from the labels. The pioneering efforts of promotion men like Mario Medious had paid off handsomely, and, by the summer of 1970, the record companies were the hip sugar daddies of the underground. Unlike Riepen, they could tolerate the most outlandish behavior; they simply wanted to get their records played.

That June, several record companies proved how eager they were to gain access to underground tastemakers regardless of circumstances when they helped underwrite the First Gathering of the Alternative Media Project, a four-day conclave of two thousand underground media types held on the campus of Goddard College in Plainfield, Vermont. The brainchild of Larry Yurdin, a Goddard graduate and college instructor who had also started alternative rock formats for radio stations in Montreal and New Jersey, the Project drew representatives from three hundred stations as well as rock writers, magazine editors, and others from all over the country. To help defray costs, Atlantic Records ponied up $2,500. In return, the label was able to showcase several acts, including J. Geils.

The Project quickly degenerated into a factional, acid-soaked free-for-all. Speakers were shouted down, and panels dissolved under the assault of various radical and special interest groups. Bob Fass, the host of a popular music and talk show on New York's listener-sponsored leftist radio station WBAI, lost control of a panel on free enterprise to a radical caucus that embraced Jerry Rubin and members of various groups representing gay liberation, women's lib, and the Liberation News Service. Fass's unsuccessful attempt to hold the floor ended when he was carried bodily out of the meeting. Another panel on comics and the alternative media was disrupted by two couples having sex in the back of the room. Afterward, the couples moved to the front of the room, where they elaborated on their agenda.

"Meetings are so stupid," opined a still-naked eighteen-year-old named Mother Earth. "If people would ball more, everything would be cool." Her message was duly recorded by *Rolling Stone,* which reported that the protester then "went to the bathroom to wipe off."

The collapse of the Project's agenda was of no concern to the record companies. Stu Werbin, who covered the conference for *Rolling Stone,* wasn't surprised to run into his buddy, the ubiquitous Mario Medious, buying pizzas, lasagna, french fries, and chocolate ice-cream sundaes for disc jockeys and Project keynote speaker Baba Ram Dass. Observes Werbin: "The record companies were willing to try anything."

The same could not be said for Riepen, who certainly wasn't going to let his businesses get hijacked by loose cannons. But rather than woo his employees, he antagonized them. WBCN kept a hot line, an unlisted phone number Riepen used whenever he wanted to speak with the disc jockey on the air. One Sunday afternoon he called John Brodie, who was new to the station, and excoriated him for playing too many songs with drum solos. Terrified, Brodie immediately switched to something Riepen thought more appropriate.

The incident likely would have ended there had the popular music director Charles Laquidara not been the DJ slated to follow Brodie. Having spent the weekend in Rhode Island taking LSD with a bunch of friends, Laquidara arrived at the station around 5:00 P.M., not quite fully recovered from the effects of either trip. He was shocked to find Brodie looking as if he'd been crying.

"Hey, man," Laquidara asked, "what the fuck is going on?"

"Ray Riepen was with his friends, and he called me on the hot line and told me that I was a hot dog," Brodie said. "He told me that nobody wants to hear drum solos on a Sunday afternoon and I should learn radio or get the fuck out of the business."

Less of a politico than many of the other staffers at WBCN, Laquidara nonetheless delighted in being an on-air brat. In Riepen, he had an obvious target and wasn't going to miss the opportunity to make him pay.

"Y'know," Laquidara said as he opened WBCN's microphone to begin his show, "we got this boss, Ray Riepen. This guy really thinks he's a hot shot. He gets his friends together and they all get drunk and he tries to impress them because he's got this radio station. He called John Brodie, the guy you just heard on the air, and told him that nobody wants to hear a drum solo on a Sunday afternoon. What do you guys think? Gimme a call." Laquidara then played every record he could think of with a drum solo, including "Sing Sing Sing" by Benny Goodman.

Riepen rose to the bait, summoning Laquidara to the station the next morning and asking him to quit. "I can't fire you because of the fucking people here," Riepen admitted, "but I'd like you to resign."

Laquidara refused. "I didn't do anything wrong," he said. "You're the guy who called Brodie. You resign."

It was a standoff—and an indication that Riepen was losing control of the station. As far as he was concerned, his caustic call to Brodie was just part of a larger attempt to make WBCN a viable alternative business. Along with the addition of the news department, Riepen had begun tightening the station's music format. WBCN's free-form style was a hit with listeners, but it had failed to make significant commercial inroads among mainstream advertisers. Looking for a middle ground, Riepen had hired a program director and begun to fire disc jockeys deemed too far out of the mainstream.

As part of the new regimen, Pete Wolf's show had been severely curtailed, a move that enraged him. Walking into the studio for what would prove to be his final show, Wolf cued up "Think" by the Five

Royales, pulled his records from the station's library, and walked out. When the single ended, the only sound to be heard over WBCN was the needle clicking over and over again in the record's last, blank groove.

But Riepen's troubles began in earnest when he hired Arnie "Woo Woo" Ginsberg, Boston's famous Top 40 disc jockey, as station manager. Ginsberg wasn't given a show; Riepen hoped his presence would make the station more professional and send a message to any advertisers who might still be nervous about it. Instead, the staff saw Ginsberg as another example of how Riepen was going to sell them out.

"I hired Woo Woo Ginsberg because he was a symbol of our triumph over Top Forty," says Riepen. "He was *the* only famous guy in Boston radio. A bunch of hippies hired the biggest name in radio in New England! And these fucking idiots said, 'Well, Woo Woo Ginsberg isn't the image we want to present.' I said, 'No, the image we want to present is over the air—it's you guys. Let me figure out how to get into the agencies.' They thought it was unhip and tragic. I thought it was fabulous. We'd finally crushed AM."

Advertising had become a particularly sore point between Riepen and the staff. Although it was Riepen who had initially limited the number of commercials on the station, they constantly and unfairly portrayed him as the enemy rather than as an ally and engaged him in ongoing battles over which ads they would accept. On other commercial stations, disc jockeys simply read whatever advertising copy was put in front of them. But WBCN was supposed to be about community and consciousness.

"The line was always changing," remembers Werbin. "Ray would agree, 'No ads for the army.' And then someone would object to saying 'we' in another commercial. Looking back twenty years, the issues seem trivial because it was really a control issue. But it was always fought on political and ideological terms, which couldn't happen today."

Riepen grew increasingly irate. "I had disc jockeys—fucking idiots who had their noses full of coke every time Mario would come up from Atlantic—who wouldn't know hip if it hit them in the nose, trying to play like I was some moneygrubbing fucking guy," he still fumes. By the end of 1970, when the Tea Party was struggling, Riepen was also fighting a full-blown war with his station's staff, and Charles Laquidara in particular.

The knockout blow was the staff's decision to unionize, a move that, while cloaked in ideology, was once again simply a power struggle. Led by Danny Schecter, who replaced Burlingham as news director and became shop steward, WBCN's employees aligned themselves with the United Electrical and Radio Machine Workers Union, an organization that had allegedly been tossed out of the AFL-CIO for being communist. Unlike most broadcast properties, where technical staff, on-air performers, and reporters all belonged to different unions, United Electrical accepted everyone, including the sales force. "It was like an auto plant," says Schecter. "We were all in the same union and supported each other in negotiations."

Contract bargaining began. But Riepen quickly came to believe that the union's goal was never to reach an agreement. Under the National Labor Relations Board's guidelines, Riepen could not fire anyone during negotiations. "They wanted to keep this going in perpetuity," says Riepen, a tactic confirmed by former union members. Riepen had been outmaneuvered. He had no recourse left except to sell his interest in WBCN, a move that left him shattered. "I invented that fucking format, and I've got guys talking to me about compromising the integrity of the radio station. I didn't even argue with them. Because I was off doing the newspaper instead of cultivating those guys, I was a businessman all of a sudden. I wasn't a businessman. I was the guy who invented the sixties."

In his defeat, some at WBCN had sympathy for him. "In the end," says Joe Rogers, "I think he underestimated that people would take his role so seriously and that they would do lots of things to get rid of him. That surprised him. Ray made himself such an easy and obvious target. You want to yell against the accessible target who isn't all that scary. That was Ray."

Riepen sold his interest in WBCN for $220,000. But his mistakes there had served to embitter rather than enlighten him. He began to vent his spleen at the *Phoenix* staff, and it wasn't long before they, too, were envisioning how much nicer life could be without him.

In May of '71, just as the paper was about to break even, Missner pulled the rug out from Riepen by resigning as publisher and threatening to sue *The Phoenix* for repayment of the $350,000 he'd invested.

Led by Riepen's friend and hand-picked editor Harper Barnes, twenty-three of the paper's thirty staffers signed a petition supporting Missner and backed up their action by continuing to put out the paper without pay. "I betrayed him," Barnes admits. "But in the end Ray becomes *so* overbearing that you'll do anything to get him off your back."

The combined loss of staff and financing was more than Riepen could combat. On May 17 he resigned as copublisher of *The Phoenix*, selling his 50 percent share in the paper to Missner for a paltry $100,000. Although he planned to finance a September '71 concert by the Rolling Stones at the Boston Garden in association with Don Law, he left Boston in defeat.

Law, like everyone else, had bristled under Riepen's management and didn't miss the opportunity presented by his departure to begin working with Barsalona and other agents on his own. "I had lunch with Don Law about the time that everything was coming apart," recalls Barnes. "He was practically in tears, which is not like Don. He said, 'I don't know what the hell to do. I owe this man a great deal, but he's just making me crazy. I can't run the business.' "

Law set up his own concert company, one that would succeed because he had the cool efficiency to capitalize on the connections he'd made through Riepen and wasn't interested in any of the counterculture baggage that came with it.

In the coming years, WBCN, *The Phoenix,* and the Boston concert business would each continue to grow and enrich their owners—but not Ray Riepen. He went to California, eventually taking some of the money he'd made selling out his positions in WBCN and *The Phoenix* and buying a crossroads town in the Sequoia National Forest, which he renamed Camp Wishon.

In the wake of his departure, his antagonists gloated. "The guy would've been worth millions," says his chief tormentor, Charles Laquidara. "Ray Riepen had *The Phoenix,* the Boston Tea Party, WBCN. He had the world by the balls. I would've committed suicide."

By the nineties Riepen was practicing law back in Kansas and presiding as a circuit court judge. And WBCN had become everything it once hated. As the rock business grew more and more structured, the station's format became increasingly limited. In the late seventies a procession of professional program directors ransacked the station's formidable library of the blues, jazz, and folk records that had formed such an important part of the programming. "They wanted to get a white rock sound," says original WBCN disc jockey Joe Rogers. Soon after tossing out Ray Riepen, the visionary with a track record for negotiating the middle ground between bohemia and business, WBCN's supposedly principled staff quickly abandoned "the American Revolution." Riepen's most cherished notion, that the underground would empower a new generation of socially and politically enlightened businessmen, had not proven practical. WBCN was just another radio station—and not a very good one.

Laquidara stayed on, riding his childish persona to local celebrity. In the mid-eighties, while negotiating a richer contract, he freely relinquished the clause that limited the number of commercials in his show to eight an hour. Like virtually every other disc jockey on FM rock radio, Laquidara now airs whatever commercials he's told to, including U.S. Army ads. "We had a motto that said, 'Ugly radio is dead.' We are now ugly radio," he admits. "I have some politics left," he maintains, "but that's over. I don't want to be too hard on myself and say I sold out because had I not compromised I wouldn't be working today. I sort of settled for the golden handcuffs." If he was willing to forgive himself for wanting to make money, Laquidara remained in no hurry to see Riepen get credit for his role in WBCN.

In April of 1993, WBCN hosted a reunion and party to mark its twenty-fifth anniversary as a rock station. Infinity Broadcasting, which had made the station the cornerstone of a national radio network of forty-six stations and syndicated disc jockey Howard Stern, didn't even bother to send an executive from its home office.* Instead, WBCN founder T. Mitchell Hastings, under whose aegis the station had been a bankrupt classical outlet, spoke.

Bo Burlingham, the station's onetime fugitive, was also there. His conspiracy charges had been dropped by the government in 1973, and—in a delicious irony that indicated just how much the times had changed—the former Weatherman was now an editor at *Inc.*, a business magazine for entrepreneurs. Recalling how Riepen had stood by him, Burlingham was horrified to hear WBCN's history being rewrit-

*Three years later, in April 1996, Infinity would move Laquidara to another of their Boston stations, WZLX, in order to air Stern's show in his WBCN morning slot.

ten. Neither Riepen nor his "American Revolution"—the belief that the new culture should redefine business and not the other way around—was even mentioned. WBCN, having become the opposite of what it had aspired to be, had no interest in celebrating its true past as a challenger to the status quo. It *was* the status quo. "Hastings kind of got up there and took credit for the founding of WBCN," says Burlingham. "Something he basically had nothing to do with."

Sitting in the audience with Laquidara, who knew the truth, Burlingham shook his head. "That's really gross," he said. "To let him get up there and do that. You know damn well that Ray Riepen did it."

"Ah, well," said Boston's premier disc jockey. "Ray's not here."

Jon Landau, *Rolling Stone* critic and aspiring record producer, whose passion for music was matched by a razor-sharp intellect and a consuming desire to succeed in the record business. "He figured out he was never going to be the best in the country at the art," said one friend, "and he became the best at the money." Boston, May 1971. MICHAEL DOBO

Jon Landau *(left)* with one of his "rabbis," Capricorn Records founder Phil Walden, in August 1971. He encouraged Walden to sign guitarist Duane Allman, who created Capricorn's most successful and important group, the Allman Brothers Band. In return, Walden tutored Landau in the dollars-and-cents realities of the business. MICHAEL DOBO

Painter-turned-singer Peter Wolf. His obsession with music made him a key player in Boston's emerging rock scene as WBCN's jive-talking, late-night disc jockey the Woofa Goofa, and as the vocalist for the J. Geils Band. "There was a feeling of moving away from bubblegum pop—AM radio and that sort of thing," recalls Wolf. "It was musicology." MICHAEL DOBO

The first mogul of the underground, Ray Riepen, creator and owner of the Boston Tea Party, underground rock station WBCN, and *The Phoenix*. A lawyer with an affinity for the emerging culture, he negotiated the no-man's-land between bohemia and business. His fall cheered his detractors, but signaled the end of the Boston underground's heyday. To Riepen, it was an adventure; to his successors, it was strictly business. MICHAEL DOBO

Don Law. As manager of the Boston Tea Party, Law succeeded Ray Riepen as the city's premier rock promoter. By the eighties, his dominance of the New England concert business had made him a wealthy man—and led the Massachusetts attorney general to charge four of Law's companies with antitrust violations. Law denied the charges in a settlement. MICHAEL DOBO

The Big M: Mario Medious *(left)*, and his protégé, Paul Ahern, at a WBCN softball game. A bookkeeper for Atlantic Records, Medious was pressed into service as the label's first FM promotion man and became their high-stepping, trash-talking goodwill ambassador to the underground. Ahern was later head of promotion for David Geffen's Asylum Records and a silent advisor to the Eagles. MICHAEL DOBO

Bob Dylan *(right)* with Pete Seeger in 1963. Dylan's appearance at the Newport Folk Festival that summer made him the shining star of the folk movement. Two years later, when he used the festival to premier his new electric rock band, Seeger threatened to take an ax to the power line. JIM MARSHALL

Bob Dylan and Robbie Robertson performing in San Francisco during Dylan's first electric tour. Roundly booed by the folk faithful everywhere he went, Dylan never retreated from his decision to play rock. JIM MARSHALL

Albert Grossman, who managed Bob Dylan, Janis Joplin, the Band, Peter, Paul and Mary, and others, near his home in Bearsville, New York. Grossman was the towering prototype for all subsequent rock managers but an enigma to his clients, who called him Cumulus Nimbus. "It was great, gray, and august," said one. "But when you went up to touch it, it wasn't there." JIM MARSHALL

Mo Ostin *(right)* and Frank Sinatra, at the offices of Warner Bros./Reprise Records in Burbank, California. Sinatra's decision in 1960 to hire Ostin, a former comptroller for the jazz label Verve, as head of Reprise, mystified everyone—including Ostin. "It was an idiotic move," the executive later said. "I absolutely was not qualified to do the job." COURTESY OF WARNER BROS. RECORDS

Mo Ostin with George Harrison, shortly after the ex-Beatle signed to Warner Bros. in 1976. The label's willingness to grant rock performers creative carte blanche was a key part of Ostin's success. Said one competing label head: "Anytime anyone gets out of a record contract now, they come to Warner Bros." COURTESY OF WARNER BROS. RECORDS

Janis Joplin and producer Paul Rothchild at Hollywood's Landmark Hotel in the summer of 1970. Rothchild, who began his career by recording a bluegrass band in a Harvard University library, played an enormous role in steering Elektra Records into the rock business. Best known for his work with the Doors, he produced Joplin's final album, *Pearl*. She died at the Landmark of a heroin overdose on October 4, 1970.
FROM THE COLLECTION OF DAN ROTHCHILD

During the early seventies, David Geffen and Elliot Roberts became
the preeminent rock managers through their association with Crosby,
Stills, Nash and Young, Joni Mitchell, Jackson Browne, the Eagles,
America, and others. Shown at the Geffen-Roberts Sunset Boulevard
office, *left to right*, Elliot Roberts, Graham Nash, David Geffen, and
Neil Young. HENRY DILTZ

Neil Young, relaxing in Los
Angeles during rehearsals for
the album *Time Fades Away*,
June 1973. His unshakable
devotion to his muse sometimes frustrated record
executives and disappointed
fans but ultimately made
him the most admired artist
among his peers. Remarked
one: "Neil Young thinks he is
the modern Shakespeare."
JOEL BERNSTEIN

"Kick out the jams—or get off the stage." The MC5 in concert in 1969. *Left to right,* Wayne Kramer, Rob Tyner, drummer Dennis Thompson, and Fred "Sonic" Smith. The band's espousal of radical politics put them in lockstep with the underground, but at odds with the increasingly professional record business. An artistic touchstone for the punk movement of the seventies, the MC5 paid dearly for their dreams. LENI SINCLAIR

When worlds collide: John Sinclair *(left)*, the poet, political agitator, marijuana activist, rock and roll propagandist, and manager of the MC5, with Jon Landau, who produced the band's album *Back in the USA*. Landau pushed them to focus on commercial success. With his prodding, the group dumped Sinclair as their manager. LENI SINCLAIR

Guitarist Joe Walsh of the Eagles at a 1975 Los Angeles concert. At the time, the band and their manager, Irving Azoff, were in a protracted battle with David Geffen to wrest back control of their music publishing, worth tens of millions of dollars. BARRY SCHULTZ/RETNA

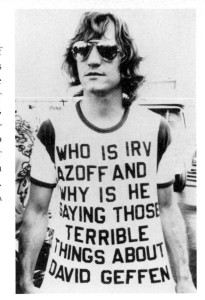

Don Henley (left) and Glenn Frey (center) of the Eagles confer with Azoff following a 1980 concert. The self-described "governing body" of the Eagles, the two ambitious musicians found a no-holds-barred advocate in Azoff, whose Frontline Management supplanted Geffen-Roberts as the leading rock management company with a roster that included the Eagles, Boz Scaggs, Steely Dan, Chicago, and Styx. HENRY DILTZ

Before the fall. The massive success of Peter Frampton's 1976 album *Frampton Comes Alive!* was the culmination of years of touring—an approach to rock marketing refined by manager Dee Anthony and booking agent Frank Barsalona. Frampton's crash would soon demonstrate the limits of that philosophy. Celebrating after Frampton's March 1976 show at Madison Square Garden are, *from left,* promoter Bill Graham, disc jockey Scott Muni, Anthony, and Frampton. WENDI LOMBARDI

At his best, Bruce Springsteen provided his fans with a chance to celebrate
rock and roll as the best part of themselves. Performing on the *Darkness on the
Edge of Town* tour, Seattle, December 1978, *from left,* Clarence Clemons, Max
Weinberg, Springsteen, Garry Tallent, Roy Bittan, and Miami Steve Van Zandt.
REX RYSTEDT

Onstage at Madison Square
Garden for the close of the
Tunnel of Love Express tour,
Jon Landau grabs a guitar
and allows himself to enjoy a
rare moment in the spot-
light. Manager, producer,
teacher, mentor, and friend
to Springsteen, he played an
enormous role in shaping
the singer's work and career.
"Jon would manipulate for
the good of the art," said
one associate. "Or for what
he felt was the good of it."
DEBRA ROTHENBERG

BOOK TWO

The
Mansion
on the
Hill

There are two reasons why a man does anything.
There's a good reason and there's the real reason.

—John Pierpont Morgan

10

Rock and Roll
Future

RAY RIEPEN'S DEPARTURE FROM BOSTON MARKED A TURNING POINT. His personal shortcomings had sped his demise, but when he proved the business potential of the underground culture his fate was sealed. Riepen's affinity for its politics and goals had led him to recognize the scene's validity. But once he had demonstrated to others that there was money to be made, appreciating the culture became irrelevant. It was a business, and the people who replaced him were concerned with running it efficiently.

As at WBCN, Riepen's forced exit from *The Phoenix* did not cure the weekly's problems. It was soon apparent that Richard Missner, Riepen's former partner, was having trouble making a go of it on his own. Missner turned to Larry Durocher, a savvy aviation executive turned business consultant who had helped devise the strategy to oust Riepen from the paper. Although he had scant publishing experience, Durocher, like Riepen, had an eye for opportunity and quickly agreed to become the paper's publisher. "When I went to *The Phoenix*, it was an idea whose time had come," says Durocher.

A political liberal, Durocher reveled in the freedom and sense of possibilities that *The Phoenix* represented. But unlike Riepen, who

211

fancied himself an enlightened capitalist, Durocher was an unrepen-
tant hustler. He saw the paper's possibilities in the bright light of opportunity rather than the warm glow of ideology.

"*The Phoenix* was a way for me to collect the berries," he says. "You
go into the forest and you'll find that any higher order of ape will always collect the berries in the shade. And they climb trees. The reason
they live in the trees is because shit falls down."

As the paper's manager, Durocher immediately did what Riepen
couldn't. He gave the editor, Harper Barnes, a free hand. "All I did
was let go of everybody," Durocher remembers, "like a sailboat that
had been reined in too close to the wind and was about to tip over. I
figured just let it go forward and the bad things will stop happening.
And that's what happened. While I was trying to do that—which was
essentially nothing—it became this enormous success." After Riepen's
taunts, having a hands-off administrator was a godsend to the staff,
which was now doing some of its best work.

Durocher's unfettered ambition was a revelation to the staff. "Larry
is one of the most thoroughly Machiavellian dudes I've ever known,"
says former *Phoenix* photo editor Jeff Albertson. "He was about as far
from an innocent as I could imagine. But you couldn't get mad at
Larry; it was like getting mad at a snake."

No one was more impressed by Durocher than Jon Landau, who
quickly cultivated a close friendship with the crafty publisher. In a young
business being invented by a small circle of ambitious and insightful businessmen riding the roller-coaster of the era's social convulsions, Landau
recognized the importance of picking the best teachers. He had already
accrued a small group of older, successful record men, including Jerry
Wexler and Phil Walden, whom he called his "rabbis," and his relationships with those men were both personal and practical. With his yen to
succeed, Landau hadn't failed to notice that both knowledge and an
entry into the business often grew out of having the right mentor, and
his rabbis offered both a buddy system and a tutorial. Durocher became
Landau's newest and most influential buddy and rabbi.

Durocher's contribution to Landau's education was unique. He had
virtually no interest in the music industry. But when it came to the ins
and outs of conducting business, the Boston wheeler-dealer could be
a heady tutor. In Landau, he recognized a kindred soul and found an
eager and engaging acolyte. Landau admired him for what he was, an

unapologetic player who kept a bemused but always acquisitive eye on the prize. Says Harper Barnes: "Jon was obviously not going to be a rock critic, and he always had a kind of mixture of art and money. He figured out he was never going to be the best in the country at art. So he became the best at the money."

"[Durocher] and Jon would get on the phone for four or five hours sometimes," recalls one writer. "These huge, long conversations. And I think Jon's thoughts were a little more innocent before he met up with this guy. They would sit around and just . . . scheme. For a non-music businessperson, he was the person Jon felt the most affinity for and understanding of."

The brand of hard-nosed business savvy that Durocher brought to the table was in short supply around *The Phoenix*. Despite Durocher's steadying influence on the day-to-day operation, an undeclared war still simmered between the young staff and Richard Missner for control of *The Phoenix*. As at WBCN, it was a complex battle: part ideology, part ego. And just as the radio station's staff had bridled under Riepen's attempts to solidify WBCN's business operations, the *Phoenix* employees were enraged when they learned that Missner planned major editorial changes.

The break came in May of '72, when Missner named himself editor in chief and fired Harper Barnes. Durocher, who supported Barnes, was also dismissed. In response, the staff presented Missner with three demands: reinstatement of Barnes, recognition of a new *Phoenix* Employees Union, and the formation of an editorial board "to protect the editorial product from the publisher's whim." Missner rejected the demands out of hand and, almost a year to the day after Barnes and the *Phoenix* staff had sided with him in the ouster of Riepen, found himself in the middle of a strike.

Durocher counseled the staff, which had thrown up pickets around the paper's office and was pressuring advertisers to withdraw support from a scab-written edition of *The Phoenix*. "I went and talked to Harper," recalls Durocher. "And I got Landau. Landau, Harper, and I sat down." Durocher wanted to find a settlement that would allow Missner to maintain face while placating the union.

With Landau acting as the go-between, Missner said he would agree to the staff's demands in return for assurances that they would work on the next issue and stop harassing the scabs. Landau arranged a meeting between Barnes and Missner in a hotel room in Harvard Square. Durocher was not at the meeting, but by leaving a telephone in the room off the hook with him on the line, Landau was able to take his cues. "Landau is talking to me during the meeting, telling me everything that's being said," Durocher says. "Harper made this wonderful speech, everything just went perfect. There's an agreement from the lawyers, it's a very simple thing. And Richard says, 'Okay, let's the two of us sign it right here in front of everybody, Harper. And let's all go back to work.' And Harper says, 'No, Richard. You read it and bring it over to work this afternoon, we'll all be there.' And Landau is freaking out! *Mistake! Big mistake!*"

Landau's fears proved well founded. Missner failed to appear at the *Phoenix* office that afternoon, sending word that the deal was off. Having played the role of conciliator, urging the angry staff to sit down with Missner, Landau was now panic-stricken that they would turn on him. He called Durocher in a frenzy. "Landau was really scared that the staff was going to kill him," says Durocher.

Indeed, the labor confrontation took a violent turn the following day when a group of twenty strikers, including Barnes, broke into the paper's production offices. "It got real ugly," admits Barnes, who was among several strikers later charged by a scab worker with assault and battery. "I did some things for which I'll forever be embarrassed."

Although Missner managed to get the paper out, support for the strikers was strong, and, by the following week, the publisher capitulated. But things had gone too far to save Barnes. At 4:30 A.M. on May 23 an exhausted Landau emerged with a signed deal that included only a six-month settlement contract as a contributing writer for Barnes. As Barnes, Durocher, and Landau saw it, it was a sacrifice that had to be made. "I finally agreed to go away, and Richard rehired everyone else," says Barnes.

Emotionally spent, Landau broke down in tears as he drove home from the meeting. And he penned an equally misty-eyed farewell to Barnes for the poststrike issue of *The Phoenix*. "I know that if I write for this paper for another twenty-five years," wrote Landau, "when someone asks me what it is like to work at *The Phoenix*, I'll tell him straight out the same thing I felt last Tuesday: 'You should have been there when Harper Barnes was the editor.' "

Landau barely hung around the paper another twenty-five days, let alone twenty-five years. Instead, he moved to New York and concentrated on working for *Rolling Stone*. Barnes didn't see much of Landau or Durocher until October, when they were reunited in Manhasset, New York, for Landau's wedding to writer Janet Maslin. And despite Landau's heartfelt tribute to him in *The Phoenix*, their relationship was winding down.

It was a familiar scenario for Landau. Invariably, he would lose contact with friends when their career paths no longer crossed, a disengagement that frequently left a bad aftertaste.

"Being social is work for Jon," Jeff Albertson says bitterly. "When Jon is social it's not because he wants to do it or is comfortable with it, he does it because he's trying to accomplish something. He's incapable of the kind of give-and-take and trust that's involved in a friendship. He always has something behind what he's doing." Says Durocher, "Jon is one of these people who doesn't form a lot of relationships. Most of the relationships are 'I just spent twenty minutes with you and you just spent twenty minutes with me and we're even.' A lot of his life is like that."

Durocher, however, continued to figure in Jon's life. With *Rolling Stone* yet to reach a firm financial footing, Landau recommended his rabbi to Jann Wenner as a business consultant. Within a few months, Durocher was publisher of *Rolling Stone*.

●

DUROCHER'S UNAPOLOGETIC OPPORTUNISM AND EGO PLAYED A HUGE ROLE in shaping Landau's business persona. But while the relationship fortified his desire to find a place for himself in the business, he remained unsure of his next move. There wasn't much more he could do as a rock critic, and his career as a record producer was a washout. Landau began to turn the laserlike focus Durocher had admired on film criticism. As a career move, it would prove a dead end, but along the way he found something as important to his future success as any lesson Larry Durocher had to offer: an artistic vision.

As he had with rock and roll, Landau quickly developed an encyclopedic knowledge of film history. Both with Maslin and on his own, he began attending screenings virtually every day and never left home without a copy of *The American Cinema*, Andrew Sarris's touchstone of modern film criticism. After just a few months, he was confident enough to begin writing in-depth film reviews for *Rolling Stone,* assuming the new custom-built title of Record and Film Editor.

Though smitten with the medium, Landau was never able to achieve the same clarity and originality in film reviews that marked his rock criticism. His assessments were sometimes way off the mark. He panned *The Godfather,* for example, and criticized the "thinness" of director Francis Ford Coppola's moviemaking. The biggest problem, however, was his inability to trust his own intuitive judgment. He seemed burdened by the weight of all the theory and history he had so diligently absorbed. While his best music reviews were marked by the delight of discovery, Landau's overwrought film critiques had all the joy and flow of a college term paper. As a discipline, rock and roll criticism had been a clean slate with no preset rules. Now, attempting to fit into an established field delineated by articulate critic/theorists like Sarris and Pauline Kael, Landau brought nothing original and, surprisingly, little that was insightful to the game.

Ironically, while *Rolling Stone*'s readers weren't benefiting from Landau's stint as a film critic, he was. Films and the viewpoints of several directors would play a profound role in shaping decisions he would make later when he returned to record producing. Landau was particularly taken with the young filmmaker John Milius, whom he had met while on assignment for *Rolling Stone.*

One of the most successful screenwriters of the late sixties and early seventies, Milius would cowrite Francis Ford Coppola's *Apocalypse Now* and had already scripted *Magnum Force, Jeremiah Johnson,* and *The Life and Times of Judge Roy Bean.* When Landau hooked up with him in the summer of '73, the twenty-nine-year-old screenwriter had just directed his first feature, *Dillinger.*

In Milius's work, Landau recognized the grandeur and legend of that most appealing and romantic of all American characters: the Outsider, the man who follows his own code. Regardless of whether they were outlaws or G-men, Landau saw Milius's protagonists as philosophical brothers, "all of them loners, people who live outside the law, creating their own way of life, and willing to pay the price for having done so." The reward for such a life, according to Milius, was to become one with the American landscape, to leave a footprint and so become inseparable from the history and legend of the land.

Milius touted legendary director John Ford, whose Western epics sought to distill the American experience. When he told Landau that Ford's *The Searchers* was his favorite film—and made special mention of several of the director's other pictures, including *How Green Was My Valley* and *My Darling Clementine*—the critic paid heed. A scant three months after interviewing Milius, Landau emerged as a full-blown Ford devotee. He offered up an in-depth appreciation of the director and Milius's favorite pictures in particular—now presented as Landau's favorites—in *Rolling Stone*.

In the films of Ford, Landau embraced a vision of the romantic hero not unlike the one espoused by Milius: "lonely men with egos so big they could make the superhuman sacrifices on which the lives and futures of lesser characters depended." Invariably, Landau found himself attracted to the films and scenes that mythologized the unrequited nature of heroic action, the loneliness that belief in one's actions can bring. None moved him more than *The Searchers* with its complex and ambiguous story of Ethan Edwards.

As played by John Wayne, Edwards is an arch figure, a former soldier and fugitive who dedicates years to tracking a group of Comanches who have carried off a young white woman and inculcated her into their society. Edwards sets out to "save" the woman from the disgrace of having joined the Indians by killing her, but ultimately returns her to her white family. Yet his triumph over his own prejudices and reacceptance of the woman earns him no redemption. Watching *The Searchers*, Landau saw Edwards as the classic, tragic American hero, "left as we found him: homeless, without family or roots, shut out from any human contact and condemned as a fugitive to wander the wilderness, this time in search of whatever solace without purpose he can find there."

Landau also found that the dramatic core and attraction of Ford's work "often rested in an individual's testing himself against a society in transition." For a young, ambitious, and creative man coming of age in the turmoil of the early 1970s, it was an appealing and resonant prescription for heroism. And it was the romantic vision Landau returned to two years later when he shaped the work and career of a rock star.

THE HARD-WON PEACE AT *THE PHOENIX* WAS SHATTERED JUST TWO MONTHS after the strike when Richard Missner quickly and quietly sold the paper to Stephen Mindich, the publisher of the rival *Boston After Dark,* for $320,000.

It was a move made in management heaven. In one stroke, Missner had gotten rid of his troublesome staff and out of publishing; Mindich, who had been locked in a life-or-death struggle for control of a market that—while potentially lucrative—could be expected to support only one weekly, now had an open field. Just as important, he had the valuable and hipper *Phoenix* name. At a press conference to announce the sale, Mindich revealed that *Boston After Dark* would cease publication and be replaced by *The Boston Phoenix,* although he was really just switching mastheads by opting to use the newly acquired name on his own weekly with the *Boston After Dark* staff. Mindich left no doubt as to what that meant for the former staff of *The Phoenix.* "Missner's employees," he said at the press conference, "are Missner's responsibility."

If Ray Riepen and Richard Missner had been disliked within the underground culture, the approval rating for Stephen Mindich was even lower. "He was just a jerk," says the normally reserved Don Law, who now had little choice but to advertise his concerts in Mindich's paper. "He had a terrible tendency to get drunk, try and pick up women, and get into fistfights." Not surprisingly, Larry Durocher liked him. "I got a kick out of him," he says. "He's not only a guy who'd take the pennies off a dead man's eyes, he'd take the flowers right off the grave. If you look up the word 'survivor' in *Webster's Unabridged Dictionary*—the big eighty-pounder—you will see a woodcut drawing of Stephen Mindich."

Missner's sale of *The Phoenix* did not, however, prove to be the knockout punch in either his battle with the staff or Mindich's drive to gain control of the market. Instead, it was to be the last rallying point for a true alternative press in Boston. Stunned and angered by what was perceived as a bad-faith sellout, Chuck Feger, head of the *Phoenix* Employees Union, stood up at the press conference and vowed that the staff would publish its own paper, to be called *The Real Phoenix.*

Although Mindich was able to prevent use of the paper's name, Feger and his coworkers proved as good as their word. On August 2, the entire former staff of *The Phoenix,* with the exception of one writer, George Kimball, who had defected to Mindich, put out the first issue of *The Real Paper.* For $320,000, all Mindich had done was shake off Missner.

Having grown directly out of the union wars at *The Phoenix*, the new staff-owned paper was conceived as a moneymaking collective, an "antibusiness business," as two of its staffers later dubbed it. Fueled by a unique mix of personal animosity toward Missner and Mindich and a belief—not unlike Ray Riepen's—that the real legacy of the underground would prove to be a new form of enlightened, cooperative capitalism, many on the staff of *The Real Paper* viewed themselves as warriors in a political and class struggle. Each of the thirty-four founders received one hundred shares of stock and equal voting rights, with the slots of publisher, editor in chief, and advertising director filled by election. Only staff members could be stockholders, and, according to the company's bylaws, they had to sell their stock back to the company if they left to prevent creating a majority shareholder. The wage scale was both modest and narrow. The publisher, at $175 a week, was the highest-paid staffer, while the receptionist made $110.

After Jeff Albertson secured $1,000 for an ad from Underground Camera, Bob Williams, the new advertising director for *The Real Paper*, honed in on the music business. "The [music] industry started *The Real Paper*," he says. "Two outfits funded it in an instant. One was Tech Hi-fi, a now defunct stereo chain. They bought fifty-two pages up front because they didn't want to have one vendor in the marketplace. So they gave us a check for five thousand dollars." Williams's second ad call was to Warner/Elektra/Atlantic, the new record distribution arm of Warner Communications, Inc. The company immediately bought five full-page ads at $1,200 apiece. "It really put us over the edge to get started," says Williams.

Staffers worked without pay for the first month, and the paper was an immediate hit. Within two months *The Real Paper* was generating a profit; within eight months, its revenue had reached $462,000 with a net profit of $53,000. Its weekly press run was fifty thousand, of which thirty thousand copies were paid for. Just as important to the staff and the credibility of the paper was that success had been achieved while maintaining a level of political and social commitment. Like the early WBCN, *The Real Paper* wouldn't accept just any ad, rejecting those considered demeaning to women or any cigarette ads. A long-term, lucrative contract for a Portuguese wine was turned down because of that country's continuing policy of colonialism in Africa.

The quick success of *The Real Paper* was beyond everyone's

expectations. "The environment was very, very heady," says Albertson, who had become associate publisher. "My father was the vice president of the Federal Reserve Bank, and he could never understand what I was doing. He used to say, 'Explain it to me again, Jeff. Tell me what it is you're doing.' And I would tell him about rock and roll, I would tell him about the underground newspaper business. I could've been talking about space travel. He didn't understand how a guy who was twenty-two could be a publisher of one of the most important publications in New England, couldn't understand how the oldest person on the paper was twenty-six. It all happened so fast—and the money was so phenomenal. We started a paper for one thousand dollars in August of '72, and by the spring of '73 we were taking in twenty-five thousand a week. These kids are saying, 'Twenty-five thousand dollars a week? My father doesn't make that in a *year*.' "

But success brought new problems. Despite *The Real Paper*'s initial focus on being a capitalist collective, it soon became apparent that certain people would be more important than others if the publication was to survive. Although Jon Landau was living in New York, he was still viewed as the most authoritative voice on the Boston music scene and a key addition if the paper wanted to solidify its early hold on rock advertising and continue to stave off Mindich. A month after *The Real Paper*'s debut, Landau agreed to contribute.

"We all thought he was the only important name," says Paul Solman, the paper's first editor. "If there was anybody whom it mattered to keep, then it was Jon more than anybody else. I don't know what percentage of that paper was music and stereo ads, but it was huge. He brought more to the paper than the paper brought to him."

Although Landau agreed to write for the paper, he had little sympathy for its cooperative structure. Like his mentor, Durocher, Landau felt no overt antipathy toward Mindich, and he took the staff to task in his first column for portraying themselves as "a small band of heroes struggling against overwhelming odds to maintain the purity of Boston's weekly press. There is some justice to this assessment," wrote Landau, "but not enough to suit my taste." What did suit Landau's taste was keeping his own options open. His most telling action when he joined *The Real Paper* was to accept his share of the weekly's stock but to avoid signing the bylaws with its stock buyback provisions. The administration was too disorganized for anyone to notice.

Aside from the credibility he was expected to bring to the weekly's music coverage, Landau's presence was seen by some of the paper's senior staff as a way to attract other critics. After all, Landau could dispense assignments for *Rolling Stone*. One of Landau's recommendations was his new friend and acolyte, Dave Marsh. A former editor of the Detroit-based rock magazine *Creem,* he was hired as music editor. If *The Real Paper* was fashioned as the antibusiness business, Marsh styled himself the anti-intellectual intellectual.

A native of Pontiac, Michigan, and a college dropout, Marsh portrayed himself as the gifted and largely self-educated product of an otherwise dull environment. "I could always write," he told an interviewer. "I was real verbal—started talking when I was eight months old. People didn't read much in Pontiac, but I found a book my father had, some collection that had writers in it like Robert Benchley and Dorothy Parker, all the Algonquin crowd. I read that book, and it made me laugh so much that when I was in eighth grade, I could write just like Robert Benchley."

In Detroit, Marsh hung around John Sinclair and became enraptured with the freedom and potential of the scene. "He was a kid who was caught up in the thing," says Sinclair. "He was one of the typical teenage White Panthers." Marsh cut his ties to Sinclair and the White Panthers after meeting Landau, correctly dismissing them as having grown irrelevant. But Sinclair's gleeful penchant for propaganda wasn't lost on him. Where conservative, thoughtful reasoning was the cornerstone of Landau's style and reputation as a reviewer, Marsh developed a cocky, shoot-from-the-lip approach similar to Sinclair's. Landau's pieces invited discussion; Marsh's armchair diatribes dismissed it.

Marsh's tenure at *The Real Paper* was brief; after six months he moved on to *Newsday* until Landau helped him land a job at *Rolling Stone*. But he was quick to toot his own horn and expound on his ambitions, and he left an impression among his Boston coworkers as a guy on the make. "He told me everything about himself," says Albertson. "All of his aspirations, all of his admiration of Landau, all of his hopes to become a music industry player. I would say he was an aspiring toady even at that point. He was just looking to get a home where he could be part of it. Obviously, he found it. To be honest with you, I kind of liked David. But he was an insecure sycophant even then."

Within *The Real Paper,* the limits of being an antibusiness business quickly became apparent. In the spring of '73 the closeness that unified the staff was rent by personal variables no one had foreseen: Albertson's wife left him and moved in with his close friend and associate, Bob Rotner—the publisher. Neither Albertson, the associate publisher, nor Rotner would resign. And since the paper's bylaws made it almost impossible for anyone to be fired, the staff was quickly divided into two camps: Rotner and management and Albertson and a core of writers.

Also unforeseen were the effects of the paper's quick success on the staff. It was conceived as a cooperative venture, begun in anger and bent on a shared vindication. But as soon as the money started to come in, the knives came out. While management received the highest salaries, they were nowhere near those of traditional companies, and the continuing prospect of having fame without fortune began to rankle. Eventually, a deal was proposed in which *The Real Paper* would acquire 49 percent of its own printing company, Arlington Offset. The other 51 percent was to be owned by a group led by Rotner.

Naturally, Albertson was the most outspoken opponent of the purchase, predicting that Rotner and management would use their salaries from the printing company to get their hands on a greater share of *The Real Paper*'s money. The decision to purchase Arlington Offset passed—by one vote. On the newsstands, *The Real Paper* was doing just fine, and its reporters were frequently complimented by the editor of *The Boston Globe.* But as the prototype for a new, enlightened form of capitalism, *The Real Paper* was a complete bust.

Disenchanted, Albertson drifted away from the paper in late '73 while continuing to collect his paycheck through the following year. He spent most of his time drinking and taking pictures at Joe's Place, a tiny Cambridge club owned by his friend Joe Spadafora.

Located in Cambridge's Inman Square, Joe's became a popular hangout for blues fans. It was also a health hazard and a firetrap. When it rained, the city sewers routinely dumped a foot of fecal matter in the basement. During shows, Albertson sat on top of the refrigerator behind the bar and took pictures, a vantage point that also protected him from the crush of listeners that flagrantly violated the occupancy rating of two hundred. "I've never been in a place that was so frighteningly crowded," says Albertson. "If somebody fell down they would've been killed."

Featuring blues legends like Howlin' Wolf, Koko Taylor, and

Muddy Waters, Joe's Place also became a popular stop for up-and-coming rock acts, despite the fact that Spadafora was infamous for not paying them. "They'd go looking for the money and Joey would've spent it, lost it, drunk it—whatever," says Albertson. Still, Spadafora would host late-night booze-and-barbecue parties at his condominium on Putnam Avenue for the acts he liked. One of them was a struggling group from New Jersey, Bruce Springsteen and the E Street Band.

SIGNED TO COLUMBIA RECORDS, BRUCE SPRINGSTEEN WAS JUST ONE OF THE hundreds of hopeful young performers to flash across Boston's rock scene in the years since Mario Medious had helped transform the city's massive student population and nascent underground into a key market for breaking new rock acts. Indeed, Springsteen's first area appearance, a showcase for Boston/Cambridge writers and disc jockeys at Paul's Mall in January of '73, went almost unremarked. "You know how it is at these press parties," says writer and disc jockey James Isaacs, who attended the showcase. "Everyone talked through it."

Isaacs went to see Springsteen again three months later when he played with Steely Dan at Oliver's, a club across the street from Fenway Park. He played there again in August and this time drew an extremely favorable review from critic Neal Vitale of *The Boston Globe*, who said he was watching "a totally brilliant, unique, soon-to-be-a-giant artist in his early days before he becomes a star." When Springsteen began a three-night stand at Joe's Place in January of '74, Isaacs was there. This time, he weighed in with a Springsteen review, the first to appear in *The Real Paper*.

Predicting that the rocker was "at the start of something large, indeed," Isaacs—under the nom de plume Henry Armetta*—followed Vitale's lead, and it was soon the sentiment of several critics around the country. In Los Angeles, writer Peter Philbin saw Springsteen play six songs at a Troubadour showcase and came away a true believer. "Let me put it to you this way," he wrote in the *Los Angeles Free Press*, "never have I been more impressed with a debuting singer than I was with Bruce Springsteen on Monday night."

*Henry Armetta had been a Hollywood character actor from the twenties to the mid-forties who specialized in bumbling, stereotyped Italian buffoons.

Although the critics couldn't know it, the growing support came at
a crucial time in Springsteen's career: his albums weren't selling and
Columbia had serious doubts about him. In addition to John Hammond at Columbia, Clive Davis, who had been the top executive at
CBS Records when Springsteen joined the roster, had been an ardent
proponent. But Davis had been forced out in September of '73 over
alleged financial improprieties, and Springsteen quickly found himself with few powerful allies within the company. Instead, Charlie
Koppelman, a music executive whose tastes tended toward far more
pop-oriented performers, was now running Columbia's A&R department. Mike Appel, Springsteen's manager, had been shocked to discover how little the new regime thought of his client when he and an
associate, Bob Spitz, played an early tape of Springsteen's second
album for Koppelman and another executive, Kip Cohen.

"Mike and I watched their faces," recalls Spitz. "And Mike looked
at me in the middle, and his eyes narrowed. He didn't say anything,
but he shook his head just about two inches. He knew that they
weren't getting it. And they turned it off and said, 'Fellas, we may
have run to the end of our days with Bruce Springsteen. This is not
an album we are going to put out.' They wanted him to be a
singer/songwriter, to go from what they thought was a very rudimentary first album to maybe being Van Morrison. When we walked out
of there Mike called A&M, Mercury, Warner Brothers—we were
ready to move Bruce."

Springsteen, however, proved far more malleable. When Appel gave
him a watered-down account of the meeting with Cohen and Koppelman, he restructured the album and gave the executives what they
wanted. "He finished the songs and got rid of the filler," says Spitz.

Landau had been dispassionately observing Springsteen's inex-
orable rise since the year before, when Clive Davis had sent him a copy
of the rocker's first album, *Greetings from Asbury Park, N.J.*, and lobbied
for a *Rolling Stone* review. It was an unusual request from the head of
a major record company, and it marked Springsteen as a Columbia
priority. Paying heed, Landau assigned critic Lester Bangs to review
the record and sent Stu Werbin to Max's Kansas City in New York to
hear Springsteen.

"Clive sent over the record," recalls Werbin. "Jon played it and
really liked it, but he wasn't ready to go himself. He brought me in,

played it, and said, 'You go check this out.' Bruce was playing upstairs at Max's. I went down, and there were like eight or nine people there." Werbin remembers being impressed enough to drag Landau down to the club the next night.

If Landau had in fact seen Springsteen that early, he wasn't ready to weigh in with an opinion. But by the time Springsteen had begun to attract attention around Boston, he had become both cognizant of the rising groundswell and a fan of the rocker's second album, *The Wild, the Innocent, and the E Street Shuffle*. With the band set to return to Boston for a series of shows at Charlie's Bar—one of which was to benefit Joe's Place, which, to no one's surprise, had burned to the ground—Landau added his voice to the growing chorus of Springsteen supporters. "I reviewed the album and timed it to appear in *The Real Paper* before the gig," Landau later recalled, "because it was a favorable review and I had been told that in Cambridge I had some marquee value."

Landau gave Springsteen a qualified thumbs-up. While taken by the spirit and level of songwriting that informed the album—he dubbed Springsteen "the most impressive new singer-songwriter since James Taylor"—he saw room for improvement, especially regarding Springsteen's choice of material and studio technique. "Next time around," wrote Landau, "he ought to work a little harder on matching the production to the material, round out a few rough edges and then just throw some more hot ones on the vinyl."

Landau's faith in his own "marquee value" proved well founded. He and Dave Marsh arrived at Charlie's Bar for Springsteen's show to find a blowup of the review displayed outside the club. Even better, Landau spied a lone T-shirted figure standing on the sidewalk reading the review. It was Springsteen. Sidling up to the performer, he asked him what he thought of the review, and, when Springsteen said he thought it was on target, Landau stuck out his hand and introduced himself.

Inside the club, Landau and Marsh sat down with Springsteen and Mike Appel. Springsteen may have been pleased with Landau's review, but Appel was not. As the coproducer of Springsteen's albums, he took Landau's criticism of the record's production as a personal affront. By the end of the evening, however, when Landau told them that the show was one of the greatest he'd ever seen, the ill will seemed to have dissipated.

Less than a month later, Landau was once again in the audience when Springsteen returned to open a show for Bonnie Raitt, and his performance more than reinforced the positive reaction Landau had had at Charlie's. Overwhelmed by what he saw and heard, Landau penned what proved to be both an extremely personal and pivotal essay. In it, he marked his own twenty-seventh birthday by celebrating Springsteen as the embodiment of all that rock and roll had meant to him. Although the piece only hinted at the depth of his problems, it was written at a moment when Landau's life was on the verge of crumbling, and its voice was that of a soul desperately in need of something to believe in.

Landau's career as a producer remained at a standstill. He continued to edit the *Rolling Stone* review section but was so unhappy in New York that he had been forced to beat a retreat to the familiar comfort of Boston. He was taking medication for Crohn's disease and was frequently in pain. Despite this, his condition was worsening and he suffered from debilitating stress-related flare-ups that frequently prevented him from working or eating. As his health continued to deteriorate, a major operation appeared to be the only solution. But perhaps even more difficult, his eighteen-month-old marriage was collapsing. Unable to view his life with clarity, Landau sought the safe and familiar harbor of his love for rock and roll. And in Bruce Springsteen he spied his beacon.

In a direct and unusually personal voice, Landau traced his involvement with rock and roll, recalling the power of epiphany that certain artists and records held for him—how, for example, he had to stop driving and pull his car off the road the first time he heard "Reach Out, I'll Be There" by the Four Tops on the radio—confessing that music had been his most cherished companion through an otherwise lonely life. But Landau also admitted that becoming a professional critic had precipitated a crisis. He had lost the spark of excitement that music had held for him, developing a professional detachment, and he likened himself to a shoe salesman who simply follows a daily routine. Yet despite his unhappiness he still held out the hope of feeling the old familiar thrill. "In my own moments of greatest need," Landau wrote, "I never give up the search for sounds that can answer every impulse, consume all emotion, cleanse and purify— all things that we have no right to expect from even the greatest works of art but which we can occasionally derive from them."

Perhaps because Landau's need at the moment was so great, Springsteen answered all those hopes for reaffirmation. "Tonight," wrote Landau, "there is someone I can write of the way I used to write, without reservation of any kind. Last Thursday, at the Harvard Square theater, I saw my rock 'n' roll past flash before my eyes. And I saw something else: I saw rock and roll future and its name is Bruce Springsteen. And on a night when I needed to feel young, he made me feel like I was hearing music for the very first time."

Intended as a kind of personal catharsis, Landau's essay became the critical coronation for Springsteen that Columbia Records had so desperately sought. In the two years since Clive Davis had begun lobbying critics for reviews, Springsteen had certainly received more than his share of favorable notices, but Landau was quite another story. His stature among other critics—of which he was keenly aware, referring to himself with a bit less humor than might be expected as "the king of rock and roll"—was predicated to a large extent on his conservatism. With Landau's unqualified endorsement of the rocker, Columbia now had both a well-respected critic on board and a great tag line to run with. They wasted no time. "I saw rock and roll future and its name is Bruce Springsteen" ran in bold, block capitals above Landau's name in the advertisement that appeared on the third page of the July 18, 1974, issue of *Rolling Stone,* right next to the magazine's masthead, where the critic's name also appeared as an editor.

Columbia's trumpeting of the *Real Paper* essay had greatly helped both men, reaffirming Landau's status as a critic while fanning the growing grass fire of support for Springsteen. Most important, Landau's review and Columbia's subsequent exploitation of it had shifted critical debate decidedly in Springsteen's favor. The question was no longer whether Springsteen was simply good—a subject upon which the jury had previously been out—but whether he was great. Even *The New Yorker*'s Ellen Willis found herself reacting directly to Landau's pronouncement when she reviewed Springsteen's show at Avery Fisher Hall earlier that month, writing, "I'm not yet ready to endorse Jon Landau's rash proclamation that Springsteen is the future of rock and roll, but in the present he sure provides a good night out."

Springsteen himself was pleased enough to surprise Landau with a telephone call. Since the beginning of his career, he had been particularly sensitive to press reactions. In the year after the release of his first album, *Greetings from Asbury Park,* his most ardent and continual support came from *Crawdaddy!* and writers Peter Knobler and Greg Mitchell in particular. In response, Springsteen became something of a fixture at the magazine's Manhattan offices. The call to Landau lasted several hours and at one point turned to the criticism Landau had raised in his review of *The Wild, the Innocent, and the E Street Shuffle.* "Listen, I got a question for you," Springsteen said. "You mention in the review that the production wasn't quite up to the material. I hear this all the time. And I don't really—it's only my second album—and I really admire a lot of producers like Phil Spector, but I'm still not exactly clear on what a record producer should be doing. What's their job as opposed to my job?"

Landau explained what he'd seen as his role when he was a producer, pointing out that various producers had different strengths—how someone with a background as a musician and arranger like Arif Mardin or Quincy Jones could be expected to place his own stamp on the sound and direction of a record while nonmusicians like Jerry Wexler or Lenny Waronker might act more like coordinators or sounding boards for the artist. Getting the right producer, Landau suggested, had a lot to do with knowing what you wanted, and it paid to know what each producer's strength was. Drawing an analogy from the film industry, he suggested to Springsteen that picking a producer was a form of casting. It was the first long, serious talk between the two.

The next would occur a few months later, on October 29, at Jeff Albertson and James Isaacs's Cambridge apartment. Springsteen had played a concert that night at the Music Hall, and the *Real Paper/*Joe's Place crowd was assembled for a postconcert party, but he did little in the way of socializing. He spent the evening off in a corner, locked in conversation with Landau.

11

Eagles Aerie:
Hoot Night
at the Troubadour

WHILE WARNER BROS. RECORDS HAD CAST ITS FATE WITH THE underground rock scene of the late sixties because it had few other options and nothing to lose, David Geffen's companies—Asylum Records and Geffen-Roberts Management—were formed to promote and exploit a rock movement whose widespread appeal was now obvious. The success of both ventures was immediate and significant. And because the rewards were now just as obvious to the musicians, a new, more professional, and money-oriented outlook emerged, supplanting the free-wheeling musical style that had characterized the Los Angeles scene in the heyday of the Sunset Strip. "We were all going to get on Asylum, make records, and be stars," says Glenn Frey.

Frey had met Jackson Browne at a benefit concert in Long Beach, and they became fast friends. Like Browne, he and his songwriting partner, J. D. Souther, had had disappointing recording experiences, and the future didn't look any better. In the summer of '68 they had formed a folk duo, Longbranch Pennywhistle, and signed to Amos Records, a small label co-owned by singer Kenny Rogers. They recorded one album before running into problems. They wanted to make a rock record and had begun to work with David Briggs, the producer of Neil Young's breakthrough record, *Everybody Knows This Is Nowhere*, but Amos was vehemently opposed to the move. Says Souther: "It wasn't really their world. They were still trying to encourage us to record songs that were well known. The fact is, we weren't writing spectacular songs—we were just starting—but I wasn't about to do anybody else's songs."

It was a standoff. Longbranch Pennywhistle wouldn't make the record Amos wanted, and Amos wouldn't fund the record the duo insisted on making. "I thought I was doing something unique," says Souther. "And my job, at whatever stumbling pace, was to embrace that artistry, not look for a way to get on the charts."

In Browne, Frey and Souther found a comrade. They were all virtual unknowns, and when Browne found a cheap apartment in Echo Park, a working-class neighborhood east of Hollywood, he suggested that Souther and Frey take a sixty-dollar-a-month flat in the same building.

Ned Doheny, who rounded out the clique, remembers the bond as "friendly competition." Primarily a guitarist, Doheny found himself pushed to develop as a songwriter. "We were constantly challenging each other," he says. "Most of the time it was friendly: 'Boy, wait until they hear this one.' It wasn't particularly vitriolic or spiteful or weird, although the competition went farther than some of us realized. That's one of the reasons the level of songwriting got so high."

When Geffen told Browne he was starting Asylum, the singer urged his new manager to sign his friends. Eager to impress his young client, he agreed. "David Geffen loved Jackson," says Frey. "And Jackson said, 'I'm going to get you guys on Asylum.' It was the unique kind of selfless act that he was and is capable of. He did his level best to get us on Asylum."

After auditioning the songwriters, Geffen offered them contracts but told Frey that he wasn't a solo act. "David Crosby is in a band," Geffen said. "You should be in a band."

Initially stung by the assessment, Frey nonetheless took the advice to heart and set about assembling a group. He wasn't exactly sure who or what he was looking for, but he had a pretty good idea where to look: the bar at the Troubadour. By the late sixties Los Angeles was no longer the musical backwater it had been just a few years before and the Troubadour had become its most important rock and folk club. Located on Santa Monica Boulevard in Hollywood, it was a popular watering hole for established stars like the Everly Brothers, Kris Kristofferson, James Taylor, Joni Mitchell, and Graham Nash, as well as managers and label executives.

"When I first got to town in the early seventies, I used to go and sit in the Troubadour bar and listen to Lou Adler and Albert Grossman and David Geffen and all those guys argue," recalls Irving Azoff. "They would sit in the front of the bar, scream and yell and holler at each other, and then they'd go next door to Dan Tana's for dinner."

Says producer John Boylan, "On any given night you could run into the pantheon of the whole country rock and roll movement. Much more vibrant than the Village folk-rock scene that I was in on just four or five years earlier. The bar was *the* hangout."

What really attracted local musicians and executives to the Troubadour was its Monday "hoot" nights. Traditionally the slowest night of the week, Mondays were set aside by club owner Doug Weston as an open-mike night for aspiring—as in cheap—talent. And while the practice had been an integral part of the earlier folk boom, the Troubadour showcase was significantly different because of the audience. You could actually get hired to play with an established artist or even land a record deal if you were good enough. "Linda [Ronstadt] would go down to the Troubadour and hang out in the bar and meet songwriters and get songs," says Peter Asher, James Taylor and Ronstadt's manager and formerly half of the British duo Peter and Gordon. "There was a sense that you were at the center of a musical movement. Certainly, when there is a movement, the outside perception is that there's a scene and everyone knows each other. Usually, that's not as true as it seems. Americans used to think of England like that—they'd ask me what Liverpool was like and I'd have to tell them that I'd actually never been there, that it's a dark, ugly town and no one goes there. But in this case, it really was true. You were aware that there was some genre of music developing."

The gatekeeper for hoot nights was Roger Perry, who opened the club doors at about six-thirty on Monday nights and then compiled the list of the eight to twelve musicians who would be allowed to play. Glenn Frey had made it his business to befriend Perry—as well as the Troubadour's waitresses and bartenders—but he left nothing to chance. On Monday afternoons he arrived in front of the club at five o'clock. The competition made for a tough crowd—and almost instant acceptance or rejection. Says Boylan, "Everybody would hang out in the bar until they'd hear somebody. The door would open and everybody would stream from the bar into the showroom to see what was happening. Then, if the act wasn't any good, they'd all be back out in the bar."

Boylan, who was putting together a band for Ronstadt in the fall of 1970, recruited Frey as one of her guitarists, offering him the then princely sum of $250 a week. They were still missing a drummer two days before rehearsals started until Frey ran into Don Henley at the Troubadour bar. Henley was the drummer for Shiloh, another band on Amos Records, and he and Frey became fast friends in Ronstadt's band. When Frey told him there was a chance to form their own band for David Geffen's new label, Henley signed on immediately.

The rest of the pieces fell into place a few months later. After the group had come off the road and scattered, Ronstadt needed to play a handful of dates. Henley and Frey were still in Los Angeles, but Boylan had to hire bassist Randy Meisner and guitarist Bernie Leadon to fill in for the others, and the quartet—with the addition of Boylan on keyboards—debuted at Disneyland. They played with Ronstadt for only a few dates before accompanying Frey on his triumphant return to David Geffen's office. While Henley would later suggest that David had no idea whether the group was any good—"Geffen himself couldn't carry a tune in an armored car," he said—the executive had no trouble making the call.

"Geffen had this saying," recalls John Hartmann, the former agent for Buffalo Springfield who had just joined Geffen-Roberts. " 'It's easy in music to tell what's good. It's hard to tell what's bad.' And it's true: music is basically good, it's fun, it's *music*. So even when it sucks, it's sort of okay. Nine out of ten acts signed to record contracts are losers, but they're signed because A and R guys say, 'Hey, I like that.' We saw the Eagles once. They were backing Linda. Then Elliot and David and I went to a little rehearsal hall at Barham and Ventura Boulevard and sat in a room where they were set up at one end with a huge pile of boxes in the middle and we were at the other end. We watched them over the boxes. And we knew and committed to them right then. It was nothing to believe in the Eagles."

Geffen's commitment to the Eagles was total. He squared away Frey's lingering contractual problems with Amos Records. He advanced the band members money to live on and sent them to his dentist to have their teeth fixed. In the fall of 1971, Geffen booked the group for an extended run at a club called the Galley in Aspen, where they could work on their repertoire and develop away from the glare of L.A. The following spring, Asylum spent $125,000 of Atlantic's money to record the group's debut album, *The Eagles,* at Olympic Studios in London. But Geffen faced an uphill battle with Atlantic, which was not enthusiastic about the band.

"At that point, David knew very little about the record business," says Paul Ahern, Asylum's first director of promotion. "However, there's one thing you can never argue about: David beat the shit out of Atlantic with the Eagles. David would come out of a meeting with all of the staff and say the Eagles were going to be bigger than Crosby, Stills and Nash. He was in there fighting for them. And the Atlantic people would say to me, 'What is he, kidding? The Eagles are going to be bigger than Crosby, Stills and Nash?' There was resistance, and he did go the distance."

A former Atlantic promotion man who had learned the ropes from Mario Medious, Ahern became one of Asylum's first employees after he told Atlantic that the label had promoted the wrong Jackson Browne track, "Rock Me on the Water," as a single. Instead, he urged them to release "Doctor My Eyes." The label took Ahern's advice, and the record reached the Top 10 on the *Billboard* singles chart in the spring of 1972, giving Asylum its first hit and the biggest single Browne would have for ten years. Ahern quickly discovered, however, that there was a good deal of tension between Atlantic and Asylum. Ever cheap, Atlantic wanted to keep Geffen and his label on a short leash.

"Asylum was nothing but David and his secretary, Linda [Loddengard]," recalls Ahern. "So Atlantic essentially called all the shots. To be realistic, I was young and impressionable, so Atlantic probably figured they could control me, too. But David, in his unique way, wanted to learn more and more about it every day and became less and less easy to control. [Atlantic] hired me to help them out but also to keep an eye on him. But David, he gets up early in the morning."

With such a small staff, Asylum depended on Atlantic's sales and promotion teams to push their roster. But the executives invariably gave any Asylum release a backseat on their own titles, and Geffen was left to do much of the job himself. Along with learning radio promotion, he pitched his acts earnestly to the rock press. At *Rolling Stone,* Geffen's taste and business acumen captivated Jon Landau, who adopted him as his newest rabbi and flattered Geffen in print as "a mensch." And Asylum's artists were delighted by the job Geffen was doing. *The Eagles* had produced three hit singles: "Take It Easy," "Witchy Woman," and "Peaceful Easy Feeling."

"It's my assumption that David Geffen called in a lot of favors in seventy-two for 'Doctor My Eyes' and 'Take It Easy,' " says Frey. "The record company happened very fast—for David Geffen and Elliot Roberts, too, who were still trying to figure it out. In retrospect, though, I think every record company president was thrilled to get David Geffen out from the other side of the desk."

Indeed, David now was on the side of the desk where his considerable negotiating skills were not always used in the service of the artists he managed. That fact would cause considerable problems as Asylum lifted off like a rocket. With Geffen-Roberts and Asylum sharing offices at 9130 Sunset Boulevard, there was never even a pretense of a boundary between Geffen's dual role as the record company and the comanager of virtually every artist on the label. John Hartmann, for example, had been hired by Geffen-Roberts when Elliot was ill, but he also worked for Asylum. "I was the very first employee of Asylum Records, and I managed all of the artists that were on the label," he says.

Much like Albert Grossman's ABG Management before it, Geffen-Roberts was a nerve center for both its clients and the emerging scene. If anything, Geffen's tastes were proving even more commercial than Grossman's. "The difference was Geffen-Roberts had big artists and tons of gold and platinum records on the wall," says Elliot Mazer, a onetime Grossman client who produced Neil Young. The office was much more focused and businesslike. "David never did any drugs," Mazer adds. The company also became adept at putting their artists on tour and getting them the best prices. "John Hartmann and I basically kept the clients working," recalls Harlan Goodman. "When he got there none of them were working, so we put everybody on the road."

Hartmann urged Geffen to place his artists with Premier, now the country's most powerful rock agency. When Neil Young's 1972 album *Harvest*—with its number one single, "Heart of Gold"—gave Young the biggest hit of his career, Geffen-Roberts cashed in with a vengeance, using Barsalona's agency to play hardball. "We decided to go for a ninety/ten split with Neil," says Hartmann. "He didn't work that often, he was very hot, and we wanted to make a killing."

Barbara Skydel at Premier argued that promoters would never agree to such a one-sided arrangement, at least, not for Young. Geffen-Roberts was adamant. "We'll fight that battle at the end," Hartmann recalls telling her. "Go ahead and book the tour."

Geffen-Roberts knew the greatest resistance would come from San Francisco's Bill Graham, the country's preeminent rock promoter. Like Geffen, he ignored industry conventions and turned a blind eye to conflict-of-interest questions when it suited his purposes. Aside from the Fillmore East and West and other venues, Graham owned the Millard Agency, the booking agent for numerous West Coast acts, and had a hand in the management of several prominent San Francisco bands, including the Grateful Dead and the Jefferson Airplane. And he was notoriously hard to get money out of. "Bill Graham was a good friend," says Harlan Goodman, "but Bill would call you up when you were making twenty-five thousand dollars a night and say, 'I got great news! I got you two shows at Winterland for twenty-five hundred dollars!' Gee, really? Can we pay our own way?" In a move that smacked of collusion, Graham told other promoters he was not going to accept Young's terms and convinced them to do the same. The scene was set for a showdown. When the day came to close the contracts and name the price, Graham called Geffen and said the deal was no good and that he wanted to negotiate. Geffen sent him back to Hartmann.

"Bill and I got into an outrageous screaming match," says Hartmann. "We carried it to a level where every person in the Geffen-Roberts building was standing in or near my office listening. When it was all said and done, I said, 'What's it going to be, Bill? Are you going to pass or take the deal?' And he took the deal. Then everybody fell. Neil deserved the money. I'm sure all the promoters cheated us, anyway."

DAVID GEFFEN SOLD ASYLUM TO HIS CLIENTS AS A REFUGE FOR SIGNIFICANT artists, a small boutique label where they would be free to create whatever they wanted. While it quickly became far more than that, he was true to his word regarding artistic freedom. "Asylum was the only record label I ever really loved," says Souther, who later made albums

for Columbia and Warner Bros. "Asylum occupied this one little plane-
tary system that seemed to be almost beyond the gravitational pull of
big business. It was a real wonderful time to be there because they
really didn't interfere with my record making."

Bones Howe, who produced singer/songwriter Tom Waits for Asylum, recalls that Geffen generally limited himself to helping artists
find the right people to work with in the studio: "David's talent was
putting people together. He had a great sense of which people would
really generate synergy. Like me and Waits. He had a sense that the
two of us together would make really good records. And his expectations never went beyond that. He just said, 'If you guys like each other,
go in the studio and make a record.' He never said what kind of
record. Once he said, 'I wish you wouldn't make a jazz record with
him, but I know you're going to.' That was the worst that ever happened. That was what he did with Joni Mitchell, with Jackson, with
everyone: 'I just want you on my label. I want you to make whatever
record you want to make.' "

As the management company, Geffen-Roberts took a similar tack.
"To their credit, David and Elliot saw what was wrong with the agency
system the minute they got in there," says John Boylan. "David was the
first mogul who was artist-oriented. Peter Asher was the first big-time
manager who could play an instrument. That had tremendous resonance within the community of musicians at large. They didn't want to
deal with the cigar guys, everybody was against that. We were all anti-
showbiz. We used to make fun of [mainstream performers] and call
them the 'costume people.' No costumes. No makeup. Forget the
smoke. You go onstage in your jeans and play the fucking music."

As a team, Geffen and Roberts had widely divergent styles and
roles. "Elliot was the happy, good-time guy, the mellow guy who just
wanted to hang around and smoke joints and watch the girls go by,"
says Don Henley. "When the groups were fighting and there was a lot
of squabbling and turmoil going on, David would send Elliot in to try
and calm everybody down."

Geffen was far more driven, both professionally and personally,
and he was eager to prove his prowess to his clients during the early
days of Asylum and Geffen-Roberts "David had this knight-in-shining-
armor syndrome," says Doheny. "He particularly liked it if he could
rescue you from a compromising situation. He really liked to rescue."

The artists were attracted to Geffen by his intelligence, his deep and cutting sense of humor, shrewd eye, and love of gossip. He was an instructive presence: funny, bright, and formidable. Still, he told his clients that he was deeply unhappy and afraid he would never find anyone to love. Says Doheny, "He loved us in a way that was based in a sense on a denial of his own reality. He took great interest in our relationships when we were in love or something like that. He really liked that. I don't think he lived vicariously, but I think that he thought we were to a certain extent 'normal.' And said to me on more than one occasion, 'I don't think I'll ever be happy.' Which I thought was amazing. There was always something kind of desperate and sad about David." Joni Mitchell captured Geffen's longings in her song "Free Man in Paris."

Among his clients, Geffen's closest personal relationships were with Mitchell—with whom he shared a house—and Jackson Browne. His professional match, however, would prove to be the Eagles. Like all great managers, Geffen was as creative in his own sphere as any of his artists were in theirs. The Eagles, conversely, took their business as seriously as they took their music, and they were the only clients whose greed and ambition matched his own. "We had seen a lot of our heroes and predecessors get ripped off and lose everything they had," says Henley. "Or in some cases not get what they had coming to them or have somebody steal it from them. Either a crooked record company, a crooked manager, a crooked accountant or business manager. It really shook us up to see that some of our heroes from the sixties didn't have a pot to piss in. So we were jaded. And we were determined to be a little bit smarter about it."

Their attitude toward music was just as professional. Recalls Frey, "When we were putting the Eagles together we didn't want any weak links, and we knew we had to become songwriters. So Don and I became the principal songwriters and, as a result, the governing body. We thought of the Eagles as the rock and roll Camaro, the best-designed car of the seventies and eighties. And we always tried to improve the basic design. We realized that rock and roll is a war of attrition. The longer you survive, the more you become an institution."

"Glenn and I were on the same team," says Henley. "It was he and I against everyone else. We felt like it was our group. Glenn and I both had pretty strong work ethics; we're both pretty anal about rehearsal.

We rehearsed *a lot*. And we were diligent about doing our homework. But, of course, we had role models—Crosby, Stills, Nash and Young and the Byrds and Buffalo Springfield. Staying together was very important to us. We saw all these groups going through temper tantrums and all the infighting between Neil and Stephen [Stills], the Byrds breaking up. We wanted to last longer than that. And we found out how fucking hard that was. A lot of our time and energy was expended on simply keeping the group together."

After the success of *The Eagles,* the band hit a rut. Their second album, *Desperado,* was a collection of songs inspired in large measure by a book on the western outlaw gang the Daltons that Doheny had given to Souther as a birthday present. The songwriters honed a metaphor that the Eagles would use to great advantage throughout their career: rock and roll as an outlaw lifestyle. If the album struck many critics as contrived, coming as it did from a group that was straightforward about its commercial aspirations, the view eventually found great resonance with fans. But at first *Desperado* was a dud. "We'd had three charting singles with our first album, and Atlantic was stoked," says Frey. "But when Atlantic president Jerry Greenberg heard *Desperado,* he said, 'They made a fucking cowboy record!' "

With their sales stalled, the Eagles blamed Geffen-Roberts and Asylum for spreading themselves too thin. "It's the old sauna story," Henley complained as he watched Asylum's roster expand while the Eagles' career hovered in a holding pattern. "Jackson, J.D., Ned, and Glenn were at David Geffen's house one day and he said, 'I want to keep Asylum Records really small. I'll never have more artists than I can fit in this sauna.' Then, all of a sudden, he was signing people right and left."

The label's quick success and hip cachet made it extremely attractive, even to established artists like Linda Ronstadt, who quickly outsold the Eagles. Even worse, Geffen-Roberts was managing the group America, a Warner Bros. trio whose light-sounding folk-rock proved commercially potent but was so unoriginal that rumors circulated that the group's first hit, "A Horse with No Name," was actually performed by Neil Young. "That grated," admits Frey, "because we felt they didn't have our substance but were having monster hits and riding in limos. We started to think about these things."

The expanded roster and ceaseless demands of the artists were also testing the limits of Geffen-Roberts hand-holding talents. There just wasn't enough love to go around, and a growing jealousy, even among the artists who were friends, now characterized the company. Joni Mitchell and Jackson Browne—the latter's role in bringing many of the others onboard notwithstanding—were perceived as Geffen's favorites. Jack Nitzsche, who wanted to make his own albums, suspected Geffen and Roberts were only interested in keeping him as a producer "at Neil's beck and call" and quit the firm. Stephen Stills, who didn't get along with Geffen, left in a huff and printed up bumper stickers that read WHO IS DAVID GEFFEN AND WHY IS HE SAYING THESE TERRIBLE THINGS ABOUT ME?

"Artists are generally a jealous bunch," says Peter Asher. "They're jealous of artists who are more successful than they are. They want to know why someone else's record came into the charts higher." But that jealousy wasn't limited to the artists. Observes Doheny: "I found Elliot very charming, very bright, and very contentious. I liked Elliot a lot, but he made me uneasy; I felt like I was being judged constantly. Also, as there is between most managers and artists at a certain point, there's a sort of natural antagonism or envy. You can always tell yourself as a manager that you're the guy making all the money and he's the one going out and getting the incurable venereal diseases, but they really can't help but envy you. Because you're *there*, you're closer to the fire. It's life once removed. Managers are a pretty hideous breed as a rule. And, of course, they hate the artist for being able to ride their sweat to glory."

●

IN THEIR PRE-ASYLUM DAYS, GEFFEN AND ROBERTS HAD BEEN ABLE TO TAP-dance around the laws governing the roles of agents and managers. But being the record company *and* management was about to prove an insurmountable challenge, even for a wheeler-dealer like Geffen. It had been easy, as the manager of a clique of young artists without record deals, for Geffen to make the argument that his record company would take the best care of them. He had proven that by browbeating Atlantic on behalf of Jackson Browne and the Eagles, making hits out of records that almost certainly would have died without his advocacy. But the fact remained that the relationships between an artist and his manager and an artist and his record company are drastically different. A manager is employed and paid by the artist, while a record company essentially hires—and as a rule owns the work—of the artist. By becoming the record company, Geffen had reversed his relationship with the Geffen-Roberts artists: instead of working for them, they worked for him. Artists who sought special deals were rebuffed. "One of David's sayings was 'You're not my partner,' " recalls Paul Ahern. "He made it pretty clear that this was not a partnership and don't pretend that it is."

As he had with Nyro, Geffen also continued the practice of becoming the music publisher for his clients. No one squawked about this arrangement, either—at first. "Let me just put it this way," says J. D. Souther. "In my case, I had no record deal that I wanted, no publishing deal that I wanted. David offered me a record deal that I wanted, a publishing deal . . . and good management. My recollection is that no one at the time balked at any of this. I was glad to be in business with him, and it seemed to me that everyone else was at the time."

But once success came, the notion of Geffen having the complete package—management, record deal, and music publishing—rankled. The argument Geffen had used for including publishing was a standard one: any money the group might make from their music publishing should be cross-collateralized against their recording advance as insurance for the label against a poorly selling record.

"Whether you give it all to Morris Levy* or give it all to David Geffen, the only thing you have to give is your songs and performances," says Frey. "There were no questions asked; we didn't think anything of it. We didn't even have lawyers. It was simply put to us that the insurance against a shitty record was publishing."

Record companies traditionally make such arguments when they sign an act—and managers just as faithfully resist them. But when the record company was Asylum, the music publisher the Geffen-owned Companion Music, and the management firm Geffen-Roberts, no such fight took place. Indeed, no one signed to Geffen's companies thought anything of it until 1972 when something happened that none of them had considered. Geffen sold Asylum Records to Warner Bros. for

*A powerful and much-feared record executive whose mob connections and mistreatment of artists were legend.

$7 million. Artists who had believed all of his talk about Asylum being a refuge thought they'd been had.

"David used us," says Doheny. "He piled us all together and leapt off us into his next venue, traded us like a Joe DiMaggio card. That embittered some of us. He parlayed a small record company; he turned all of us over to Warner Brothers. Those of us he had no use for he simply discarded without a great deal of care for feeling or sentiment."

Geffen later said that Warner Communications, Inc., chief Steve Ross had simply materialized one day and expressed an earnest and pressing desire to own Asylum Records, and, being an obliging sort, he had agreed. The sale price was simply the highest number he could think of. But Warners was said to be worried about its liability under the California Labor Code because of Geffen's role as both the label and the management company.

Regardless of Ross's motives or tactics, the deal looked huge. Geffen and Roberts received 121,952 common shares worth $4,750,000 at the time of the sale. Also included was $400,000 in cash and $1.6 million in promissory notes convertible into common stock. The sale covered Asylum as well as music publishing and Geffen's and Roberts's interests in the royalties of some of their artists. Geffen accepted a five-year employment contract with WCI and turned over his 75 percent interest in Geffen-Roberts to Elliot. John Hartmann and Harlan Goodman were told they would be running the day-to-day operations at the management firm, but, behind the scenes, Geffen continued to call the shots.

A meeting was planned at which Geffen, Roberts, Hartmann, and Goodman would present the new setup to the clients as a fait accompli. But if the move was seen as a way to dampen a powder keg of conflicts before it exploded, Glenn Frey and Don Henley lit a match.

Disgruntled about his career, Ned Doheny had begun to wonder aloud to the others about Geffen having all the cards. In conversations with Hartmann and the Eagles, he particularly questioned the propriety of Geffen owning their publishing, which prompted Henley and Frey to poll others in the business about the structure of their deal. "I had a lot of great advice from Paul [Ahern] and Bob Buziak, who was at Capitol at the time," says Frey. "They became silent advisers to the Eagles." Neither man thought the Eagles' deal was advantageous for the band. To complicate matters, the Eagles' business manager and lawyer also handled Geffen-Roberts. How, they asked Frey, is Geffen's business manager going to look after your interests *and* his?

Frey made that argument to Jerry Rubinstein, the business manager for the Eagles and Geffen-Roberts. Was it right that his record company was also his management? He noted that he hadn't been paid for a recent tour and had never had an outside attorney look at his deal. Frey and Henley also discussed leaving Geffen-Roberts with Hartmann. "They said, 'Leave Geffen and be our manager,' " recalls Hartmann. "I said okay. We were drinking, we were stoned, I didn't know if this was real or not. But the next morning Geffen came to me and said, 'How dare you?' "

Caught off guard, Hartmann tried to convince Geffen that he wasn't leaving. Goodman, on the road with Crosby and Nash, hurried back to Los Angeles to try and help smooth things over. "David had thought it was John who put Glenn up to seeing Jerry Rubinstein," says Goodman. "It wasn't. The Eagles knew they were going to be big, but it just wasn't coming fast enough." As tempers rose, any attempts at intervention became academic. "David fucks people who betray him, and he fired John," says Goodman.

If Hartmann expected to be taking the Eagles with him, he soon found that this was not the case. He believes Geffen was able to pressure the band into staying. "He went to them and said, 'If you go with them I'll bury you,' " says Hartmann. " 'And I own your records and your publishing.' So I ended up without the act."

Amid the staff shuffling at Geffen-Roberts, a joker turned up in the deck. Irving Azoff, a young hustler from Illinois who had built a name for himself as a regional booking agent and promoter, had joined the firm, much to the surprise of Goodman. Arriving at the office in the midst of the Hartmann beheading, he was shocked to see Azoff.

"What are *you* doing here?" Goodman asked.

"Funny," said Azoff.

"What do you mean?"

"What do I mean? You guys don't know I'm coming here? They didn't talk to you about this?" Azoff added that he had brought his client Joe Walsh with him to Geffen-Roberts because the guitarist was interested in working with Goodman and Hartmann.

"Well," said Goodman, who had decided he would eventually follow

Hartmann out the door, "if breaking up the team bothers you, you're more than welcome to come with us."

It was an invitation Goodman would soon regret. "Irving mentioned to David that I had offered him a job—as only Irving can—and David said, 'How dare you sit there and take Elliot's money and try and steal our employees?' David thought I was going to stay and run the company. I said, 'David, we don't have to do this. I don't want to stay here and have you wind up doing to me what you did to John. If you want me out, I'll just go.' "

Teaming up, Hartmann and Goodman began managing the country rock band Poco, which had recently fired Geffen-Roberts after learning Geffen wanted to take Richie Furay out of the band and pair him with J. D. Souther and former Byrds bassist Chris Hillman to form a new supergroup. Managing the group was an open challenge to Geffen-Roberts, but Hartmann and Goodman were lucky enough to find an ally in Frank Barsalona at Premier Talent, who was the band's booking agent.

"Elliot called Premier trying to get them to drop us," says Goodman. But it was a measure of Barsalona's own power that he was willing to lose several good acts, including Neil Young, rather than be dictated to by Geffen-Roberts. "Frank, the godfather, didn't take either call. And Elliot pulled his acts because they kept Poco." Within two years, however, Hartmann and Goodman found a measure of revenge: David Crosby, Graham Nash, and the group America were spirited away from Geffen-Roberts. Without Geffen in the picture, Stephen Stills agreed to reunite with Crosby and Nash.

But the satisfaction Hartmann and Goodman got from eating off Geffen and Roberts's plate was small potatoes compared to the feast Irving Azoff was about to enjoy. Henley and Frey were still in the market for a manager of their own, someone who would kill for the Eagles the way that Crosby, Stills, Nash and Young had believed David and Elliot would kill for them.

At five-foot four, Azoff was a screaming record industry Napoleon straight from central casting. "He bonded with the Eagles," says Goodman. "Those guys appreciate blood, and they'd never met anyone like him. Somebody wants to play? Well, how big do you want to play? In those circumstances, Irv is the biggest guy on the planet."

Azoff listened carefully as the Eagles listed their grievances against

Geffen and Roberts. They didn't like the way the *Desperado* album had turned out. Producer Glyn Johns had been good for the band when they first started working with him, but now the group felt hemmed in by his approach, which emphasized the laid-back Asylum singer/songwriter style at the expense of more hard-edged material. "Glyn didn't think U.S. bands could rock, and he wanted us to be a folk group," says Frey. "Meanwhile, we're taking a beating opening for Jethro Tull, and our feeling was 'We gotta have kick-ass songs.'" The band was also bothered by the fact that they had made no money on the *Desperado* tour; the receipts had been used to pay back commissions owed to Geffen-Roberts. "I realized I didn't have any money to speak of," says Frey.

The Eagles broached the conflict-of-interest issue to Geffen and Roberts. Their answer was direct. "They kicked us out," says Henley. "When we brought up the conflict-of-interest issue, that scared the hell out of them. They said, 'We're dissolving the company now, and you guys have to go.' They kept Neil and America and Joni Mitchell, but they perceived us to be troublemakers." Much to Geffen's chagrin, Azoff, who claimed Geffen-Roberts had reneged on his compensation agreement, went with them.

Taking on the most powerful management firm in the business was a dicey move, but Azoff quickly proved that the Eagles had not traded down. During a two-day break in the Eagles' 1974 tour, Henley and Frey flew to the Bahamas on a gambling spree. Accompanied by Azoff and a girlfriend of Henley's, they arrived in the islands by private jet and quickly ran into trouble at customs: an agent found rolling papers in the woman's bag. The group was pulled aside for a search. Azoff, who was carrying Valiums in his boot, knew they were in for trouble. He could probably talk his way into the clear, but Frey had half an ounce of marijuana with him. Thinking quickly, Azoff volunteered to be searched first.

Disappearing into the search room with the customs agent, Azoff immediately produced the bag of Valiums. "This is what you're looking for from me," he said, adding that while he didn't have a prescription, his father was a pharmacist. He then "accidentally" flashed the $5,000 he'd brought for Frey and Henley to gamble with. When the customs agent didn't rise to the bribe, Azoff—cognizant of the fact that Paul McCartney had recently been barred from performing in several countries because of a marijuana bust in Japan—foresaw a nightmare world in which many lucrative foreign markets would be closed to the Eagles. He began talking as fast as he could: "There's a kid out there with a blue shirt on who has gold records all over his wall. He's a rock star. He's just got a couple of joints with him. If you bust him here he can't play in the U.K., Australia, Japan. You're gonna end his career."

After talking it over, the agents decided to search Henley, who Azoff said was clean, but skip Frey. They were off the hook.

"Irving brought boundless ambition to the job," Frey would marvel years later. "Irv had no fear." The Eagles had found their killer.

As a manager, Azoff would not make the same mistake that Geffen had. He served just one master, and he did it with an abrasive glee. As the Eagles solidified into one of rock's top-selling acts, Azoff was always there to get them a better deal. Renegotiating the group's recording contract became an annual event as the band reached new commercial peaks. By the mid-seventies, the Eagles were selling an incredible one million albums a month, a pace they managed to maintain for two years. And, on tour, the band was able to dictate unheard-of terms. Instead of Neil Young's ninety/ten split, the Eagles insisted on 97.5 percent of the gate. And, as Frey remembers, there was a simple answer for any promoter who didn't want to work for a measly 2.5 percent. "We said, 'Shut up, we're going to sell out.' "

Success, along with a shared cynicism about the business, had given the Eagles a jaded attitude that was light-years from the spirit of artistic camaraderie that had marked the early days when Frey, Souther, and Browne were living hand-to-mouth in Echo Park and making fun of the "costume people." "Everybody sort of went their own way," says Doheny. "And the whole scene got a lot more desperate as a result. You can hear a lot of it on the Eagles records; there's a lot of bile in those records, a lot of arrogance. 'Everybody else is doing it, so what the fuck.' And also being kind of bedazzled: you're with this actress and that producer and all of a sudden it becomes kind of racy and fun. It becomes the same grinding-out-your-cigar-on-the-outstretched-palms-of-the-poor that you fought so desperately to deny yourself when you were starting."

In 1977, with Azoff out in front on their behalf, the Eagles went to court against Geffen and Warner Bros. It was the final act in a long struggle to wrest back control of their music publishing. The suit, which sought to invalidate the group's publishing contract—by now one of the most valuable in the industry—was meant as a body blow to Geffen. "We sued David Geffen under the assumption that he didn't like bad ink," admits Frey.

For a self-described artists' champion like Geffen, the Eagles' suit was a public relations disaster. In it, the group made public their initial contracts with Asylum and Companion Music and charged that the two separate deals had been tied together illegally. Additionally, the suit alleged that Geffen had always intended to sell Asylum and the publishing companies and make a huge profit for himself at his clients' expense. Cutting to the heart of the conflict-of-interest issue, the suit charged that "Geffen failed and refused to disclose to plaintiffs at any time that his role as their personal manager and fiduciary was in conflict with his role as an executive and owner of Asylum Records and Companion Music and failed to obtain on their behalf independent advice and counsel as to the merits of the foregoing agreements and plaintiffs' rights." The suit sought $10 million in damages and return of the copyrights.

Although Geffen was the familiar enemy, the real target—the deep-pockets target and the one with the most to lose—proved to be Warner Bros. Having absorbed Asylum, it was making the profit from the one million albums a month the band was selling. And while Azoff was careful to make kissing sounds in the press about how happy the group was to be recording for the company, behind the scenes he had Warner Bros. up against the wall.

While record companies traditionally viewed copyrights as rock-bottom assets and didn't want to set a bad precedent by letting them go, there were other issues—like their future profits from the Eagles—at stake. Without the band's goodwill, it didn't look as if the label was going to get any more records. Warner Bros. was a public company—how could management explain to stockholders that they had lost the future income on one of their biggest acts because they wouldn't let go of a deal that appeared to be patently unfair? It was a lose/lose scenario for the company.

After two years of bickering, Warner Bros. caved in, and, in an out-of-court settlement, the Eagles retrieved their publishing rights. If it was WCI that ponied up, the victory was viewed—at least in some industry quarters—as coming at Geffen's expense. "Other people ate [the publishing deal] because they wouldn't fuck with Geffen," says Hartmann. "But Irving decided to make it fucking with Geffen. And tried to *be* Geffen."

In the coming years, Azoff's Front Line Management quickly supplanted Geffen-Roberts and its successor firm, Elliot Roberts's Lookout Management, as the premier rock management company with a client roster that boasted the Eagles, Boz Scaggs, Steely Dan, Stevie Nicks, Jimmy Buffett, Styx, and Chicago. If Azoff's heavy-handed tactics earned him the enmity of label heads and concert promoters, he never made his performers feel that he was getting rich at their expense the way Geffen had. And, as a result, they didn't begrudge him his piece of the action. "Irving's fifteen percent of everybody turned out to be worth more than everyone's eighty-five percent of themselves," J. D. Souther observes with amusement.

Years later, when he would once again mimic Geffen by starting his own label, Giant Records, Azoff mused on how they had both climbed from management into the corporate tower. "There wasn't so much a void when I came out to L.A. as a sense of having gone from accelerated college classes with geniuses to being thrown in with a bunch of illiterates," he said, looking even smaller than usual as he peered over his big desk in the corner office of a building he owned on Wilshire Boulevard. "It was such a fucking seat-of-your-pants, invent-the-rules-as-you-go business. And David invented a lot of the rules. For anyone with any sort of gift of gab and business sense it was easy to beat. Then the manager thing became real entrepreneurial; it was the next step for idiots who wanted to own or operate our own businesses. Being a manager was the way to go."

Azoff paused and looked out the window at Beverly Hills. "Management is a terrible business," he said finally with a grin. "Who wants an artist to take eighty-five percent of his money?"

●

DAVID GEFFEN'S EUPHORIA AT HIS $7 MILLION SCORE FROM WARNER BROS. was short-lived. In Asylum's first year at Warner Bros., albums by Linda Ronstadt and the Eagles alone earned more than that for the company. David had committed the uncharacteristic error of underestimating the true value of his assets.

If Geffen had been quick to rebuff an Asylum artist looking to

participate in the success of the label with a cry of "You're not my partner," he seemed to entertain no such notion about his relationship
with Warner Bros. The company was tied to him for a long time to
come. Aside from the purchase price, his deal included a five-year employment contract that effectively bound him to Warners for much of
the decade. It was bad enough that he had sold too cheaply, but there
was also the problem of how the purchase price was paid since much
of it was in volatile WCI stock. When the deal was consummated in
1972, David received shares worth more than $4.5 million. Six months
later, their value had plummeted to just $800,000.

In a panic, Geffen went back to Ross and asked him to make him
whole. Ross obliged by pledging to pay David the difference between
the market price of the stock and its value at the time of the Asylum
purchase over a period of five years. In return, though, he wanted Geffen to oversee an expanded record company. Prior to purchasing Asylum, WCI had bought Jac Holzman's Elektra in 1970 for $10 million.
If the price for the label, which boasted the Doors, Carly Simon,
Queen, Harry Chapin, and Judy Collins as well as its outstanding folk
and classical catalogs, wasn't enough of a steal, WCI's accountants immediately took advantage of a little-known aspect of the tax code that
enabled them to write up the value of their new assets to $20 million.
"I did much better for Ross than I did for myself," says Holzman. "He
got his money back from that deal right away. They ended up paying
virtually nothing for Elektra."

Holzman ran the label for two years, but it wasn't the same business
he had entered fresh out of college with $600 in bar mitzvah money.
After twenty years, he was, by his own admission, "burned out." But
Ross also made him part of a seven-man brain trust to investigate opportunities being presented by new technologies, a job that Holzman
loved. The fact that he wanted to move to Hawaii didn't faze Ross.
Holzman didn't foresee any problem working on the technologies
from there, but Elektra was another matter. In Geffen, he saw the solution to his problem. "I couldn't tell them I was going without giving
an avenue," says Holzman. "And the avenue was take Geffen's Asylum
away from Atlantic, put it together with Elektra to get some critical
mass, and let David run it."

Put in charge of a combined Elektra/Asylum in July of '73, Geffen
slashed Elektra's artist roster from thirty-five to ten and fired its entire

promotion, publicity, and production staff. Publicly, David trumpeted that he'd single-handedly transformed Elektra from a pauper to a prince. But, privately, he fumed that running a record company for someone else wasn't really what he'd envisioned when he'd sold Asylum. "David was very pissed off at me because he felt I had saddled him with this thing," says Holzman. "He took a lot of potshots at me in the first year or so."

Unhappy, Geffen was on the make again. He suggested to Ahmet Ertegun that Atlantic be combined with Elektra/Asylum and they become cochairmen. Ertegun was receptive. He had not been happy when Asylum was taken away from Atlantic and merged with Elektra, a move that cost Atlantic the additional billing that Asylum provided, and this was a way to get it—and more—back. For Geffen, combining his operation with Atlantic meant a bigger power base for him. Together, the operation would have $100 million in sales, the majority coming from Atlantic.

The merger hit a snag when a group of key Atlantic executives who saw their own stature diminished by the deal, including Jerry Wexler, who continued to loathe Geffen, begged Ertegun to reconsider. "One day you'll cry tears of blood from this wonder boy of yours," Wexler warned him. The merger died.

Looking for opportunities outside WCI, Geffen thought he saw an opening in the L.A. club business. As a manager, he had bristled at the booking policies of the Troubadour, where owner Doug Weston demanded tough terms when it came to options, a contract clause that obligated performers to play the club again. Running the most important club in Los Angeles, Weston frequently insisted on several future appearances in return for a first-time booking. And, of course, there was the issue of money. Weston had been unable to carve a piece of the burgeoning concert business for himself and had no place to put acts that could sell out a ballroom or concert hall. Instead, they were forced to either buy out their option—as Elton John did, paying $25,000 for his three remaining dates—or play in a club that couldn't possibly accommodate all the people who wanted to see them. That often meant working two or three shows a night for six days. And while established stars could command more than the standard $4.50 cover charge, it was a lot more work than they were used to. Geffen portrayed Weston's practices as the most onerous among L.A. club owners. Nine months later, he and a group of partners opened the Roxy to compete with the Troubadour, just a few blocks away.

The other backers of the five-hundred-seat club included Elliot Roberts and Ode Records president Lou Adler, and it was booked by Bill Graham. The opening acts were Cheech and Chong, who were signed to Adler's label, and Graham Nash and Neil Young, both managed by Roberts. Between sets, a group of dancers from the television show *Soul Train* shimmied up and down the aisles—definitely not a Bill Graham touch. But by 1978 its shows were sporadic. By the mid-eighties it was being rented out to promoters on a freelance basis.

Geffen faded out of the Roxy partnership, but he had other irons in the fire. He had been earnestly courting Bob Dylan, whose Columbia recording contract was up, for Elektra/Asylum. Getting next to the reclusive Dylan was not easy, even though he had left Woodstock to live in Malibu, which prompted Geffen to buy a beach house nearby. Geffen ultimately surmised that the Band's Robbie Robertson had Dylan's ear, and Robertson, until then a faithful disciple of Albert Grossman's, could see that his new friend was far more driven than his old mentor. He immediately became a Geffen convert and passed the word along to Dylan.

No longer managed by Grossman, Dylan was unable to get Columbia to write him the lucrative new recording contract he wanted—"Dylan doesn't seem to realize that we're not a nonprofit organization," CBS Records Group president Goddard Lieberson bitterly complained—and he signed with Elektra/Asylum in late '73. Geffen orchestrated a national forty-date concert tour that reunited Dylan with the Band and earned the singer $2.5 million.

It was classic Geffen. The tour coincided with the release of Dylan's Asylum debut, *Planet Waves,* and the attendant publicity drove the record to the top of the charts, making it Dylan's first number one album and a coup for Geffen and Asylum. CBS Records, with the strongest distribution and marketing machine in the business, had never had the same kind of out-of-the-box success with a Dylan album. As an added bonus, Geffen could point to the $2.5 million from the concert tour that the singer wouldn't have made without him, a sweetener that didn't have to come out of the WCI coffers.

If Geffen expected a number one album and a huge payday to make Dylan happy, he had the wrong man. Part of the problem was that

Geffen and tour coordinator Bill Graham, who put together a controversial plan that gave himself a lucrative deal while offering a pittance to local promoters, had succeeded *too* well at conveying the eagerness with which the public had clamored for concert tickets. Initial ticket requests had been so strong that Graham publicly estimated that Dylan could have sold twenty times as many tickets as were available. If so many millions wanted to see him, Dylan reportedly wondered, then why hadn't Geffen sold more copies of *Planet Waves*? Two other Elektra/Asylum albums released around the same time, Carly Simon's *Hotcakes* and Joni Mitchell's *Court and Spark*, had gone on to sell far better.

More to the point, there were rumors that Dylan personally disliked Geffen. "He thought Geffen was just interested in being a celebrity," one source told *Rolling Stone*. Geffen denied the rumors, but the star would be back at Columbia after just a year, signing a deal that reportedly paid him sixty cents a record more than Asylum and gave him a new, improved royalty on his back catalog.

Stung by the rejection, Geffen lashed out at Dylan. "Bob Dylan has made a decision to bet on his past," he said. "I was more interested in his future. He should thank me. At the time he went with me, they weren't that interested in him."

Such carping was mild compared with his complaints to executives at WCI. Without the benefit of the bigger fiefdom that a combined Elektra/Asylum/Atlantic operation would have given him, Geffen was bored. And despite public protestations to the contrary, he was still disgruntled about the way his sale of Asylum had tallied. "He lost enthusiasm for Elektra," recalls one Warner executive. "He was bitter and twisted about how he'd blown his shot at the big score. He made no secret about his discomfiture."

Although the Atlantic merger had fallen through, Ertegun remained sympathetic, as did Warner Bros. Records chairman Mo Ostin. "Mo kind of sided with him," says record producer Joe Boyd. "His attitude was 'This is a very talented guy, we've got to make him happy.' And I think Ahmet felt the same way: Let's make David happy."

There were other reasons for making Geffen happy besides admiration and goodwill. "David Geffen wanted to be out of there in the worst way," recalled Joe Smith, then president of Warner Bros. Records. "He made them crazy to the point that they were going to have to let him out or face a maniac all the time."

In late 1975, Steve Ross named Smith the new chairman of Elektra/Asylum, and Geffen, who had been lobbying in the press for the top studio job at Warner Bros., just about got his wish. He was named vice chairman of the film company, reporting to his old talent agency boss, Ted Ashley. It was a tremendous show of support for someone who had no prior studio experience. But as a studio chieftain, he would prove a washout.

Part of the problem was a matter of style. David had prospered as the head of his own companies and as a label chairman for Ross in large measure because those situations gave him the freedom to follow his own gut instincts and make quick decisions. At the studio, Geffen had to contend with a laborious group process for approving projects. "I hated those meetings," Geffen later said. "I'm ready to be responsible for everything; I'm not good unless I'm responsible. I'm not good unless my deciding to do it is the last decision that has to be made."

Nor did Geffen approach the job with the same focus as the other film executives. "He didn't read!" says Boyd. "You used to see [vice president of production] John Calley going out every night with a stack of scripts, and he'd come back in the next morning with little bits of paper stuck in all of them with notes. David, the idea of him leaving the studio with a stack of reading for the night was anathema. So he couldn't make head or tail of the whole thing and left with his tail between his legs."

Ashley soft-pedals the quick end that came to Geffen's Warner Bros. Pictures career. "This wasn't one of those somebody-fired-somebody kind of things," he says. "It was 'David, you're a superstar. But you should never work for anybody. Never.' " As Ashley remembers, the parting, which took place at an est meeting, was a love fest, ending with the requisite Hollywood Hug.

Geffen was essentially phased out of the WCI loop. On November 10, 1976, a company press release said that Geffen had resigned as vice chairman of the studio and was going to become executive assistant to Steve Ross. With nominal roles on the boards of the film and record companies, it appeared to be a position designed largely to allow him to sit out the remainder of his contract. And although Geffen said he would be involved in possible acquisitions, he resisted Ross's suggestion that he move to New York, where the chairman normally parked executives he wasn't sure what to do with.

By the following year, however, he moved east on his own, just as his five-year contract with Warner Bros. expired. Save for teaching a two-day-a-week course at Yale on the music business, Geffen, for all intents and purposes, had retired. It had been a tremendous ascent and a disappointing end. At thirty-four, David Geffen had an entertainment career that, if not dead, was no longer the unblemished track record of a wunderkind. For the first time, he seemed unsure of himself.

"I have no plans," he told *Variety* as his WCI contract lapsed. "None whatsoever, although I intend to leave Warner Bros. I've had a lot of offers, but I'm not interested in any of them now. Teaching is a lot of fun and I enjoy it. And until I figure out something I think I will enjoy equally as much, I'd just as soon teach."

His downfall was greeted with undisguised glee in many quarters, not just Hollywood. *The New Yorker* writer and Ertegun hagiographer George Trow haughtily dismissed the executive with a one-sentence put-down worthy of Ertegun himself. "There was," he wrote, "a brief vogue for David Geffen." But the truth was David still had admirers and supporters within the business who were willing to recognize his brilliance, not the least of whom were Mo Ostin and Steve Ross. David Geffen would be back. And this time, *he'd* be Chief of the World.

12

THE PLAYER

BRUCE SPRINGSTEEN'S MANAGER, MIKE APPEL, WAS NO DAVID GEF-FEN. A failed musician looking for a way to stay in the business, he had drifted into songwriting and producing. He found a writing partner, Jim Cretecos, and a job in New York with an old-style Tin Pan Alley jingle factory, the Wes Farrell Organization. For $300 a week, Appel cranked out commercials for Kleenex tissues and Mr. Pibb soda and songs for middle-of-the-road singers like Paul Anka and the made-for-television bubblegum group the Partridge Family. When one of Appel's Partridge Family songs, "Doesn't Somebody Want to Be Wanted," became a million-selling Top 10 hit, it didn't make him rich, as his salary was recoupable against royalties. Worse, you didn't have to be David Geffen to see that the Farrell Organization was the kind of music business schlock house that was fast becoming an anachronism. At a time when the artist-oriented Asylum was the record industry bellwether and its founder a millionaire, writing songs for the Partridge Family wasn't the kind of thing you bragged about.

In a bid to get closer to the action, Appel and Cretecos sought out rock bands to work with. The results proved farcical. In 1969, they cowrote and produced songs for an early heavy metal trio from Brooklyn named Sir Lord Baltimore. The owner of the New Jersey studio where the band was recording introduced Appel to someone who could get the band a label contract: Dee Anthony.

"He says he thinks he can do something to help us out," Appel recalls. " 'My word is my bond, Mike,' and he shakes my hand. I was a kid then, I didn't know any better. He took my tapes out of that studio, sold them to Mercury, took the entire advance. I never got anything except some kind of credit."

Were he not convinced he'd been had, Appel might have considered himself lucky to be out of the picture. Anthony, who disputes Appel's recollection (he says the Mercury advance was used to pay the band's studio bill and that he never made any money off Sir Lord Baltimore), took the band straight to Frank Barsalona at Premier, who booked them into Bill Graham's Fillmore East. There, the group instantly attained legendary status—as one of the worst bands to ever play the storied hall. Summoned to Graham's office after the group's first set, Anthony and Barsalona were told by the furious promoter that Sir Lord Baltimore was, in a word, "pus." Anthony quickly beat his own retreat, calling the band "horrible" and claiming he'd only gotten involved with them as a favor for a friend.

Appel and Cretecos's other flyer into the world of progressive rock was a Crosby, Stills and Nash knock-off band named Montana Flintlock, which, if possible, fared even worse than Sir Lord Baltimore. Yet Montana Flintlock would pay Appel an unexpected dividend. On the road, the band used a soundman named Carl "Tinker" West. Tinker, who built surfboards on the New Jersey shore, had also dabbled a little in band management. In the fall of '71, he heard that Appel and Cretecos were looking for other acts to work with—preferably acts that wrote their own songs so Appel wouldn't have to give the publishing to Wes Farrell—and he told Appel he should hear one of the kids who'd played in a couple of bands he had managed, a prolific songwriter named Bruce Springsteen.

When Tinker brought Springsteen to the Wes Farrell office, he didn't make much of an impression on Appel. Dressed in a T-shirt and torn dungarees, Springsteen was thin and almost painfully shy. He played two songs at the piano as if his life depended upon it, but Mike found him obtuse and wordy. "They were the worst two songs I ever heard in my life," Appel told writer Charles Cross. "The only thing memorable about one of the songs was that he was dancing with a girl who was deaf, dumb, and blind. And there was reference to the fact that he was dancing to a silent orchestra. I thought it was kind of interesting and offbeat."

Appel told Springsteen he'd have to write more commercial songs if he wanted a record deal. "There's just nothing here that anyone is going to get excited about," Appel told him. "It's gonna flop." Springsteen said he was going to California to visit his family for a couple of months, but that he'd be back in touch. Appel promptly forgot all about him.

Four months later, when the receptionist buzzed Appel to say Bruce Springsteen was on the line, Appel told her he'd never heard of him, and only the mention of Tinker's name jogged his memory. This time, when Springsteen played a new song called "It's Hard to Be a Saint in the City," Appel was floored. After making him sing the song a second time, Appel and Cretecos quickly said they'd manage him. "The second time," Appel recalled, "as he was singing that song with those lyrics, I said, 'Why me, Lord?' I'm a guy with all this candy-assed pop commercial kind of records that I've been involved in all my life, like the Partridge Family. Why would I get a guy like this?" It was an excellent question.

AFTER THE SCREWING THEY BELIEVED THEY'D TAKEN ON SIR LORD BALTImore, Appel and Cretecos weren't going to trust anyone else near Springsteen. No well-connected middleman like Dee Anthony was going to be invited in, and they certainly weren't going to risk the publishing income by letting Wes Farrell—who was still paying their salaries—get the faintest whiff of Springsteen. "They were scamming under Wes's nose," says Bob Spitz.

A publishing administrator for Farrell, Spitz was yet another would-be performer who had drifted to the business side after admitting a recording career wasn't in his future. Cretecos and Appel told him they were going to leave Farrell to produce and manage Springsteen and suggested he come with them. One listen was all it took to convince Spitz. "They'd just gotten a tape of Bruce's," he recalls. "The next day Bruce was in the office; he sat on a chair in Wes's office and played a song for me he'd just written called 'No Need.' "

Quiet and reserved, Springsteen hadn't made much of a first impression, but when he began to sing, Spitz, only too aware of his own shortcomings as a musician and songwriter, marveled at his ability to reinvent himself.

"He was nothing in a social situation," says Spitz. "He was shy. Bruce was like a social misfit—he couldn't handle his own stuff. He had a little mousy girlfriend who did all his talking for him, and he had a different one every week. But they were all of the same variety: very mousy, very New Jersey, very Gentile, very uneducated. But in 'No Need' he had the line 'You know I stumble when I talk, so she says, "Babe, don't talk at all, just sing." ' I thought, 'This guy knows what he's all about.' I knew right away this was the most amazing stuff I'd ever heard."

It was also impossible to argue with Appel's enthusiasm for his new discovery. Recalled Spitz, "Mike had just had his second daughter, and Wes Farrell was his lifeline. Not only for a check every week; his insurance was paid. But he was sold on Bruce enough to know right away that he was ditching it all. And he never thought he was rolling the dice: he knew what he had. I remember that as vividly as anything—Mike knew what he had."

It soon became apparent that they wouldn't have to wait long before Springsteen had enough material for an album. Keyboardist and band mate Danny Federici, who had played with Springsteen since they were teenagers and even lived with him at Tinker's surfboard factory, had been overwhelmed by how productive he could be. "Bruce was incredibly energetic," Federici told writer Robert Santelli. "He was writing an unbelievable amount of songs—five or ten a day. And they were epics . . . The most amazing thing was that one night, say a Friday, we'd do a thirty-song set. The next night, Saturday, we'd do an entirely different thirty-song set—all written that week."

Not all of the songs were gems, though. Appel, abrasive and impulsive by nature, was not the kind of person to hold his tongue if he thought Springsteen had written something that was subpar, and he relished his role as the bad cop. "One of the reasons that most artists—most of the good ones—slip into this indolence, this sloth of ordinary material, is because there's no cattle prod around," he says. "No prick like Mike Appel. I'd say, 'I can't *stand* this song!' "

With no solid connections and only his belief in Springsteen to work with, Appel simply decided to bulldoze his way into an audition for his client. One afternoon, just a few months after they had begun working with Springsteen, Appel, Cretecos, and Spitz commandeered the office of Farrell's administrator, Vel Thornton, while she was out to lunch and placed a call to John Hammond, the legendary A&R executive at Columbia, who had signed Bob Dylan. His career as a talent scout for the label went back to the thirties, when he had signed blues great Bessie Smith and jazz giants Count Basie, Billie Holiday, Teddy Wilson, Charlie Christian, and Benny Goodman. In later years, he brought Aretha Franklin, George Benson, and Stevie Ray Vaughan to the record company. Privileged and erudite, he was everything Appel was not. They immediately hated each other.

During that first telephone call, Appel went out of his way to denigrate Hammond, even as he was begging the A&R man's secretary for an audition. "He said, 'I hear [Hammond] has ears, and I just want to see if that's true,'" recalls Spitz. "Jimmy [Cretecos] and I looked at each other—I wanted to fall off the chair. I thought he was out of his fucking mind." Nevertheless, Hammond's secretary scheduled an audition.

Performing in Hammond's office for two hours with an acoustic guitar, Springsteen played several of his most recent songs, including "It's Hard to Be a Saint in the City," "Growin' Up," and "If I Were the Priest," a song about the Virgin Mary running a whorehouse in the Old West with Jesus as a customer. His cascading tumult of lyrics and religious imagery immediately grabbed Hammond, who pegged Springsteen as a refugee from a parochial school education. "That's the damndest song I've ever heard," Hammond later recalled telling Springsteen. "Were you brought up by nuns?" The guess was on the money.

Springsteen's childhood had been bracketed by two strict and unapproving bookends, Catholic school and his father. Springsteen had loathed school, "the big hate," he called it. When he thought of his formal education, it wasn't learning or friendship that came to mind but humiliation and rejection. And what he remembered most clearly was the punishment meted out by the nuns. When he was thirteen, he'd been made to sit in a first-grade class after wising off. "Show this young man what we do to people who smile in this classroom," a nun had said to one six-year-old boy, who promptly walked over to Springsteen and slapped him across the face. He could still feel the sting, just as he could not forget the time a nun had stuffed him in a garbage pail or all the days that he'd been forced to wait after school for his parents to come and pick him up. The stale odors of the convent had made him throw up, and he came to think of them as the smell of religion.

He remained an outsider even after leaving parochial school to attend Freehold Regional High. But he found a refuge in rock and roll. "Nothing hit me until I was about fourteen," he told writer Peter Knobler. "And when it did, it hit me completely, took over my whole life. Everything from then on revolved around music. Everything." At fifteen he joined a local band, the Castiles, named for a popular shampoo, and discovered that being in a rock group conferred the status and cachet that had otherwise always eluded him. Although his skin was badly pitted with acne scars, he suddenly found himself surrounded by girls whenever they played a dance. Just as important, the group provided him with a new family: Tex Vinyard, who managed the Castiles and numerous other local groups, was a generous man who opened his house to the young musicians, buying them equipment and lending them money. He had a special affection for Springsteen and gave him the keys to the house. Springsteen soon took to calling Tex's wife, Marion, "Mom" and sometimes lived with them.

It was a vast improvement over his real family. Springsteen had been running away from home since he was eleven. The tension between him and his father, Douglas, was constant, and they couldn't seem to agree on anything, especially Bruce's infatuation with music. "When I was growing up there were two things that were unpopular in my house," he would say years later. "One was me, the other was my guitar." In the faded, blue-collar resort towns of central New Jersey, Douglas Springsteen took work as he could find it, as a gardener, a worker in a Nestlé's factory, a prison guard. Music, as far as he could see, was a waste of time and a dead end. "Bruce's dad was rough," says Spitz. "And Bruce needed a dad."

Bruce's mother, Adele, was left to negotiate the unhappy ground between her son and her husband. When Bruce ran away to Greenwich Village on the eve of a school graduation, she'd been able to talk him back by reminding him of a party planned at the house and promising there wouldn't be a fight when he came home. But as soon as he got there, his father yanked him into the house, leaving a girl Bruce had brought with him standing outside, and threw him into his room. Removing all the lightbulbs, Douglas Springsteen left his son sitting in the dark to ponder both his sins and his future.

By the time Bruce had turned eighteen, the family had moved to San Mateo, California, without him, and within a month he was evicted from the house. He attended Ocean County Community College for two months but dropped out when the school psychiatrist invited him in for a talk after classmates complained about him. With the Vietnam War on, that meant the end of his student deferment, although he would later say that the army similarly turned up its nose at him "for reasons of weirdness."

Like Spitz, Hammond recognized that Springsteen had used rock and roll to reinvent himself, to defeat a life that was otherwise painful and meaningless. Deeply moved by the results, Hammond virtually agreed to sign Springsteen on the spot. A live showcase was arranged for that evening at the Gaslight in the Village, and Springsteen and Appel were asked to return the next day to record a studio demo.

On the street in front of the CBS building, Appel and Springsteen gave each other an ecstatic hug. A record deal! Now the new life they'd each dreamed of would begin. "We were gonna be a whole family," says Spitz. "Mike had already been my dad. Now he was gonna adopt Bruce, too."

BRUCE SPRINGSTEEN WASN'T THE ONLY MEMBER OF THE NEW "FAMILY" VINdicated by the Columbia Records signing. Mike Appel could also see his dreams coming true. He was going to be a player. Dee Anthony may have squeezed him out of the picture with Sir Lord Baltimore, but Appel envied his power and that of other successful rock managers. "That was Mike's pantheon," says Spitz. "Power guys. Guys who could push. Mike's idols either screwed him or were tough talkers. Albert Grossman was an idol of Mike's. And Mike believed all the lore and wanted to be just like Albert, he wanted to be just like Dee Anthony. He wanted to ride like a steamroller over people. And yet he didn't have it in him."

When too many calls came into the Farrell Organization regarding Springsteen, the family quickly folded its tent. They crashed at Spitz's Twelfth Street studio apartment before moving into the midtown office of Appel's attorney, Jules Kurz. And when Springsteen's advance money finally came through from Columbia, Appel decided it was time to step up in the world and get his own offices. As far as he was concerned, there was only one address worth having: 75 East Fifty-fifth Street, where Albert B. Grossman Management had its offices. "Mike wanted to fuck where Albert fucked," says Spitz. "That was the only building we went to see. Albert was on the fourth floor, we were upstairs. But we got close enough that Mike could smell it."

In June, CBS Records sent Appel two checks totaling $25,000 as an advance against future Springsteen royalties. Appel had followed the general and onerous industry practice favored by the managers he admired and signed Springsteen to concurrent management, production, and music publishing agreements. What he didn't bother to do was open a business account. Instead, he deposited the two checks into the personal account he maintained at a small bank near the office.

Although Springsteen's production contract with Appel and Cretecos's Laurel Canyon Ltd. entitled him to approximately one third of all royalties due from Columbia Records, it made no specific mention of how advances were to be distributed. And, in keeping with standard industry practice, Appel's company had the right to deduct all costs from Springsteen's share. "Some of that was Bruce's money," Spitz says of the advance. "But it was never Bruce's money. [Appel] gave him a little for his apartment rent."

Springsteen didn't care. He bought a new guitar and, for the first time in his life, rented his own apartment, a small, disheveled place in the shore town of Bradley Beach. More important, Mike Appel had helped him to get what he wanted most in the world: a recording contract and a shot at becoming a rock star.

John Hammond, fearing the worst regarding Appel and his business arrangements with Springsteen, had convinced the reluctant manager to show the contracts to a leading copyright lawyer. According to Hammond, the attorney had pronounced it "a slave contract." Yet the talent scout had to admit that if Appel remained unmoved, so did Springsteen. His warnings to the young rocker fell on deaf ears. "I tried to tell it to Bruce," said Hammond, "but Bruce was loyal."

It was not really a question of loyalty. Springsteen was ecstatic to have a recording contract, but he was willfully ignorant of the business. "Bruce," says Spitz, "was a happy guy. Bruce felt like Mike was taking care of him because he wanted to make a record, and he got to make a record." When Spitz tried to get Springsteen to copyright a notebook full of unrecorded songs, Bruce was uninterested. The concept of protecting his work was alien; he wanted to get a record. He wanted to take himself to the next step.

Springsteen's disinterest in money made life simple for Appel. Nearly half of the Columbia advance went to setting up Laurel Canyon's new offices. Unleashed, Appel and Spitz went on a shopping spree, spending $12,000 on office furniture at Macy's.

Spitz, who was keeping the books, such as they were, began to grow leery. "Mike wanted everything," says Spitz. "He wanted to look great. Michael wore a jean jacket, and that money went into the front flap of his jean jacket and he did everything in cash for a while. Or he'd write a check out of our account. None of it went to Bruce. I'd say, 'Mike, we have to start putting accounts in order.' And he'd say, 'Don't worry about it. Theoretically, everything is for Bruce's good, anyway.' "

If neither Springsteen nor Appel had any idea of what they were supposed to be doing with the advance, they were both eager to get going on recording an album. The entire advance of $25,000 was hardly an extravagant budget—and, of course, now there was nowhere near that amount available for studio time. So instead of working with a topflight Manhattan recorder, Appel booked Springsteen into Studio 914 in tiny Blauvelt, New York, because it was owned by an acquaintance of Appel's, engineer Brooks Arthur, who was willing to extend unlimited time and credit to them. The basic tracks on all nine songs were recorded in a single day, and the entire process took only about a week. Coproduced by Appel, Cretecos, and Springsteen in the summer of '72, *Greetings from Asbury Park, N.J.* was released by Columbia in January of the following year.

The five months between recording and release left a huge gap during which no money was coming in, and they began to think about rustling up some gigs. For that, they would need an agent. Spitz, who had promoted concerts as a college student, knew how tough it could be just to get the attention of an agency. The only one to take Spitz seriously—even when he had money to spend on talent—was a junior agent at the William Morris Agency in New York named Sam McKeith. In late August, when Springsteen had a show slated for Max's Kansas City, Spitz called him. The agent remembered him immediately.

"You're in the music business now?" McKeith asked.

"Yeah," said Spitz, "and I got a kid."

The agent was unimpressed. "Everybody's got a kid," he said.

"This guy's been signed to Columbia. You should come hear him."

McKeith did, but Springsteen's acoustic performance, with Spitz accompanying him poorly on second guitar, left the agent unconvinced. "I could tell that this guy was very talented," he said, "but I found the stuff he was playing to be very depressing."

Appel and Spitz kept after him, coming up to the William Morris office with a tape of three of the songs Springsteen had cut for *Greetings from Asbury Park, N.J.* Whether it was the band arrangements, the performances, or the lyrics—which reminded the agent by turns of Dylan, Van Morrison, and the Byrds—the tape turned the trick. McKeith decided to sign him.

What Spitz and Appel didn't know was that an unspoken variable regarding the internal politics of the William Morris Agency weighed even heavier in McKeith's mind. He liked Springsteen and thought he was talented, and it certainly helped that the singer had been signed to Columbia and had the powerful backing of Clive Davis as well as Hammond. But Bruce Springsteen was a white rock and roll act, and McKeith was the only black agent at William Morris.

In the late sixties, the agency had begun to take a lot of heat from the African-American community for its absence of black executives. William Morris had traditionally handled black acts, including Ray Charles and the entire Motown Records roster, but its only black agent had been Wally Amos, and he had left the company to form Famous Amos cookies.

McKeith was recruited in 1968—the year Geffen left the agency—as a one-man affirmative action program. Not surprisingly, he was never considered for William Morris's tonier departments like television, motion pictures, or theater. Instead, he was dumped on Steve Leber, head of the music department. Already bent out of shape over his department's lack of status at William Morris and looking to get out, Leber was livid.

"Were they going to make a black guy a movie agent?" asks Leber. "A television agent? Are you kidding? There was prejudice and a feeling that these guys weren't competent enough to become television or motion picture agents. They should only be music agents. They never respected the music department."

Leber took McKeith on as his own assistant. But the embittered Leber pulled no punches with his new trainee. "You're the house nigger," he announced flatly. This wasn't exactly news to McKeith, but he was willing to put in the hours and do the hump work and within a few months found that he actually liked it. And along with whatever lessons Leber would have imparted to any trainee, he had one more for McKeith. A large measure of Wally Amos's success at William Morris, Leber told him, had come as a result of signing Simon and Garfunkel, which, more than anything else, had validated Amos in the eyes of the agency's senior executives.

"Sam," Leber told him, "I want you to promise me one thing. They're going to try to get you to sign black acts and give you all the black acts when I leave. Do me one favor, please. Make sure you go out and get a white act. Because the only way you're ever going to be big in their eyes is to get a white group."

In Bruce Springsteen, Sam McKeith saw his white act and professional salvation. He called Appel the day after receiving the three-song tape and said he wanted to represent him.

Appel, meanwhile, wondered how he had gotten involved with what appeared to be the world's only black rock and roll agent. Sensing the way things worked at William Morris, Appel went to see McKeith and asked him point-blank if he really had the leverage to get Springsteen in front of white audiences. "What am I going to do?" Appel later recalled. "Have Bruce open for Teddy Pendergrass?"

McKeith, who had by now decided that he *had* to have Springsteen, believed it was a fair question. He had heard that the rival ICM agency also wanted Springsteen and fretted about how Columbia might counsel Appel. William Morris had not done a good job recently for several of its acts, and the label was steering its artists to other agencies. He quickly tried to allay Appel's fears and close the deal. "He was asking the right questions," McKeith says. "I'm talking about what we can do, how we're going to do it. I had the territory for him. I wanted Bruce Springsteen."

What McKeith didn't tell Appel was that while he had helped Stevie Wonder build a white audience by encouraging him to play important rock venues like the Troubadour and laid the groundwork for the big crossover success Wonder would enjoy in 1972 with the album *Talking Book* and his opening slot on the Rolling Stones' American tour that year, he didn't have much experience working with white acts. Still, he did have something unique to offer. Leber had initially encouraged him to concentrate on booking gigs for acts already signed to the agency rather than focus on being a talent scout. McKeith had inherited the northeast territory when another agent left and knew all its colleges and clubs cold. He also knew from experience that the region was a particularly difficult one for black artists and was convinced that he could sell Springsteen like no other act he'd handled before. Pledging that he would work his tail off and put Springsteen on bills only with white acts, McKeith finally convinced Appel that he was the right man for the job. Where a more established agent with other opportunities would have given Springsteen only the attention that an untried, unknown act whose first two singles sold virtually no copies deserved, Sam McKeith literally booked Bruce Springsteen as if his career depended upon it. If Springsteen had any idea how lucky he was, he never said. But Appel and Spitz were quickly convinced they'd made the right move. "Sam laid his life on the line," says Spitz. "The day Bruce came into that office, he booked Bruce blind."

It was the financial lifeline Appel and Springsteen needed. For $1,500 a show, Springsteen began to work the northeast college and club circuit, beginning in November of '72 with a show at York College in York, Pennsylvania, that also marked the debut of Bruce's new group, the E Street Band. The following January, when Columbia released *Greetings from Asbury Park, N.J.,* Springsteen played his showcase for Boston critics at Paul's Mall. McKeith, who still hadn't gotten Springsteen to sign his William Morris contract, followed him up to the club to try and close the deal. He was puzzled to discover the same indifference to business that Spitz had seen.

"It was so hard getting all the papers signed by this guy," says McKeith. "Now I'm up in Boston, I had the papers with me. I go, 'Bruce—you gotta sign this, you didn't do this. I gotta get it done.' He looks me straight in the face and says, 'I dunno . . . All these papers . . . I tell you what I'm gonna do. I'm gonna trust you.' " Without reading the contract, Springsteen signed it.

When it came to performing, however, Springsteen didn't need anyone to tell him how to be an entertainer. Recalls Spitz, "When Bruce got on a stage, Mike and I would sit there and say, 'Where are all these stories coming from?' Bruce didn't get onstage and kick ass— Bruce got onstage and was *funny.* He'd introduce a song for five minutes. People would roll in the aisles, and then he'd play the song. That was all intact when we met him. Bruce had his persona, he knew what he wanted to do. As much as I'd like to believe that Mike and Jimmy shaped Bruce, Bruce was Bruce. Underneath that reticence was a guy who really had a good grasp of where he wanted to go."

Performing was a way for Springsteen to be the person he had never been as a kid. In real life, he was a loser, the poor kid from the wrong side of the tracks who always seemed to be walking with his head down, the disappointing son, the teenager left behind by his family, the guarded, socially inept young man who preferred to let his girlfriends do his talking. But in front of a crowd, with a guitar strapped across his shoulder, Bruce Springsteen was dynamic, self-assured, and powerful. The transformation grew out of a deep need to repudiate a painful past and bleak future and seemed, to those who met him, purely emotional. "So frequently the artistic need is completely unconnected to intellectual ability," observes Jeff Albertson, who hung around with Springsteen whenever the rocker came to Boston. "One of the important things to remember about Bruce is that he isn't very bright—all you have to do is listen to him for fifteen or twenty minutes. And the lack of self-doubt that comes with not being that bright is a very, very useful thing to guys like that."

The easy confidence that was always a part of Springsteen's show was not, however, evident in the recording studio. Beginning with his first album, Bruce developed a pattern of last-minute perseveration, always second-guessing his own creative decisions. After test pressings of *Greetings from Asbury Park, N.J.* had been distributed, Springsteen listened to the album and decided he wanted to replace two songs, including "It's Hard to Be a Saint in the City." Appel, who was on a business trip to Los Angeles at the time, had to spend over three hours on the telephone convincing Springsteen to let the record stand.

Appel's faith in Springsteen never flagged. Certainly his own success would be tied up with his client's, but, financial irresponsibility notwithstanding, he served Springsteen heart and soul. He saw his job as taking care of him and ensuring that he became a star, and he did it with gusto. "When Clarence [Clemons] first got into the band, we bailed him out of jail for nonpayment of child support," says Spitz, and "Vini [drummer Vini Lopez] for fighting. I'd say to Mike, 'That's their problem.' He'd say, 'Do it. No ruffles for Bruce. I want Bruce to see we're taking care of everything. He's to create, he's to make music, that's what Bruce does.' And Mike protected him." Still, there was something undeniably abrasive and self-destructive about Appel. Like his client, he hungered for the chance to be someone else; he looked with uncontained glee toward the day when Bruce Springsteen would be the mammoth star that he, Mike Appel, had been the first to recognize. And then he was going to rub everybody's nose in it. On a trip to Los Angeles in the summer of '72 to meet Peter Golden, William Morris's influential West Coast music agent, Appel decided to have a little fun.

"Bobby," he said to Spitz, "go make a tape copy of the test pressing."

"What for?" Spitz asked.

"We're going to shop Bruce. Let's take it around and see if other people hear it."

At A&M, Appel and Spitz played the tape of *Greetings from Asbury Park, N.J.*, pretending it was a demo they were peddling rather than a completed album by an artist signed to a rival label. They made similar stops at ABC/Dunhill and Mercury, all with one hope: to collect rejection letters on Bruce Springsteen. They weren't disappointed.

"Mike wanted to shop him to have those letters so he could later throw it in everybody's faces," recalls Spitz. "They were on our wall for a long time."

Appel's thirst for vindication was somewhat more constructive when it came to Columbia. He was constantly badgering the label to support his client, but, aside from Hammond and Davis, Springsteen initially found few champions there. Typical was the reaction of Tom Werman, an influential Epic Records producer and A&R executive, who went away from one of Springsteen's early shows scratching his head. "You got the craziest guy in the world," Appel recalls him saying. "I don't know what that guy was."

One of the few true believers at Columbia was publicist Peter Philbin. Indeed, Springsteen was the sole reason he was at the label. While working as a freelance journalist, Philbin had penned an early and well-publicized rave review of Springsteen's February '73 showcase at the Troubadour, which had led to a friendship with Appel and Springsteen. A few months later he moved to New York and began palling around with Springsteen. Scuffling for work as a writer, he landed a job writing artist bios for CBS Records' international division and eventually became part of the publicity department. "I thought, 'Great—now I can work on Bruce's albums.' " Along with Ron Oberman, a young publicist at Columbia, Philbin preached the gospel according to Bruce. Most just didn't get it.

"I saw Bruce clear Max's Kansas City," says Philbin. "I had seen Bruce the night before, and he was great. So I brought ten people from Columbia down. At the end of the evening, Mike and I were the only ones there. Everyone else said, 'You're nuts,' and left."

Appel understood only too well from his own experiences as a musician and songwriter that nine out of ten artists signed to major record company contracts failed, and he was willing to do anything to make sure his client was the exception rather than the rule. When *Greetings from Asbury Park, N.J.* sold a disappointing twenty thousand copies, he responded by pushing Columbia as loudly and arrogantly as he could, making himself a pariah at the label. "Mike burned a lot of bridges," says Philbin.

Springsteen's growing popularity as a club act was one of the few good cards that Appel and Springsteen held. "*Asbury Park* fizzled out," recalls McKeith, "and Bruce got a little gun-shy." Aside from the poor sales, reviews had been generally good but far from overwhelming, with many critics resisting the hype Clive Davis was feeding them and not quite sure what to make of Springsteen's tangled imagery and endless barrage of lyrics, even when they appeared to like them. Writing what was meant to be a flattering review in *Creem*, Dave Marsh crowned Springsteen "the obvious heir-apparent to the throne of Scuzz King of Rock 'n' Roll" and a man who "doesn't give a shit how big a fool he makes of himself."

Such pronouncements couldn't have been cheering to Columbia or Springsteen. But the commercial failure of *Greetings from Asbury Park, N.J.* turned the heat up a notch, and for his next album Springsteen put together a collection of seven songs that, with the exception of its final track, "Wild Billy's Circus Story," hung together loosely as a conceptual collection. *The Wild, the Innocent, and the E Street Shuffle* was Springsteen's romantic vision of life on the streets. Lyrically, it was as bombastic and overloaded as the first album, but it gave a real indication that Springsteen was a rock and roller. More raucous and band-oriented than its predecessor, it was a step forward.

It didn't sell either. Support at Columbia was quickly evaporating.

With Davis gone and Hammond on the verge of mandatory retirement, the doubts that Charlie Koppelman and Kip Cohen had expressed when they rejected the original tapes of *The Wild, the Innocent, and the E Street Shuffle* were indicative of Columbia's general attitude toward Springsteen. In the wake of the album's commercial failure, those doubts were intensifying. Koppelman wanted Springsteen to back away from the harder rock edge that he was working and record in Nashville as a solo act. Even Hammond called the new album "a disaster" and believed Springsteen's recordings were misdirected, failing to convey his passion and intensity.

Appel was livid. "Mike said, 'You know the only reason John Hammond gets guys like Bruce?' " says Spitz. " 'It's because we throw them in his lap. He's a lucky guy.' " Philbin, Oberman, and the small cadre of Springsteen fans at Columbia lobbied to keep him, arguing that he should be allowed to make records the way he wanted to.

If Springsteen's appeal wasn't evident in his record sales, it was a different story on the road, where McKeith's club bookings and Springsteen's onstage abilities were producing a small but rabid following. McKeith and Appel pulled some strings just prior to the recording of *The Wild, the Innocent, and the E Street Shuffle* and got Springsteen the opening slot on an arena tour by Chicago, then at the height of their popularity. The twelve-date tour would allow him to play to his largest audiences yet—between ten and fifteen thousand per show.

Initially, the dates went well. But when the band played the Spectrum in Philadelphia, a city Springsteen considered his home territory, it proved a frustrating and humbling experience. "Kids were throwing rolls of toilet paper during 'For You,' " Appel recalls. When a beach ball landed on his piano, Springsteen had had enough. Kicking over a chair backstage, he vowed he'd never open another tour. "Mike, we can't do this anymore," he yelled. "We can't *do* this! When this tour ends, we'll call it quits and go back to the clubs and start from zero!"

Although he feared McKeith might lose some of his enthusiasm, Appel had no choice. But the agent took it in stride, and the energy and length of Springsteen's shows soon became the talk of the rock scene and a key part of his ultimate success. More important, his faith in his own abilities as a performer appeared unshakable when he knew that the audience, no matter how small, was there to see *him*. "I've known artists who couldn't play to empty seats," says Philbin. "It drove Bruce. I've seen him play shows to seven people where he killed."

But at Columbia the pressure was on Springsteen and Appel to prove that he could have a hit single. Just two months after the release of *The Wild, the Innocent, and the E Street Shuffle*, Springsteen and Appel began to talk about how they could craft a single from the long, largely introspective material that Springsteen had been writing. Ironically, the man who was constantly being compared with Dylan, who liberated rock from the tyranny of the 45, had to find his way back into that format. And as far as Springsteen was concerned, no one had done more with it than Phil Spector. Ingeniously layered, hopelessly ambitious, the producer's singles featured textures and depths of sound far in advance of what the studio technology of the early sixties should have allowed. They were deliciously over the top and as immediate as the roar of a motorcycle. None excited Springsteen or suggested the still-to-be-discovered frontiers of rock music to him more than "Be My Baby" by the Ronettes. Maybe, he suggested, a Ronettes-inspired sound would work on a song he was working on called "Born to Run."

Springsteen's desire to replicate Spector's "wall of sound" meant extensive overdubbing, recording numerous versions of a part and piling them one on top of the other. It was a new and laborious style of recording. *Greetings from Asbury Park, N.J.* had taken a week to record, *The Wild, the Innocent, and the E Street Shuffle* two months. Springsteen and Appel worked on the song "Born to Run" for three months, never losing sight of the fact that it had to fit into a Top 40 radio station's format. Playing a completed version of it one night for *Crawdaddy!* editor Peter Knobler, Bruce seemed finally satisfied with the results. "WABC!" Springsteen chimed in at the tape's conclusion, imitating the powerhouse New York station's jingle. Knobler had to admit it sounded like a pop hit.

Columbia, despite having just fortified Springsteen with the ad campaign built around Landau's review, wasn't so sure. They didn't want to release "Born to Run" as a single, especially when there was no album to promote with it. In desperation, Appel sent tapes of the song to disc jockeys around the country who had been supportive of Springsteen. It was an open challenge to the label and could have further eroded the already shaky relationship, but the gambit paid off.

Listener response to "Born to Run" was immediate, and fans turned up at record stores looking for a record that didn't exist. It was an embarrassment for Columbia but proof nonetheless that Springsteen could have a hit record. Suddenly the label was eager to get his next album.

But Springsteen had band problems. Earlier in the year he had fired drummer Vini Lopez, replacing him with Ernest "Boom" Carter, a friend of keyboardist Davey Sancious. Then, in August, as they began to cut "Born to Run," Sancious and Carter quit. Epic's Tom Werman, who had once characterized Springsteen as "the craziest guy in the world," had offered Sancious his own contract. Carter went with him. The double loss was a disaster musically. Worse, Springsteen couldn't tour without a band, and the departures precipitated a financial crisis. "By the end of seventy-four Sam McKeith had become the most important factor in our lives," says Appel. "He was getting us three or four college dates a week. We would run out of money, and he would keep us alive so we wouldn't die. And we'd use the money to go into the studio and make records. That's how we kept ourselves going while we did *Born to Run*."

Appel had lost all his credit cards, yet when Springsteen insisted on spending months holding open auditions for band replacements at a Manhattan rehearsal hall, he never balked. If anything, his faith in Springsteen's ultimate success became even more fervent as their financial problems compounded. By comparison, Cretecos had bailed out of the partnership in January of '74, selling his half interest in Springsteen's publishing to Appel for $1,500.

Appel was always belligerent, but now, as if he needed to reinforce his own belief in Springsteen as well as the rest of the world's, he was maniacal. One night, while driving to a band audition, he picked a fight with Philbin.

"How big will Bruce be?" Appel asked him.

Philbin, who was without doubt one of the two or three rabid Springsteen partisans at Columbia, was surprised by the question—his attraction to Bruce was emotional and artistic. To him, Springsteen was an icon of teenage rebellion whose style and persona placed him alongside James Dean and Bob Dylan.

"Kids are going to walk like Bruce," Philbin rhapsodized. "They're going to identify with him."

"Yeah," Appel said impatiently, "but how *big* is he going to be?"

Philbin thought for a minute. Since the Landau-inspired ad campaign, sales of the first two records had finally begun to creep upward. Still, beyond his growing draw as a live act and the recording of "Born to Run," there was nothing other than Bruce's promise to suggest he could become one of rock's commercial elite by "going gold," industry parlance for selling 500,000 copies of an album. But Philbin had enough belief in Springsteen to go out on a limb.

"Gee, I don't know," he said hopefully. "Bruce's next album could sell between five hundred thousand and eight hundred thousand copies."

Appel slammed on the brakes. "Get out of the car!" he screamed. Philbin stared at him. "Get out of the car!" Stunned, Philbin did as he was told. Without another word, Appel reached across the front seat, slammed the door closed, and sped off in a rage.

Nearly twenty years later, after Bruce Springsteen had become a star far beyond what any of his other early advocates had ever imagined, Philbin would look back at Mike Appel with a mixture of anger and admiration. "That guy slammed the door on me and drove away," he says. "But he was right. Mike Appel had a vision, and it was the right one, even though he alienated a ton of people. He saw it when no one else did. He saw what Bruce could be. Bruce later played the Los Angeles Coliseum. I never saw Elvis play the Coliseum. He signed Bruce for all the right reasons, and he was pure of heart."

Decidedly less pure was what Mike Appel envisioned Bruce Springsteen doing for him. He believed to his toes that Springsteen was a star, but he also saw him as the springboard for his own career as a power in the business. Publicly, Appel would term Springsteen "an all-consuming artist," but, quietly, he and Spitz had been searching for other acts to manage, believing that Springsteen's ultimate success would give them the leverage to create a stable of stars. Pulling a page from his own short playbook, he signed an unknown songwriter from New Jersey named Floyd Marcus and rechristened him Penman Floyd. Although he never told Springsteen, he planned to have Floyd tour as his opening act.

If Appel expected lightning to strike twice, he was badly mistaken. A good songwriter with a sweet voice, "[Marcus] couldn't perform his way out of a paper bag," says Spitz. "It was like watching my dentist play." Fearing that Marcus's weakness as a performer would prevent him from getting a record deal, Appel made what Spitz describes as "a very expensive tape—using Bruce Springsteen money."

Still, no one was willing to sign Marcus without seeing him perform. Afraid to put him in a club, Appel rented Columbia Studios on Fifty-third Street and distracted the executives with a lavish catered meal. The sleight of hand didn't fool anyone. Says Spitz, "Mike spent a fortune, all of our money. The guys came in from Epic. They listened; they ate; they left. And that was the end of Penman Floyd."

Like Dee Anthony, who would close his eyes in reverie as if plumbing the depths of a great truth when listening to the witless Sir Lord Baltimore, Appel's flier with Penman Floyd suggested a basic inability to discriminate between a good and a bad act. Appel had been able to recognize Springsteen's talent the first time he heard "It's Hard to Be a Saint in the City," but his second reaction—"why me?"—was just as on target. Only coincidence and circumstance had brought him Bruce Springsteen, and it was now obvious that all of Appel's eggs were in that fateful basket.

Handed the chance to work with Springsteen, Appel had given it his all. But for all his pushing, for all his bluster, for all his work, he would be totally unprepared for Springsteen's success when it came. Trained in the old school of the Wes Farrell Organization, where the company held all the assets while the performers and writers were replaceable cogs, Appel might envy Albert Grossman his power, his influence, and his office furniture, but he never understood what set him apart. Grossman not only said his clients were artists, he believed it, and they, and not the manager or the record company, set the artistic and commercial agendas. As an advocate for the unknown Bruce Springsteen, Mike Appel was superb, hammering away at a largely indifferent record company, saying over and over and over again that his client had to be heard. But in his rush to be an industry player, Appel proved breathtakingly shortsighted. The management, production, and publishing contracts that he placed before his client didn't rectify Springsteen's ignorance and disinterest regarding business, they took advantage of it. Blinded by his own ambitions, Appel had opted not to see the contradiction in treating Bruce Springsteen like one of Wes Farrell's disposable bubblegum acts. That was fine when no one else saw Bruce's promise—then Mike could have him under any conditions he wanted. But once the rest of the world came around and agreed that Springsteen was special, there would be no shortage of potential managers willing to give him a fair shake. With success, it would all have to come crashing down. "You have to envision the success," Philbin says, reflecting on Appel's failing. "You have to try to envision the room you will wind up in. Mike recognized Bruce's talent—he saw rock and roll future years before Jon Landau. But he didn't think it through."

13

THE GURU

IN THE FALL OF 1974, JON LANDAU'S CAREER AS A PRODUCER WAS AT a standstill, but his record reviews for *The Real Paper* and *Rolling Stone* reflected his continuing interest in the business. The passion that had fueled his earlier and best music criticism had been largely replaced by an acute awareness of how music was made and promoted. Landau was far more interested in the role of the behind-the-scene professional than most critics, and his reviews were liberally peppered with observations on studio technique and business trends. He was now concerned not just with the question of whether a recording was good, but why it succeeded or failed with the public. The change in subject matter was indicative of Landau's change in perspective. He was not a fan anymore, he was a record maker, albeit, an unsuccessful one, and his reviews took on the tone of an industry prognosticator biding his time until he could find an appropriate home.

Newly divorced, Landau moved to New York and began scouting job opportunities. He made it a point to rekindle his relationship with Springsteen, whom he had continued to praise in *Rolling Stone*. Together, they might take in a movie, grab a bite to eat, or just hang around Landau's apartment playing and discussing favorite records.

Invariably, the conversation would turn to the problems Bruce was having putting together his next album, *Born to Run*.

Springsteen had been grateful for Landau's heartfelt endorsement in *The Real Paper*, but hadn't foreseen the weight of expectation that the subsequent $50,000 advertising campaign and tag of being "rock and roll future" would create. "The whole episode was a big drag for me," Springsteen fumed. "I mean, who wants to come out onstage and be the future every night? Not me. You know, let somebody else, let the guy who thought up using it in the ad come out and do it! You know? See how he likes it."

The public's high expectations were matched by those at the label. It claimed to be $150,000 in the red on Springsteen's albums, and the undeniable critical buzz coupled with the strong listener response to "Born to Run" was all the encouragement it needed to believe Springsteen's commercial future was at hand.

It was more pressure than Springsteen was prepared to deal with. He had been playing versions of some of the new songs at his concerts and they seemed to go over well, but he just couldn't get them to work in the studio. Springsteen knew he wanted to make a hard-driving record, but he wasn't quite sure how to get there. "The only concept that was around *Born to Run* was that I wanted to make a *big* record, you know," he told Peter Knobler. "Just like a car. Straight ahead, that when that sucker comes on it's like *wide open*. No holds barred!" For the first time in his career, it looked as if Springsteen had written a check his guitar couldn't cash. At a loss as to how to turn things around, he gravitated to Landau for answers.

Landau spoke confidently about the process. There were unnecessary and irritating glitches in the recordings made at 914 Studios. Hadn't Bruce noticed, for example, that the foot pedals on the studio's piano were exceptionally noisy and could be plainly heard during solo piano passages? How could he possibly make a top-notch album without the proper tools? Why was he making it unnecessarily hard on himself? He belonged in a state-of-the-art studio with a seasoned engineer. Springsteen found Landau's logic inescapable and told Appel, who was reluctant to spend the money, to book him into the Record Plant in Manhattan. He was paired with engineer Jimmy Iovine, a young phenom who had already worked with John Lennon and Phil Spector, but even then Springsteen continued to falter. Appel, ever short on tact, had his own antidote: all Springsteen needed was a sharp kick in the ass. "Duke Ellington used to say, 'I don't need more time, I need a deadline,' and I subscribe to that," Appel says. "I don't mean you rush it out; you're not going to create *Sergeant Pepper* in two weeks. But you'd be surprised how quick it can go with a gun to your head." Appel manufactured fights on demand. When Springsteen struggled to complete the lyrics to a section of "Jungleland," the extended, near operatic song intended to close the album, Appel belittled his efforts. "All these lyrics," he said dismissively. "I coulda wrote 'em."

"Well," Springsteen replied, "I was trying to create an idea rather than be specific, and it was sort of a general feeling . . ."

"Supposing the general feeling sucks," Appel retorted sharply. "What then?"

Taken aback, Springsteen said nothing. Appel, realizing he had overstepped his bounds, was relieved when Springsteen brought a new set of lyrics to the next session. He quickly gave them his seal of approval. "Bruce Springsteen again," Appel said when he heard the new verses. "There it is—that's Bruce. For a minute I thought you gave the lyrics to Mike Appel and he wrote them. You trying to give me some writer credits?"

They laughed off the incident, but Appel remained incapable of being political. He clung stubbornly to the belief that Springsteen was and would remain *his* discovery, *his* exclusive property. Landau, on the other hand, recognized that fame would liberate Springsteen from such claims, indeed, that Bruce's success would be the only fact of any consequence. Once the outside world recognized Springsteen, Appel's goading and challenges would be an irritant and an anachronism.

Appel was eager to have his opinions acknowledged; Landau was always cautious. If Springsteen asked him what he thought about a particular song or piece of a recording, he might venture a reaction but was always certain to turn the question back on *him*—to ask what *he* heard or thought. Unlike Appel, he was subtle enough to make his feelings known while reinforcing Springsteen's self-image and belief in his own abilities, and the approach proved helpful. After one particular night of discussion with Landau, Springsteen found himself reenergized about a song that had confounded him. The following evening he telephoned Landau from a rehearsal session. "Listen to this," he said. Putting the receiver down, he led the group through

"Tenth Avenue Freeze-out." Convinced that Landau was the man to help him iron out the album's problems, Springsteen told a none-too-pleased Appel that Landau would be joining them as a coproducer.

It quickly became apparent to Springsteen that Landau knew less about the practical aspects of making records than advertised. "He don't know nothing about the studio," Springsteen remarked, "but he's a smart guy, Landau." Aside from urging drummer Max Weinberg to simplify his playing for recording purposes, Landau made few musical suggestions. But such shortcomings were immaterial. The role that Landau was playing was a new and sorely needed one for Springsteen. He could define the context, and he did.

Springsteen later explained, "He came up with the idea 'Let's make a rock and roll record.' Things had fallen down internally. He got things on their feet again. He was able to point out reasons why we weren't progressing ... Jon was a super-important figure." Bruce Springsteen had found a guru.

In stark contrast to Appel, he was able to help Springsteen define the missing framework for his vision. As a critic, one of his primary tenets had been that an album had to hang together as a whole with a beginning, middle, and end. Springsteen began to consider the interrelation of the songs and their overall impression. At one point he even considered presenting the album as a cycle of songs that—beginning with the sound of an alarm clock—would loosely chronicle the events of one day from morning to late at night. Although the more obvious elements were eventually discarded, the finished album, *Born to Run*, would still suggest that cohesion and movement.

Springsteen's relief at having Landau on board was mirrored by Appel's anxiety. The last thing he wanted was competition. After resisting hiring Landau as coproducer, Appel insultingly offered to pay him $200 a week—the same salary the members of the E Street Band were each making—rather than the "points," or percentage, that producers normally received. But Landau was no stranger to producer contracts. He had received 3 percent of the retail price of the albums he had produced for Livingston Taylor and the MC5 and eventually settled on a fee of 2 percent for his work on *Born to Run*, half of which was to be paid by Appel and the remainder by CBS Records.

Whatever aura of confidence Landau projected, he was not without his own doubts regarding how he would fare as a producer after his previous projects had failed to generate much interest. But his Boston rabbi, Larry Durocher, encouraged him to put those doubts aside. "Jon had produced a couple of other things," says Durocher, "but they were always these semikooky little things that no one would ever have any reasonable expectation to do well. I couldn't imagine why he would even consider being a producer. I know that Landau believed there was a direct parallel between his experience with Springsteen and my experience with both *The Phoenix* and *Rolling Stone.* And my experience was if you stopped fucking these things up they would go forward on their own momentum. There was part of him that was afraid of producing, but he had such a belief in Springsteen that I think the theory was 'Let Springsteen be Springsteen and you can't lose.' "

It was a frustrating, draining process. Bowing to the pressures to complete the album, marathon sessions began at three in the afternoon and ended at 6 A.M. But sometimes the recordings went around the clock, with Springsteen wandering from one studio to another, rehearsing the band in one room, adding a vocal to a previously recorded track in another, and mixing a different song in a third. Visitors to the Record Plant found the sessions characterized by long periods of angry lethargy, punctuated by occasional bursts of energy as Appel, Landau, and Iovine—frequently at a loss for what to do—simply waited for Springsteen to come up with ideas.

Although he hadn't forgotten Appel's reluctance to let him coproduce the album, Landau—perhaps in deference to his own limitations in the studio—had to admit that he was not without talent. And when it came time to winnow the album down to eight songs, he was crucial. Landau and Springsteen viewed a midtempo love song about a topless dancer, "Linda Let Me Be the One," as their best shot at a pop single. Appel, however, dismissed the suggestion with his usual tact: "Are you guys kidding me? I don't know what we need in terms of a pop song. I would love to have a hit. But please, not this. It's terrible. I mean, it's like Peter Philbin went home one night, took his guitar, and wrote a song."

At a moment when his client was buckling under the weight of expectations, Appel's confrontational style and need for recognition compounded the doubts rather than alleviating them. Landau, by comparison, acted as a filter, placing himself between Springsteen and the record company, which gave Bruce some needed breathing room. He could continue to pretend that the business didn't matter.

"Bruce was not especially interested in business," says Karen Darvin, then Springsteen's girlfriend. When nearly a dozen eager executives from CBS Records poured into the studio to listen to the final version of *Born to Run*, Springsteen virtually ignored them. "He and I laid on the floor of the studio and laughed at how seriously everyone was taking it."

Being a friend, liaison, and gatekeeper enhanced Landau's position. More important, Springsteen was convinced that he had helped him break the creative logjam at a crucial juncture in his career. Still, he continued to be plagued by doubts. As with his first album, he decided at the last minute that he was unhappy with *Born to Run* and wanted to scrap it in favor of recording the songs live in concert. But where it had previously fallen to Appel to shore up his confidence, Landau now got the call. After four torturous months in the studio, he wasn't about to let Springsteen shelve the album, which was also beginning to shape up as a very good payday for Landau as advance orders came in. He convinced Springsteen that the record was finished and it was time to let it go. "I know what's on there," a reassured Springsteen affirmed three months later, "because I died on the damn thing graduating. I *believe* that record."

Just how much stock Springsteen was putting in Landau's opinion—and how deeply Landau believed in his potential—wasn't lost on Appel. Having shed his partnership with Jim Cretecos, he hadn't counted on sharing his property with Jon Landau.

●

BRUCE SPRINGSTEEN HAD FINALLY BEEN MOTIVATED BY LANDAU TO LIVE UP to the artistic promise of his first two albums, but he wasn't prepared for *Born to Run*'s success. Still bitter over being encumbered by the baggage of Columbia's early hype—first as "the new Dylan" and then as "rock and roll future"—he now had to deal with being the label's top priority. Having stood by Springsteen through the disappointing sales of his first two albums, Columbia sensed its payoff was finally at hand and wasn't going to blow it.

In September of 1975, when *Born to Run* was released, CBS Records was the undisputed heavyweight champion of an industry that on the back of rock albums had grown to $2.2 billion annually. Unlike Mo Ostin's Warner Bros. Records, there was no ideology at CBS Records, only product, and the company's large marketing and sales departments were a smooth machine. Into its waiting maw Columbia now fed *Born to Run*. What came out the other side was a Rock Star.

CBS had hyped its own staff into a frenzy. "You don't go right to the public to sell a new performer," Columbia president Bruce Lundvall told *Business Week* for a self-congratulatory story on Springsteen entitled "The Merchandising of a Superstar." "You sell him to your own company first, then to the trade, and then to the record buyers." Months before *Born to Run* was released, CBS brought in its promotion staff to hear the album and made it clear that radio and retail were to be told that "something big is coming." In New York and Los Angeles, the extended dates that Springsteen played at the Bottom Line and the Roxy became events. He had graduated to concert halls even before *Born to Run* was released, regularly drawing thousands of listeners, especially in the Northeast, where Sam McKeith was able to arrange more bookings—and the unsatisfied demand for tickets became a story in itself. (Just to be on the safe side, CBS bought 25 percent of the tickets for the ten Bottom Line shows; in Los Angeles, the first of four shows at the Roxy was a private party for industry trade magazine *Billboard* and closed to the public.) With guaranteed sell-outs, CBS arranged live radio broadcasts over local stations, all of which heightened the moment.

Live, Springsteen delivered. Both *The Village Voice* and *The New York Times* weighed in with ecstatic reviews, as did Landau's protégé Dave Marsh, who covered the Bottom Line shows for *Rolling Stone*. If his earlier critical pronouncements regarding Springsteen had left something to be desired, Marsh now declared him "the living culmination of twenty years of rock and roll tradition," while failing to mention that Springsteen had dedicated a version of "Born to Run" at one of the shows to Marsh and his girlfriend, Barbara Carr, a rock publicist who was soon to become both Marsh's wife and Landau's business associate.

The results were almost instantaneous: *Born to Run* was released September 1, 1975, two weeks after the Bottom Line shows, and became an instant hit. Within two months, it had sold 700,000 copies. At a time when selling 500,000 albums was a rare achievement that earned performers "gold" album awards, *Born to Run* would became the first album certified for the industry's new "platinum" award, which signified sales of one million copies. Even Bruce Lundvall, while quick to add that he believed Springsteen would last, had to wonder how much meat was in the sandwich. "Is it all publicity?" he asked rhetorically. "Some of it is, sure."

In early October, Appel and Columbia parlayed queries from *Newsweek* and *Time* into concurrent cover stories. Springsteen, already leery about all the coverage, was loath to do the interviews. Landau, who was getting approximately eleven cents for every copy of *Born to Run* sold and had no problem doing the math, was all for it, but smart enough to let Appel badger him into it.

The coverage in the two magazines split down the middle on the issue of hype. *Time,* which had published earlier stories on Springsteen and considered him "theirs," was completely laudatory. *Newsweek*'s Maureen Orth, while bowled over by a Springsteen show in Red Bank, New Jersey, remained a bit more skeptical, concerned about all the clanking she heard from the PR machine—particularly from Appel, whom she viewed as a raving lunatic. When she finally went to Springsteen's home to meet him, she had been working on the story for ten days. "He had no idea I was coming—they just sprung it on him," she says. "He had Johnny Ace playing on the phonograph and was packing to go on tour. Packing consisted of throwing six T-shirts into an old piece of luggage. And there I was on his doorstep."

Telling Orth that the Johnny Ace record was "the sound of universes colliding," Springsteen asked her to dance with him. Instead, she suggested they go for a stroll on the boardwalk, where she asked about how he'd drawn on his own experiences to create the characters in his songs. Stopping in one of the arcades, she beat him at one of the games, winning a black plastic scorpion. After a while, he said he had to go to Manhattan and offered to drive her back.

During the ride, Orth asked about his relationship with John Hammond and why he had declined to participate in a television tribute, *The World of John Hammond,* that had featured many of the record man's discoveries, including Bob Dylan. Unaware that Appel had turned down a request for him to appear on the show, Springsteen was stunned to learn that Hammond was deeply hurt by the snub. "His mouth dropped," says Orth. "He was extremely naive at that point."

More unsettling was discovering that Springsteen was going to Manhattan to have his picture taken for *Time.* "He was trying to be nice [but] was really uncomfortable; he obviously had something on his mind he didn't tell me. When we got off the Jersey Turnpike he finally revealed to me he was supposed to be on his way to get his picture taken for *Time*."

Orth tried to talk Springsteen out of doing the *Time* story, arguing emphatically that all the attention would create a backlash. "You should pick one cover or the other," she said. "You're not big enough yet to do both covers, and it's going to backfire." Naturally, she urged him to pick *Newsweek*. "If you do both," she said, "you'll be in trouble."

Springsteen was noncommittal, but Orth's comments obviously hit a nerve. She was later told that he put his fist through a wall at the *Time* photo session. "CBS and *Time* were furious with me because they said I had riled him up," she recalls.

Newsweek's coverage of Springsteen would ultimately cause other bad feelings. The magazine misidentified Landau in a photo caption as Springsteen's manager; the error was Appel's worst nightmare—in print, no less. He incorrectly suspected Orth, who had nothing to do with writing photo captions, of doing him dirt at Landau's behest. And if Appel wanted proof that she wasn't operating hand in glove with Landau, he need look only as far as Dave Marsh, Landau's friend and budding advance man. Despite being wowed by Springsteen's talent, Orth had dared to raise the issue of hype. For the crime of not genuflecting deeply enough before the shrine of St. Bruce the Immaculate, Orth was pilloried by Marsh, who wrote that "her style is about as compatible with rock as cannibalism is with missionary work" and dressed her in mud as "a glamour sniper recently returned from a European vacation."

Such personal attacks were a hallmark of Marsh's work. Actually, Orth's credentials included previous cover stories on Stevie Wonder and Bob Dylan, and she had just returned to the magazine after a five-month leave of absence. During that time, she had worked as an assistant to Italian director Lina Wertmuller on the film *Seven Beauties*. The parallels between journalist Orth's five-month leave to work with Wertmuller and critic Landau's five-month stint as Springsteen's co-producer were striking, although Marsh never came close to characterizing his friend's work on *Born to Run* as a "vacation." And well he shouldn't have. Landau didn't stop contributing to *Rolling Stone* while he worked on *Born to Run*. Despite producing an album for Columbia Records, Landau continued to be listed as editor of the magazine's record review section through June of '75, which, if true, would be a blatant conflict of interests. During that period, he personally reviewed albums on MCA, A&M, and Apple by Elton John, Nils Lofgren, and John Lennon respectively. He also wrote glowing reviews of a live performance by Jackson Browne—whom he would soon be producing—and the book *Mystery Train* by his former *Rolling Stone* associate, critic Greil Marcus. Marsh, whom Landau had recommended to replace him as record review editor, then tapped Marcus to review *Born to Run* for *Rolling Stone*. Marcus loved the album.

Such incestuous behavior was less obvious to the public at large than the widely debated issue of record company hype. But it did not go unnoticed, and it tarnished Springsteen's image. John Sinclair, Marsh's old propaganda teacher from his White Panther days, pegged Marsh and Landau as coconspirators on a massive Springsteen hype. Sinclair, who still had an ax to grind about being pushed aside when Landau began working with the MC5, didn't miss the opportunity for a particularly scathing review in the *Ann Arbor Sun*. In his view, Springsteen was a good but highly derivative rocker whose material owed more thematically to *West Side Story* than to the cultural roots of rock and roll. His elevation into the ranks of rock's great writers and performers, Sinclair believed, had more to do with CBS's marketing might and Springsteen's romantic appeal to several self-serving rock critics whose conception of "the streets" was decidedly secondhand.

"Springsteen's are not songs of direct experience compellingly told as acts of cathartic artistic release," Sinclair wrote. "They are tales of a mythic urban grease scene which, taken together, form a script for a third-rate television treatment of delinquent white youngsters of the slums. It is easy to fool persons such as Landau and Marsh regarding the authenticity of such a fantastic proposition, since the streets are not where they feel most comfortable; and it is equally easy to convince well-heeled young college students of today, desperate for an identity separate from that of their despicable parents, that what they are seeing and hearing is the true reflection of the young thugs of the worser parts of town, whose dead-end existence is somehow more exciting than their own." Decrying Landau and Marsh's outsized influence in elevating Springsteen's work to "the effervescence of the True Rock Gospel," Sinclair ended by saying that while he didn't begrudge Springsteen his success, all the hype and insider maneuvering had forced him to take a pass. "I have never been paid enough by any agency of the recording industry to persuade me to love the thing which they are determined I love," he wrote. "And, to paraphrase the great Jon Landau, 'It's too late to start now.' "*

Most critics disagreed with Sinclair and generally hailed *Born to Run* and Springsteen as the real item. But if Springsteen was everything advertised, he'd have no trouble taking whatever critical licks came his way. Shielding him—either through apology or personal attacks on critics—only suggested the opposite. It was, however, something that Marsh and Landau could offer him as a show of power and friendship.

Once admiring of Springsteen, Landau had turned reverential. The task of separating his admiration from his own self-interest had become impossible. In 1974, at the height of his influence as a journalist, Landau's work for *Rolling Stone* and *The Real Paper* had provided a yearly income of approximately $30,000. It was, in all likelihood, more than any other rock critic in the country was making, but it paled alongside what he now made as Springsteen's producer. In the year following its release, *Born to Run* earned over $100,000 for Landau, a figure made even more attractive by the fact that it represented only a few months' work and would continue to increase for many years as the album went on selling, providing him with an annuity. His relationship with Springsteen now had a very powerful financial component. Appel, who had never wanted Landau working on *Born to Run* to begin with, didn't relish the thought of the producer as a permanent fixture. But with Springsteen convinced that Landau had been integral to the album's success, his involvement was beginning to assume a new permanence. After pursuing possible staff positions with several record companies, including Columbia, Clive Davis's Arista, and David Geffen's Asylum, Landau suddenly told the labels that he was now more interested in continuing to work with Springsteen. It was a development that made Appel nervous. He wanted to follow *Born to Run* with a live album. Aside from capitalizing on Springsteen's

*In 1972, Landau had published a collection of criticism entitled *It's Too Late to Stop Now: A Rock and Roll Journal.*

currency as a concert attraction and saving the time normally needed to work up new material, the strategy would ape the formula Dee Anthony had used to build Joe Cocker, Humble Pie, and J. Geils.

It was also a way to cut Landau out of the equation. Who needed him to make a live album? In a not-so-rare show of bad judgment, Appel made a point of telling Landau that he'd get the call next time Springsteen went into the studio but that he wouldn't be needed for the live album. Landau, still putting the final touches on *Born to Run*, saw the plan for what it was, and the revelation was enough to shatter his normal composure. He almost came to blows with Appel in the course of a screaming match on the roof of the Record Plant. An uneasy rapprochement was reached. Two months after the release of *Born to Run*, Landau joined Appel and Iovine as part of the production crew when Springsteen's shows at the Roxy were recorded for a possible live album.

With the success of *Born to Run*, Landau had at last arrived as a producer. Jackson Browne, who admired Springsteen and wanted to toughen his own sound, hired him to produce *The Pretender*. A literate songwriter, Browne wanted Landau to help him negotiate a more rock-oriented sound. Landau was proud of the results, and his friend Dave Marsh heaped praise on him in *Rolling Stone* for rescuing the songwriter from "a hodgepodge of California studio effects." But while the album sold well and Browne and Landau remained friendly, they never worked together again. For good or bad, *The Pretender* would prove to be the only time in his career that Jackson Browne completely turned the production reins over to someone else.

Although Landau remained eager to see his relationship with Springsteen continue, his work with another artist should have cheered Appel, who could have played to Landau's voluble ego by suggesting that his role as Bruce's coproducer, though more limited than Landau might like, was a valuable calling card for the successful, independent career he hungered for. Instead, he saw Landau as a carpetbagger. Worse, his own ego prevented him from recognizing that Springsteen, whose opinion was the only one that really mattered, didn't share that view. Appel had shepherded his tribe through the desert and could now, with the success of *Born to Run*, see the promised land of power, wealth, and prestige that he had so long sought. Under his management, Bruce Springsteen had gone from an unknown to a million-selling artist, which was a great incentive for other performers to want to sign with Appel. But he was unable to set aside his personal jealousies and take an accurate read of his client. Mike Appel was about to slit his own throat.

THE SEEDS OF APPEL'S DOWNFALL WERE PLANTED IN THE CONTRACTS HE had presented to Springsteen long before Landau arrived on the scene. When Springsteen had come to him and Cretecos four years earlier, in the spring of 1972, it was agreed that the team would act as managers, producers, and publishers. The arrangement, while fraught with potential conflicts, was far from unique. Albert Grossman had pioneered the structuring of publishing and production deals for his clients a decade earlier and had found unique ways to participate personally; David Geffen, whose early standing as a comer in the music industry owed much to the original way he had used his role as a partner on Laura Nyro's publishing to cut himself a large piece of her value as a recording artist, had taken the formula to greater heights at Asylum by establishing himself as the manager, the publisher, and the record company. Indeed, the troubles Geffen experienced with the Eagles bore a striking similarity to those between Appel and Springsteen. Once eager for a deal—any deal—both acts gladly signed contracts they would later view as one-sided. But, unlike Geffen, Appel wasn't smart enough to see that the balance of power shifted with success.

Springsteen, whose indifference to business had alarmed Spitz, Hammond, McKeith, and others, had been willing to sign *anything*—an early management contract signed in May of '72 would have paid Cretecos and Appel a 50 percent commission. The deal, which was superseded a few months later by a contract that paid a more standard 20 percent, was scrapped only after Hammond insisted that the contract be read by an outside attorney, who found the deal unconscionable.

Along with the management deal, Springsteen signed publishing and production contracts. A standard if onerous arrangement, the production contract set Appel and Cretecos up as Laurel Canyon Productions and gave that company the authority to make a deal with a label. Under the terms of the contract, the company would advance money to make recordings and pay Springsteen a royalty of 3 percent of any record's retail price. When Laurel Canyon later made a deal with CBS Records, the production company received a royalty rate of 18 percent of wholesale, roughly equivalent at the time to 9 percent of retail. Since it had pledged to pay Springsteen only 3 percent of retail, double that amount was left for Appel and Cretecos. Additionally, while it was pledged to lay out the money for recording, which it could do only by getting an advance from the record label, all costs would ultimately have to be recouped out of Springsteen's share.

Economically, production deals simply extended concepts engendered by standard record company contracts, in particular, that the artist pays for everything even though the company owns the recordings. Record companies like CBS could argue, with some justification, that nine out of ten artists fail and such recoupment clauses help protect their exposure. But Laurel Canyon had no money to lose; the production deal loaded the debt solely onto Springsteen. While Appel could point out that he took "only" 20 percent as manager, his production company stood to make better than 200 percent more in royalties than the artist he was managing. Such machinations were not unusual but made sense only for throwaway pop acts like the ones Appel had worked with at Wes Farrell or performers who failed to make it big. In the months preceding the release of *Born to Run*, Appel realized that his initial management contract had only one more year to go and approached Springsteen about making a new, improved deal. Springsteen was more than amenable.

With the release and immediate success of *Born to Run* in September, the contract talks remained vague and amiable, but that changed in November when Appel asked for and received a $500,000 advance against the album's royalties from CBS. Rather than simply divvy up the money, Appel decided to use it as an inducement to get Springsteen to sign a new contract, and he told him he could have a share at a new, improved royalty rate if he re-upped. If not, he would hold him to the old contracts, which meant Springsteen would receive one third of the money minus costs. Springsteen, with a million-selling record and just $3,000 in his bank account, began to have some doubts about Appel. He brought his contracts to Landau and asked him to recommend a lawyer. Landau took him to his own attorney,

Myron "Mike" Mayer, who had negotiated his deal on *Born to Run*. The attorney told Springsteen that he had signed a bad deal.

"It was our take on Appel's relationship with Bruce that it was overbearing and really exploitive," says Mayer. "He was signed for the whole nine yards." Still, he adds, "Bruce did not say, 'Okay, let's go get rid of this guy.' He became unhappy with the arrangement. He wanted to restructure it and keep Appel in on a reasonable basis."

A request from Mayer for a complete audit showed what Spitz and others had long known. "Appel kept no books," says Mayer. "He had a good accountant, but the books consisted of two shopping bags full of paper, and he gave Bruce handouts. I don't think he was stealing; [it was] just a very unprofessional way of doing things." The audit, meant to serve notice that Springsteen was serious about renegotiating, succeeded only in raising Appel's hackles. When he and Mayer sat down to discuss a new management contract, they got nowhere. "He was unwilling to even come back and moderate [the financial arrangement]," says Mayer. "I mean, still take the lion's share. But he wouldn't even talk about it. So it went downhill from there."

Appel saw the selection of Mayer to renegotiate the deal as further mingling Landau's and Springsteen's interests. When the attorney told him that Springsteen wanted Landau to produce the next album, Appel went ballistic. "This was the moment when I realized that Landau had, in effect, taken over," he told writer Marc Eliot.

Mayer admits that representing both Springsteen and Landau may not have been the best idea but says the arrangement began innocently: "Jon did not push for the breakup. If anything, he did encourage Bruce to find out more of what was happening with the business aspects of his career. Because he saw Bruce's evolution and development. He knew that this was going to be something. As a friend, Jon had genuine affection for Bruce. [He] loved the music and was interested in producing the records. He didn't want to be manager, he was doing pretty well on his royalties from the records. Jon is interested in business, he's interested in making money. From Appel's point of view, getting rid of him was some sort of nefarious plot on the part of Jon. That's not true."

In early July, Appel went on the offensive. In a letter to CBS Records, he warned that his Laurel Canyon Productions would use its exclusive production rights to block any attempt by the label or Springsteen to designate Landau as the producer of Bruce's next album.

Three weeks later, Springsteen responded with a lawsuit to break Appel's management, production, and publishing contracts. More unusual than the suit's charges of fraud, undue influence, breach of trust, and breach of contract were the filing's last two causes of action. Together, they sought $1 million in damages for blocking the hiring of Landau as Springsteen's producer and for Appel's refusal as music publisher to grant clearances for Dave Marsh to use lyrics from Bruce's songs in a quickie biography. Like Landau, Marsh was not a plaintiff in the suit but was represented in other matters by Mayer.

Appel quickly filed his own suit against Springsteen, Landau, and CBS aimed at upholding his rights as Laurel Canyon Productions. The action was intended to tie up Springsteen's career and did not address any of the charges of fiduciary malfeasance Springsteen had lodged against him.

Mayer had led Springsteen and Landau to expect a quick capitulation from Appel. In August, they were shocked when New York Supreme Court Judge Arnold L. Fein found for him and granted a preliminary injunction barring Landau from producing Springsteen. Most damaging, Fein ruled that Landau had "no rights" under the Laurel Canyon Productions agreement, while Springsteen was not legally entitled to appoint or approve his producer. It was a rude awakening. Not only were Springsteen and Landau barred from working together, effectively putting Springsteen's career on hold, but the judge's decision, which was upheld twice on appeal, only enhanced Bruce's anger and frustration regarding how much control Appel had over him. It also soured him and Landau on Mayer.

"We hadn't prepared Bruce with the realities of litigation that sometimes you win, sometimes you lose," Mayer says. "I was starstruck with Bruce, and I protected him too much. We lost that motion, but litigation goes that way. I think he was upset about that; he felt frustrated. Also, Jon was—how shall I put it?—very unhappy that he was foreclosed from doing the production. I suspect Jon wanted to get another opinion, and that tore it."

Devastated that he couldn't record—and that Appel was also seeking an injunction in New Jersey to tie up the box-office receipts from a series of shows—Springsteen was now eager to reach a settlement. Bob Spitz, who had left Appel's employ and hadn't spoken with either Springsteen or Appel in over two years, suddenly found himself pressed

into a role as intermediary when the singer showed up one night at
Spitz's Greenwich Village apartment. Spitz took him to a nearby restaurant for a hamburger, where the rocker poured out his frustrations.

"There's no money left," he told Spitz. "Mike's taken everything,
he's keeping me from playing. Do you remember anything that went
on? I need help."

Spitz, who'd always found Springsteen cavalier when it came to finances, was shocked at how distressed he was. "I don't know if Bruce
will admit it," he says, "but he was in tears. He saw the dream crumbling. And he told me that night, 'If he'd only be fair, I'd go back.' "

Spitz agreed to relay that information to Appel. But emboldened by
the fact that the court's rulings were all going his way, Appel dismissed
the opportunity. He wasn't just worried about Landau's continued involvement, he was bent on retaining a huge share. "Bob, I'm telling
you right now," Spitz recalls him saying, "I know what I've brought to
this: I've brought fifty percent worth. If I don't get fifty percent, fuck
him. I'll get fifty percent." Spitz suggested that neither Springsteen
nor a judge would find that equitable. "Mike," he said, "you're going
to lose him." Appel wasn't interested.*

Sam McKeith had also made a failed attempt to patch things up. In
some ways, he was in the same boat as Appel. He had focused all of his
energies on building Springsteen's career, and now the agency's deal
with the star was about to expire. It was crucial to McKeith's career
that he keep him as a client. "I called Appel up and said, 'Listen,
you're in trouble with this guy, and I might be the only one who can
help you out,' " recalls McKeith. " 'I don't want to be his manager. I
want to keep him as an agent. Give me his home phone number. I'll
let you know what the conversations are like.' "

McKeith drove to Asbury Park and met with Springsteen, who was
in a feisty mood. "Look, I like Mike," Springsteen told him. "But one
hundred percent of my publishing?† People are telling me I'm being
ripped off, and I don't like this."

Still, Springsteen told McKeith he wanted to patch things up with

---

*Spitz later gave a deposition in support of Springsteen in which he outlined the way finan-
cial matters had been handled when he worked for Appel.

†Under the terms of the publishing agreement, Springsteen received 50 percent of the royalties due to the publisher for recordings, but the songs were wholly controlled by Appel.

Appel. He also said he wanted to go back on the road but needed money to mount a tour; McKeith promised to secure a $25,000 loan if he re-upped with the agency. Bruce waffled. Because of all the hassles with Appel, he told McKeith, he didn't want to sign a new deal until things shook out. Eager to accommodate him, McKeith offered to float the same loan under different conditions: he didn't have to sign a contract extension, just pay back the loan during his next two tours. Springsteen was agreeable, although McKeith remembers him saying that he also had a deal working at Columbia to get money. But the loan papers William Morris's attorneys sent to Mike Mayer were based on Spring-steen's agreeing to a new contract. When McKeith heard about it, he im-mediately sided with Springsteen. But his loyalty and the role he played in launching his career would prove insufficient to keep him as a client.

With Appel effectively out of the day-to-day picture, McKeith was finding it more and more difficult to get a hold of Springsteen. His road crew and assistants were now working out of his home—Boss Acres—in Holmdel, New Jersey, and McKeith couldn't penetrate the retinue of friends and employees. Barry Bell, an assistant at William Morris, had become friendly with Springsteen and, unbeknownst to McKeith, had discussed forming a new agency in partnership with Appel to handle Springsteen and a few other acts when the agency contract expired. But once it became obvious to Bell that Springsteen and Appel would not reconcile, he moved to Frank Barsalona's Pre-mier Talent Agency, bringing Springsteen with him. Where McKeith had offered Bruce a $25,000 loan, Premier now loaned him $100,000.

It was a bitter pill for McKeith. "There was a great deal of tension between Barry and me for years after Springsteen left the agency," he says. "Quite frankly, I believed he did a Jon Landau on me." The falling-out with William Morris and the loss of Springsteen sent him into a tailspin. "When Bruce left him it ruined his life," says McKeith's former mentor, Steve Leber. Following Springsteen's defection to Pre-mier, McKeith was fired and suffered a breakdown that literally landed him on the streets. He never spoke to Springsteen again.

THE PROTRACTED BATTLE WITH APPEL LEFT SPRINGSTEEN HIGH AND DRY. Not only was he prevented from recording with Landau, but he had no management to handle his business affairs and help arrange tours.

To fill the administrative gap, Landau suggested that Springsteen hire entertainment attorney Michael Tannen. Tannen did work for the Rolling Stones, John Lennon, and Stephen Stills, but his key client was Paul Simon. An unusually savvy student of the business, Simon had worked in music publishing, first as a songwriter for hire and then as a song plugger, and when Simon and Garfunkel hit it big in the mid-sixties, his acumen helped make him one of the wealthiest artists in the business. Jon Landau befriended him in the early seventies, and his admiration soon came to encompass Tannen as well.

"I knew Landau through Paul," says Tannen. "The Appel litigation had gone from awful to impossible. Bruce was bankrupt and enjoined from going into the studio. And I give Landau great credit because he came to me—I wasn't [acting as] a lawyer, but more like an outside agent—and he said, 'Could you help Bruce? Could you represent Bruce? What should we do?' "

Tannen advised Landau to dump Mayer. Although Mayer had begun his career as a litigator, his firm, Mayer, Nussbaum, & Katz, had become specialists in entertainment contracts and rarely handled courtroom work. It was a big distinction, but one that Landau hadn't recognized, and now he and Springsteen were paying the price. Says Tannen, "Jon had the balls, with my support, to fire [Mayer]."

As Mayer recalls, however, the task of firing him actually fell to Springsteen. "Bruce was a real man about it," he says. "He came up and he talked to me. Financially there was no problem; he straightened out what he owed us. It was a loss, but I learned two things: never be a fan of your client and don't give the guy rose-colored glasses. If I'd won that lawsuit," Mayer adds with a bitter laugh, "we'd probably still be representing him today."

Mayer's replacement was Peter Parcher, a former partner of Tannen's and a seasoned litigator. While Parcher looked for a way to turn the case around, Tannen took over the de facto management of Springsteen's career, with Landau operating as his key adviser.

"For about a year all of Bruce's affairs were run out of my office, including his tours, which I hated," says Tannen. "I was virtually the only person representing Bruce. So I was a little bit manager, a lot adviser, nonlitigating lawyer. But my collaborator in all of this was Jon . . . He had left *Rolling Stone,* and that was his life at that point: 'I do this thing with Bruce.' "

Landau's sharply honed careerism notwithstanding, there was much about Springsteen beyond the magnitude of his onstage abilities that Landau and others found appealing, even seductive. At a time when rock and roll acts were looking and sounding more and more like product, Springsteen held himself out as the real thing. Despite being the beneficiary of one of the costliest, most sophisticated marketing campaigns the record industry could produce, he remained a naïf. The reasons were twofold. Artistically, and especially in concert, he could deliver. More important, he insisted that he was not a rock star, but a man doing a job, and he wore his New Jersey working-class roots on his sleeve. On that issue of faith turned much of Springsteen's appeal.

"The pressures of the business are powerless in the face of what is real," Springsteen declared to *Crawdaddy!* founder Paul Williams, and that belief extended to the image of his E Street Band. Although formed specifically to back Springsteen after he had signed to Columbia, the group's original members had played with Springsteen in various unsuccessful bands over the years. That shared history of scuffling around the bars of the Jersey Shore created a mythology built on a blue-collar, lunch-bucket ethic. No one in the E Street Band personified or extolled that attitude more than guitarist and record producer Steve Van Zandt. Van Zandt had very definite ideas about what rock should aspire to and how a musician approached that challenge. "Bruce and the rest of us have many years of being musicians and that's the job," he said just after the release of *Born to Run.* "Our ambition is still the same: to enjoy it and make sure the people come and enjoy it. Even big success can never affect Bruce or me or the band. Listen, we've gotten into a lifestyle, and it's hardly gonna change. We have no temptation to do things for money."

In the wake of such pronouncements, Springsteen was heralded as the keeper of the promise that rock—despite surrendering its ties to an anticorporate counterculture—was still about something more than acquiring the trappings of success. It proved a very powerful mystique. Springsteen had attracted a core of loyalists who served as an adjunct to the E Street Band and included journalists, record executives, fans, and employees. David McGee, a business reporter and music critic, was among them. A writer for the trade magazine *Record World,* McGee was a good deal savvier about the realities of the music business than most rock critics. He initially viewed Springsteen with skepticism.

"I wasn't real thrilled about the first album, and like everybody else I saw Jon's review and all the hype," McGee says. "But when I saw Bruce I was just overwhelmed. I believed every word that Jon wrote after that. I felt the same kick in my stomach seeing Bruce that first time as the first time I heard Elvis or the Beatles. A real legit feeling— the guy was *for real*."

McGee wrote glowing reviews of a Springsteen concert and the first Southside Johnny and the Asbury Jukes album that Van Zandt produced. He was soon hanging around the Stone Pony, the Asbury Park bar where the Jukes often played, and found Springsteen surprisingly accessible and refreshingly indifferent to his status. The E Street Kings, a softball team comprised of Springsteen and members of the E Street Band and the Jukes, played games in Central Park, and McGee would run into Springsteen on the streets or sitting alone at the Bottom Line watching a band. Even when Springsteen was working, the situation was much the same. While visiting his mother in Carbon Hill, Alabama, McGee hooked up with him in nearby Birmingham, where he was playing the following evening. They spent Springsteen's off night just driving around the countryside. His employees and crew viewed Springsteen with similar admiration. "Bruce was really sweet back then," says lighting designer Marc Brickman. "He just wanted to have fun, and he wanted to make people have fun. Everything he wanted was positive. I don't think there was a negative bone in his body."

Brickman was just twenty-one when he saw Springsteen perform in Bryn Mawr, Pennsylvania, and he later talked his way into a job providing the lights for one of Bruce's shows at a nearby college by offering to do it fifty dollars cheaper than the company the promoter had already lined up. Brickman showed up with a small, homemade system, and Springsteen and Appel were pleased with the results. Although Appel said he couldn't afford to hire him, Brickman began working gigs throughout the region. After Clive Davis complimented Appel on the lighting when Springsteen played the Bottom Line in July of '74, Brickman was hired for an upcoming West Coast tour.

During the break with Appel, the crew and band set up an office at Springsteen's house and coordinated dates with Tannen. A pecking order began to emerge, with status validated by nicknames. "Everyone had a name, everyone was a character," recalls McGee. "Those guys had a kind of Jersey Shore Mafia thing about them. Everybody was 'Guido' or something." Springsteen, of course, was "The Boss," while Landau, who already referred to himself as "the king of rock and roll," had his name shortened to "The King." Dave Marsh became "The Duke," his girlfriend, Barbara Carr, "The Duchess," and McGee was "The Baron." "It was like royalty," says McGee. "We were the ones in the inner circle."

While a strong support group helped Springsteen to remain focused through the legal battle with Appel, Landau continued to rely on Larry Durocher in Boston for advice and encouragement. "I had to listen to that bullshit for two hours every day," says Durocher. "I couldn't start or end my day without a report from Landau. It was some very bitter goings-on."

Tannen's strategy was essentially the same as Mayer's: to use Parcher's litigation to force a settlement. But he wasn't certain Springsteen would go for it since Appel's continuing legal victories had him at a distinct disadvantage. With things at their bleakest, Landau and Tannen met with Springsteen before a show in Boston to discuss whether to proceed with the lawsuit. "I said, 'Look—here it is: I think we should fight this, but it's your life,' " recalls Tannen. "And he said—very unemotionally—'I'm fighting this to the end. If it takes another ten years, I don't care.' It gave us the power to do whatever we had to do. Although I'm very proud of what I did, it was his litigation, and he won it because he stood up and said 'I'm not giving in and this is the way things have to be.' "

When it came time for Springsteen to be deposed by Appel's attorney, Leonard Marks, the seasoned litigator found himself in the rare position of opposing, rather than representing, a performer. And aside from whatever personal sympathies Marks felt for artists, he was also an astute observer of entertainment business realities. Unlike Appel, he recognized that it was highly unlikely a successful artist could be forced to accept a business arrangement against his will. From the beginning, he had counseled Appel to accept Springsteen's departure as irreversible. It was an opinion that Springsteen's behavior during the depositions only reinforced.

Springsteen was belligerent beyond belief. Peppering his responses with a flood of profanities that he appeared unable to control until the judge told him that a jury could be made aware of his testimony if the case went to trial, he made it clear at every turn that he felt Appel had cheated and abused him. His dramatic behavior, including standing on a table and screaming at Marks, reinforced Marks's belief that the rift between Appel and Springsteen was unbridgeable. And while admitting that Appel's decision to hold on to the $500,000 advance had ignited Springsteen, Marks did not think the situation would have come to a head without the intervention of Landau and others. "A series of advisers and producers were whispering in his ear," he says. "They made the continuation of the Mike Appel relationship impossible. [Appel] was shocked when I told him I thought it was very unlikely the relationship would continue."

Appel, who had spurned Springsteen's initial efforts to restructure their contracts, now found the tables turned. Bruce was not willing to re-sign with him under any circumstances. And what would it mean if Appel ultimately won the lawsuit? Very little. He might be entitled to damages, but his management contract was expiring even as the suit dragged on, and Springsteen had proven willing to let his recording career atrophy rather than submit to the conditions of the Laurel Canyon production deal.

The only strong card Appel had was the publishing agreement. It, too, was about to expire and leave Springsteen free to start his own publishing company for any new songs he wrote, but it still gave Appel ownership of any songs written over the last five years. Although Peter Parcher had dropped the causes of action pertaining to the blocking of Landau's selection as producer and the refusal to grant lyric clearance to Marsh for use in his biography, during Marks's questioning Springsteen remained incensed over not controlling his own songs.

Walter Yetnikoff, who had taken over as head of CBS Records, had told Landau and Tannen that he was willing to renegotiate Springsteen's recording contract. Without Appel's large cut, and with Springsteen's newfound status as a star, it would obviously be a far more lucrative deal. But before he could negotiate a settlement with Appel, Tannen would have to know *how* lucrative. Recalls Tannen, "The only thing I have in my mind is to get Walter to agree to a royalty. I got him to pay one dollar, which was the superstar royalty. It was a casual conversation, it wasn't like a negotiation. And that was it. Once we had that it was downhill."

In April of 1977, Appel's incentive to settle was heightened. Springsteen had filed his suit in federal court; Appel had obtained his injunction barring any recording with Landau in state court. Now Springsteen's attorneys argued that the state suit was essentially a counterclaim to Springsteen's charges of mismanagement and should have been joined to his prior federal case. If the state court agreed, Appel would be forced to defend himself against Springsteen's charges of mismanagement. Serious settlement discussions began almost immediately. The intense animosity that Springsteen had exhibited during the depositions vanished as quickly as Mike Appel.

"Bruce, in my conversations with him, said he was never mad at Appel," Tannen says. "And I don't think he ever was. He never hated him. I think he thought Appel didn't do the right thing by him, but I never heard any angry words about Appel. Sometimes you settle and the person writing the check is *really* pissed off. But when Bruce paid Mike, he felt he was paying what was fair and didn't begrudge him the money."

There was no reason to: Appel sold his interests far too cheaply. In return for giving up his production and management rights to Springsteen, Appel received $800,000 over five years, all of it laid out by CBS as advances against Springsteen's new, vastly improved royalty rate. His cut as coproducer of the first three albums, which in some cases had been as high as 6 percent, was reduced to 2 percent. As music publisher, Appel retained a 50 percent interest in the twenty-seven songs that Springsteen had recorded and released while he was his manager but relinquished any rights he held on the singer's future songs. Six years later, a cash-strapped Appel sold Springsteen his remaining interest in the publishing for $425,000. To Tannen, who was well aware of the potential value of Springsteen's publishing, Appel's decision to part with his share was "amazing."

14

DEE ANTHONY'S
THREE RULES
OF SUCCESS

W**ITHIN A WEEK OF THE SETTLEMENT WITH** A**PPEL,** L**ANDAU AND** Springsteen returned to the studio to work on the next album, *Darkness on the Edge of Town.* As the album took shape over the next eleven months, Landau's influence on Springsteen became plain. The media hoopla and charges of hype that attended the release of *Born to Run* had left Springsteen loath to make another record as grandiose. Instead, he began by crafting smaller songs about an environment he knew intimately, the faded, blue-collar towns of New Jersey that he still called home. In essence, he was embracing the cardinal rule of any introductory creative writing course: write about what you know.

Whether Landau's background as an editor was the spur for such a common-sense approach, the new songs dovetailed neatly with his rock and roll philosophies. As a critic, Landau had championed the approach that less is more. He had derided the extended, long-form jams of the psychedelic era as excessive and unfocused and declared the vast majority of performers unequipped to handle the liberation from the 45 rpm single format that Dylan had championed. With the MC5, that view had resulted in a slavish adherence to two-

and three-minute tracks on *Back in the U.S.A.*, a regressive preference that was completely Landau's and would be reflected in the albums he produced with Springsteen. Mike Appel had been enraptured with Springsteen's unusual and ornate lyrics and had encouraged the dense, epic song-stories that highlighted the first three albums. Landau, who preached simplicity and liked records that were frankly commercial, did not. The long form vanished from Springsteen's work.

Unlike the MC5, Springsteen had no interest—real or imagined—in politics. A community college dropout, he was not much of a reader, and his early albums reflected his ability to communicate on a gut level. Landau, however, was an intellectual. And while his tastes were comparatively conservative, he had—unlike Springsteen—arrived at them through a carefully weighed aesthetic system rather than instinct. "I think Bruce saw something in him he never was," says lighting director Marc Brickman. "It was his tutor. It was his mentor. He was going to open the other side of the world that he really didn't have any knowledge of." Landau was soon exposing Springsteen to the records that had shaped his views as well as the novels and short stories of Flannery O'Connor and the movies of John Ford. The rocker devoured them and began referring to them frequently in interviews as inspiration for his own work.

Just how deep an impression Landau was making on Springsteen became apparent with the release of *Darkness on the Edge of Town*. Aside from cleaving to Landau's preference for rock's traditional short-song format, the album was loaded with imagery and debts to sources Landau had discovered as a film critic. The motion picture based on John Steinbeck's *East of Eden* was, for example, the touchstone for the song "Adam Raised a Cain." But more striking was the way Springsteen himself had been refined and recast: *Darkness* was a subtler, if no less romantic, evocation of the outsider portrayed on *Born to Run*. Now, however, Springsteen's small-scale snapshots dealt with the working class and the suburban world that he was actually familiar with rather than the romanticized cityscape of the first three albums, the "mythic urban grease" that John Sinclair had lampooned. Springsteen's previous songs told stories about ex-girlfriends who had run off with street hustlers and "city dudes"; on *Darkness on the Edge of Town* those same women still rejected him, but now they were married and fading into the anonymity of suburban life in towns with comfortable, bourgeois names like Fairview while Springsteen prowled the less predictable perimeters of that world as an outcast in search of some redemption unnamed and unknown. In the end, the album did nothing so much as re-create Springsteen as a modern Ethan Edwards, the main character in Landau's favorite film, John Ford's *The Searchers*. Indeed, Springsteen's new persona hewed precisely to the vision Landau had expounded years earlier in *Rolling Stone* of Edwards as the archetypal tragic American hero: "homeless, without family or roots, shut out from any human contact and condemned as a fugitive to wander the wilderness, this time in search of whatever solace without purpose he can find there."

To promote the new album, released in April of '78, Springsteen launched a four-month tour in May with a show at a 3,500-seat theater in Buffalo, New York. In the three years since the release of *Born to Run*, Springsteen had been largely out of the public's eye and its attention had turned to other performers. *Darkness on the Edge of Town* did not come close to selling as well as *Born to Run*, and the tour got off to a disappointing start. Just who would turn things around was unclear. Mike Tannen wanted to become a film producer and had little interest in doing the things that Appel had done like setting up Springsteen's tours, particularly once he had been paid for ending the litigation. Within such a vacuum, Landau was the obvious choice.

"Landau kept saying he didn't want to be manager," recalls Brickman. "But he'd always be around. He laid back; he calculated and watched. The way he did it was he said, 'I don't want it, I don't want it,' and finally we went out on *Darkness* and it wasn't happening, there were problems monetarily. Suddenly *we* all said to him—and obviously Bruce—'Why don't you be the manager?' And everyone went, 'Oh, what a great relief. God, Jon Landau is gonna be our manager now!' Which was basically the beginning of the end for everyone."

Effecting the business side of Springsteen's career presented a stiffer challenge to Landau's powers of persuasion than helping him devise an artistic point of view. Despite all he'd been through in the Appel lawsuit, Springsteen's feelings regarding fame and success remained ambiguous and a bit naive. He'd courted fame, but remained fearful of being seen as a sellout. When *Born to Run* raced onto the charts—potentially making him a wealthy man—he couldn't conceive of how its success might affect his life or his work.

"The guy that Mike Appel met actually scorned money," recalls Peter Philbin, who had become Springsteen's A&R man at Columbia. "I had an expense account, and I would take him out and pay for the meal. No big deal—they were all broke. And at the end of the meal, Bruce would act like 'You have money—that's not hip.' I think he just grew up without money and found an alternative energy source."

Springsteen had similar problems with the way the record company presented his work and built his image. When Columbia had initially promoted him as the "new Dylan," he found the comparison nothing but a burden. But the record industry Springsteen was forced to deal with was far more sophisticated than the one Dylan had come of age in, and it was a much bigger factor in his career. Columbia did not "make" Dylan. His reputation owed everything to his artistic genius and Grossman's view that Dylan should be in charge of his own career; it owed virtually nothing to the then primitive marketing department at Columbia Records. Springsteen, the merits of his work notwithstanding, was quite a different story. By the seventies the record companies had recognized the massive commercial rewards that the music had to offer, and they had learned a great deal about how to sell it. Once they finally got behind Springsteen, that marketing might generated much of his success. Columbia had spent $40,000 in initial advertising for his first album, an additional $50,000 to promote Landau's coronation of him as "rock and roll future," and a whopping $250,000 for tour support. Still, he had trouble reconciling his own artistic aims with the record company's purely commercial decisions— or at least wanted to keep the company at arm's distance. "It's okay as long as it stays out of the way and *helps*," he told journalist Ray Coleman as Columbia beat its marketing drums for *Born to Run*. "Otherwise it's [got] me freaked out, so why bother with the whole thing? I get upset by it sometimes, you know—I just don't wanna go and get lost in a bunch of stuff that don't mean nothing to me." In the face of these contradictions, Springsteen continued instead to preach the gospel of the rock and roll faithful. Explicitly and forcefully, he insisted that CBS's promotional and commercial concerns were not his concerns. "This is the reason to live," he said of the music. "It ain't a job and it ain't a business."

Springsteen might declare that making music was an act of faith rather than a commercial enterprise, but Landau had a decidedly different take and was no longer just the producer. Rock managers in the decade since Albert Grossman had redefined the role acted as the bridge between the artist and the business, promoting and protecting their clients' credibility as artists while negotiating the best possible business deal. Like Grossman, Landau's intelligence, careerism, knowledge of the business, and eagerness to embrace the main chance made him a good choice for manager, and both men held the requisite near religious belief in the talent and ultimate success of their clients. But Landau's role in his client's career was vastly different from Grossman's in that he was responsible for far more than facilitating the exposure of the work. As producer, he helped enunciate it. And, as tutor and mentor, he frequently defined it, supplying the subject matter and raw material and pushing the work in a particular direction. Just as important, he was not contemptuous of the record companies the way Grossman was. On the contrary, he admired David Geffen, Jerry Wexler, and Phil Walden at least as much as he admired their artists—and he certainly had nothing against money or commercialism. Springsteen's acute fear of being seen as a sellout was an issue that Landau had long ago dismissed as self-deception, as the MC5 could attest.

Among his coworkers at *The Phoenix* and *The Real Paper*, Landau was always the hard-nosed realist, the one whose overdeveloped sense of logic and the bottom line wouldn't permit him to indulge in any counterculture pipe dreams. As Springsteen's friend, producer, manager, and teacher, Landau would prove completely unapologetic about looking for a big score and shape the work toward that goal. Even as a young fan, his love of Otis Redding was coupled with an admiration for Redding's willingness to consider himself an entertainer rather than an artist and to be, in Landau's words, "openly and honestly concerned with pleasing crowds and being successful." Indeed, as Landau somewhat crassly summed up Redding's approach to his career, "his personal credo was 'make that buck' and before he died in a plane crash in December of 1967, he had earned millions of them."

While Landau's client was certainly as eager as Redding to please his fans, being motivated by money remained a prickly issue. A case in point was Springsteen's adamant refusal to play large arenas, which he viewed solely as a moneymaking proposition and inconsistent with the intimacy and credibility he wanted to have with his audience. "I couldn't play those big places," a frustrated Springsteen had said after his brief stint as an opening act for Chicago. "It had nothing to do with anything that had anything to do with me, those big arenas. So I won't go to those places again." In the wake of the hysteria that attended *Born to Run,* Springsteen had managed to remain idealistic. "Bruce has already said he doesn't want to play fifty-five-thousand-seater stadiums, which would mean people on the seventeenth tier of the balcony having to read in the newspaper to find out what went on at the concert," Steve Van Zandt said dismissively in the weeks following the album's release.

Springsteen's resistance to accepting music as a business proposition heightened his reputation among fans as the genuine article, the antidote to rock's creeping commercialism. His oft-stated indifference to the record business machine, to the trappings of fame, to anything but the power of rock and roll to invest a humdrum life with meaning was apolitical but still echoed the aspirations of the earlier underground movement and resonated deeply with his fans. At a time when rock music was increasingly synonymous with the business of selling rock records, they saw him as the cherished exception, the one who had risen but remained true. The covenant was explicit: it was about music and community, not money or stardom. Looking at Bruce Springsteen, his fans saw and heard not just themselves but a celebration of rock and roll as the best part of themselves.

Mike Appel's inability to convince Springsteen to play bigger halls had proven financially disastrous. At a time when Springsteen's exploding popularity should have wiped out all debts, Appel was going broke. When he had suggested that Springsteen play a show at Philadelphia's huge JFK Stadium, the singer had bristled with indignation.* Nor would Springsteen allow Appel to put him in the developing and highly lucrative market for T-shirts and other concert souvenirs. When Appel printed T-shirts for one show in conjunction with a promoter, Springsteen refused to let him sell them.

---

*Years later he would play there as the headliner on Amnesty International's Human Rights Now! Tour.

Where Appel's ego and fantasies about being an industry heavy-weight created unnecessary confrontations, Landau could get Spring-steen to change the way he viewed business. It was the difference between a slap and a caress. "A good manager has to have a feel for his band," says Peter Philbin. "Jon Landau systematically convinced Bruce Springsteen that he was letting his fans down and had to play bigger shows. He provided Bruce with an explanation to change the things he'd said in the past."

Whether Springsteen really had an artistic obligation to meet con-sumer demand, commercially and economically the logic was un-avoidable. "We were doing eight, nine months in America once it went to *arenas*," recalls Van Zandt. In essence all Landau had done that Appel could not was get Springsteen to admit that his career was as important to him as his music was. But that admission was huge, an ac-ceptance, at least in private, of Landau's conviction that rock was as much a business as an art. Contrary to what he'd said earlier, Spring-steen was now ready to accept that rock and roll *was* a job. "Jon Lan-dau came in, and his eye was on the money," says Philbin.

As Landau was well aware, the financial rewards for accepting those compromises were staggering. During the years between *Born to Run* and *Darkness on the Edge of Town*, the record industry had ex-perienced the greatest growth in its history. In 1975, *Born to Run* became the first rock album certified "platinum" for sales of one million copies. Within three years, rock albums by the Eagles, Fleet-wood Mac, and Peter Frampton would each sell over ten million copies. And, like the labels, the concert business also grew in size and sophistication until it bore little resemblance to the psychedelic ball-room circuit of the late sixties. As early as 1971, rock's shifting eco-nomics had led to the shuttering of many of the smaller rock venues like the Tea Party and the Fillmore East and West. And where they survived, they were no longer the apex of the circuit. The goal now was to play sports arenas.

The changes were particularly obvious in Boston, where Ray Riepen's protégé and successor, Don Law, had grown wealthy by transforming the loose underground scene into a legitimate, struc-tured business. In 1971, he parlayed his job at the Tea Party and rela-tionship with Frank Barsalona into the Don Law Company, which staged its first show at the 15,500-seat Boston Garden. By the end of the decade, Law's dominance of the New England concert market was beyond challenge. From 1977 to 1980, the Garden presented seventy-six pop and rock concerts, and Law promoted all but three of them. Over the same period, he produced all but one of the forty-five pop shows at the 7,200-seat Cape Cod Coliseum. By 1981, his hegemony was such that the Massachusetts attorney general charged four of Law's companies with violating the state's antitrust act. Without admitting guilt, Law paid $20,000 and signed a five-year decree agreeing not to engage in what the Commonwealth characterized as monopolistic practices.*

For the performers, the financial rewards were just as apparent and irresistible. In 1968, Premier had charged the Tea Party $1,250 for its first booking, a three-night stand by Procol Harum. Just eight years later, Premier's top act, Peter Frampton, was paid $250,000 for one stadium show in Philadelphia.

Monetarily, the marriage of the music and the business was an extraordinary success. But artistically and socially, it was a complete reversal of the values that had spawned the music. The underground scene started in earnest when rock assumed the mantle of meaning and intent from folk music, and it was founded on a search for authenticity and an explicit rejection of consumerism and mainstream values. But the resonance and appeal of that message had proven broad enough to supply the impetus for a new business—and that business had taken on a life of its own. When Frank Barsalona and Dee Anthony preached professionalism and a respect for show business homilies, they nurtured a commercial star system that had nothing to do with the original underground ideal. By the late seventies, they—and the record companies—had succeeded to such an extent that the modern rock scene became the antithesis of what it had originally aspired to be. Jon Landau was correct in recognizing that rock was a business. The problem was that the music no longer drove the business, the business drove the music.

---

*In the early nineties Law was still the only New England rock promoter of any consequence, and his network of venues ran the gamut from clubs to stadiums in Massachusetts, Rhode Island, Maine, and New Hampshire. His personal holdings included a twenty-two-acre estate in Dover, Massachusetts, a $1.4 million summer home on Cape Cod, and a fleet of ten luxury cars. He also owned three New England radio stations in partnership with Frank Barsalona.

The pitfalls of that new equation were about to become apparent. In 1976, the year Springsteen switched to Premier, the agency was a well-oiled machine, lubricated by the extraordinary success of its longtime client, former Humble Pie guitarist Peter Frampton. The ultimate embodiment of the Premier philosophy, Frampton owed a great deal of his success to the guidance of both Frank Barsalona and his manager, Dee Anthony. But in the coming year, the perils of focusing solely on the acquisition of fame and ever-greater amounts of money would become all too clear. Frampton was about to go into free fall.

IN 1967 PETER FRAMPTON'S BLOND GOOD LOOKS BRIEFLY MADE HIM A teen pop idol in England, but he responded to his newfound fame by drinking too much. Looking for a clean start and recognition as a musician, in 1969 he hooked up with guitarist Steve Marriott, who had left the band Small Faces to form Humble Pie. Also on board were bassist Greg Ridley from the group Spooky Tooth and drummer Jerry Shirley. The band recorded two albums for England's Immediate Records and were managed by the label's co-owner, Andrew Loog Oldham. When Immediate went bust, Oldham introduced the band to Jerry Moss at A&M Records, who gave the group a $400,000, seven-record deal and urged them to hire a strong American manager. Dee Anthony, who had been the U.S. management representative for Spooky Tooth, seemed an obvious choice.

The band was keenly aware of Anthony's close relationship with Frank Barsalona, whose track record for booking and building British bands in America was peerless. Despite having heard rumors that money had a way of disappearing around Anthony, Shirley says the band "chose to turn a blind eye" to the stories. "We were very impressed with their American rah-rah-let's-go-do-this approach. And Frank, as we used to say, was frank. He was a heavyweight and knew how and where to do what had to be done." The band was sold. On top of their commissions—20 percent for Anthony and 10 percent for Premier for bookings—the musicians were so pleased that they made a lavish pledge to their new American handlers. "We said, 'When we get to headline, we'll buy you each a Rolls-Royce,' " recalls Shirley.

Barsalona and Anthony, as they had done with other bands, put Humble Pie on the road and kept them there. The idea, of course, was to build credibility and recognition through exposure. And to translate box-office success into album sales, Anthony added his own wrinkle to the Premier formula of endless touring. Once his acts had built sufficient credibility on the road, he urged them to capitalize on it by recording a live concert album. It was a plan he soon applied with great success to the careers of his three most important clients, J. Geils, Joe Cocker, and Humble Pie.

"Dee got that formula from Woodstock," says Jerry Shirley. "He saw the results [from the film and its sound-track album] for the bands he had on that bill. Dee knew if he could get what he saw happening night after night after night onto a record and translate it over the airwaves, then he had an almost racing certainty of a hit. It was just a matter of time before it would break. And once you'd had your live record, hopefully you could sustain and go on and have several more hits."

In 1971, after eighteen months of nearly nonstop touring, Humble Pie released *Performance—Rockin' the Fillmore*, a live album that brought the band to new commercial heights. Having slowly worked their way up from making $500 to $1,000 as the opening act on a Premier package tour, Humble Pie were now commanding between $3,500 and $5,000 a night. With the album's release, the group's guarantee immediately jumped to $10,000. In December of '71, they went out on a brief ten-show tour as a headliner and took home $25,000 from just one show at the Spectrum in Philadelphia. That Christmas, Barsalona and Anthony got their Rolls-Royces.

Frampton wasn't there to enjoy the ride. He had quit on the eve of *Performance*'s release, having lost a struggle with Marriott for control of the group's direction. The remaining members were instantly drunk on their success. Recalls Shirley, "Suddenly any equipment we wanted, transport needs, or hotel wants—all the things we had aspired to we pretty much did." It wasn't unusual for Marriott to run up an $800 telephone bill in a $15 motel room.

Anthony was not the person to stop them. His considerable abilities as a packager and motivator of talent did not extend to financial management. In an increasingly sophisticated business, his sense of fiscal responsibility was crude. If anything, he was a willing beneficiary of

Humble Pie's free-spending habits, and he had the car to prove it. It was obvious to Anthony's associate, Vince Mauro, that more money was leaving Bandana than coming in. "Tremendous money was being made at the time," he says. "But there were IRS processors coming to Bandana."*

Still, Anthony was admired in the industry. "Dee might have messed over his acts—I don't really know the internal of it—but with me Dee was always a cat I could respect," says Mario Medious. Indeed, when Medious left Atlantic in 1973 to become the American manager of an act Anthony had once been associated with, Emerson, Lake and Palmer, he sought out Anthony's counsel.

While returning to New York from a concert in New Haven, Connecticut, Medious snorted cocaine in the back of a limousine and listened attentively as Anthony imparted his formula for successful artist management.

"Let me tell you something, Mario," Medious recalls Anthony saying. "There's three things you got to remember if you're gonna manage anybody. The first thing is, uh, get the money."

"Yeah, yeah," the stoned Medious said eagerly. "What's the next?"

"Let that sit for a while, man. Let it melt in, soak into your brain." Leaning back, Medious drifted into a coke haze.

"Mario!" Anthony barked fifteen minutes later, snapping him out of his reverie. "The second thing you've gotta remember if you're gonna manage anyone in this music business is to remember to get the money!"

Twenty minutes and several lines of cocaine later, the lecture concluded. "The third thing you gotta remember," Anthony said, "is don't forget to always remember to get the money."

Getting the money and holding on to it were two different issues, however. Once Humble Pie was a headliner, Anthony's plans became increasingly grandiose and he lost sight of what he was good at. "Dee was incredible, terrific," says former Bandana employee John Doumainian, but "always fucked things up. He just had this thing in his head that he was an Irving Azoff. He wasn't. He was a motivator, in the trenches. And that's where he should've stayed."

---

*Anthony and Mauro eventually wound up suing each other over the details of a loan agreement.

In the summer of '72, Humble Pie headlined a tour with Alice Cooper. To manage their money, Anthony introduced the band to Bert Padell, a well-known entertainment industry accountant who was also his financial adviser. At Padell's suggestion, Humble Pie set up a corporation, Oven Development. According to Jerry Shirley, Anthony became the company's sole officer and the band members were listed as employees in order to reduce their taxes. When Anthony negotiated a new A&M recording deal in the summer of '72, Oven Development, rather than the band members, became the direct recipient of royalties. Among the corporation's investments was five acres of beachfront property with six cottages in Nassau. The idea was to live there or rent out the cottages to other rock bands when Humble Pie was touring, although that rarely happened. Says Shirley, "It was literally this wonderful toy we couldn't afford. We were spending it like we were going out of style. On the surface, it was probably the best time the band ever had, [but] troubles were brewing that went way deeper. It had to do with drugs and all the trappings that came with rock and roll that you didn't know the long terms of, you didn't see unless you were way more interested in the future than we were. We weren't businessmen. It was an ugly word. Little did we know we'd one day be middle-aged men with daughters who have to go to college."

Eat It, the first album under the band's new contract, was going to be the big payday. A huge marketing and promotion campaign was plotted, including billboards in Times Square, a tour of Japan, and a headlining show at Madison Square Garden. No one took a good listen to the record or cared that the band was crumbling. "Steve was overworked and overdrugged," remembers Shirley. "We just needed to stop and let him put his life back together. Instead, we made a shitty record, and no one stopped us from releasing it." *Eat It* quickly lived up to its name. Says Shirley, "It went up; it went down. Like an early rocket."

The album's obvious failure didn't alter Anthony's grandiose plans, chief among them to film Humble Pie's upcoming tour of Japan for theatrical release. Two years earlier, A&M had backed the filming of Joe Cocker's American tour with a large ad hoc group, Mad Dogs and Englishmen, and the resulting documentary and sound-track album had been Cocker's critical and commercial peak. Anthony now proposed to do the same thing with Humble Pie.

The half-baked plan had farcical results. Anthony chartered a Boeing 707, but when the plane left for Japan, the forty passengers included the band and their three female backup singers as well as the road crew, a couple of music journalists, Jerry Shirley's brother, Anthony's family, and Anthony's new English chauffeur, Ernie—but no film crew.

The cost for the Japanese jaunt, which covered five shows in ten days, was staggering. "We got a forty-thousand-dollar guarantee and were probably spending a thousand dollars a day each just on cameras and eating," says Shirley. "Figure it out. It was out of control." When the tour continued in America, the group leased two custom Lear jets, one for the band and one for their baggage. It all seemed a grand lark until Bert Padell informed the band that the tour had run up $100,000 in debts. While willing to accept his share of the blame for wasting money, Shirley was nonetheless chagrined to hear Padell, who had backed Anthony's plans for the Japanese tour and film, suddenly preaching austerity.

By the fall, the group was back in the studio, but their tenuous finances cast a heavy pall. After years of playing any and every rock venue in America, they had nothing to show. "Steve was devastated," recalls Shirley. "Then the mess really started. It was like a mini-Elvis."

Financially and creatively broke, Humble Pie soon disbanded. In the coming years, A&M released some of the group's recordings on compact disc, but Shirley received no royalties, and his inquiries about money were greeted with the news that Oven Development remained in the red. In 1991 Marriott burned to death at home when he passed out with a lit cigarette in his hand after a night of heavy drinking.

●

DURING HUMBLE PIE'S BRIEF GLORY DAYS, FRAMPTON STRUGGLED. Although he had achieved some of the critical acclaim he hungered for—*The New York Times* had dubbed him one of rock's ten best guitarists—three solo albums for A&M had created little beyond a seemingly insurmountable debt. In 1975, as he prepared to record *Frampton,* the future looked so bleak that he considered becoming a session musician. "It got to the point where I couldn't afford to borrow any more money to lose," he said. By the time he had finished recording the album, he was $175,000 in the hole.

To promote the album, A&M and Bandana focused on San Francisco. Yet despite a live broadcast on local rock station KSAN, A&M was unable to interest any of the city's major press outlets in talking to the guitarist and had to settle for interviews with college and high school papers. Still, Frampton was articulate and likable, and local sales showed an immediate increase. Although far from a runaway hit, *Frampton* handily outsold his previous albums. Fortified, Frampton began headlining regularly, and the timing appeared right for Anthony's usual coup de grâce, a live album. This time Anthony's gambler's instincts brought in a jackpot.

Upon its release in January of 1976, the two-record *Frampton Comes Alive!* was a hit. In Detroit, where Frampton was slated to begin a tour with a one-nighter at Cobo Hall, four more shows had to be added. By April 10, the album reached number one on the *Billboard* chart, where it stayed for ten weeks, eventually selling over twelve million copies. Radio embraced several pop singles from the album, including "Show Me the Way" and "Baby, I Love Your Way." The industry as a whole was enjoying a healthy period, but the years of constant touring provided Frampton with a following and produced the explosive sales. Recalls John Doumainian, who had been on the road with him since '73, "It didn't go from nothing to a hundred thousand dollars a night. There were times we'd ask Peter to do a show for two hundred dollars."

Like Springsteen, Frampton was almost rueful about dealing with money. "I don't really realize how much there is," he said after *People* magazine estimated that his album and tour had generated $50 million. "I don't want to know. It's a staggering amount, unfortunately." Yet Frampton had become the ultimate subject of Frank Barsalona and Dee Anthony's strategy for marketing rock acts.

The recent crash of Humble Pie should have served as a cautionary tale, but having worked hard for success, Frampton and Anthony proved remarkably unprepared for it. From the first days of the tour in Detroit, where Peter played to five times as many fans as originally anticipated, the only philosophy driving the juggernaut was Dee's third rule of success: "Don't forget to always remember to get the money." Promoter Bill Graham added a second concert at the fifty-thousand-seat Oakland Coliseum. In Philadelphia, 118,000 tickets were sold for a show at JFK Stadium that also featured the group Yes.

Frampton's handling had all the earmarks of a cash-out. Although Premier's bands were admonished to work long and hard if they expected to succeed, Barsalona had originally urged them to guard their credibility by controlling their exposure and not milking the last dime out of every market. "They were very ethical in the way they went about it," Boston promoter Don Law says of Premier's early days. "It was 'Let's do what makes the most sense. Let's do what's going to build this, what's going to make it exciting. Let's not push it. Let's undersell it in every case and make sure it sells out.' " More to the point, the strategy enhanced and preserved careers. By underselling the market, the demand for the act remained unsatisfied and appeared greater than it might be. Most important, whether it was true or not, the musician did not appear motivated by greed and could not be tagged a sellout by either the fans or the rock press.

This had become the core tension in the evolving world of rock and roll. The success of the music as a business was indisputable. But much of rock's popular appeal for its audience remained its rebellious nature: rebellion against conformity, rebellion against the mainstream, and rebellion against expectations. Bob Dylan and the folk-rock artists of the mid-sixties had amplified that rebellion and given it an explicitly political and intellectual component, and it had been celebrated as a key part of the counterculture by the rock underground of the late sixties. Even as the radical politics and more extreme cultural positions of that period faded in the seventies with the resolution of the Vietnam War and the broader acceptance of such central issues as individual freedom and lifestyle choices, on at least an emotional level rock continued to be the music of the outsider.

It was a point that Anthony, with his roots in traditional show business, missed. Instead, he treated Frampton's fame like the big score. Rather than practicing restraint, Frampton was frequently performing seven nights a week, and virtually all publicity opportunities were accepted indiscriminately. He appeared twice on *The Mike Douglas Show*, an afternoon television talk and variety program that catered to housewives. After posing shirtless for the covers of *Rolling Stone* and *People*, Frampton was shocked to find himself devoid of any critical currency and spurned by the fans who had initially embraced him. He was right back where he'd started eight years earlier. He wasn't a musician, he was a teen heartthrob—a joke. He responded exactly as he had years before: he got loaded. This time, his drinking was exacerbated by cocaine use. He would later complain sarcastically that no great effort was made to stop him, but he lacked the self-confidence to challenge Anthony's three rules of success. "Peter had a lot of problems," says Mauro. "His judgment was to go with what Dee and Jerry Moss told him to do. Peter was a victim, but he allowed himself to be."

Any press coverage of Frampton that mentioned Anthony at the time portrayed them as a close-knit pair, an earnest, hardworking, likable young artist and his dedicated, paternal manager. (Indeed, because of Anthony's intense focus on Frampton the J. Geils Band dropped him as their manager.) Yet if the relentless promotion made Frampton nervous, it always seemed to fall short of Anthony's aspirations. Fifteen years after Frampton's appearance before 118,000 paying fans at Philadelphia's JFK Stadium, Anthony could only lament about how much more they would have made if the concert were held in the nineties, after ticket prices had skyrocketed. "Peter's take was about $250,000," Anthony recalled. "You know what you would get today with 118,000 people at JFK? They won't let you put in more than 100,000 today. But 118,000 today—*God Almighty!* You could've taken out three million bucks. For one show! You see the difference in numbers?"

Instead of extending Frampton's career by giving his audience a chance to rest after *Frampton Comes Alive!*, Anthony insisted he go back into the studio immediately and cut a follow-up album. It was a poor strategy since there was no way Frampton could be expected to duplicate the success of the live album. Exhausted from the touring, Frampton proved hard-pressed to come up with enough original material and was forced to round out the album with covers. Released in the spring of '77, *I'm in You* quickly fell on its face. "We sold three million copies," says Doumainian. "And they probably took back two million. It was a failure."

As the summer tour for *I'm in You* progressed, so did Frampton's depression. Slated to play two shows at the Aladdin Hotel in Las Vegas—an inappropriate booking to begin with—Frampton called Anthony from his room at the casino and told him he wanted to go home. "No one really thought about my health," Frampton would later complain, "except that I was starting to consider the fact that here I am alone in a room with a bottle of Remy Martin drinking myself to sleep. Thinking, 'Let's get to the next gig.' Let's get it over with, you know?"

Anthony dispatched Mauro to talk some sense into Frampton. He urged the star to get professional help, but told him it would be a mistake to cancel the tour. "All you have left is your career," Mauro said. "Your personal life is in shambles. If you throw this away, you have nothing. This is the only satisfaction you have—why destroy it?" Frampton played that night and gave a professional but completely rote performance that one reviewer termed "duller than nails."

WHATEVER DAMAGE *I'M IN YOU* DID TO FRAMPTON'S CAREER, IT WAS NOTHing compared with the next project Anthony championed. At the height of *Frampton Comes Alive!*, Peter was signed to star in a movie based on the Beatles' watershed album *Sgt. Pepper's Lonely Hearts Club Band*. As the lead, he would have no speaking lines but would perform six songs. Along with the potential to introduce Frampton to an even bigger audience, the film was Anthony's chance to be a mogul. In return for delivering his client, he was named executive producer of the film. The real producer was British rock impresario Robert Stigwood, whose power and prestige Anthony greatly admired.

During the seventies, the film operation of the Robert Stigwood Organisation (RSO) was responsible for several blockbusters, including *Saturday Night Fever* and *Grease*, while RSO Records scored worldwide hits with the sound-track albums to those films as well as albums by Derek and the Dominos, Eric Clapton, and the Bee Gees.

Filming began in October of '77, a month after Frampton had concluded the *I'm in You* tour. Turned loose in Hollywood, Anthony rented a bungalow at the Beverly Hills Hotel—he preferred the one that Elizabeth Taylor used—and took to greeting guests in a toga. However, Frampton's unhappiness and self-doubts lingered, and they were evident on the set. "He was overwhelmed by his instant success and felt he was not deserving of it," recalls the film's director, Michael Schultz. "He was an excellent musician, but I don't think he knew how good he was."

After filming was completed, Frampton took a vacation in Nassau and drove Anthony's Rolls-Royce into a tree. He broke an arm, three ribs, and sustained a head injury that required twelve stitches. From his hospital bed in New York, he watched the televised premiere of *Sgt. Pepper's*. It was just as well that he didn't have to be there and see the senior executives from his record company, A&M, get up and leave the theater long before the film was over. It wasn't just a bomb, it was a critical wasteland. "This isn't a movie," *New York Times* critic Janet Maslin concluded, "it's a business deal set to music."

In November, Frampton was back on the road, but, much like Humble Pie, he suddenly discovered he didn't have as much money as he'd thought. He soon severed his ties with Anthony. As part of their settlement, they agreed not to discuss their differences, a commitment Frampton has clung to largely out of fear. "He put me down in one article," Anthony says of him, "and I sent the word back to him. I said the next goddamn time he puts me down again, I'll do an exposé on him that'll scare the shit out of him. If you can't say something nice about someone, don't say it."

Anthony can't quite seem to follow his own advice. As he tells it, his client's fall had nothing to do with greed, overexposure, managerial incompetence, or indifference to credibility. "He lived out in Bel Air," says Anthony. "Man, he had a great home. Two Mercedes. He had everything going, but . . ." Anthony pauses long enough to tap his nose dramatically and sniff deeply. Dropped by A&M in 1982—just five years after *Frampton Comes Alive!* became the biggest seller in the company's history—Frampton never got his career back on track.

Anthony, however, did. Although Frampton's collapse effectively ended his reign as a leading rock manager, he was still in business in the nineties. His daughter, Michelle Anthony, had become a senior executive at Sony Music, and Anthony was managing two of the company's acts. "Artists go out there and do a thing, and they don't know how a manager's mind thinks," he says. "I can give you the secret of how a guy like Frampton could come back again. But let me tell you: he should know it. He knew it ten years ago. He's tried with three or four different managers. It must be frustrating. And I love that kid— he's a fabulous little talent. There should've been a niche for him."

By the light of the smoldering wreck that had once been Peter Frampton's career, the music business was forced to confront an inconvenient truth: professionalism had its limits. Frampton had followed every dictate of the Premier/Bandana philosophy, and the end result was a brief and extraordinary commercial success followed by an insurmountable artistic bankruptcy. "Respecting the boards" just wasn't enough, even if you viewed rock only as a business. Although the quest for authenticity and the rejection of mainstream values of the folk movement and the early rock underground had been succeeded by a commercial industry and a class of professional performers whose overriding concern was the preservation of their careers, one thing hadn't changed: the residue of that original ethos remained rock's core appeal, and you couldn't maintain a career without at least a nod to it. Peter Frampton and his handlers forgot that he had to have something to say. Record buyers didn't. Nor would Jon Landau. While pushing Springsteen to accept the music as a business, he would encourage him to acquire a more explicitly political and social voice—a voice that echoed the work of earlier artists who clearly hadn't been motivated by commerce.

15

KING DAVID,
ACT TWO

I T HAD BEEN THREE YEARS SINCE DAVID GEFFEN MOVED FROM
Elektra/Asylum to Warner Bros. Pictures, two since he'd resigned
from the film company. Jobless, he'd continued to receive a
salary from Steve Ross for another year, but it was only in the last year,
1978, that he'd been without a contract or a paycheck. Now, as 1979
approached, Geffen took his first tentative step back into the Warners
fold as a consultant. He joined the record group's five top executives—label heads Ahmet Ertegun, Mo Ostin, and Joe Smith and distribution executives Henry Droz and Nesuhi Ertegun—for a
once-a-month policy meeting. He initially downplayed the significance of his return in the trades. "It's a way to get nominally back into
the music business," he told *Variety*. "But I wouldn't want to get back
on the street; I wouldn't want to run a company again."

If Geffen actually felt that way, it wasn't for long. His abrupt
departure from Warner Bros. Pictures had branded him a failure, and
the following winter, while vacationing in Barbados with Paul Simon
and television producer Lorne Michaels, he agonized over how to
mount a full-scale return to the entertainment industry. With inescapable logic, Simon suggested he simply begin again by doing what

he had done best, concentrating on music. Asylum had been an un-qualified success, and even if his subsequent flier at the film studio wasn't, at least it had opened the door. Geffen took to the idea. His time off hadn't dulled his self-assurance when it came to running a label—or his contempt for most of the people who would be his com-petitors. "I felt then, as I do now, that the same people I was compet-ing against in 1970 when I started Asylum Records were the same people I'd be competing against in 1980," Geffen said. "They were considerably older, and I was still pretty young. I thought, if I could do it then, I can do it now." Geffen asked Ross to put him back in the record business.

Having made a fortune with David Geffen's first record company, the WCI chief was more than open to the idea, even when the terms that Geffen proposed were far stiffer than previous label start-up deals. Despite claiming a personal worth of $30 million, Geffen in-sisted that Warners put up all the money—$25 million—in return for a 50 percent stake in the company. Aside from a split on any profits the label generated, Warners would also be able to make money on a five-year exclusive distribution arrangement. Of course, the proposed company had only one asset: David Geffen. But Ross quickly agreed to fund the label, dubbed Geffen Records, and administer it through Mo Ostin's Warner Bros. Records.

By industry standards, the deal was extravagant and could only make sense within the corporate culture that Steve Ross had built. He believed in executive compensation the way a missionary believes in conversion. For the top record executives, the magnitude of the change was not just unexpected, it was almost unimaginable. "When Steve Ross came in with Kinney, benefits became religious," says Stan Cornyn, who was then vice president of creative services at Warner Bros. Records. "I think I was making fifty thousand dollars a year and feeling very rich. And the first time I really got a bonus, Mo and Joe called me into their office and gave me twenty-five thousand. This is a major change in lifestyle. They were making all kinds of money. *All kinds of money.*"

Within WCI, Ross had embraced a system of empowerment that gave a wide berth to company heads like Ostin and Ertegun while lav-ishly rewarding them. The system worked: under his direction, the op-erating revenues of the record operation that included Warners,

Atlantic, and Elektra grew from $200 million a year in 1969 to over $3.2 billion in 1992, the year of Ross's death. But such a system also made it easier for Ross to reward himself while creating an aura of the beneficent father. Paying homage to that aura was as much a part of the WCI culture as hefty bonuses, and Geffen—like everyone else at the company—was clearly willing to do so. Whether Ross's extravagance with his shareholders' money ever won over Geffen as convincingly as it did other executives, however, is doubtful.

Whatever talents key record executives like Smith and Ostin brought to the table—and in Ostin's case they were unique and undeniable—the two men remained quite different from Geffen in their approach to business in that they always were and always would remain employees. David Geffen was in business for himself, with or without partners, and he did not need a leader to follow or a father to believe in. He already believed in David Geffen.*

Geffen's score with Ross was even more impressive because he was able to reserve worldwide distribution outside of North America for himself. In this feature, Geffen Records harkened back to the deal he had made ten years earlier for Asylum, which had been distributed by Atlantic in North America only and by EMI in the rest of the world. During the seventies, however, WCI had worked hard to build its own domestic and international record distribution companies. Now, despite the facts that the new distribution companies could have used the additional product and that he was the sole source of financing for Geffen Records, Ross wasn't even getting to plug the new label into his own growing international network.

It was clear that Ross valued the opportunity to be in business with Geffen but that even he went out of his way to avoid fighting with him. Joe Smith, then the head of Elektra/Asylum, discovered to his dismay that one of his label's most prestigious artists, Joni Mitchell, was being transferred to the new Geffen label. Of course, Geffen and Mitchell had a long history, and she continued to be managed by Elliot Roberts.

*Connie Bruck, in her biography of Steve Ross, *Master of the Game,* notes that Geffen and Ross had "a long and complicated relationship" but suggests that Geffen was able to disregard the myth that enveloped Ross whenever it was time to do business. "The prevalent view in the upper strata of WCI," writes Bruck, "was that David Geffen did better in his negotiations with Ross than anyone else in the company did; that, as several said, he 'had Steve's number.'"

But, in Smith's view, she was making the move because of what he deemed "excruciating pressure" from Geffen. Even worse, Smith viewed the transfer as absurd from a financial standpoint and wanted Ross to block it. "I tried to explain to Steve Ross what it meant when Geffen took Joni from me at Elektra," says Smith. "First, you're financing that label with Geffen, and, second, it's a joint venture with Geffen so you're only getting half the profit. So you're financing somebody who's stealing from us. He shrugged. He didn't want to take on Geffen."

When Geffen did make an international distribution deal, it was with CBS Records at a time when there was a virtual state of war between CBS and Warner Records. Walter Yetnikoff, who had become president of the CBS Record Group in 1975, had made the rise of Warners a rallying cry for his troops, hoping to ignite the company and create an identity for himself as an audacious leader. At the CBS Records convention that year, he had distributed GI boots to employees and had signs posted that read FUCK THE BUNNY (Bugs Bunny, one of Warner Bros.' most recognizable cartoon characters, had been elevated to something of a corporate mascot). The following year Yetnikoff lured away one of Warners' most successful and prestigious artists, James Taylor; Ostin soon returned the favor by making a deal for Paul Simon, a key Columbia performer who detested Yetnikoff.

In the midst of this antagonism, Geffen struck gold. Over the objections of the head of his own international division, Dick Asher, Yetnikoff offered to pay $17 million for foreign distribution rights for Geffen Records. It was a sum that even Nesuhi Ertegun, the head of WCI's overseas record operation, proved unwilling to match. Within the industry, Yetnikoff's largess was seen as motivated by both his admiration for Geffen's abilities and as a way to tweak Warners.

If Geffen was unwilling to pump his own fortune into his new record company, he lost little time spending Ross's. He went after several established superstars, most notably Donna Summer, Elton John, and John Lennon. Lennon's murder brought a quick and tragic end to the relationship after just one album, *Double Fantasy*, which he recorded with his wife, Yoko Ono, while the Summer and John contracts—each worth a hefty $1.5 million per album—proved a misstep. Indeed, moving to Geffen produced a pronounced downturn in the careers of both performers. Summer's stay proved particularly disastrous; her biggest hit while signed to Geffen was for another label. "She Works Hard for the Money," a top-ten hit, was released by Mercury in 1983 to settle an old contract dispute.

In comparison to Asylum, which had focused almost exclusively on a core of Los Angeles singer/songwriters, Geffen Records was intended as a broad-based record company—more like Clive Davis's Arista, which had become the industry's most successful start-up during Geffen's sabbatical—pursuing pop, rock, black, and sound-track projects with equal vigor. Within the tight focus of Asylum, Geffen's feel for the scene had been all but infallible; Geffen Records seemed ill defined and out of touch. Badly in need of a shot of credibility, in the spring of 1982 Geffen set out to woo an artist whose credentials were impeccable: Neil Young.

●

BY THE EARLY SEVENTIES, YOUNG HAD GOTTEN EXACTLY WHAT HE'D TOLD producer Jack Nitzsche he wanted: "lots of money and star fame." He had scored a number one record with "Heart of Gold" and the albums *Everybody Knows This Is Nowhere, After the Goldrush,* and *Harvest* had sold a combined five million copies. His membership in the supergroup Crosby, Stills, Nash and Young had brought him even more money and almost unparalleled status. Their 1970 album, *Déjà Vu,* sold 2.5 million copies, and the group's popularity continued unabated for years despite the absence of any new studio recordings. When the quartet re-formed for a 1974 tour, it played two dozen stadium shows.

Young had no trouble embracing the trappings of rock stardom. He soon had a beach house in Malibu, a large ranch in Northern California, a Danish-built double-masted schooner, and a fleet of rare antique cars. And as one of Reprise Records' biggest moneymakers, he expected Warner Bros. and Mo Ostin to indulge him. When it came time to sign a new contract with the label in the mid-seventies, Young wanted to meet in an Old West frontier town like Tombstone, Arizona. Instead, Ostin convinced him to settle for the Western Street set on the Warner Bros. Pictures back lot in Burbank. Young was so taken with the set that it later became the focal point of an even stranger request. When rumors circulated that an apocalyptic earthquake was about to strike the San Andreas Fault, Young called Stan Cornyn, then the label's executive vice president of artist relations, and said he wanted to drive his airstream trailer onto the set and sit out the earthquake. Parking a trailer on the lot over the weekend was against OSHA rules, but Cornyn called Frank Wells, the president of the motion picture company, and made it clear that Warner Bros. Records wanted whatever Neil Young wanted. "Frank," said Cornyn, "this is one of those times when we're talking an artist, maybe thirty million dollars. I permit no questions to follow what I'm about to say. I *need* Neil Young in a trailer on the back lot, Western Street, this weekend. Will you do it?" The regulation was ignored.

Whatever indulgences and eccentricities Young allowed himself as a rock star, he took his responsibilities as an artist seriously. Unlike Peter Frampton, he had complete faith in his own abilities and vision. He had no need for a manager who would teach him how to move onstage, mold him to a tried-and-true business program, or tell him when and what to record. Nor did he require a tutor and mentor like Jon Landau to sharpen his ideas and expose him to new resources. His relationship with his own manager, Elliot Roberts, was a complex combination of both friendship and business, but there was never any question of who was in charge. Young found himself less interested in preserving and solidifying his status than with exploring the medium. By his own admission, his biggest hit, "Heart of Gold," had put him "in the middle of the road"—and the view wasn't particularly interesting. "Travelling there soon became a bore so I headed for the ditch," he observed. "A rougher ride but I saw more interesting people there."

From his new vantage point as a star, integrity was not something Young viewed as a luxury item. It was paramount. "Nobody expected *Time Fades Away* and I'm not sorry I put it out," Young said of a vibrant but commercially disappointing collection of rough-hewn, mostly live recordings. "I didn't need the money, I didn't need the fame. You gotta keep changing. Shirts, old ladies, whatever. I'd rather keep changing and lose a lot of people along the way. If that's the price, I'll pay it. I don't give a shit if my audience is a hundred or a hundred million. It doesn't make any difference to me."

By 1975, Young was careening from style to style and band to band with increasing speed. *Homegrown,* a country album in the vein of the commercially successful *Harvest*, was recorded with Nashville musicians and shelved on the eve of release in favor of an expanded version of *Tonight's the Night*. The following album, *Zuma*, reteamed him with the rock group Crazy Horse, with whom he then set off on a world tour. But during a break, Young recorded a reunion album with Stephen Stills, *Long May You Run*, and scotched the rest of the tour in favor of hitting the road with Stills and his band. A month into that tour, which was greeted with mixed reviews, Young abruptly went home.

Young's fits and starts presented a challenge to Warner Bros./ Reprise, which had grown from a money-losing record company into an industry powerhouse based in large part on its willingness to take its underground rockers seriously and follow their lead artistically. Mo Ostin proved remarkably open to letting Young pursue his increasingly labyrinthine path, even when it looked like career suicide. In 1977, Young put together *Decade*, a three-record compilation of both familiar and previously unreleased songs, to sum up the first ten years of his recording career. But the week before it shipped, he telephoned Elliot Roberts and announced that he wanted to put out an album of new material instead. With advance orders of 300,000 copies—heady numbers for a triple album by an artist whose sales had been in steady decline—*Decade* had looked as if it could reestablish Young's commercial credentials while providing a windfall to the record company. Two days after Young called Roberts, Ostin went to see him. After listening to new tracks Young wanted to release as *American Stars 'n Bars*, Ostin agreed to postpone *Decade* for a year in favor of the new album. And by the time *American Stars 'n Bars* was delivered to Reprise four months later, it was drastically different from the album Ostin had heard.

Financially, Young proved willing to pay the costs for his artistic detours. After finally completing a country album he was willing to release, 1978's *Comes a Time*, Neil decided after the album was pressed and ready to be shipped that he had made a mistake in sequencing its songs. Rather than release an album he was unhappy with, he arranged to buy all 200,000 copies at a cost of $160,000 in return for Reprise re-ordering the tracks.

By the following year, when he cut his fourteenth solo album, *Rust Never Sleeps*, it was clear that Young's decision to veer musically from the more commercial middle of the road was being vindicated artistically. Self-indulgent, egotistical, given to whim, and frequently drugged or drunk, Young's behavior was a catalog of rock star clichés. Buffalo Springfield had made him a rock star, which was what he had wanted to be. But his work with that group, and on his first four solo albums, culminating in *Harvest,* had also established him as one of rock's most ambitious and influential singer/songwriters and stylists. If, as he had told his producer, Jack Nitzsche, he had simply recognized that there was a gap in rock and roll waiting to be filled by someone who could combine the music of the Rolling Stones and Dylan, Young had been more than crafty. He had been successful. By 1979, critics were beginning to accord Young a new heft.

"For my money," wrote *Rolling Stone* album review editor Paul Nelson of *Rust Never Sleeps,* "Neil Young can outwrite, outsing, outplay, outthink, outfeel and outlast anybody in rock & roll today. Of all the major artists who started in the Sixties (Bob Dylan, the Rolling Stones, the Who, et al.), he's the only one who's consistently better now than he was then."

Young had served as a touchstone and inspiration for the younger set of Southern California singer/songwriters like Henley, Frey, Souther, Browne, and Doheny who made up the Geffen/Roberts talent roster. But unlike the Eagles, who had dealt with the contradiction inherent in the commercial success of their outlaw image by contriving a world-weary cynicism, Young was finding he could still present something fresh and wide-eyed, even as his musical palette darkened.

Like the Eagles and Peter Frampton, Young was a successful rock star whose tours tended to focus on large sports arenas. Yet unlike virtually every other rock star, he was not threatened by the punk movement's implication that arena rock was the vapid, puerile product of an overwhelming and crass business machine. The reason was simple. By casting his creative net wide and daring to fail in public, Young had produced the work and won the credibility that forgave whatever rockstar whimsies he indulged in, whimsies he embraced not for the sake of the record company or the public but to feed the work and his own monumental ego. "Neil never sold out," says former Geffen/Roberts associate John Hartmann, "and he never will. Neil Young thinks he is the modern Shakespeare."

But after thirteen years with Reprise, Young's relationship with the label had finally grown strained. For all his faith in following the artist, Ostin didn't always say yes. He still ran a tight ship financially and was loath to green-light a sure money-loser, even if the artist was Neil Young. Young's 1981 album, *Re*ac*tor*, included a song entitled "Surfer Joe and Moe the Sleaze"—an apparent dig at Ostin and his former second in command, Joe Smith—and Young and Roberts decided to leave Reprise for RCA records, which, unlike Warner Bros., had been all but devastated by its inability to deal meaningfully with rock's commercial ascendancy. In the early eighties, when the label was going through one of its periodic and invariably unsuccessful attempts to catch up with the CBS and Warners labels, it shelled out $15 million to sign singer Diana Ross away from Motown. Even if Young made some albums that didn't sell, his presence could only raise RCA's profile and credibility with other artists.

The deal RCA offered Young looked good. With a guarantee of approximately $1.5 million per album—a tremendous amount for an artist who frequently demonstrated his indifference to commercial considerations—it was far richer than Young's former Reprise contract or anything else on the table, including an offer from Geffen Records. By the spring of '82, the contracts were drawn, but the day Young was to sign them, David Geffen called Roberts and asked his former partner to bring Young to see him first.

Geffen portrayed RCA's big-money offer as a millstone. Did Neil really think RCA would just let him make whatever kind of records he wanted if it was losing money? He took a page from Mo Ostin and pledged that Young would be free to make whatever records he wanted without commercial constraint if he took a smaller deal from him. And who knew? In the more artist-friendly environment of Geffen Records he'd do better work and maybe make even more money at the end of the day. The pitch hit home. Roberts was so gung-ho on the Geffen deal that he publicly trumpeted that the agreement he had made for his client was worth $6 million less than RCA's offer. (Elliot was only half as oblivious to money as he made out; the actual difference between the offers was really $3,025,000—still a powerful testament to Geffen's persuasiveness.) Instead, he argued that what clinched the deal was Geffen's dedication to artistic integrity.

"Other companies can offer you money up the ass," Roberts said, "but not many people can offer you love and respectability from the point that they really do treat Neil as a great artist. It's never a question of 'Hey, we gave you three million and the album only sold half a million so the next one better be more commercial, fella.' You play an album for David and he genuinely loves it. He's not concerned with sales on that level because you must remember that David Geffen is a very wealthy person . . . He's doing this record company because he loves music . . . This is not a company that's looking at the bottom line . . . He's looking to put out fine records . . . When you do business with those kind of people, in the long run you make more money."

What Roberts was saying was true. Unfortunately, he was describing Mo Ostin, whom he and Young had opted to leave. But Geffen Records now had its credible artist.

●

IN THE SIXTIES AND SEVENTIES, GEFFEN HAD PARLAYED HIS FEEL FOR THE underground into ever-greater show business opportunities. The William Morris Agency had led him to music, Laura Nyro into management, and Asylum to an association with Steve Ross and the chance to be a movie mogul. That he had failed as vice chairman of Warner Bros. Pictures did not prevent him from following the same plotline in the second act of his career. Geffen Records was intended to provide its chairman and CEO with a wedge into other entertainment areas, including film and theater. This time David Geffen would not fail.

When he landed the original cast album for a hot Broadway musical like *Dreamgirls,* he used it to widen his purview by becoming the show's coproducer in a partnership with the Shubert Organization, ABC, and Metromedia. By 1982, *Dreamgirls* was taking in $400,000 a week, of which Geffen's take was $40,000. That same year, the partnership spent $4.5 million to bring Andrew Lloyd Webber's London show *Cats* to New York. Even Geffen wouldn't defend the show as a work of art, but it was soon providing him with annual profits in excess of $5 million.

Geffen Records wasn't the immediate success that Asylum had been, but it was becoming clear that Geffen's touch was back—indeed, his Broadway successes, real estate ventures, art acquisitions, and a tentative foray into film production suggested his skills and reach might extend far beyond the world of rock. Having regained his perch as the industry *wunderkind,* Geffen was asked by reporters why he'd ever left the business to begin with. His explanation was a surprise: he had been seriously ill. Or, at least, he had believed he was.

He had stopped working only, he said, after being diagnosed with an unnamed terminal illness, adding that he'd decided to return to work three years later when a second battery of tests revealed that he'd "never even been sick at all." Slowly, over a series of subsequent interviews, he offered more and more details. Five months after revealing he had been sick Geffen still wouldn't specify what had been wrong with him but said that he'd checked into Los Angeles's Cedars-Sinai Medical Center for a relatively minor operation, only to be informed by the doctor afterward that he was very seriously ill and would eventually lose his bladder. The "nightmare" ended, he said, when he checked into a New York hospital three years later—having been told that his condition was unstable—only to learn that there had never really been anything wrong with him. With time and repeated telling, Geffen disclosed that he'd been misdiagnosed with cancer.

Even Geffen had to admit that the obtuse manner in which he chose to reveal the story raised as many questions as it answered. "If they think I had a nervous breakdown," he said, "I don't give a shit." Some wondered if he had. "It's a hard one," allows Ted Ashley, Geffen's former boss. "He was not yet a satisfied human being. You work your ass off, you're a superstar, you achieve an uncommon amount of progress. And somehow you wake up in the morning and you don't feel good and you're not very happy with yourself. If that's the case, I think it's more in keeping with his personality to attribute it to something less personal—meaning cancer, an outside agent."

Friends and associates, including Elliot Roberts and agent Sue Mengers, attested to seeing Geffen in the hospital or emotionally shattered during this period. Still, he was uncharacteristically reticent, referring to the physician whose misdiagnosis had produced years of unnecessary agony only as a "legitimate" Beverly Hills doctor. And despite saying that his mother and friends believed he should bring legal action, he was remarkably forgiving. He had no desire to sue the doctor or Cedars-Sinai hospital for robbing him of those years. He just wanted to put it all behind him.

The reaction was distinctly out of character, or at least didn't fit his public persona. Geffen's growing reputation beyond the record business as a man not to be trifled with was based in part on how unpleas-

ant he could be when he put his mind to it. "When David feels maligned, he feels more maligned than anybody I've ever met," his former employee and sometime antagonist Irving Azoff observed. While
it was duly noted around town that even Steve Ross didn't want to fight
with him, Geffen's status as an unforgiving opponent was cemented by
a protracted, vicious fight with one of Hollywood's most successful
screenwriters, Robert Towne.

Towne was the author of *Chinatown*—for which he had won an
Academy Award—and *Shampoo*. In 1979, he had convinced Warner
Bros. to let him direct an original screenplay, *Personal Best*. Shooting
had begun the following year but was suspended when the Screen Actors Guild went on strike in July. Geffen, who had set up a joint venture with Warner Bros. Pictures to parallel his record agreement,
agreed to finance the completion of the film as an independent
project, sidestepping the strike. But as a subsequent $155 million
lawsuit brought by Towne would attest, it was the last thing he and
Geffen agreed on.

According to Towne, Geffen made his life unbearable, interfering
with the production and publicly boasting that he would "completely
destroy" the filmmaker. Those actions, the suit charged, had a financial motive and were aimed at forcing Towne to renegotiate his deal:
Geffen had sought a reduction in Towne's share in the gross receipts
and an increase in his own, he wanted to charge him for any cost overruns, and he tried to ram through a takeover provision if the film was
late or over cost. For his part, Geffen maintained that Towne had a cocaine problem and couldn't properly supervise the film or its budget.
Even before filming could be completed, Towne claimed, Geffen had
closed down the production and padlocked the facilities in a bid to finish the film without him. Towne, who says he was able to line up alternate financing and get Geffen off the financial hook, would insist
that Geffen had threatened to sue anyone who paid for *Personal Best*'s
completion. Eventually, he agreed to Geffen's financial concessions
and ceded Warner Bros. first rights to two of his screenplays, *Greystoke*
and *Tequila Sunrise*.

The battle was hardly over. According to Towne, Geffen eventually
had his director's cut seized from one optical lab and transferred to
another in order to have his name placed at the beginning of the film
and posted armed guards outside the projection booths at the New

York and Los Angeles premieres of the movie to keep Towne out. In case the fight wasn't personal enough, Geffen gave a scathing deposition against Towne in his divorce case, portraying him as a cocaine addict. Towne pointedly used his own suit to paint Geffen as a serial slanderer. "This is not an isolated instance of Geffen using libel, slander, and other vindictive and coercive tactics to punish and coerce those with whom he deals and has disputes," Towne charged. "Indeed, it is Geffen's practice to launch vicious, defamatory attacks and to employ other coercive tactics to gain his end in such situations. Accordingly, an award of exemplary damages is particularly appropriate."

If Towne's arrows ever hit their mark, Geffen didn't show it. Rather, he treated the lawsuit as proof of his importance. "You're looking at the man who's just been sued for $155 million," he crowed to a group of writers and producers on the day Towne filed the suit.

For all the venom, the case was eventually settled quietly out of court. But Geffen was impressed enough by Towne's attorney, Bert Fields, to hire him. A much feared Los Angeles litigator, Fields would become a valuable and long-standing member of Geffen's legal team. (In one of the suit's most humorous and telling moments he had belittled Geffen's charge that Towne was unstable because he was seeing a psychiatrist by pointing out that Geffen only knew of Towne's therapy because he was being treated by the same doctor.) And, in what could be considered the final insult to Towne, *Personal Best* wound up not costing Geffen a dime. Before the film was released, Warners took it back and absorbed the production costs when Geffen complained that he couldn't afford the financial or mental anguish of having a flop with his first picture. Towne had cast himself as a brave fighter for artistic freedom taking on a well-known bully, but the suit did Geffen no lasting damage. His next movie was *Risky Business*, which made Tom Cruise a star, cleared Geffen $7 million, and established him as a producer of consequence.

Geffen had managed in just three years to accomplish what had eluded him in his first Warner Bros. tenure: he had proven that he was more than a music executive. No other entertainment executive could boast of having film, theater, and record operations. Having used his relationship with the artists he managed in the sixties and seventies to make himself a power in the record business with Asylum and Warner

Bros., he had brilliantly expanded his realms of influence and made himself into a new brand of mogul. Yet he was far from finished. In the coming years, Geffen would use his entertainment industry success as a piton to scale undreamed-of business peaks and show that he was a visionary deal maker whose turf was not limited to the record business or even Hollywood.

16

A Great Marketing Experience

FOLLOWING THE FINANCIAL BOOM OF THE LATE SEVENTIES WITH THE big sound-track albums and massive hits by Frampton, the Eagles, and Fleetwood Mac, the industry paid dearly for its commercial overreach, and sales and profits crashed. Bruce Springsteen also had real cash-flow problems. The protracted legal battle with Mike Appel had ultimately cost him $800,000, not including lawyers' fees. CBS Records had advanced the money, but Springsteen had to pay it back out of his record royalties. The *Darkness on the Edge of Town* tour had put him in the black—but just. When E Street Band guitarist Steve Van Zandt joined Jon Landau as coproducer on Springsteen's next album, *The River,* in April of '79, they hoped to remedy that. Says Van Zandt, "The first thing I produced I very consciously wanted to be a hit."

That song, "Hungry Heart," was a flat-out attempt to craft a pop single. "I did a lot of things on that record to make sure it could be played on the radio," says Van Zandt. Among them were speeding up the recording to make it sound more exciting and bringing in the former lead vocalists with the Turtles, Mark Volman and Howard Kaylan, to give the background parts a Top 40 patina. If such manipulations for commercial ends seemed at odds with the spirit of Springsteen's previous public pronouncements, Van Zandt could offer spirited if somewhat obtuse justifications for what he called "significant" singles. "I knew it was the right time, the right song, it was not a compromise," says Van Zandt. "It came out of his work." Springsteen, though irked that he'd never had a hit single while other performers, including Patti Smith and the Pointer Sisters, had enjoyed commercial success with his songs, nursed enough reservations about "Hungry Heart" to want to keep it off *The River,* and it was only included at Landau's insistence. The song ultimately reached number 5 on Billboard's Top 100 pop singles chart.

Springsteen's ambivalence was a source of frustration for CBS Records, which had been hit particularly hard by the record business recession. While industry-wide sales dropped 11 percent in 1979, the company's pretax earnings plummeted to an embarrassingly narrow $51 million on sales of over $1 billion—a 46 percent slide. As work on *The River* dragged on, the label's blunt president and CEO, Walter Yetnikoff, visited Springsteen in the studio, begging him to "finish the fucking record." Yet after assembling ten tracks as a single album entitled *The Ties That Bind,* he opted to continue recording until he had more than thirty songs. Springsteen's indecision baffled and frustrated his friend and Columbia A&R man, Peter Philbin, particularly when the rocker played him seventeen different mixes of the song "The River." "I'm sitting there thinking 'What is this?' " Philbin recalls. "And then Bruce goes, 'Now which one is better?' *Which one is better?* Hey, flip a coin!"

Chuck Plotkin, a former Asylum executive Landau had met while working on *The Pretender,* was tapped to sift through the minutiae of technical detail. "Chuck has the energy and mind-set that equals Bruce on this," says Philbin. "He will literally go through it with a magnifying glass and come up with an enthusiasm for which of these seventeen mixes are best. So Jon was very shrewd inserting Chuck. But all in all, Jon would manipulate for the good of the art. Or for what he felt was the good of it."

Van Zandt had a far more romantic approach than Landau to Springsteen's music. Although he had crafted "Hungry Heart" as a single, he preferred to record the band as live as possible, equating an unretouched performance with artistic credibility. "It was that lack of compromise that I felt he was capable of and wanted to do from the start," Van Zandt says. "If we're the best band in the world, let's prove it." But the differences between Van Zandt and Landau ran far deeper than how to conduct a studio session—they went to the core of their divergent expectations for Springsteen.

As the producer for the MC5, Landau had urged that band to focus on the work at hand, to accept making records as a business, and to sever their ties with John Sinclair and the White Panthers, whom he viewed as excess baggage. Now, he was forced to contend with a circle of friends and employees whose relationships with Springsteen were unusually complicated and emotional and who were in their own way just as doctrinaire as the White Panthers. The romance and cama- raderie of Springsteen's blue-collar approach, the notion that the music was a street-corner communion, resonated as deeply with friends and associates as it did with his fans. "A lot of people were there early on and from their hearts because they saw a talent and fell in love with an artist," says Philbin. "The work first, and then him. Bruce was able to gather almost disciples around him. And you know, he never asked. He never promised anything. He just let people do it." Says lighting director Marc Brickman, "Unrequited love was what it always was. Everyone, the whole band. You just loved what this guy was so much and what he stood for and what he believed in by his songs that nothing else mattered. He never understood that. He never believed anybody loved him that much."

The relationships had been a source for some of Springsteen's work. A few months after Brickman got married, he was surprised to hear Springsteen introduce the song "Stolen Car" in concert with a story about the wedding. The monologue soon became a fixture of the show, and, when Brickman asked about it, Bruce said the marriage had fig- ured in the writing of several songs on *The River*. Brickman was flat- tered, although he later discovered that there was a downside to being grist for Springsteen's mill. "When I got divorced two years later he got pissed off because I ruined his songs," Brickman says with a bitter laugh.

For all the bonhomie, Springsteen could concentrate on work and cut people off, a propensity Landau encouraged as he assumed more and more responsibility and power. Philbin saw the tenor of Spring- steen's organization and career changing: "Jon is very manipulative. When he came in he made pretty much a conscious decision to cut Bruce apart from anyone who was close to him in the business sense and really, one by one, cut him off. Now, it wasn't like he forced Bruce; he just went about doing it. I was not involved in day-to-day things, and as time went on, I found access was limited. Whereas coming up, Mike Appel never had a problem with anybody reaching Bruce—and it was a different point in the career—Jon really did cut people off." Before long, he was feared.

Van Zandt, by comparison, was the person the band and crew members turned to as a mediator. His friendship with Springsteen predated his involvement in the band, and he had his ear. That role only served to heighten the tension between him and Landau. Having fought to carve out his own niche as a producer when Mike Appel was the manager, Landau now appeared cool to having Van Zandt as a collaborator, reportedly fighting with him over royalties and production credits.

"Steve and Jon clashed constantly," recalls Philbin. "It was an issue over Bruce's affections you might say, over power. I think more perceived than real. But Steve Van Zandt is an interesting personality, and a lot of it is that he had a strong self-agenda. So did Jon. And Jon is infinitely the brighter guy."

Landau appeared particularly loath to give a leg up to Marc Brickman, killing a plan to make him Springsteen's video director. His antipathy toward the talented and outspoken lighting director had been apparent early on. In the steady stream of rave reviews for Springsteen's live shows the lighting often received special mention, but it deflected some of the credit for the show's success away from Springsteen and appeared to be a calling card that Landau could live without. When writer David McGee profiled Brickman in the music business trade magazine *Record World,* he was shocked by Landau's reaction. "Why didn't you get him to say he wrote the songs, too?" Landau asked sarcastically.

The following week Brickman was summoned backstage by Springsteen after a show. Landau was with him.

"Y'know," Springsteen said, "I think the lights are too busy."

"Too busy?" Brickman asked.

"Yeah. I think we need to have it . . . more straightforward."

Perplexed, Brickman simply agreed. But boarding the crew bus later, he had a sinking feeling when he looked out the window and saw Landau and Springsteen leaving together.

"I knew that I was targeted," he later recalled, "that this was coming from Landau. This is way before *The River,* even before Jon became manager. He had it in for me."

Even those on the periphery saw a change. Landau's old *Real Paper* colleague, Boston photographer and now publishing executive Jeff Albertson, who had cohosted the all-night parties in the mid-seventies when Springsteen was playing Joe's Place, suddenly found he wasn't even allowed to talk to his old friend. Loading his camera backstage before a show at Boston's Music Hall in 1978, Albertson spied Springsteen tuning his guitar in a dressing room and went in to say hello. After a few minutes, he saw Landau standing in the doorway staring at him. With a crook of the finger, Landau summoned him over.

"Look, will you leave Bruce alone right now?" Landau asked. "He wants to tune."

Albertson looked at Springsteen. "Do you want me to leave?" he asked.

"No," Bruce said.

Landau stared at Springsteen.

"Well," Springsteen said to Albertson, "maybe we'll talk later."

Albertson didn't speak to Springsteen again that night—or ever. But more than anything, the encounter left him thinking about Landau.

"I never aspired to a friendship with Jon," he says. "To be honest, it was the other way around. I didn't want anything from Jon, I didn't need anything from Jon, and I still don't . . . This is a guy who was close friends with me and a lot of people in the New England music business. And as soon as Bruce hit, you couldn't find him with a search warrant . . . The overweening ambition and the paranoia really changed Jon's ability to be a friend to anyone."

THE RIVER WAS FINALLY COMPLETED AFTER SIXTEEN MONTHS AND PROVED to be an important product for CBS Records. A lavishly packaged double album, it was released in October of 1980, just in time for the all-important Christmas sales season, which can account for as much as 40 percent of annual record industry income. As a work, it was ambitious if uneven. The lyrics to the title track were deeper and more sharply drawn than anything else Springsteen had recorded before, although the words to many of the collection's other nineteen songs were mind-numbingly redundant and featured more cars than the Indianapolis 500. The arrangements were decidedly retrogressive, not surprising considering the affinity that Springsteen, Van Zandt, and Landau all felt for fifties rock and roll.

Nevertheless, with Landau's guidance, Springsteen's reference points were becoming more socially explicit and political. Touring in support of the album, Springsteen received a rave review from John Rockwell in *The New York Times,* who paid tribute to Landau's role in his development and suggested that he might grow into a transcendent artist who could "help inspire the country as a whole." Shortly after the review appeared, Landau gave Springsteen a copy of *Woody Guthrie: A Life,* written by Landau's former *Phoenix* associate Joe Klein. Two months later, Springsteen added Guthrie's "This Land Is Your Land" to his show. Simultaneously, Landau's own aspirations for Springsteen were becoming grandiose, which became apparent when *The River* tour played a difficult date in Barcelona, Spain, on April 21, 1981.

Dictator Francisco Franco had died more than five years earlier, and the country was still taking its first lurching steps toward democracy. Spain hadn't rolled out the welcome mat for rock tours under Franco, and support facilities remained minimal. Worse, secret police followed the band and crew, and machine guns were positioned on the roof of the arena, Palacio de Deportes. The paranoia and lack of proper tools came to a head when the stage collapsed while the crew was setting up for the show.

"What the fuck are we even doing here?" Brickman asked when he buttonholed Landau. Even given their mutual dislike, Brickman was not prepared for the answer he got.

"You just shut up," he recalls being told. "I'll tell you what we're doing here. Bruce Springsteen's going to play here tonight. Bruce is going to change the lives of these people. Even if he doesn't change the lives of everyone in this audience, if he changes one kid's life in this audience, in this fascist state, and gives him a reason to live, a reason to believe in what we talk about, then it's worth playing here. Do you understand?"

Brickman was flabbergasted. "Are you kidding me?" he said. "Most of the kids don't even understand *English*! They're coming because it's a rock concert and they haven't had any!"

Springsteen's work began to show this populist intent when he turned his attention toward his next record, *Nebraska*. Working at home, he cut ten songs in September of 1981 accompanying himself on acoustic guitar. The simplicity of the tracks bore a strong resemblance to the kind of raw, solo "field recordings" that earlier folk and blues artists had made during the thirties and forties.

The collection of songs gave a new twist to Springsteen's persona as the outsider while offering more than a glimpse of the borrowed ingredients. Aside from their classic folk feel, the songs included a bastardized rewrite of the Hank Williams ballad "A Mansion on the Hill"; also raided was Terrence Malick's film *Badlands*, about mass murderer Charles Starkweather and his teenage girlfriend, which provided the spur for the song "Nebraska." Jumbled with the new influences were troubadour-style reworkings of some of Bruce's most familiar themes: the rift between fathers and sons ("My Father's House"), growing up working-class poor ("Used Cars"), and "Atlantic City," a gangster fantasy reminiscent of his earlier "Meeting Across the River." And while there was an undeniable sameness in the minimal instrumentation and the mournful cadence of Springsteen's nearly monochromatic vocals, the songs were clearly the work of someone trying to expand his artistic vocabulary.

The rough-hewn album did not cheer CBS Records head Walter Yetnikoff, who, while grateful to have any new Bruce Springsteen record, would have preferred one the company could actually market. As he recounted later, he viewed it as an album "you made in your garage, thank you. We'll do the best we can."

Releasing a small album carried positive and negative implications. Its down-and-out dust-bowl imagery elaborated the Guthrie connection that John Rockwell had first intimated in *The New York Times* and that Springsteen had subsequently made in concert. That, along with its modesty, showed that Springsteen wasn't focused solely on scoring pop hits, boosting his long-term credibility. But *Nebraska* hadn't excited CBS and virtually guaranteed that the next album he gave them would have to be a big record. Privately, both Springsteen and Landau feared that he would lose his audience unless he put out an overtly commercial album.

Work on that record was proceeding even as *Nebraska* was released, and, as on *The River*, Steve Van Zandt handled much of the production on the early sessions. But his rocky relationship with Landau and interest in pursuing a solo career had made his departure inevitable. He quit the band in '83, and Landau and Plotkin continued without him. Even with approximately one hundred songs to choose from, the sessions hadn't produced what Landau was looking for: a bona fide pop single to get the album's sales rolling. Frustrated, he confronted Springsteen and virtually demanded a more commercial single, couching it in an aesthetic argument that the album was otherwise artistically incomplete.

Still haunted by the specter of the *Born to Run* hype, Springsteen balked. But he had given Landau a double-edged sword to cut a swath between art and business, and from a business standpoint it was impossible to argue with the results. Landau had brought a focus to Springsteen's career that it had not had under Mike Appel, and he was eager to take it even further. Whether that was necessary was a matter of some debate. *The River* had sold three million copies, and the band was selling out arenas. By any standard, Bruce Springsteen was fabulously successful. "You can make a very good living—a *very* good living—selling a couple of million records and selling out arenas," says Van Zandt. "I don't think we needed to be any more successful. And didn't think we would be."

Landau, however, was about to prove that like his rabbi David Geffen, he could see over the next rise. Springsteen relented and came up with the leadoff single Landau wanted, "Dancing in the Dark." Still unhappy with the songs they had agreed on, Springsteen wanted to keep working. But with his prize firmly in hand, Landau called a halt and told CBS the album was ready.

However disappointed CBS Records' executives had been by *Nebraska*, they were ecstatic with the new album, *Born in the U.S.A.* As proof of the record's importance to the company, Columbia's highest-ranking executive, senior vice president and general manager Al Teller, personally acted as point man for the album's marketing plan. Listening to *Born in the U.S.A.*, Teller knew that Bruce Springsteen, who had crossed handily into CBS's dividend column years earlier with *Born to Run*, was about to become a gold-plated annuity. "Record companies earn their way on big, big hit albums and catalog," says Teller. "Everything else in the middle is what I call the investment money."

In the early seventies, when Springsteen had begun his recording career, record companies—the smart ones, at least, like Warner Bros. and CBS—walked a marketing tightrope. They wanted the acts they signed to be a commercial success, but being perceived as commercially motivated was career death for a rock artist. The increasing marketing sophistication of the labels, typified by the pioneering work of promotion men like Mario Medious, had brilliantly parlayed both the growing influence of the alternative media like *Rolling Stone* and WBCN and the willing careerism of its artists into a new hip capitalism. Teller, who held an M.B.A. from the Harvard Business School, had contrived a concrete, commercial game plan for building careers without making rock stars look as if they were motivated by commercial interests. Columbia marketed bands gradually, letting them establish their legitimacy through touring and a few critically well received albums before looking for the payoff. "Then, when we dropped the hammer, everything was in place," Teller says. "The credibility, the live audience base, we had a catalog to sell and could survive the critics' difficulty with a group having a hit single."

By the mid-eighties, however, the rules had changed. Along with airplay and touring, a new and extremely influential component, music videos, had been added to the marketing picture. MTV debuted in August of 1981 offering cable viewers rock videos twenty-four hours a day. Although the initial selection was limited, the new medium proved valuable for breaking visually arresting acts like Boy George and Culture Club. And as the channel's subscribers multiplied exponentially from 2.1 million in its first year to 16.2 million in 1983, its audience took on real clout. "When MTV came along I thought two things," recalls Teller. "What a great marketing tool, and this can prove to be a disaster. Unfortunately, number one is true *and* number two is true."

Control of image and exposure had been paramount throughout the seventies, whether it was Frank Barsalona attempting to keep ticket availability for his acts lagging just slightly behind the demand and admonishing his clients not to appear on television, or the record companies attempting to forge a consensus among critics for an artist's credibility. But music videos in general and MTV in particular were offering immediate rewards for mass exposure. Artists and labels could reap a quick financial bonanza, but no one was sure what the effect of all the exposure would be on the long-term health of careers.

"We used to literally have debates about whether it was smart for the same artist to come back and play dates to an additional two thousand people in the same market in the same *year*," says Teller. "Fearing overexposure. Now we want thirty spins a week on the video."

Videos could also help established stars increase their record sales dramatically. By taking the traditional components of record market-ing—airplay and touring—and adding videos, record companies were extending the shelf life of albums significantly. Presented with the possibility of a huge payoff, the record companies' traditional fear of consumer burnout, which tended to limit the release of singles from a best-selling album to two or three in order to preserve long-term in-terest in performers, fell by the wayside. Suddenly record companies were going four, five, and even seven singles deep on video-friendly performers. Nowhere were the financial rewards more apparent than with Michael Jackson, on Columbia's sister label, Epic.

When his album *Thriller* debuted in the last week of 1982, Jack-son released slick, expensive videos directed by Bob Giraldi, who'd made his reputation in commercials. The clips helped make Michael Jackson a phenomenon, and *Thriller* produced seven hit singles en route to selling forty million albums, making it the biggest-selling album in pop history. "What we focused on pretty rapidly was trying to pull all of these elements together to try and create an extended mega-explosion," says Teller. "It wasn't just a question of going many singles deep, but coming up with visual images to go with those singles from a video perspective and keeping an act touring and tour-ing and touring and touring and touring. Just creating a vibe and in-tensity and a desire for a particular record in as many ways as possible. It turned out to be a very potent combination. That was the game."

Obviously, having the right record to work with was no minor de-tail. "You can't invent this shit out of nothing," admits Teller. "When a record would come to us—primarily from an already established, major artist where you come out of the chute with a flying start—and we'd listen to it and say, 'We're four deep, we're five deep, we're po-tentially six singles deep,' we knew we could architect a game plan that could run the better part of a year and a half if not two years."

With "Dancing in the Dark," Landau was certain he had the single to get that kind of blockbuster album rolling. So was Teller. "It just had the smell to me of an absolute monster single," he says. "In fact, I made the mistake of turning to Landau and saying 'That's the first single and that's a number one record. I guarantee you.' Now, in this business, too many things can go wrong to guarantee anyone a number one single, but I felt so strongly about it that I just blurted it out."

Ironically, "Dancing in the Dark" never did get to number one on the pop charts because of the concurrent success of another artist's breakthrough single, Prince's visceral "When Doves Cry." Unlike "Dancing in the Dark," which bore a striking resemblance rhythmically to the biggest hit of the preceding year, the Police's "Every Breath You Take," and further aped what was happening on the charts by embellishing Springsteen's sound with the then popular patina of synthesizers, Prince's single was so radically constructed that it didn't even have a bass part. But the fact that "Dancing in the Dark" was ultimately boxed out of the top slot on the pop chart would prove a technicality in the overall success of *Born in the U.S.A.* When Landau invited Teller to the studio to hear the album, the executive correctly assessed the album's commercial potential.

"We're going to sell ten million of this in the U.S.," Teller told Landau. "It's going to take Bruce to a whole new level in terms of record sales, having mass appeal hits, and ultimately on the touring side as well. We've got at least five big hit records here, and now all we have to do is cleverly stage them, the sequence of them, the touring—and nobody tours better than Bruce—and basically put together a two-year plan."

Landau simply smiled and fetched Springsteen and had Teller repeat his enthusiastic predictions. "Bruce sort of smiled and chuckled when I said this," Teller recalls. " 'Well! Well . . . you're kiddin'.' Like he'd be the last to believe this. I said, 'No, I'm not kidding. But you don't have to worry about this. Go out and do what you do great.' Which is really the way that we all work together."

Landau and Teller immediately began working on *Born in the U.S.A.*'s marketing plan, focusing on the industry's new holy trinity: videos, touring, and label promotion. The heart of Columbia's strategy was to keep the album in front of the public for as long as possible by earmarking it as the label's top marketing priority for an unusually long period of time. Teller did that by emphasizing over and over again to his staff that the goal was not simply to have a hit but to sell ten million copies of the album.

"I didn't simply want to go from single to single and have somebody say, 'Wow, didn't we do great,' " Teller says. "I very much wanted to set out objectives and benchmarks for us to achieve. It's too easy to say to yourself, 'We've sold three million or four million records' and just pat yourself on the back and whatever it's going to sell after that is from a catalog perspective. We aggressively marketed that record for a solid two-year period. It never stopped being a marketing priority or a promotion priority. We were always coming up with new programs for the field guys to take to accounts, and this record was handled as a new release for two years. All the marketing meetings specifically designed to come up with the next phase of the Springsteen campaign were done with that in mind. And I kept saying 'Remember, folks, we've set out to sell ten million copies of this record in this country. And we're going to continue to march toward that objective.' "

In Landau, Teller and CBS had an eager and inventive partner. "Jon, in my opinion, is one of the great managers," Teller says. "He had an incredibly deep understanding of music and the marketplace. And particularly of his client. It was a treat. He and I would get together and brainstorm frequently . . . every once in a while we'd go off and have a long lunch and just take stock of where we are and come to some generalized agreement of what we're going to accomplish over the next three to six months."

Springsteen never had a problem mounting a convincing tour, a fact at the heart of Teller's admonishment to "go out and do what you do great." But the *Born in the U.S.A.* tour, intended to catapult Springsteen to superstardom, would go out without one of the stalwarts of Bruce's crew, Marc Brickman. The reason, ostensibly, was a scheduling conflict. Brickman was handling lights for bass guitarist Roger Waters, but Springsteen's schedule had changed, and Brickman couldn't make four days of rehearsals. After twelve years as Springsteen's lighting director, he found the reason for his dismissal ludicrous. "I've been with you I don't know how many years," Brickman pleaded with Springsteen. "You used to not have a set list. You used to just tug your ear or turn around and wink or move your elbow and that was the cue. Now how can you tell me after I've done five hundred shows with you that I won't know the show? How can you possibly say that?" But the plans for the stage show were far more structured than anything the band had done before, and Springsteen was unmoved. "He said to me, 'It doesn't matter,' " recalls Brickman.

Brickman saw the scheduling conflict as a ruse. "Before these conversations we were negotiating for money," he says. "There was a budget for every night, and on an eighteen-month tour, considerable amounts of money. Somebody was going to make a profit on this. Why not me after all these years? They didn't want me to have that profit. That was the bottom line. They gave that money to strangers."

Six months into the tour, Brickman swallowed his pride and had a "Dear Bruce" note hand delivered backstage. "I said, 'I'm really heartbroken. My life feels weird without it.' Landau almost fired the guy who brought the letter to Bruce in his dressing room."

Landau telephoned Brickman the next morning. "He started screaming at me," Brickman says. "Told me I was a worthless piece of shit—his actual quote. That I'd be lucky if I ever worked again. I mean, the guy was out of control."

So, too, was Brickman. He'd developed a bad cocaine habit after being bounced off the tour, and it was beginning to look as if his career was indeed over. "No one would hire me," he says, "because I wasn't with Bruce anymore. Rumors circulated—Jon did have some influence in ruining my reputation."

Brickman eventually landed on his feet as the lighting director for Pink Floyd, Paul McCartney, and the Olympics, but he was living in the past: the *Born in the U.S.A.* tour was a business proposition, not a reward for old friends. "Marc was there for the great days and went up against Landau and lost," observes Peter Philbin. "Marc Brickman had a passion for Bruce Springsteen and a genius for lighting rock concerts. Bruce benefitted from both Marc's talent and his allegiance. Unfortunately for Marc, that allegiance didn't cut both ways."

If Landau got any satisfaction out of Brickman's departure, he had bigger things to worry about than a vanquished and heartbroken former employee. As 1985 ticked down, both the tour and the marketing program for the album were reaching a critical commercial juncture. In the fall, Teller had proposed making the song "Born in the U.S.A." the album's third single. Landau fretted that if radio deemed the anthem too rough and rejected it, album sales could lose a lot of momentum, and that was the last thing Landau wanted to happen. Discussions were under way to move the show from arenas to stadiums the next summer, which would increase earnings exponentially. But Teller made a strong marketing argument, pointing out that if the single was a hit it would boost album sales significantly during the all-important Christmas season. "To show you how carefully we thought this out, I very specifically wanted to go with the title track to take us into the Christmas holidays," he says. "Because if you have a title track as a smash single at the holiday season, it's a very powerful marketing pull. People say, 'Wow, this is what I'm hearing' at a time when you get that huge thundering herd of consumers."

Teller's strategy paid off handsomely. After two stadium shows in Syracuse, the tour took a three-month break, then played a month in the Far East and a month in Europe, giving the U.S. concert market a pause while the record continued to sell. Says Teller, "We had a huge Christmas the first year, came roaring out of the holiday, and Bruce was doing arenas and planning that huge stadium tour for the next summer. All this was laid out in advance.

"That was a great marketing experience," he adds, evincing more than a twinge of pride and no hint of irony. "A very powerful experience." For some of the members of Springsteen's band, the conclusion was the same but the reaction markedly different. "We started out as a band," E Street organist Danny Federici observed after the tour, "which turned into a super, giant corporate money-making machine."

BORN IN THE U.S.A. WAS PEDDLED AS A GENEROUS SLICE OF AMERICANA, A rock and roll state of the union. But compared to *Nebraska*, little between the first and last tracks of the album was explicitly political or social in content. The opening title track was a bitter indictment of both America's involvement in Vietnam and the country's treatment of the war's veterans. It also suggested a shrinking American vista, a sentiment echoed wistfully in the album's heartfelt closing song, "My Hometown." Sandwiched between them were ten songs that dealt with such standard rock and pop song topics as love, sex, growing up, loneliness, getting into trouble, friendship, and playing in a band, and it was all wrapped in the powerful iconography of the American flag gracing the album cover. An enormous American flag—large enough to provide a backdrop for the entire stage at the outdoor stadium shows—provided the concerts' most conspicuous prop and tied in neatly with the album graphics.

The American flag had appeared on a number of album covers, most notably Sly and the Family Stone's *There's a Riot Goin' On,* the Jefferson Airplane's *Volunteers,* and—certainly not lost on Landau—the MC5's *Kick Out the Jams.* But for the earlier bands, the use of the flag had been an act of defiance. It was impossible in 1984 to imagine Bruce Springsteen ripping up an American flag onstage as MC5 vocalist Rob Tyner had done at the Grande Ballroom in 1968. Whatever excess and self-delusion characterized the MC5 and their audience, they proclaimed themselves in opposition to the values of mainstream America—and subverting the flag was a striking symbol of that open challenge.

Sixteen years later Ronald Reagan was president, and just as it had in the sixties, rock reflected the mood of the country. Rock bands were no longer philosophically at odds with the business the way the MC5 had been—they were indistinguishable from it. As Al Teller aptly observes, Bruce Springsteen and CBS were "very much on the same page." The album was the creation of a mainstream, commercial performer who, a few nods to mildly liberal politics notwithstanding, was as safe as milk.

Various local charities, frequently food banks associated with unions, were invited by Jon Landau Associates to set up information tables in the stadium hallways. During the show, Springsteen would encourage concertgoers to visit the tables or make donations, as he did, often giving the selected local charity as much as $10,000. "This is your hometown," he told the audience each night, completing his pitch for the local charity as the band seamlessly launched into the opening vamp of "My Hometown."

The gesture was admirable, but it wasn't altruistic and it bore little resemblance to the wide-eyed populism of the folk scene and the early rock underground. It was inseparable from the carefully constructed marketing campaign for the album and tour, which were decidely not charity ventures. Covering 155 shows worldwide including twenty-eight stadium dates in the U.S. and Canada, the tour grossed a reported $117 million in ticket sales alone. Sales of souvenir merchandise—T-shirts, caps, programs, and other items—provided an additional $30 million, while Springsteen's share of record royalties on the twenty million copies of *Born in the U.S.A.* that CBS claimed to have sold worldwide would easily equal that figure. Delivered from that platform, Springsteen's charitable donations were both generously observed and financially modest.

Landau had succinctly expressed his own view of charity's place in the rock and roll business when he was a critic. It was a bottom-line function. "Naturally, the intelligent groups play occasional benefits to keep the image up," he wrote in his *Phoenix* column years before, "but who is going to play for fifty thousand dollars when he can get seventy-five thousand?"

The benefits derived by the various local charities selected by Dave Marsh and his wife, Barbara Carr, who was Landau's business associate, were real. And so was the goodwill generated for Springsteen. "Promotion is, more than anything, an art of self-suggestion," rock critic Richard Goldstein had observed back in 1968. "And I don't mean concentrated word of mouth. I mean the concerted effort to identify product with ethos and thus to render it sacred—above criticism." However earnest the Springsteen organization was about the causes themselves, they were at least as earnest about instituting a program that followed Goldstein's dictum.

Creatively and financially, Landau's influence had been profound, providing many of Springsteen's artistic touchstones and the framework for his new civic and social consciousness. But with Springsteen, it was increasingly difficult to tell what was personal and what was persona. As a performer he was making millions of dollars putting on shows in football stadiums that ended with the benediction "Let freedom ring—that's what we're here for, even if we have to fight for it every day." But pressed on his own sense of civic responsibility by *Rolling Stone* reporter Kurt Loder, Springsteen couldn't remember ever voting in an election, although he vaguely offered that he had probably voted for George McGovern.

Similarly, Springsteen's embrace of the Vietnam War and its veterans appeared by turns to be both heartfelt and carefully constructed. The song "Born in the U.S.A.," like much of what Springsteen was writing at the time, had its basis in someone else's work, in this case, Vietnam veteran Ron Kovic's memoir *Born on the Fourth of July* and a script by filmmaker Paul Schrader entitled *Born in the U.S.A.* His interest in the subject ran concurrent with a spate of popular films that captured the public's imagination by offering a veteran's-eye view of the Vietnam experience that included *Platoon, Apocalypse Now!, The Deerhunter,* and even *Rambo.*

By his own admission, he had reacted to the Vietnam War with antipathy. He had not been an antiwar activist but was straightforward in his admission that, like many others, he had done everything possible to avoid service. A decade earlier, before his career took on a political cast, he had repeatedly implied that he had been rejected as psychologically unfit for service, and told a story—à la Arlo Guthrie's "Alice's Restaurant"—in which he claimed he'd avoided the draft by being as outrageous as possible during his preinduction physical. The line had been picked up by Dave Marsh. In *Born to Run: The Bruce Springsteen Story,* the biographer wrote:

> Bruce actually beat the draft in the classic Sixties fashion. "They gave me the forms and I checked everything. Even said I was a homo, and all that. Then this guy calls me into his office, talks to me for about three minutes and tells me to go home."

Certainly Springsteen was free to grow as a person and as an artist, and regardless of how he came to acquire his interests, it would be perfectly natural for him to be concerned with issues at thirty-five that held no power for him at eighteen. But it was nonetheless startling eight years later to see just how much the times and the spin had changed. A second Marsh biography of Springsteen, *Glory Days: Bruce Springsteen in the 1980s,* acknowledged that Bruce "did his best to get out of serving" but now reported that he was classified 4-F, or physically unfit, as a result of a motorcycle accident in which he had received a concussion and badly damaged his leg. There was no more bragging about outsmarting the draft or any mention of feigned homosexuality. As for the damage he'd suffered in the motorcycle accident, it never prevented Springsteen, who was a renowned gym rat, from giving one of the most physically draining shows in rock.

As his biographer, Marsh elected to celebrate Springsteen's work—and the work that his wife, Barbara, and his friend Jon Landau had done—by erecting a myth in place of the man. Marsh's disinterest in accuracy was doubly if unintentionally evident from the very first sentence of his Introduction to *Glory Days:* "When the legend becomes fact, print the legend, not the fact," he wrote, misquoting the newspaper editor in John Ford's *The Man Who Shot Liberty Valance.*

In Marsh's hands, Springsteen's career was more than a commercial triumph, it was a story of unparalleled artistic and moral achievement in which there were no compromises or contradictions. Marsh had a particularly self-serving flair for transforming the mundane into the monumental. Although, for example, rock acts frequently perform versions of old Motown hits, when Springsteen added a cover of one of Landau's favorites to his show, Edwin Starr's "War," Marsh termed it "an extremely bold choice" and "the one song that could make every implication of U.S. policy unmistakably explicit," an absurd claim and an unlikely motive for someone who, by his own admission, couldn't even be bothered to vote. Marsh later compared one of Springsteen's more modest songs, "If I Should Fall Behind," to Rousseau's social contract. As Goldstein's prescription might put it, Marsh and the Springsteen organization had identified everything the singer did with ethos, making it sacred and above criticism.

It was hard to overestimate how seriously Marsh went about beatifying Springsteen. When publisher and filmmaker Michael Moore, who shared Marsh's background in Michigan's alternative press, sought the author's help in gaining clearance to use Springsteen's "My Hometown" for his offbeat documentary *Roger & Me*, Marsh refused. According to Moore, Marsh proved thin-skinned and berated him for publishing a column in his paper *The Michigan Voice* in which General Motors assembly worker Ben Hamper poked fun at the way several wealthy rock stars, including Springsteen, wrote in the voice of "da average man, man." Hamper's irreverent potshot was just one small item in a long-running, powerful firsthand account of the drudgery and meanness of life on the GM line, and it didn't matter that Hamper actually lived in the world Springsteen conjured in songs like "Factory." "You were irresponsible for running such a thing," Moore recalled Marsh saying before he showed him the door. "Ben Hamper is my ideological enemy." When Moore later got permission to use the song with the help of Warner Bros., which was both the film's distributor and the administrator of Springsteen's music publishing company, the irony wasn't lost on him. Moore noted that Warner Bros. was the largest media conglomerate in the world, "but apparently no one's 'ideological enemy.'"

Wisely, Marsh staked no claim to objectivity and implied that he didn't believe it existed. In that regard, he could certainly point to journalistic precedent. Serious rock reporting had initially flowered in the hothouse of the underground press as the adjunct arts coverage to the left-wing politics and community reporting of papers like *The Phoenix*. Many of those papers, following the lead of the *Los Angeles Free Press,* had rejected some of the basic tenets of mainstream journalism, particularly objectivity, arguing that what appeared to be neutrality in mainstream papers was actually a perpetuation of establishment values. It was, however, an argument aimed at expanding political and social dialogue in reporting—not justifying feather-bedding. Publicly, Marsh vociferously defended himself against any conflict of interest despite the fact that *Glory Days* was copyrighted to a corporation co-owned by his wife, who was part of Springsteen's management team. "History," he maintained, "will prove me right."

That Marsh was generally tolerated as a credible voice on Springsteen was a sad commentary on the deevolution of rock journalism. Despite its early alliance with the overtly left-wing underground press, as rock moved to the mainstream and became largely indistinguishable from an increasingly formidable music business, the rock press—like the artists—took more and more of its cues from the record companies, which were always ready to aid in the preparation of a story by doling out meals, plane tickets, and hotel rooms. By the late seventies, the fawning performer profiles that were the stock-in-trade of a commercial successor to the underground like *Rolling Stone* were virtually indistinguishable from the pieces that traditional general interest and entertainment magazines ran on movie stars and sports heroes, although to its credit even *Rolling Stone* found Marsh's relationship with Springsteen unpalatable. If there was a parallel in journalism to the way Marsh covered Springsteen, it could be found in the glowing biographies of popular baseball players, books that fed the legends around men like Babe Ruth, Joe DiMaggio, and Mickey Mantle and portrayed them as larger-than-life American heroes.*

If anything, the grotesque puffery Marsh cranked out only served to cast further doubt on Springsteen's work. As a concert attraction, he

---

*Journalist David Halberstam, in his 1989 baseball book *Summer of '49,* offers numerous examples of the code of behavior baseball beat reporters followed during that era. In Halberstam's view, sports reporting was "even more timid" than the general reporting of the era, with writers beholden to clubs for their expenses and careful not to offend players. By the seventies, the relationship between rock journalists and record companies was strikingly similar.

was powerful enough to carry the live shows in the biggest stadiums, and his performances were universally praised by reviewers. And while Springsteen was cleaning up financially, he had a moderate top ticket price, declined product endorsements and corporate sponsorships, and treated his fans fairly. If not wholly convincing as an artist of conscience, he had provided entertainment value in an extremely ethical manner. In the end, Marsh did Springsteen no favors.

There was, however, another way to read *Glory Days:* as an insider's plea to Springsteen to accept and appreciate where all the imaging, guidance, and direction of Landau and company had landed him. Underpinning the book was the partisan notion that at the end of the day, Springsteen's "friends," who clearly included the author, had delivered fame and fortune while keeping his integrity intact. "Was it too much to think that he'd really beaten the system?" Marsh asked rhetorically toward the end of *Glory Days.* "Not at all. Just as long as you understood that he hadn't done it alone."

There were obvious reasons to be nervous. The frank commercial aspiration of *Born in the U.S.A.* and its tour were hopelessly knotted with symbols and artistic traditions that touched a deep nerve and suggested quests that had nothing to do with the acquisition of wealth and fame. Springsteen had become rock's premiere figure of the eighties and deservedly so. His ultimate embrace of music as business made it impossible to separate the acts of faith from the acts of fortune or to tell which one was pursued in the service of the other. As a business strategy it was superb, imbuing what was at its core a business plan to keep an album on the charts for two years with credibility and protecting it. But as an action, its meaning was completely different from that of the protest movement, to which it owed so much of its persona. *Born in the U.S.A.* wasn't undertaken to question authority or the supremacy of commercialism but to achieve it. It now spoke for the aspirations of rock.

"There's an old saying," Bob Dylan remarked in 1985, the year Bruce Springsteen was selling out stadiums. It had been twenty years since his own performance at Newport placed the mantle of artistic intention firmly on the shoulders of a new music and a new generation that swore itself forever different. " 'If you want to defeat your enemy, sing his song' and that's pretty much still true. I think it's happened and nobody knows the difference . . . The great folk music and the great rock & roll, you might not hear it again. Like the horse and buggy."

A CAPTAIN
OF INDUSTRY

ARMED WITH YOUTH'S TWO GREATEST ASSETS, PASSION AND NAIVETÉ, Bruce Springsteen had once declared that "the pressures of the business are powerless in the face of what is real"—and he had meant it. Later, with Jon Landau's help, Springsteen had evolved a much more complex, professional, and adult view of just what constituted "real." Following the commercial triumph of *Born in the U.S.A.*, he purchased a $14 million mansion on Beverly Hills' exclusive Tower Drive and went into semiretirement. Whatever Springsteen said onstage about community and the need to fight the good fight in your own hometown, he celebrated a distinctively different vision of the American Dream in his private life and now made his home in David Geffen's community. It was an honest and appropriate move. Accepting rock as a business was an admission that its goals were no longer to question the assumptions of the mainstream entertainment industry but to reap its rewards. If rock was still as capable as any other commercial entertainment of expressing the most noble sentiments, the buyer had better beware that it was just that—entertainment—and not life and death.

The passion and naiveté of the next generation remained rock's best hope. But those born of the underground had found the massive financial rewards of their commercial success overwhelming and misspent the better part of the music's artistic currency. That failure of nerve had simply and tragically reduced rock's practical power to the power of the business. Within that context, David Geffen was rock's greatest success. None of the rock stars he had helped to make famous, and upon whose work he had constructed his own far greater wealth, had his appreciation of the power the music had given him. And unlike the rock stars whom he had helped to make successful, he would soon turn his energies toward something greater than simple wealth and the maintenance of fame. As always, he could see farther than any other businessman, and he was going to get the most with it by using rock to transform himself into the kind of power broker the music had once taken as its sworn enemy. Geffen, at the still young age of forty-seven, was about to prove himself the great robber baron of pop culture, a man whose immense philanthropic and political power would invite comparison not to Albert Grossman, but to a Gould, a Ford, or a Rockefeller.

●

WHILE SPRINGSTEEN WAS HITTING HIS COMMERCIAL PEAK IN 1986, DAVID Geffen's high-ticket signings of Donna Summer and Elton John had not panned out and the early promise of acts like Asia and Quarterflash proved fleeting. For the three years beginning with 1984, Geffen Records was a losing proposition. Geffen's own taste was not enough to guarantee the label's success, and the failure of his initial strategy—to use pricey superstar signings to signal his return to the industry and attract other talent—had made him look uncharacteristically out of touch. He had to concede that being older and off the scene may have dulled his feel for the marketplace and that the new label's roster could not succeed simply as an expression of his own tastes. To his credit, he shifted his focus from developing creative talent to developing a professional staff capable of accomplishing what he could not.

He and Eddie Rosenblatt, Geffen Records' president, assembled what would prove beyond doubt to be the best A&R staff in the business. John David Kalodner signed Asia, the hard-rock band Whitesnake, and two very successful reclamation projects, Geffen's former paramour Cher and the down-on-their-luck rock group Aerosmith. The A&R department soon included two other important executives, Gary Gersh and Tom Zutaut. Gersh, an industry veteran, would sign the extraordinarily successful and influential Seattle band Nirvana, whose label debut, *Nevermind,* generated over $80 million for the company. Zutaut, who came from Elektra, quickly hit his stride with the wildly successful Los Angeles hard-rock band Guns n' Roses.

Yet even as his new staff began to correct the label's direction, Geffen was forced to confront his own apparent signing mistake, Neil Young. Geffen may have told the artist and his manager, Elliot Roberts, that he could make up in love and respect whatever his offer lacked in money, but the honeymoon was extraordinarily brief. In November of 1983, Geffen sued Young for fraud and breach of agreement. The backbone of Geffen's claim was extraordinarily brash considering the way he'd sold Young and Roberts on signing with the label. He had specifically bragged that his role—as compared to that of other record executives—was to eliminate the possibility of an artist being abused or cheated, and he had promised them that commercial considerations were all but irrelevant to him. But he now charged Young had failed to make "commercial" records. Roberts's initial justification for signing with Geffen Records—that David was "not concerned" with sales and had undertaken the label "because he loves music"—was proving willfully naive. David was now enraged by the records Young was delivering and by the notion that he wasn't getting value for his money.

Although Geffen had used the courts as a tool to wrest artistic control away from director Robert Towne during the making of *Personal Best,* the suit against Young was both arrogant and troubling. Geffen demanded Young repay the nearly $3 million he had received for a couple of albums that had sold poorly, a demand for which there was virtually no legal precedent.

Still, he cast his actions in the most flattering light. "The truth is I fought with him because I wanted him to do better work," Geffen said later of Young. "Because I love him. I would like him to have the success that good work brings with it. When you make records in four days and you want to put them out it's a ripoff . . . We spend more money on our records, I think, than any record company in the world. And when they're not good we give them more money to make them better. Some people don't want to make them better, they want to spend as little as possible so they can keep the difference and put it in their pocket, you know." As Young's former manager, Geffen had to know that he frequently worked in a spontaneous and slapdash manner. Now, however, Geffen was footing the bill.

Young took Geffen's actions to heart. "When he signed me in the eighties he didn't seem to comprehend how . . . uh, diverse my musical career could become," he said. "So he took it personally when I handed him a straight country album or a rockabilly album. He thought I was making those albums to laugh at him, as a joke at his expense."

Young was anything but joking, however, even if the results weren't very satisfying. Creatively, the seventies had been an extremely fertile period for him, but his personal fortunes turned black at the end of the decade when his infant son, Ben, became severely disabled with cerebral palsy. His older child, Zeke, born to actress Carrie Snodgress, also had the disability. Young and his wife, Pegi, were devastated by the diagnosis, and it had an immediate impact on his work.

"It was too big a picture to comprehend," he said. "Too big. Pegi's heartbroken, we're both shocked. I couldn't believe it. There were two different mothers. It couldn't have happened twice . . . I remember looking at the sky, looking for a sign, wondering, 'What the fuck is going on? Why are the kids in this situation? What the hell caused this? What did I do? There must be something wrong with *me*.' "

To help Ben, the Youngs enrolled in a demanding eighty-four-hour-a-week home patterning program that centered on physical manipulation. For eighteen months they rarely left home, spending hour after hour after hour trying to help Ben simulate crawling. During this period Young wrote and recorded *Re*ac*tor*, its maddeningly repetitive music and lyrics mirroring the physical therapy program.

Young's first album for Geffen, *Trans*, was a direct result of Ben's handicap and therapy. Young turned the experience of teaching his nonverbal child to communicate with the aid of a push-button machine into an intensely personal concept album about people and computers, using electronics to alter his voice into an unintelligible, machinelike croak. Even more obscure than *Re*ac*tor,* it was all but impossible for listeners to deduce why Young was being purposely indecipherable or to gauge the intense personal frustrations behind it. "*Trans* is about communication but it's not getting through," Young later explained. "And that's what my son is. You gotta realize—you can't understand the words on *Trans,* and I can't understand my son's words. So feel *that.*"

When Geffen pledged to honor Young as an artist, he didn't expect to be releasing intimate records that no one but Young could appreciate. As Young began work on his next album, a collection of country duets entitled *Old Ways,* the relationship should have righted itself. But Geffen refused to release it unless the label approved the producer and the songs, an arrangement anathema to Young and one he was certain to refuse. Most likely the real problem was that the record company didn't have a country music staff and couldn't possibly promote it. Geffen wanted a rock and roll record the label could actually sell.

Young ultimately relented—sort of. He had recorded a rockabilly-inflected collection of songs under the *nom du disque* of Neil and the Shocking Pinks intended to satisfy his obligation to deliver one more record to Reprise. Geffen arranged to buy the album from Reprise for $500,000, with money from Young's $1.25 million-per-album guarantee. The remaining $750,000 was to be paid directly to Young. On paper, it looked like a good deal. Unfortunately, the record—dubbed *Everybody's Rockin'*—wasn't very good and sold poorly. Following its release, Young charged that Geffen had stiffed him out of $250,000.

If Geffen expected a lawsuit would goad Young into giving him what he wanted, he was mistaken. Young countersued for $21 million, charging breach of contract and fraud. But the dollar figure wasn't the only barb aimed to hit Geffen where it hurt: Young alleged that the promises of artistic freedom were a charade to dupe him into signing with the label. The label's "secret intention," Young charged, was to back him into a corner financially, strip him of creative control, and force him to make records he didn't want to make.

Geffen's gambit was widely seen for what it was, an attempt to break a contract that he had lobbied hard to get and to impose artistic controls on an artist who, bad albums notwithstanding, was widely regarded as an uncompromising visionary—or, at the very least, someone who certainly didn't need a record executive to tell him how to make music.

The futility of Geffen's suit became evident, and he and Young agreed to drop their actions in early 1985. He eventually laid the blame for the suit on the top executive of his company, Eric Eisner, and ascribed only the most altruistic motives to his own actions. "I was trying to save Neil from destroying his career," he said, "and I was ill advised by Eric Eisner to sue Neil, and I'm sorry that I did it. It was a big mistake. I was taking too much of a fatherly role in his life, and it wasn't appropriate."

Young's five-album contract with the label was honored, but his stay on Geffen Records would prove a commercial and artistic low point. Yet whatever momentum his career lost during the period, his artistic standing hardly diminished. And when he eventually returned to Warner/Reprise, he experienced a creative resurgence. By that time, Geffen Records had turned the corner as well. In 1987, Geffen's music, film, and theater projects rang up earnings of nearly $19 million on $88 million in revenues, a whopping 21 percent profit margin. By the following year, *Forbes* estimated the value of the David Geffen Company at over $300 million.

IN RETURN FOR THE GENEROUS FINANCIAL REWARDS HE BESTOWED ON HIS executives, WCI chairman Steve Ross asked for just two things: strong business results and fealty to the myth of Ross as the company's great paternal benefactor. Many had become wealthy as a result of Ross's generosity, and his laissez-faire style of management allowed the heads of Warner Communications' three wholly owned record operations—Ahmet Ertegun at Atlantic, Bob Krasnow at Elektra, and Mo Ostin at Warner Bros.—to operate as if they were independent entrepreneurs.

Ross's relationship with Geffen and the relationship between WCI and the David Geffen Company were a good deal more complicated. Geffen's film and record operations were set up as a fifty/fifty partnership with WCI wherein Ross put up the cash and Geffen provided the sweat, which meant that unlike the heads of the other WCI record operations David really was an entrepreneur. Such an arrangement, which placed Geffen's voluble ego on a collision course with

Ross's own need to be the ultimate architect of WCI's success, could only lead to trouble. After all, while Geffen was justifiably proud of his track record as a money maker for others—claiming that he always made sure his partners did well and that several of his employees had become millionaires—the true nature of his relationship with WCI was that he was working with Ross, not for him. As Geffen candidly put it, he was "in the David Geffen business." And as Geffen artists like Don Henley could attest, he could be niggardly when it came to sharing credit or power. "He was seminal in our career," Henley says of the Eagles. "The difference between me and David is that I'm willing to admit he was very important in our career, where he in turn is not willing to admit that we are in large part responsible for putting him where he is today. That's the kind of guy he is. David had everything to do with everyone's success, and nobody had anything to do with his success except him."

Ross, who seemed to enjoy feeling that he had the upper hand, was still careful to give Geffen a long leash. As part of the financing, Geffen Records was not compelled to distribute its records overseas through WCI-owned channels and was allowed to make a deal with archrival CBS Records. When Geffen wanted to rid himself of the financially messy *Personal Best,* Ross took it off his hands. Geffen was allowed to play by special rules, rules he obviously felt he was entitled to based on his past performance.

Yet all of Ross's largess, even if fueled by a desire to benefit from Geffen's acumen while avoiding confrontations, paled compared with the deal the WCI chief agreed to in 1984. As part of the original arrangement to finance Geffen Records, the label was sold in the United States by WEA, the distribution arm of the Warner Records Group, and administered by Warner Bros. Records. When the term of that distribution agreement was up, Geffen seized the opportunity the renewal negotiations presented.

Ross pledged to give him WCI's 50 percent take in Geffen Records in six years if he agreed to renew his distribution agreement for that period. That Ross would agree to such a generous deal is almost inexplicable, but it was most likely a vote of no confidence. Geffen Records was still two years away from turning the corner, and Ross had already refused a request from Geffen for a $5 million-a-year advance. Even the *Los Angeles Times* had made the label the butt of a well-worn industry joke. "What's the difference between the *Titanic* and Geffen Records?" entertainment reporter Patrick Goldstein asked in a year-end analysis. "The *Titanic* had a band." The public jibe humiliated and enraged Geffen. When he spied Goldstein at a film premiere a few nights later, Geffen gave the audience an unexpected show. "Patrick Goldstein!" he yelled. "You're such an *idiot*! You don't know what you're talking about!"

Even Geffen ultimately portrayed his new deal as an indication of how little faith Ross had in him. "Steve Ross wasn't willing to bet on me," Geffen later remarked. "But I was happy to bet on myself." And why not? He was still making the bet with Ross's money.

Within two years, Geffen's faith in himself was rewarded. And by 1989, Geffen Records was growing fat on a steady diet of blockbuster albums. Guns n' Roses in particular sold thirteen million copies of its Geffen debut, *Appetite for Destruction,* in the United States alone. By the end of the year, the label would post sales of $225 million and claim a catalog containing fifty gold, twenty-two platinum, and nine multiplatinum albums. It was an astounding comeback. No other executive had ever built two labels of Asylum and Geffen Records' commercial scope from scratch. And it was further tribute to Geffen's diversity and intelligence that he had been able to achieve each success in a radically different way: Asylum had largely been a reflection of his own tastes, while Geffen Records relied on his ability to assemble and empower a top-notch staff.

But for all his success, he had been unable to wring a big payday from Ross. Twice he offered to sell the label back to WCI, once for $50 million and again later for $100 million. Both times Ross demurred, offering counterproposals that Geffen deemed insultingly low. He lashed out at Ross, shredding the elder man's cherished reputation as a paternal figure. "Steve never took a fatherly interest," Geffen would complain after Ross's death. "I was an asset of his."* The posturing was disingenuous on both sides. The bottom line was that whatever father-and-son relationship existed between the two, it never precluded either from playing financial hardball. "You can't make a deal about money and then make believe money isn't an issue," Ted Ashley observed of Ross and Geffen. "Who are we kidding?"

Whatever bitterness Geffen felt regarding Ross's unwillingness to

*Geffen would later seek to distance himself from the remark with a letter to the magazine's editor.

buy him out was compounded in 1989 with the proposed merger of
WCI and Time Inc. Geffen owed more than a little of his mystique as
a Hollywood player to his storied reputation for being tightly plugged
in to all action around town. But Ross, who had been having ex-
ploratory merger meetings with Time Inc. for several months, had
managed to keep Geffen and others from finding out. Not to know
that such a mammoth deal was in the works at his own company was
tremendously embarrassing to Geffen. To add to the insult, Ross—
with his well-known penchant for recognizing who to give the biggest
tip to—had used the pending merger to reward several high-profile
loyalists. Clint Eastwood, Steven Spielberg, and Barbra Streisand were
among those gifted with stock options. Geffen was not.

"Here I was an associate for twenty years and I didn't have a single
option," he fumed. "Steve always told me that when the company got
sold, he would buy my record company and I would be there for the
ride . . . But in the end no one thought that I should be included in
the benefits from the success of the company."

Geffen's belief that he had been done a gross injustice by Ross was
not universally shared. After all, Ross had already given him 100 percent ownership of a company WCI had financed. "Is it possible David
felt he should've been treated like Streisand?" Ted Ashley asks with a
laugh. "I don't know. In the case of David, he was already immensely
wealthy and owned a business. What Steve was doing—we have to be
talking about the three people he was closest to of all the artists
around. It was a way of giving them a taste that they never get."

When the Time Warner merger was completed in January of 1990,
Steve Ross stood astride the largest American media company, and
David Geffen, who had once been viewed as an heir apparent to Ross,
was largely out of the loop. He was the owner of just one of several
highly successful record companies distributed by Ross—and a comparatively small one at that.

Yet if Ross believed he had Geffen boxed into a corner, it was only
because he was unable to imagine Geffen cutting his ties to Warners.
In fact, Geffen Records' exclusive distribution agreement was about
to expire, and this time, Time Warner would have no leverage in the
renegotiation. Ross had already given Geffen 100 percent ownership
of the company. If he was relying on goodwill and a twenty-year history to carry the day, he had been sucked in by his own sales pitch

and grossly underrated his protégé. Ironically, Ross had been able to engineer a merger with Time Inc. because the entertainment industry had begun to consider the importance of worldwide distribution systems to sell an array of integrated media and entertainment products. Yet Ross had failed to realize that those same changes had made Geffen's record company extremely valuable to Time Warner's competitors. Ross—whether due to stupidity, greed, ego, or an aversion to taking on David Geffen—had done the younger executive an incredible favor by relinquishing WCI's equity in Geffen Records.

THE TAKEOVER MANIA OF THE EIGHTIES HAD INITIALLY LEFT THE MUSIC industry untouched, largely because Wall Street never understood or paid much attention to rock music or the record business. When it finally arrived in the latter part of the decade, virtually every major American-owned record company was sold, merged, or buying other labels within three years.

The factors that put each company into play were unique, but they shared two underlying and related elements: the media and financial community's lack of appreciation for the value of American popular music and the numerous foreign conglomerates who, in stark contrast to the indifference of domestic companies, could look at the popularity of American music, film, and television in their home markets and recognize them as unique and valuable commodities they couldn't possibly produce on their own.

Ironically, American record companies had played a large role in developing that appreciation. Throughout the sixties and seventies, when rock emerged as the driving commercial force in the record business, the more far-thinking companies had begun to develop foreign markets. CBS Records had been the leader, establishing CBS Records U.K. and creating a joint venture in Japan with Sony in 1967. WCI, though at first nowhere near as effective as CBS outside the United States, followed suit and created local record companies around the world through its WEA International operation. Two European companies, Britain's Thorn-EMI and Phonogram, initially a Dutch-German joint venture, were among the earliest to recognize the worldwide appeal of American music and acquired Capitol and

Mercury records respectively. To a large extent, those American beachheads soon came to define the identities of the parent labels.

In the early eighties, two new factors emerged to make U.S. record companies even more appealing to foreign firms: the invention of the compact disc and the realization that a worldwide market for pop culture was rapidly emerging.

The compact disc would ultimately provide a massive cash infusion for the music industry. Positioned as a premium audiophile product, the CD hit the market with a $15.98 list price, nearly double the standard $8.98 list price for vinyl LPs. Although initially hampered by high manufacturing costs and slower-than-expected sales, the new configuration dominated recorded music by the end of the decade, allowing record companies effectively to double their wholesale prices in a relatively short period of time. While CD manufacturing costs dropped dramatically, eventually approximating that for vinyl records, wholesale and consumer prices never fell. Record labels, which had charged retailers approximately five dollars for an LP at the beginning of the decade, continued to charge around ten dollars for CDs, even when the market matured and costs dropped. Even sweeter was the way the new configuration breathed life into a moribund back catalog. As more consumers purchased CD players, they replaced favorite vinyl LPs with CD versions.

The financial benefits to be reaped by the compact disc were particularly obvious to Sony, which, as the coinventor of the technology and a leading manufacturer of CD players, received a royalty on the patent. Perhaps even more enticing was the thought of expanding from hardware into software and enjoying the repeat business that its technology had created. Aside from the CD, Sony's Walkman line of portable high-quality cassette players had boosted worldwide sales of prerecorded cassettes dramatically, another windfall for the record companies but one that Sony derived only limited benefit from via its Japanese coventure with CBS records.

Sony also had been badly beaten by its competitors in the home video market during the seventies. The company had developed its own videotape format, Betamax, but a consortium of competitors had ultimately prevailed with the VHS format, in large measure by convincing Hollywood studios that they had the winning configuration. With a meaningful catalog of software, Sony could be in a better position to introduce and dictate technologies *and* make a profit on the catalog every time it did so.

In the second half of the equation, the worldwide market for music was growing rapidly. Despite the presence of local or national stars in virtually every foreign market, English remained the language of rock and American culture its wellspring. By the mid-eighties, Michael Jackson and Madonna had become as recognizable in Toulouse, France, as they were in Toledo, Ohio. For any foreign company with designs on the worldwide pop music market, an American record label was absolutely essential.

In December 1985, General Electric bought RCA for $6.4 billion. But asked during the press conference announcing the purchase how GE viewed its acquisition of one of the largest record companies in the world, Jack Welch, the CEO of GE, allowed only that it was "too soon" to say, focusing instead on the good fit between the appliance divisions of the two companies. The value and importance of RCA's broadcast operation, NBC, however, was acknowledged and embraced. Before long RCA Records was quietly spun off for $600 million to the German media conglomerate Bertelsmann, which already had a controlling interest in Clive Davis's Arista Records.

Similar events were unfolding just nine blocks north at CBS Inc.'s West Fifty-second Street headquarters. Reeling from an unwanted 1985 takeover bid by Ted Turner, CBS had welcomed Loews Corporation chairman Laurence Tisch as a white knight; in short order, Tisch amassed a nearly 25 percent stake in the media company and, by the fall of 1987, had effectively accomplished what Turner had failed to do: wrest control of CBS from its ailing founder, William Paley. Tisch kept his eyes fixed unblinkingly on the bottom line and immediately set about to strip the company down to its core broadcasting and network operations, turning most of its other assets into cash.

CBS Records head Walter Yetnikoff was only too happy to oblige. Yetnikoff had long bridled under the directorship of CBS and its board, and he was eager to see them sell the record company, preferably to a group under his direction. In a quick demonstration of how the music operation could be converted into cash, Yetnikoff sold CBS Songs, the record group's music publishing operation, to a group headed by investor Stephen Swid and music executives Charlie Koppelman (the same executive who had rejected the first version of

Bruce Springsteen's *The Wild, the Innocent, and the E Street Shuffle* while an A&R man at Columbia) and Martin Bandier for $125 million. If the sale price got Tisch's attention, the deal wouldn't win Yetnikoff many points at the end of the day. Swid and his partners quickly resold the publisher, now dubbed SBK Music, and gussied up to include a new label, to Thorn-EMI for $295 million.

When Yetnikoff failed to put together his own consortium to buy the record company, he turned to Sony, with whom he had a long-standing relationship. As a young corporate lawyer for CBS in 1967, he had helped negotiate the creation of the CBS/Sony Records coventure in Japan. In November of 1986, Sony proved eager to meet Tisch's asking price of $1.25 billion. But Paley, who viewed the record company as an integral part of CBS, argued successfully against the sale. Ten months later, however, when the issue was again brought before the board—this time for $2 billion—an ailing Paley agreed.

If Tisch had no appreciation of the financial value or cultural legacy of CBS Records, he was not alone. The company, with its storied Columbia imprint, was the largest, most important collection of popular American music in the world, including contemporary masters like Bob Dylan and Paul Simon and American folk art by Robert Johnson, Billie Holiday, Leonard Bernstein, Johnny Cash, Benny Goodman, Count Basie, Charlie Parker, Lester Young, Son House, Miles Davis, and Frank Sinatra. But the fact that the world's premier catalog of American music had passed into foreign hands didn't even make the front page of *The New York Times*. *Newsweek* noted the sale of America's largest and most successful record company to Sony with a modest story on page 53; yet when Sony purchased Columbia Pictures less than two years later, it was the magazine's cover story—replete with requisite flag waving and teeth gnashing about foreign takeovers. It was another indication of how far behind the times the mainstream American media remained when it came to gauging the cultural and financial value of rock music. Columbia Pictures, though associated with the glamour of Hollywood, was a studio with deep financial problems; CBS Records was a lucrative company.

The indifference was particularly striking in light of the growing anger in the United States about the gains made by foreign companies, especially those owned by the Japanese, into American businesses and real estate. By contrast, American entertainment companies comprised one of the few industries showing a big trade surplus year in and year out. The reason was obvious. Unlike U.S. steel companies, auto manufacturers, or microchip firms, entertainment companies were packaging and selling a product no foreign competitor could manufacture: American popular culture. Carried out against the backdrop of an increasingly hysterical jingoism, the sale of numerous profitable and high-profile entertainment companies to foreign firms put the lie to that pose, showing that American companies were willing accomplices rather than hapless victims in many of their defeats in the world's markets. Here was an industry in which no one could compete with American firms, yet with the global franchise for entertainment well in hand, U.S. corporations opted instead for the cash. It was an incredibly short-sighted move, one that betrayed American companies' unwillingness to bet on their own businesses. Just as embarrassing was the fact that foreign corporations were more willing than their U.S. counterparts to recognize the value, both fiscal and cultural, of popular American music.

"I think Sony is a better company and a better caretaker of that heritage and will serve it better than the current CBS Inc. would," Walter Yetnikoff said a few months after the sale. And while he had engineered the sale and been lavishly rewarded by Sony—his postsale bonus from the Japanese company was said to be $20 million—and was anything but a disinterested observer, his self-serving assessment still had the ring of truth: "Do you think CBS Inc. is a first-class company today? It's got a lot of cash. Is that your definition of a first-class company? If you want to preserve the cultural heritage of all these records we've produced? Equate cash with good things? Cash is not bad. My problem with the stewardship of CBS Inc. is that it seems to be the only thing that matters."

The sales of RCA and CBS Records left Time Warner as the only American-owned international record company,* a stunning development considering the dominance of the U.S. market, which, aside from providing the lion's share of the world's largest pop acts, accounted for 60 percent of the world's record sales through the eighties.

Those deals set off a second round of purchases as the other majors

---

*MCA Corp., which owned MCA Records and Universal Pictures, did not have record operations outside the United States and relied on other companies to distribute its titles overseas.

sought to shore up their positions by buying market share—some-times, it seemed, at any cost. England's Thorn-EMI, which had done a poor job in America with Capitol Records, funded the launch of SBK Records and acquired the U.K.-based Chrysalis Records, whose roster included Billy Idol, Sinéad O'Connor, Blondie, Jethro Tull, Procol Harum, and Pat Benatar for $160 million. In Holland, PolyGram paid $460 million for A&M Records, whose roster included Sting, Janet Jackson, Suzanne Vega, and Soundgarden, and $272 million for Is-land Records, a staggering sum considering its only bona fide hit act at the time was Ireland's U2. Even MCA Records got into the act, pur-chasing the independent jazz label, GRP, for $50 million and briefly acquiring the storied Motown label for $60 million in partnership with Boston Ventures, a private investment company.

David Geffen watched the shopping spree with more than a passing interest. Prior to Thorn-EMI's purchase of Chrysalis, he had bought 10 percent of the smaller label's stock for $6 million, a move that would ultimately net him a neat profit of $10 million. But despite the easy windfall, he denigrated Chrysalis's management for electing to sell to traditionally weak EMI. "I don't think they considered what was the best thing for their artists or they certainly wouldn't have sold it to EMI," he sneered. In fact, David had entertained the notion of making his own deal for Chrysalis—not a purchase, per se; he really didn't have the pockets for that. Rather, he had hoped to acquire its artist contracts and masters and bring them under the Geffen Records umbrella. "I didn't think it was run effectively," he said of Chrysalis, "and I thought we could do a better job."

Indeed, Geffen had harbored large-scale dreams of acquisition, claiming in 1987 that he had attempted to purchase several major la-bels, including both PolyGram and EMI. "I'm looking to own any one of the existing companies that I can buy for a price that I think I could make more money than they are. Which," he correctly boasted, "is any record company that exists." But with historically high prices now being offered for labels, Geffen quickly changed his tune. Instead of buying, he wanted to sell.

A spate of flattering and well-timed magazine and newspaper pro-files appeared just as Geffen was about to become 100 percent owner of Geffen Records. The message was clear: the *Titanic* had risen. As label president Eddie Rosenblatt noted, Geffen didn't have the catalog of an A&M or even an Island. Nor did it have any real presence outside the United States. But it did have the hits and a top-notch staff. Even more important to potential buyers was Geffen's 8 percent share of the U.S. market, a sizable chunk that would significantly boost the billing and prestige of a buyer and made even sweeter by coming at the expense of market leader WEA. But topping all variables was Geffen's timing. With the exception of England's Virgin Records, Geffen Records was the last significant independent pop and rock label out there. Any major record company looking to solidify its place in the shifting marketplace through an acquisition—or to prevent Geffen from going to a competitor—would have to come in. And it would have to pay top dollar.

Britain's Thorn-EMI was more than eager to do just that. Despite having paid $8.5 million in 1955 for a controlling interest in Capitol Records, EMI had badly botched its obvious advantage in having established record labels in both London and Hollywood. While rock fueled the growth of WEA and CBS, Capitol was slow to switch gears. The most stunning example of its intransigence had been its initial refusal to release records by the Beatles, who, in the assessment of Capitol A&R executive Dave Dexter, were "nothin'." Since the Beatles were signed to EMI Records in England, Capitol had rights of first refusal to the group's releases in the States, and refuse them Dexter did—until the first couple of singles became hits for the tiny Swan and Vee Jay labels and made Capitol the laughingstock of the industry. Even in the mid-seventies, when every other major label was aggressively pursuing FM airplay for rock albums as a matter of course, Capitol gave it only lip service. Paul Ahern, who had been the first promotion man for Asylum, joined Capitol briefly in 1974 but left when he couldn't interest the company in a demo by a band he was managing, Boston. Signed to Epic, the group's debut album sold eight million copies.

This was the company that wanted to buy Geffen Records, and the disdain David had expressed for Thorn-EMI following its purchase of Chrysalis was completely justified. Still, he entered into serious negotiations with the firm. Word of the talks soon leaked out, and on March 2, 1990, the British newspaper *The Independent* reported the sale of the David Geffen Company to Thorn-EMI for $750 million, with David joining the company as head of the EMI Records operation. In the United States, the story was quickly picked up by *The Wall Street Journal*.

The Independent had jumped the gun. Thorn's offer was on the table but not a done deal. But the leak appeared to help Geffen's lawyers in their negotiations with several other companies, including Paramount and Time Warner. If Geffen had little real desire to hook up with EMI, a company he rightly deemed inferior, its now public offer could still be expected to raise the ante from a company like Time Warner that he did respect. Steve Ross, however, was heading a conglomerate saddled with a $12 billion debt from its costly merger with Time Inc. Besides, it was unlikely he would ever be in a mood to pay top dollar for a company he had financed and then given away, especially to David Geffen. "If we had paid what he wanted, it would have valued the Warners record business at $10 billion," A Time Warner spokesman told *The New York Times* lamely, "which is too high."

News of Thorn-EMI's bid did produce a new, significant player. MCA was willing to make David Geffen its largest shareholder in exchange for complete ownership of Geffen Records and its music publishing operation. Specifically, Geffen would receive 980,000 shares of a new preferred stock, each convertible to ten shares of MCA common stock. With MCA shares trading at $54.60, the deal was worth over $535 million, a good deal less than the $750 million Thorn-EMI had reportedly offered. But it didn't include Geffen's film and theater properties and was, according to Geffen, structured as a stock swap to insulate him from immediately paying taxes. There was, of course, the issue of his low regard for EMI and the very real question of whether he would fit into that company's corporate culture if he took over its record division. Although an additional $215 million, tax considerations notwithstanding, would appear to be a good enough reason to try and get along with EMI's stuffed shirts in London, Geffen quickly concluded the deal with MCA. The reason was soon apparent: he was betting that MCA's offer would prove to be worth at least as much money as the others in the near future. "When I made the deal," he would tell *The New York Times* several months later, "I believed MCA was a company that would be sold in the next thirty-six months."

Whether Geffen was clairvoyant or simply well informed is open to debate. MCA's chairman and majority stockholder, Lew Wasserman, had long resisted the notion of selling the entertainment company, but several factors suggested he would have to change his thinking. First, several of MCA's competitors in the film business, including Columbia Pictures and Warner Bros., were now divisions of global, multimedia conglomerates and conceivably in a position to outmaneuver MCA in the developing marketplace. MCA Records was a good indication of the problem. The acquisition of Geffen Records had effectively doubled its market share, but it remained the only major U.S. record company without an international operation, a grievous problem when foreign sales were fueling a greater portion of the industry's growth than ever before.

The second factor was the presence of so many serious potential buyers. But perhaps most important, Wasserman was now seventy-eight years old, and while he hadn't lost his grip on the company, time—and the patience of other MCA stockholders—was running out. When he was hospitalized in 1987, the news had sent the price of MCA stock up more than 10 percent.

Following the sale of CBS Records to Sony, one of the Japanese company's fiercest rivals, the Matsushita Electric Industrial Company—whose brand names include Panasonic—began scouting for an American entertainment company. Like MCA, it was concerned about being left behind by competitors. In 1975 it was on the winning side of the Betamax-VHS format battle with Sony and did not relish the notion of its rival being able to use its software holdings to dictate preferences for new technology. To help identify possible properties, the company hired Michael Ovitz, the powerful head of Creative Artists Agency, who had advised Sony on its purchase of Columbia Pictures.

The raffling off of Geffen Records coincided neatly with deepening discussions between MCA and Matsushita. Five months before the sale of Geffen Records to MCA, Ovitz had met with Masahiko Hirata, Matsushita's second in command, and recommended MCA as the Japanese company's target; five months after the sale of Geffen Records, Matsushita entered into serious negotiations to purchase MCA. At the intersection of these two deals, David Geffen emerged— from a nearly twenty-year relationship with another company—as the person with the most to gain financially.

Perhaps chastened by the rise in MCA's stock price during his hospitalization, Wasserman, who had reportedly believed MCA could fetch as much as $100 a share when it came time to sell, was now ready to lower his sights. The revised price was said to be $75, still more than double the $34.50 at which MCA was trading. When the hard bargaining with Matsushita began in early November, there was good reason to doubt that a middle ground could be found between Wasserman's trenchant and dictatorial style and Matsushita's penchant for careful, long-term planning—the Japanese firm maintained a five-hundred-year plan. A forty-dollar-per-share price gap could easily be a deal killer. As luck would have it, the negotiations got a little nudge from an anonymous source.

Matsushita had been nothing if not fanatical about maintaining the utmost secrecy regarding its talks with MCA. The company was low-key by nature, and sale talks invariably had a way of attracting other potential buyers and bidding up the price, as recently witnessed by the way Paramount's attempt to come between Time and Warner Bros. had caused the merger to be restructured in a far more costly arrangement. Within MCA, the only ones president Sid Sheinberg made aware of the possible sale were the board of directors and the company's largest shareholder, David Geffen.

The negotiations didn't stay secret for long. On March 5, *The Wall Street Journal* trumpeted the talks with a prominent piece. The leak had an immediate effect: MCA's stock shot up to $54.25. Although the source of the leak was never identified, most eyes turned toward Geffen. Writing in *Vanity Fair,* reporter Peter J. Boyer voiced a widely held consensus when he noted that the one-day jump in MCA's stock price was "a leap in value of $197 million to someone who had, say, ten million shares of MCA stock." To hammer home the point, Boyer reported that Sheinberg stopped informing Geffen of the progress of talks following the *Journal* story and also quoted an unnamed friend of Geffen's relaying gleefully that the leak was orchestrated by "someone who knew that once it was out in the open, in the spotlight, Lew couldn't quietly back away from it one night." Indeed, Wasserman had spurned other offers in the past, but it wouldn't be easy to explain away the inevitable dip in stock price if he walked away from this one. Although he never got his seventy-five-dollar-per-share price, Wasserman ultimately agreed to a sale price equal to $71. Or, if you were David Geffen, $710 million.

The sale price didn't satisfy all of MCA's stockholders, but it undoubtedly made Geffen deliriously happy. With timing and cunning—and someone else's money—he had taken a ten-year-old record company with a strong staff and artist roster but no real catalog to speak of and grabbed a bigger payday than either Lew Wasserman or Steve Ross.

"He always sees the target," Geffen's friend and disciple Jon Landau said admiringly after the MCA sale closed. And if estimates that
Geffen was now a billionaire were a bit overblown, it was obvious that
at forty-seven he had the momentum and financial mass to get there.

His commitment was straightforward: Geffen Records president
Eddie Rosenblatt would continue to run the day-to-day label operations, and David—under a four-year contract—would continue to look
over his shoulder and pull down an annual salary of $660,000. And
after that? Well, Geffen wasn't sure. "I started the 1980s worth thirty
million dollars," he said in the wake of the MCA sale. "In one decade
I turned it into a billion dollars. The world is presenting itself for
people who have cash."

THE NEW ROLE OF THE NEW DAVID GEFFEN WAS THAT OF A LEADING PHIL-
anthropist. Endowing the David Geffen Foundation, which would distribute between $5 and $8 million per year to social, political, and
charitable causes, he began to lay the groundwork for turning his
wealth into real power. He began to talk to Mickey Kantor, Bill Clinton's campaign chairman after watching coverage of the '92 Republi-
can National Convention. "Really, it scared me," he told reporter
Bernard Weinraub. "They didn't care about anybody but white, Christian, heterosexual males." His contribution of $120,000 to the Demo-
cratic National Committee was one of the largest personal donations
the campaign received. More significant, it was $10,000 more than
Clinton received from Lew Wasserman, widely regarded as Hollywood's political kingmaker.

Among the Foundation's earliest beneficiaries was *The War Room,* a
fascinating and largely flattering documentary on the Clinton campaign's chief strategists, James Carville and George Stephanopoulos,
which it helped underwrite.*

One of the first assignments for Bob Burkett, the head of the Foundation, was to spend a week in Washington, D.C., lobbying against the
ban on gays in the military. Geffen paid for full-page advertisements in

*The 1993 film was directed by D. A. Pennebaker, who had given the public a firsthand
glimpse into the relationship between Bob Dylan and Albert Grossman more than twenty-
five years earlier in *Don't Look Back.*

The New York Times and *The Washington Post* supporting Clinton's initiative, although the issue proved something of a political quagmire for the new administration. Geffen was attacking his new role as a philanthropist, social activist, and political power broker with typical zest, but did not bring the same aplomb to public policy that had served him well in his own companies. "I can't for the life of me figure out why anyone would want to serve in the military," he candidly told the *Los Angeles Times,* "but if people who happen to be gay want to serve their country they should have the right to do so." The following week the *Times* ran letters lambasting him. Without responding to the issue Geffen was seeking to promote—that the government's policy toward gays in the military was wrong—readers instead expressed outrage that a billionaire could belittle anyone who wanted to aid in the defense of the country that had made him rich. It was obvious that negotiating national policy required somewhat more tact than negotiating with rock stars.

HIS FIRST STEPS TOWARD INFLUENCING PUBLIC POLICY WERE STUMBLING, BUT Geffen exercised power adroitly in the entertainment business. "David will do anything for you if you're his friend," producer Howard Rosenman, who counted Geffen as a friend, told *The New York Times.* "But if you're his enemy, well, you might as well kill yourself." Indeed, when Sony ousted Walter Yetnikoff as the head of its music operation, Geffen was widely credited with having had a hand in his downfall.

Since the sale of CBS Records to Sony, the hard-drinking Yetnikoff had alienated everyone who came in contact with him. Although the barbs were frequently aimed at his own artists, Geffen was not spared. After first angering him by refusing to grant Geffen Records permission to include a song by Sony's most popular artist, Michael Jackson, in the sound-track album for the film *Days of Thunder,* Yetnikoff taunted Geffen by telling one of his employees that he would arrange for Sony to purchase Geffen Records for $1 billion if Geffen would teach Yetnikoff's girlfriend how to fellate him. When the remark got back to Geffen—as Yetnikoff had to know it would—he soon found he had more trouble than he could handle.

A story in *The Wall Street Journal,* relying on anonymous sources, suggested that a new contract Yetnikoff had signed with Sony would be his last. Although Geffen denied he had anything to do with the spin the press was taking, Yetnikoff was certain that he was behind it. "Events will prove that I'm hardly a lame duck," Yetnikoff said a few days later. "Are there people who want to bring me down? Probably . . . And you know who always comes sort of head to head with us. And pretty much consistently loses, and we know why he's angry. And we know he's spiritually bankrupt—don't we? Don't we? And we know he is upset when I call him a cocksucker. Don't we? . . . If he thinks I'm gonna stop calling him a cocksucker, he's wrong."

If Yetnikoff couldn't tie Geffen to the negative spin the press was taking on his new contract, Geffen's fingerprints were all over Yetnikoff's sudden fallouts with his two biggest acts, Jackson and Springsteen. Geffen had reportedly pointed out to Jackson that CBS had made money on his feature-length video flop, *Moonwalker,* while the singer lost $16 million, and Jackson was soon cleaning house, replacing his business adviser, who had close relationships with Yetnikoff, with Geffen confidants. Frank Dileo, a former Epic Records promotion man and Yetnikoff ally who had served as Jackson's manager, was fired. Jackson also severed his ties with attorney John Branca, with whom Yetnikoff also enjoyed a close relationship. Dileo's replacement was Geffen's close friend Sandy Gallin, while Branca's successor was Allen Grubman, an attorney whom Yetnikoff had helped build up in the industry before Grubman grew secure in his power and tired of taking Yetnikoff's abuse. Before acquiring Jackson, Grubman's most important clients had been David Geffen and Bruce Springsteen, with Landau hiring Grubman on Geffen's recommendation. Rumors soon abounded that Jackson would be departing Sony for Geffen Records or MCA.

Jon Landau and Bruce Springsteen joined Grubman and Geffen at Yetnikoff's beheading. "Walter Yetnikoff was a good friend to Bruce Springsteen and me for many, many years," began the carefully worded statement Landau released to *Billboard* on August 22. "We enjoyed a superb professional relationship and a pleasant social one. For reasons that remain obscure to us, the relationship ended not long after CBS was purchased by Sony. Neither Bruce nor I have had a significant conversation with him in nearly two years."

To say the press release was out of character for Landau would be a gross understatement. He liked to maintain an air of mystery and remained so far behind the scenes that, unlike many managers, he wouldn't even attend negotiating sessions for his client's recording contracts, sending attorneys instead and having them report back to him. To release such a statement, the ever-cautious Landau had to be either under tremendous pressure or convinced that Yetnikoff was already on his last legs. As it had with Jackson, the press soon became rife with speculation that Springsteen would eventually land on either Geffen or MCA Records.

By early September, Yetnikoff had been removed by Sony. Privately ecstatic, Geffen publicly professed amazement that anyone would consider pointing a finger at him for abetting the action. "Walter slit his own throat," he told one reporter. "How could I be responsible for what Sony—a company run by people I've never met—does about management? It's insane to think it. Insane." Protestations aside, Yetnikoff's downfall only added to Geffen's lore as a man not to be crossed.

IN 1988, GEFFEN AND CLIVE DAVIS HAD AGREED TO HELP ORGANIZE AN AIDS benefit in New York for the Gay Men's Health Crisis. Geffen, whose relationship with Davis remained shot through with competitiveness, quickly arranged for an appearance by the biggest act on his label, the wildly popular heavy metal band Guns n' Roses. Unfortunately, shortly after the band's participation was announced GMHC decided it didn't want them as part of the show. The band had recorded a song, "One in a Million," that included racist and homophobic lyrics about "Immigrants and faggots," spreading "some fucking disease."

It was likely that Geffen, who by his own admission now listened to Mozart at home, was unaware of the song and only knew that he was offering GMHC one of the biggest rock bands in the world as a drawing card. But he compounded the problem by refusing to be contrite. "If you need a blood donor and the only person who can give you a transfusion is Adolf Hitler, you take the blood," Geffen said, employing an analogy that couldn't have pleased Axl Rose, the singer/songwriter for Guns n' Roses. In the wake of the controversy, Geffen resigned from the benefit's committee and the hard-rock show was scrapped. Davis and Arista mounted a more mainstream concert featuring Whitney Houston, Carly Simon, and Barry Manilow that was broadcast on CBS and raised $1.5 million.

In an abortive effort to defuse criticism, Geffen gave an interview to *Village Voice* columnist Michael Musto but called GMHC "a bunch of assholes" for spurning his help. Burying himself up to the neck, Geffen demurred when Musto asked him if he was gay. "For your column or your personal knowledge?" Geffen asked. Told it was for the column, Geffen replied that he was "not interested in saying," a reply that Musto duly noted for his readers.

As a gay man living in the age of AIDS, Geffen had to be aware of the rising tide of gay militancy and the presence of factions in the gay movement and press who, as a result of the health crisis, divided the world into two camps: friends and enemies. None were more outspoken or dogmatic than Michelangelo Signorile, the features editor of the lesbian and gay news magazine, *OutWeek*. Through his otherwise innocuously titled column "Gossip Watch," Signorile had become the primary proponent and practitioner of "outing," or exposing the homosexuality of closeted public figures. Claiming his activities were necessary to force action against AIDS and show young closeted gays that there was nothing "queer" about being gay, he spewed poisonous copy worthy of Senator Joseph McCarthy, threatening to destroy people who disagreed with him by publishing files he claimed to have compiled on their private lives. Geffen's assessment of GMHC as "assholes" was all Signorile had to hear.

Ripping into Geffen as "a self-hating man of power and privilege," Signorile demanded that Geffen Records drop Guns n' Roses and comedian Andrew Dice Clay for their alleged homophobia. "I don't care how much blood money you've given to fight AIDS," he continued. "You, David Geffen, are the most horrifying kind of nightmare I've come to study in the grotesque mosaic of the media swirl." If Geffen didn't comply, Signorile urged readers to telephone Geffen Records. For good measure, he threatened to put any journalist friendly to Geffen on his hit list.

After death threats were reportedly phoned in to the record company and gay guerrillas in Los Angeles pasted Geffen's photograph onto bus stop benches, Geffen quickly dropped the not-so-lucrative

Andrew Dice Clay and a controversial and commercially marginal rap group, the Geto Boys. Claiming a position on the high road, Geffen said the cuts were a result of his own sense of outrage and had nothing to do with censorship. "I'm not saying the artist hasn't got a right to make these records. I have a right to say I won't make money selling these messages. I'm not going to make money off records that talk about mutilating women and cutting off their tits and fucking their dead bodies." However, Guns n' Roses—the label's primary cash cow—remained.

Signorile's attack also produced another change: Geffen slowly came out of the closet, describing himself as a bisexual. The following March, Geffen gave $1 million to AIDS Project Los Angeles (APLA). It was announced as the largest individual donation ever made to an AIDS service organization, and David soon matched it with a donation to GMHC in New York, thus ending his battle with them. A few months later when Geffen received an award from APLA, he described himself as a gay man, adding that he'd "come a long way to be here tonight." A leading gay magazine, *The Advocate,* followed up the honor by naming Geffen its 1992 "Man of the Year." By then Signorile was calling him "a hero."

As a philanthropist and power broker, Geffen liked to maintain that he had no agenda, especially when the Washington press corp belittled him and other Hollywood Clinton supporters for trying to muscle their way into White House business. But claiming he was the highest taxpayer in the country in 1990, he obviously believed he was entitled to exert as much influence as he could. And besides, couldn't Mack McLarty, the White House chief of staff whom Geffen spoke with regularly, use his insights? "I've made a billion dollars," he told Kim Masters of *The Washington Post* with a mixture of smugness and defensiveness. "My only agenda is to see if I can do any good. I'm not calling and trying to change legislation or looking for a tax break."

Still, the White House was proving responsive to those in the industry who had helped the campaign. In a broad initiative, Clinton's federal trade representative—Mickey Kantor—threatened trade sanctions against China in 1994. Although the new administration refused to make a trade issue of the Chinese government's political and human rights abuses, it was ready to play hardball to stop the manufacture of unlicensed compact discs and videos. The commercial piracy, which the entertainment industry estimated cost it as much as

$2 billion a year, was the kind of issue that was near and dear to the hearts of Geffen and Time Warner, who had given the Democratic National Committee a whopping $400,000 in 1992. Nor was Geffen limiting his focus to the White House. Numerous Democrats in the U.S. Senate, including Ted Kennedy of Massachusetts, Joseph Lieberman of Connecticut, and Bob Kerrey of Nebraska, received a financial boost from the Geffen Foundation.

And would he turn down an administration job if it were offered? "No one's asked me," he coyly told *The New York Times*. "If somebody felt there was a job I could actually do I would consider it—not out of any ambition to be in Washington, but I do want to rise to the occasion of serving there if warranted."

GEFFEN'S VIBRANT SENSE OF CIVIC DUTY DIDN'T DETER HIM FROM CONtinuing to take care of business, and opportunities continued to present themselves. In late 1994, just as Geffen's employment contract with Matsushita was about to expire, his close friend, Disney Studios chief Jeffrey Katzenberg, walked away from his job after a long-running battle with his boss, Michael Eisner. Geffen, who had encouraged Katzenberg to strike out on his own, soon formed a partnership with him and the most successful film director in Hollywood, Steven Spielberg. The new firm, dubbed Dreamworks SKG, was touted as a full-service entertainment company complete with studio, record label, and cutting-edge multimedia and computer operations.

Institutional investors, who had once turned up their noses at the pop world that Geffen so brilliantly promoted and exploited, lined up immediately, but, on the whole, their services were superfluous. Largely on the strength of limited joint ventures with computer magnates like Bill Gates and Paul Allen, the company was soon capitalized to the tune of $1 billion. Geffen, Katzenberg, and Spielberg each ponied up $30 million—although the surfeit of willing investors made it obvious that they didn't have to put up a dime—and retained majority control. Before the plans for Dreamworks were even set, the trio landed on the cover of *Time*. Everybody wanted to be in business with David Geffen.

Even Mo Ostin, whose faith in artistic freedom had made him the most admired executive in the record business, would wind up work-

ing for Geffen. Warner Communications Inc. was gone and its successor, Time Warner, was being run largely by Time executives who appeared more interested in refocusing the conglomerate to compete
with telephone and cable companies than with the financial might of
their own record operation. When Ostin was put on a tighter leash by
his new bosses, he opted to leave the company, and, shortly after
his Warners contract expired in April of 1995, he was named the head
of Dreamworks Records. And while it was no surprise that David
Geffen could recognize talent and opportunity when his competitors
couldn't, Hollywood history seemed to be repeating itself. Ostin, who
had patterned his own career on the visionary studio executive Irving
Thalberg, was now working for the man who as a teenager had
idolized Thalberg's dictatorial boss, Louis. B. Mayer.

In the five years following his ascendancy to the ranks of America's
financial elite, Geffen and his partners in Dreamworks would become
the nation's largest contributors to the Democratic Party with donations totalling over $2 million. Now in possession of real power, the
man who had once vied for status with his own artists evinced a new
modesty.

"I don't want to present myself as a person who has influence,"
David Geffen said one afternoon in his Hollywood office. "I neither
have it nor seek it." Then, he proceeded to return telephone calls to
Michael Ovitz, Lew Wasserman, Barry Diller, Ted Field, and several
others, arranging for them to meet President Clinton when he passed
through Los Angeles the following night.

ACKNOWLEDGMENTS

Approximately two hundred people were interviewed for this book. With the exception of the few who wished to remain in the background, they are credited in the notes section; my thanks to all.

Two interviews proved key in shaping my thoughts for this book, and they deserve special mention. Although the conclusions are my own, they would not have been the same if I had not spoken with Stan Cornyn and the late Paul Rothchild. They each had a different perspective regarding the time, the music, and the business, but had spent an extraordinary amount of time mulling over their experiences. The generosity with which they shared those insights deeply affected me and my work.

Some of the research for this book was conducted in the public library systems of New York City, Boston, Santa Monica, and Westchester and Woodstock, New York, as well as private holdings of the Academy of Motion Picture Arts and Sciences, the University of California at Los Angeles, and *Rolling Stone* magazine. Please support your local public library.

I owe a debt to the following people for their help in arranging interviews and obtaining information: Pat Baird, Ken Barnes, Harriet Barovick, Carrie Campos, Bernice Capitano, Beth Cohen, Charles Cross, Cameron Crowe, Robert Draper, Pete Fornatele, Mimi Fox, David Granoff, Lauren Iossa, Alan Jenkins, Gary Kenton, Howard Levitt, Dan Loggins, Mary Mac, Bob Merlis, Chris Mundy, Bruce Mohl, Kim Neely, Alexandra Peers, Bob Wallace, and Chuck White.

Jeff Smith's painstaking copyediting, along with his personal knowledge and appreciation of the subject, vastly improved this book. I'm also grateful for the enthusiasm of everyone at Times Books and Random House—particularly Carie Freimuth, Beth Thomas, Mary Beth

Roche, Diane Henry, and Dennis Ambrose. Thanks to Kevin W. Goering of Coudert Brothers for both his diligent legal review and his penchant for enlightening and entertaining late-night conversation. For their friendship and encouragement, a special thank you to Betsy Alexander, Paula Batson, Laurie Berke, Crescenzo Capece, Dan Doyle, Jim and Pam Eigo, Bill Flanagan, Paul Fox, Myra Friedman, Steve Gett, Franne Golde, Andrew Goldmark, Diane Goldner, Linda Goldstein, Ron Goldstein, Richard and Elaine Goodman, David Handelman, Linda Moleski Hill, Joe Levy, Jamie Malanowski, Susan Morrison, Jack and Barbara Orentzel, Bob Porter, Sheila Rogers, Evelyn Rossi, Chip Stern, Michael Sukin, Sam Sutherland, John Swenson, and Jean-Pierre Weiller.

I am particularly indebted to four friends and colleagues. Although neither one of them knows it, the conversations I've enjoyed over the years with Jeffrey Ressner and Adam White played no small part in my decision to write this book. I owe a different debt to two equally generous writers. Bob Frenay was the first editor and publisher of a music magazine to give me a shot. Fredric Dannen, through his friendship and professional example, encouraged me to do more with that shot.

I worked for several years as a reporter and editor at *Rolling Stone* and many good things came of that tenure. The best was getting to know Jodi Peckman, who helped me research and assemble the photos for this book. When I first met Jodi, I treated her rudely. She has spent the subsequent years embarrassing the hell out of me by proving a true friend. I hope she never stops taking her revenge.

Special thanks to Paul Feinman, Kitchen Boy Supreme, for his friendship and wise counsel. Eddie Karp, my friend and a master linguist of the secret language, had to listen to me rant about this book ad nauseum; it's just amazing what some people will do for a free dinner (it's a cardinal principle of record promotion). The love and enthusiasm of my sons, Warne and Joshua, sustained and inspired me in ways I simply can't describe.

Finally, this book would not exist without Ruth Fecych and my agent, Chuck Verrill. Ruth is a rare and great editor—hard to satisfy and impossible to alienate. Her passion, dedication, hard work, intelligence, and downright stubbornness are what I read on every page of this book. Chuck has done the most that any friend and partner can: he believed in me and told me the truth.

NOTES

1: Cambridge and the Battle of Newport (pages 3–20)

pages 3–4: Details of Paul Rothchild's production of the Charles River Valley Boys and the formation of Mt. Auburn Records taken from the author's interview with Paul Rothchild, 6/23/92.

pages 4–5: The history of the Cambridge folk scene and the early coffeehouses is chronicled in depth in Eric von Schmidt and Jim Rooney, *Baby, Let Me Follow You Down: The Illustrated Story of the Cambridge Folk Years* (Garden City, N.Y.: Doubleday, Anchor Books, 1979). The book has subsequently been republished by Harvard University Press. It is a source for this synopsis of the development of the Cambridge coffeehouses, while several interviews, including those with Rothchild, Joe Boyd, Peter Wolf, and Rooney, helped form the reporting.

pages 4–5: Rothchild's employment and recording projects for Prestige and Elektra: Rothchild, 6/23/92, op. cit.

page 5: "Boston was a spawning ground": Author's interview with Jac Holzman, 12/15/92. Holzman is also the source for the history of Elektra.

page 6: Folk fans viewing Top 40 with disdain: Peter Wolf told the author, "Folk music became this sort of sensibility. It was this noncommercial thing; it was musicology. Somehow the jazz and folk aspects worked together. There was a feeling of this moving away from bubblegum pop—AM radio and the Good Guys and that sort of thing. There was an alternative, a real alternative." Author interview with Peter Wolf, 8/7/92.

page 7: Early attempts at folk-rock and discovery of the Butterfield Blues Band: Author's interview with Joe Boyd, 11/14/95. All subsequent quotations from Boyd are from the author's interviews.

page 7: Biographical information on Butterfield band taken from Ed Ward, *Michael Bloomfield: The Rise and Fall of an American Guitar Hero* (New York: Cherry Lane Books, 1983).

page 8: Details of Dylan's performances at the 1963 Newport Festival taken from Robert Shelton, *No Direction Home: The Life and Music of Bob Dylan* (New York: William Morrow, Birch Tree Books, 1986).

page 8: "There were lots of battles": Author's interview with Peter Yarrow, 11/27/95. All subsequent quotes from Yarrow are from the author's interviews.

page 8: "This was the last outpost": Author's interview with Barry Goldberg, 6/4/92.

page 8: Lomax's introduction and dustup with Grossman: The description of Lomax's remarks are based on the recollections of Paul Rothchild in *Baby, Let Me Follow You Down*. Michael Bloomfield recounts events essentially the same in Ward's biography. The details of the subsequent fight with Grossman are taken from the author's interview with Boyd, who witnessed it.

page 9: "Goddamnit, it's terrible!": Author's interview with Pete Seeger, 11/16/95.

page 9: Butterfield at Club 47: "I gave Butterfield one hundred dollars for the night. I said, 'Paul, we've never paid anybody this much before!' " Author interview with Jim Rooney, manager of Club 47, 2/18/93. Ramifications of performance from author's interview with Peter Wolf, 8/7/92: "And then in came Butterfield. And when Butterfield came in it was like young cats that just sort of were accepted by the folkies. Dylan had just played electric. When that first [Butterfield] album came out, a lot of young cats went 'Wow!' The Blues Project was starting up. The Vagrants. The Magicians. The Lost with Willie Alexander. The Barbarians. These groups started forming, and people started getting into groups as far as songs. The Mods, the Rockers. And the folk scene started to be put aside, and a lot of the excitement started moving toward the electric stuff."

pages 10–11: Background on Jon Landau and his passion for music drawn from several essays by Landau, including "The Baptism of Brandeis U," originally published in *US* #1, edited by Richard Goldstein, 1969, and "Growing Young with Rock and Roll," *The Real Paper*, 5/22/74. Other information culled from "Fusion Interview: Jon Landau, parts 1 & 2" by Robert Somma, *Fusion*, 10/16/70 and 10/30/70. Additional information provided by a confidential source.

page 11: History of *Crawdaddy!*: Author's interview with Paul Williams, 7/9/92. All subsequent quotes from Williams are taken from his interview.

page 12: "I can do better than this stuff.": "Fusion Interview," op. cit.

pages 12–13: History of the Remains: Author's interview with Barry Tashian, 8/30/92. All subsequent quotes from Tashian are taken from this interview. Tashian, in his role as musical guru for the emerging Boston underground rock scene, also produced the first record by Peter Wolf's band, the Hallucinations, "Love's Not So Easily Had."

pages 13–14: Don Law, Sr., and Don Law, Jr.: Author's interview with Don Law, Jr., 3/4/93, Barry Tashian, 8/30/92, and Peter Wolf, 8/7/92.

page 14: " 'We can't have her—she's got dirty feet!' ": Author's interview with John Sdoucus, 9/11/92.

page 14: The Remains at Brandeis and Landau's subsequent rave reviews and relationship with Tashian: "Fusion Interview," op. cit.; Jon Landau, "The Remains: Epic 24214," *Crawdaddy!* #7, undated; author's interview with John Sdoucus, 9/11/92. op. cit.

page 15: "Don was never a young guy": Confidential source.

page 15: "They both had an ambition": Author's interview with Robert Somma, 6/25/93.

page 15: Meeting of Wolf and Landau and details of Wolf's history: Author's interview with Wolf, 8/7/92. All direct quotes are from this interview.

page 17: Breakup of Jellyroll: As one of Landau's Boston acquaintances put it to the author: "I don't think he ever thought to himself, 'I'm going to be some kind of entrepreneur in this business,' but when you think of him as a musician, he was certainly not the pot-smoking, wild abandon–type musician. He was very systematic even then. I'm sure he's the guy who got the band to rehearsal at the same time and made sure they wore the right things. He had a very strong need to control things."

page 17: Landau didn't have the confidence to go to the audition: Confidential source.

page 18: Crawdaddy! writers thrown out of the Cafe Au Go Go and Landau's reaction: "Fusion Interview," op. cit.

page 18: "There was all this kind of arcane stuff there": Author's interview with Jann Wenner, 12/2/92.

page 18: "I got the flash that he was serious": "Fusion Interview," op. cit.

page 19: Landau's Hendrix review: "Hendrix and Clapton," *Rolling Stone,* 11/9/67. Landau wasn't the only rock critic to fail to take the true measure of Hendrix's originality. Robert Christgau, who was emerging in New York as that city's most influential rock critic, also gave Hendrix a thumbs-down. He preferred Alvin Lee, the blazing fast guitarist with Ten Years After.

page 19: Landau's antipathy toward psychedelia and arguments with Wenner: As Wenner said to the author: "Oh, he and I used to fight about it all the time. He didn't like the San Francisco bands, he liked the r and b stuff."

pages 19–20: Landau's conversation with Wexler: Confidential source. Confirmed by Wexler.

2: The Tea Party (pages 21–41)

page 21: Paul Williams leaving *Crawdaddy!:* Author's interview.

pages 21–22: The history of the Lyman Family: David Felton, "The Lyman Family's Holy Siege of America," *Rolling Stone,* 12/23/71.

page 23: Ray Riepen and the opening of the Boston Tea Party: Author's interviews with Riepen, 3/9, 3/11/93 and 11/4/93. All quotes are from these interviews.

page 24: "That wasn't the glamour part of the agency business": Author's interview with Frank Barsalona, 12/2/92. The subsequent history of the Premier Talent Agency is culled from this interview, as are all Barsalona quotes unless otherwise indicated.

page 25: Barsalona fired from GAC: "Premier Talent Agency: Twenty Years of Rock 'n' Roll," *Billboard,* 8/18/84. Advertising supplement.

page 26: At least two public dances in San Francisco each week: Ralph J. Gleason, *The Jefferson Airplane and the San Francisco Sound* (New York: Ballantine Books, 1969). Pages 1–81 offer a thorough history of the San Francisco psychedelic rock scene.

pages 26–27: Brian Rohan and the San Francisco attitude toward business: Author's interview with Rohan, 8/27/92.

page 27: Premier's roster: "Premier Talent Agency: Twenty Years of Rock 'n' Roll," op. cit.

page 27: "When the West Coast acts came through": Author's interview with Don Law, 3/4/93. All Law's quotes are from this interview unless otherwise noted.

page 28: "Bill Graham had written to us": Author's interview with Ric Lee, 5/24/93.

page 29: "His genius is seeing things that other people can't see": Author's interview with Harper Barnes, 10/11/93.

page 29: "He had stacks and stacks of books": Author's interview with Joe Rogers, 10/18/93.

page 31: Landau's reaction to concert interruptions: Jon Landau, "A Free Concert in Boston," originally published in *The Phoenix,* June 1971, reprinted in Landau, *It's Too Late to Stop Now: A Rock and Roll Journal* (San Francisco: Straight Arrow Books, 1972), p. 140.

page 32: "I used to go down to cover the shows": Jon Landau, "Memoirs of a Rock Critic Turned Superstar Manager," *Billboard* advertising supplement, op. cit.

page 32: Landau's relationship with business types viewed dimly by many of his peers: The following was said to the author by a Boston acquaintance who knew Landau well: "If I go back and look at the people in the record business I knew back then, it would've been impossible to know who would make a career out of it and who was just collecting eight thousand records in his basement. Since there were no precedents for what the careers might be, it was not clear who was headed in what direction. On the other hand, there was a perception that Jon was hustling very early when nobody else was and he was very interested in making money and all of that. That's true—and he was . . . It was perceived that [he was networking], and he was quite resented by some of his more creative Brandeis classmates and colleagues who wondered how he was so different from them even early on."

page 32: "He was never a laid-back, vague person": The speaker wishes to remain anonymous.

page 33: Continuing argument with Wenner over Grateful Dead and San Francisco bands: Chet Flippo, "Rock Journalism and *Rolling Stone*" (master of arts diss., University of Texas at Austin, 1974), p. 75.

page 33: "The question is not *whether* there is a hype": Jon Landau, "The Sound of Boston: 'Kerplop,' " *Rolling Stone,* 4/6/68.

page 34: "It is hard to tell whether such a performance": Jon Landau, "The Newport Folk Festival," *Rolling Stone,* 8/24/68.

page 34: Cream review and Clapton's reaction: Jon Landau, "Cream," *Rolling Stone,* 7/20/68. There were other, more colorful versions of Clapton's reaction to Landau's review. In his interview with the author, Harper Barnes offered a version in which Clapton supposedly first read the review over lunch. "I heard he saw it and then went outside and threw up," said Barnes. "I never could eat in that Mexican restaurant after that."

page 34: Jon Landau, "Rock & Art": *Rolling Stone,* 7/20/68.

page 36: Details of Tom Donahue's life and career are from Ben Fong-Torres, "Farewell to Tom Donahue," *Rolling Stone,* 6/5/75, and by Rachel Donahue, "Tom Donahue," in "The AOR Story," an undated supplement published by *Radio & Records.*

page 37: The early development of FM is chronicled in Peter Fornatale and Joshua E. Mills, *Radio in the Television Age* (Woodstock, N.Y.: Overlook Press, 1980).

page 37: Ray Riepen's involvement with WBCN and the launch of "The American Revolution" is from a combination of many sources, including interviews with Riepen, Wolf, and Rogers. The date of the format's debut was recounted in James Isaacs, "Joe Mississippi Harold Wilson Fats Rogers Is Back," *The Real Paper,* 8/30/72.

page 38: Dramatically improved sales on albums: Author's interview with Joe Rogers, 10/18/93.

page 38: "If you've got ten thousand dollars you can come in": Author's interview with Peter Wolf, 8/7/92.

page 40: Details of the rivalry with the Crosstown Bus from author's interviews with Ray Riepen, 3/9/93 and Don Law, 3/4/93.

3: Purely Pragmatic Business (pages 42–60)

page 42: Details of Fugazi Hall party from author's interviews with Stan Cornyn, 6/17/92, and Dennis McNally, publicist and biographer of the Grateful Dead, 7/26/95.

page 43: Many of the details of the history of Warner Bros. Records and some quotes are culled from an unpublished manuscript, "What a Long, Strange Trip It's Been (An Authorized History of Warner Brothers Records)," compiled and written by Ellen Pelissero and Stan Cornyn in 1981. At the time, Cornyn was the director of creative services for the company and Pelissero was his assistant, and the project was undertaken as an official company history. Exhaustive (it fills two bound volumes), it never saw the light of day—perhaps, I suspect, because unlike most in-house corporate histories it is not wholly flattering. The author is grateful to Stan Cornyn for providing access to it and encouraging its use. All direct quotes from the manuscript are credited where they appear.

page 44: Record sales figures: Adam White, ed., *Inside the Recording Industry: An Introduction to America's Music Business* (pamphlet) (Washington, D.C.: Recording Industry Association of America, Inc., 1988), pp. 56–58.

page 48: Warner Bros. memo quotes: Pelissero and Cornyn.

page 48: "Warner Brothers was a great name, but a shitty company": Quoted in Pelissero and Cornyn.

page 50: "It was an idiotic move": Author's interview with Mo Ostin, 12/26/94.

page 51: "Before there is any discussion": Pelissero and Cornyn.

page 51: "I got the feeling": Pelissero and Cornyn.

page 52: "There was an active folk movement": Author's interview with Paul Rothchild, 6/23/92.

page 53: "This was an outpost": Author's interview with Joe Smith, 6/17/92.

page 53: "There was this strange feeling in there": Quoted in Jerry Hopkins, "Lou Adler," *Rolling Stone,* 12/21/68.

page 54: Details of Billy James's career, meeting with Lieberson, and quotes are from the author's interview with Billy James, 6/26/92.

page 55: Lieberson's credits are taken from a discography compiled by Mort Goode and included in *Goddard Lieberson: 1911–77,* a tribute album assembled by CBS Records.

page 57: "It was becoming quite clear that those acts": Author's interview with Stan Cornyn, 12/7/92.

page 57: "I felt strongly": Author's interview with Mo Ostin, 12/26/94.

page 57: "Mo Ostin and I were really close": Author's interview with Jack Nitzsche, 9/19/93.

page 57: "Greene and Stone wore dollar signs on gold chains": Author's interview with John Hartmann, 8/26/93.

page 57: Background on Charlie Greene and Brian Stone, their dealings with Sonny and Cher and Mo Ostin, and all Brian Stone quotes from author's interviews with Stone, 9/17 and 9/21/93.

page 59: Exchange between Bono and Greene and Stone. Ibid.

page 59: "I listened and said, 'This is great' ": Author's interview with Ostin, 12/26/94.

page 59: Reprise dropped Caesar and Cleo because they wouldn't drop Greene and Stone: Author's interview with Ostin, 12/26/94.

page 60: Derek Taylor accused Sonny and Cher of ripping off the Byrds: John Rogan, *Timeless Flight: The Definitive Biography of The Byrds* (London: Scorpion, Dark Star, 1981), p. 31. The quote is from Rogan's interview with Taylor.

page 60: Dylan disappointed by Cher's success superseding the Byrds': Shelton, *No Direction Home*, p. 356.

4: Riot on the Sunset Strip (pages 61–81)

page 61: Formation of Buffalo Springfield: There have been various accounts of Stills and Young running into each other on Sunset Boulevard, all essentially the same but with minor differences. In recollections given in interviews over the years by Stills, Furay, and Young, there's disagreement over who spots whom, whether they are going in the same or opposite directions, etc. Neither Stills nor Furay has mentioned that Friedman was with them at the time but both Friedman and Palmer say he was. This reconstruction is drawn primarily from the author's interview with Friedman (née Frazier Mohawk), 5/13/93, and Dick Davis, 11/8/93, but also used information from Allan R. McDougall, "A Conversation with Stephen Stills," *Rolling Stone*, 3/4/71; Cameron Crowe, "So Hard to Make Arrangements for Yourself: The Rolling Stone Interview with Neil Young," *Rolling Stone*, 8/14/75; and Scott Young, *Neil and Me: The Neil Young Story* (Toronto: McClelland & Steward Ltd., 1984).

page 62: "The first thing we noticed": Author's interview with Friedman, 5/13/93. All subsequent quotes are taken from this interview.

pages 62–63: Details of Young's Canadian years and trip to California from John Einarson, "Neil Young: A Rock Legend Talks About His Early Days," *Goldmine*, 1/30/87. Einarson, who has chronicled the history of the rock scene in Winnipeg, expanded his research on Young into a biography, *Neil Young: Don't Be Denied* (Kingston, Ontario: Quarry Press, 1992), which covers the rocker's early years in great detail.

page 63: "I loved the hearse": Crowe, op. cit.

page 63: "I wrote all new melodies": Ibid.

page 63: "an interesting key": Einarson, op. cit.

page 63: "I knew my only chance to be heard": Crowe, op. cit.

page 63: "I was happy to see fucking *anybody* I knew": Ibid.

page 64: "They wanted the trappings, the associations of success": Author's interview with Davis, 11/8/93.

page 65: "My father's attitude was always": Author's interview with Michael Ostin, 12/14/92.

page 66: "Lenny wanted them very, very badly": Author's interview with Mo Ostin, 12/26/94.

page 66: "In those days": Author's interview with Jerry Wexler, 3/6/93.

page 67: Young's seizures: According to his father, Neil suffered seizures before his arrival in Los Angeles: Young, *Neil and Me,* pp. 68–69. Information on the UCLA tests from author's interview with Brian Stone, op. cit., medications from author's interview with Dick Davis, 11/8/93.

page 68: The "freak sanctuary": "Freak Out Hot Spots!" A map of Los Angeles prepared by Frank Zappa, *Los Angeles Free Press,* 11/11/66.

page 68: Demonstrations: Art Kunkin's "Youth Want Place to Meet and Talk; Want Equal Rights as Human Beings," *Los Angeles Free Press,* 11/18/66. The *Free Press* is the source for much of the background material on the Sunset Boulevard confrontations.

page 71: "We were all sitting in front of the fire": Author's interview with Robin Lane, 12/3/92.

page 71: "Fabulous!" he enthused: Author's interview with Stone, 9/17/93.

page 74: Conversation between Smith and Donahue: Pelissero and Cornyn.

page 74: "How could I hang out with the Dead?": Author's interview with Joe Smith, 6/17/92.

page 74: The Dead slipped Bill Graham a hit of LSD: Bill Graham and Robert Greenfield, *Bill Graham Presents: My Life Inside Rock and Out* (New York: Doubleday, 1992), pp. 243–45.

page 75: "They always told Tom Donahue": Quoted in Jann Wenner, "The Record Company Executive Thing," *Rolling Stone,* 7/8/71.

page 75: "They were really the springboard": Quoted in Pelissero and Cornyn.

page 76: Robert Christgau's coverage of Monterey, "Anatomy of a Love Festival," appeared in *Esquire,* January 1968. It was reprinted in Robert Christgau, *Any Old Way You Choose It: Rock and Other Pop Music, 1967–1973* (Baltimore: Penguin, 1973).

page 77: Signing prices reported in *Rolling Stone* #2, 11/23/67.

page 78: Jim Fouratt bankrolling the underground press: Abe Peck, *Uncovering the Sixties: The Life and Times of the Underground Press* (New York: Pantheon, 1985), p. 169.

page 79: Response to Fugs contest: Pelissero and Cornyn.

page 80: "lots of money and star fame": Author's interview with Nitzsche, 9/19/93.

page 80: "Everyone thought of the group": Author's interview with Davis, 11/8/93.

5: Cumulus Nimbus (pages 82–111)

page 82: Details of Grossman memorial dinner from author interviews with Bob Krasnow, 8/17/92, and David Braun, undated. All direct quotes attributed to them are from these interviews unless otherwise indicated.

page 83: "The first impression I had of him": Author's interview with Suze Rotolo, 6/5/92. All Rotolo quotes are from this interview.

page 84: Details of Grossman's early years: Author's interviews with Vinny Fusco, 5/14/92, and Bob Gibson, 6/9/92, as well as Rory O'Connor, "Albert Grossman's Ghost," *Musician,* June 1987 and Michael Goldberg, "Albert Grossman: 1926–1986," *Rolling Stone,* 3/13/86. All Gibson and Fusco quotes are from author's interviews.

page 85: "There was a whole bunch of gospel people there": Author's interview with Paul Rothchild, 6/23/93.

page 85: "We got to hang out every night": Author's interview with George Wein, fall 1992. All Wein quotes are from this interview.

page 85: "Albert offered me a job": Author's interview with Allan Ribback (née Moses Moon), 6/12/92.

page 86: "Albert was the first guy to insist": Author's interview with Jim Rooney, 2/18/93.

page 87 "He was very intuitive": Author's interview with Peter Yarrow, November 1992. All Yarrow quotes are from this interview unless otherwise noted.

page 88: "Grossman brought me Peter, Paul and Mary": Author's interview with Jerry Wexler, 6/4/92. All Wexler quotes in this chapter are from this interview.

page 88: "Of course, the record hit big": Author's interview with Artie Mogull, 1/18/93.

page 89: "They would take as long as they wanted": Author's interview with Stan Cornyn, 12/7/92.

page 90: The size of Dylan's publishing advance: Shelton, *No Direction Home.*

page 91: "The guy had unbelievable connections": Author's interview with Nick Gravenites, 6/4/92. All subsequent Gravenites quotes are from this interview.

page 92: "The thing that I recollect": Author's interview with Dan Weiner, 6/12/92.

page 92: "Albert was the first guy": Author's interview with Jonathan Taplin, 6/2/92. All Taplin quotes are from this interview.

page 92: "Everybody was at the mercy of the labels": Author's interview with Mike Friedman, 6/5/92. All Friedman quotes are from this interview.

page 92 "He was quite inarticulate, actually": Author's interview with Milton Glaser, 6/8/92. All Glaser quotes are from this interview.

page 93: "I couldn't believe what went down": Author's interview with D. A. Pennebaker, May 1992. All Pennebaker quotes are from this interview.

page 96: "Grossman used to wear a five-button suit": Author's interview with Joe Smith, 6/17/92.

page 97: "That scene around Dylan was strange": Author's interview with Peter Coyote, 7/30/92. All Coyote quotes are from this interview.

page 97: "assuming freedom" and background on the Diggers' history and philosophy is taken from Charles Perry, *The Haight-Ashbury: A History* (New York: Rolling Stone Press/ Random House, 1984), pp. 108–110.

page 98: Details of Dylan's meeting with Otto Preminger and reconstructed dialogue are from the author's interview with Mike Friedman, 6/5/92.

page 101: Dylan, Grossman, and the Warhol lithograph: Details of Dylan's meeting with Warhol are from "Dylan and Warhol: Gerard Malanga Interviewed by John Bauldie," in *Wanted Man: In Search of Bob Dylan,* edited by John Bauldie (New York: Citadel Underground/Carol Publishing Group, 1990). The story of the trade of the picture for the sofa is in an affidavit of support by Steve Constant, Grossman's accountant and coexecutor of his estate, in papers relating to the settling of the estate filed with the Ulster, N.Y., County Clerk, Kingston, N.Y. At the time of Grossman's death, the painting was in the possession of Bob Krasnow. A series of letters in the file, viewed by the author, suggests that Grossman loaned the painting to Krasnow, who kept it in his Gramercy Park home in Manhattan and was slow to return it upon Grossman's death despite repeated requests from

Albert's widow, Sally. The correspondence ends with a letter on October 5, 1987—twenty months after Grossman's death—from Ulster Surrogate Court Judge Joseph J. Traficanti ordering Krasnow to return the picture to Sally.

page 101: Details of Grossman's wedding are from two of the guests, who wish to remain anonymous.

page 102: Shelton's account of the motorcycle accident appears in *No Direction Home.* Al Aronowitz's recollection is from an interview with author, 9/4/92.

page 102: "If it hadn't been for Albert": Rock and Roll Hall of Fame induction dinner, 1/19/94.

page 102: Details of Dylan and Grossman's contractual arrangements and disagreements are taken from *Albert B. Grossman, Albert B. Grossman Management Inc. and Grossman Glotzer Management Corp.* vs. *Bob Dylan,* Case #14403/81. Filed 7/1/81 in Supreme Court of the State of New York, County of New York. The suit, plus additional affidavits, depositions, and motions attached to the case, are included in the Grossman estate file in the Ulster County Clerk's office, Kingston, N.Y.

page 105: "Bob . . . You think you're right": Author's interview with Bob Gordon, undated.

page 106: "He once said, 'If you listen to me' ": Author's interview with Barry Goldberg, 6/4/92.

page 108: "He didn't want to confront things": Author's interview with Myra Friedman, 5/15/92.

page 108: "He was the baron of Bearsville": Author's interview with Michael Lang, 5/18/92.

page 109: Grossman helped Manuel through detox: Dakota Lane, "As His Friends Saw Him," *Woodstock Times,* 1/30/86.

page 109: The source of the story of Goldberg's visit to Grossman's house is from the author's interview with Goldberg, 6/4/92.

6. The Man from the Wiliam Morris Agency (King David) (pages 112–129)

page 113: "David expanded the Machiavellian book": Author's interview with Paul Rothchild, 6/23/93.

page 114: "I could see for myself": Don Shewey, "On the Go with David Geffen," *The New York Times Magazine,* 7/21/85.

page 114: "The Explanation": Shewey, op. cit.

page 114: "You've got to put blinders on": Transcript of interview with *Rolling Stone's* Jeffrey Ressner, May 1989.

page 114: "My mother taught me how not to get hustled": Lisa Gubernick and Peter Newcomb, "The Richest Man in Hollywood," *Forbes,* 12/24/90.

page 114 Flunking out at Texas: John Duka, "The Ego and the Art of David Geffen," *The New York Times,* 10/3/82.

page 115: Background details on the William Morris Agency culled from Deborah Haber, "Close Up: William Morris," *Television Magazine,* September 1964, and Lisa Gubernick, "Living Off the Past," *Forbes,* 6/12/89.

page 116: "We all think alike": Haber, op. cit.

page 116: "to tell the truth": Duka, op. cit.

page 116: "It was either give William Morris": Duka, op. cit.

page 116: Sandy Gallin's subterfuge and subsequent bragging: Fred Goodman, "Handholder to the Stars," *M,* August 1991.

page 117: The *New York Times* article mentioned in John Duka's article cited above.

page 117: The 1988 Geffen interview was with Joe Smith and appears in Joe Smith, *Off the Record: An Oral History of Popular Music,* edited by Mitchell Fink (New York: Warner Books, 1988).

page 117: Elaine Dutka, "Little Shop of Winners," *Time,* 12/12/88.

page 117: Ertegun loan: Christian Williams, "David Geffen's Touch of Gold," *The Washington Post,* 5/6/92; Ertegun's insistence on the story's veracity: Patrick Goldstein, "Geffen: From a Minor to a Mogul," *Los Angeles Times,* 12/12/82.

page 117: "wits and instinct": Julie Baumgold, "The Winning of Cher," *Esquire,* February 1975.

page 117: "He, in his mind": Author's interview with Irving Azoff, 6/23/92.

page 118: "The music industry was invented": Author's interview with John Hartmann, 8/26/93.

page 118: "He is a driving": Haber, op. cit.

page 119: "You took a few weeks": Johanna Schneller, "Is This the Next Mike Ovitz?", *GQ,* May 1992.

page 119: Geffen fabricated a stint as an assistant on *The Danny Kaye Show:* Smith, *Off the Record.*

page 119: "I didn't know": Author's interview with Jerry Brandt, 9/15/93.

page 121: Cameo Parkway stock: Author's interview with Steve Leber, 5/20/93, and conversation with David Geffen, 9/16/96.

page 122: "David is a very seductive person": Goldstein, op. cit.

page 122: The description of Nyro is from Geffen's interview with Smith, *Off the Record.*

page 122: "She was weird": Author's interview with Artie Mogull, 1/18/93.

page 123: Monterey stage patter from William Kloman, "Laura Nyro: She's the Hippest—and Maybe the Hottest?," *The New York Times,* 10/6/68.

page 123: "almost as bad as Laura Nyro": Ibid.

page 123: "[Mogull] put her down terribly": Quoted in Smith, *Off the Record.*

page 124: "The others are business": Michael Etchison, "Soul . . . For Laura Nyro 'Love Is Surely Gospel,' " *Los Angeles Herald Examiner,* 10/8/68.

page 124: "I wanted her to be the biggest star": Robert Sam Anson, "David Geffen Talks a Little," *Esquire,* November 1982.

page 124: "that fat freak": Etchison, op. cit.

page 124: Nyro's contracts: *Nigro v. Celestial Music/Milton T. Okun Inc./MGM Inc.,* Index #16286/1968. Filed April 15, 1969, in Supreme Court, State of New York, Hon. Samuel H. Hoftadter.

page 125: Geffen as 50 percent owner of Tuna Fish Music: Clive Davis, with James Willwerth, *Clive: Inside the Record Business* (New York: William Morrow, 1974), p. 116.

page 125: "I kept her incommunicado for two years": Maggie Paley, "The Funky Madonna of New York Soul," *Life,* 1/30/70.

page 126: Kamen stock: Gubernick, op. cit.

page 126: "I decided I was getting": Haber, op. cit.

page 127: "I once asked him": Lisa Gubernick, "Roots: The Man Who Discovered Chaplin and the World's Fastest Golfer," *Forbes,* 6/12/89.

page 127: Geffen quit Ashley Famous to manage Nyro: Fredric Dannen's interview with Geffen, 7/27/87.

page 127: Details of Nyro deal from Davis, *Clive.*

page 128: "While they were acting and working together": Author's interview with Richard Barovick, 5/28/93.

7. Chiefs and Indians (pages 130–151)

page 130: "An artist never got involved": Author's interview with Peter Wolf, 8/7/92.

page 131: "Geffen was an opportunist": Author's interview with Joe Smith, 6/17/92.

page 131: Geffen's ongoing relationship with Clive Davis and his role in alerting the CBS Records executives to several acts: Davis, *Clive,* p. 117.

page 131: Elliot Roberts: Details of the early career of Elliot Roberts and his relationship with David Geffen are from David Crosby and Carl Gottlieb, *Long Time Gone, The Autobiography of David Crosby* (New York: Doubleday, 1988), p. 131; Robert's Rules of Order were named after him: Author's interview with Elliot Mazer, 1/24/94; Elliot Rabinowitz name change: Filed Los Angeles, Calif., Case #906339, 3/27/67.

page 131: "She was a jumble of creative clutter": From "Rock 'n' Roll's Leading Lady," *Time,* 12/16/74.

page 132: Roberts and Buffalo Springfield: Jerry Hopkins, *The Rock Story* (New York: Signet, 1970), p. 207.

page 132: Young asked Roberts to manage him as a solo artist: Young, *Neil and Me,* p. 84.

page 132: "Neil is a king": Author's interview with Harlan Goodman, 8/20/93. All subsequent Goodman quotes are from this interview.

page 132: "Neil needs somebody": Author's interview with Will Hinds, 12/21/92. All subsequent Hinds quotes are from this interview.

page 133: "Elliot has many strengths . . ." Author's interview with John Hartmann, 8/26/93.

page 133: "You're dealing with a true eccentric": Author's interview with Mo Ostin, 12/26/94.

page 133: Details of Crosby and Roberts's bust: Crosby and Gottlieb, *Long Time Gone,* p. 136.

page 134: "I don't remember them ever working": Author's interview with Robin Lane, 12/3/92.

page 134: "Sebastian had blown up the Lovin' Spoonful": Author's interview with Paul Rothchild, 6/23/92. All subsequent Rothchild quotes are from this interview.

page 135: Roberts turned to Geffen: Crosby and Gottlieb, *Long Time Gone,* p. 142–3.

page 136: "Ahmet really played [Clive]": Author's interview with Bob Rolontz, 2/18/93. All subsequent Rolontz quotes are from this interview.

page 136: "Six hundred thousand dollars": Author's interview with Jerry Wexler, 3/6/93. All subsequent Wexler quotes are from this interview.

page 136: "He was the most charming person": Smith, *Off the Record,* p. 304.

page 136: "When I first met him": Quoted in George W. S. Trow, Jr., "Ahmet Ertegun: Eclectic, Reminiscent, Amused, Fickle, Perverse, pt. 1," *The New Yorker*, 5/29/78.

page 136: "I think David Geffen": Author's interview with Ned Doheny, 3/17/93.

page 138: Ertegun's three-day trip: Author's interview with Joe Boyd, 3/22/93.

page 138: "It was as if the *Pasadena News*": Quoted in Jann Wenner, "The Record Company Executive Thing," *Rolling Stone*, 7/8/71.

page 138: Various sales culminating in the creation of Warner Communications, Inc.: Background taken from author's interviews with Ahmet Ertegun, 12/21/94; Ted Ashley, 9/9/93; and Smith, Wexler, Rolontz, Cornyn, op. cit. Also Connie Bruck, *Master of the Game: Steve Ross and the Creation of Time Warner* (New York: Simon & Schuster, 1994) and Pelissero and Cornyn, unpublished manuscript.

page 138: Atlantic nearly sold to Paramount for $1 million: Author's interview with Wexler, 3/6/93.

page 139: "When Steve Ross first bought the company": Author's interview with Ahmet Ertegun, 12/21/94.

page 139: "You realize": Quoted in Pelissero and Cornyn.

page 139: "I called Ahmet one day": Author's interview with Ted Ashley, 9/9/93. All subsequent Ashley quotes are from this interview.

page 140: "I've lived with this.": Caesar Kimmel, quoted in "He Has His World, I Have Mine," *Forbes* 6/1/70.

page 140: Meeting between Ertegun and Ross at 21: Ross told this story repeatedly over the years. The author's source is Tony Schwartz, "Steve Ross on the Spot," *New York*, 1/24/83.

page 141: "Everybody wants to be Ahmet": Author's interview with Brian Stone, 9/17/93.

page 141: Crosby's feelings regarding Geffen: Crosby and Gottlieb, *Long Time Gone*, p. 140.

page 141: "I read Crosby, Stills and Nash's existing contract": Author's interview with John Hartmann, 8/26/93.

page 142: Geffen's version of Crosby, Stills, Nash and Young's success: Quoted in "Golden Boy," *Newsweek*, 11/20/72.

page 143: "This is one of the few places.": Quoted in "Geffen's Golden Touch," *Time*, 2/25/74.

page 143: Geffen haranguing Tobias reported in Andrew Tobias, "The Middle-Aged Turk of the Pop Music Business," *New York*, 7/16/73.

page 143: Incident at Schrafft's: Ibid.

page 143: "France is like Brooklyn": Trow, op. cit.

page 143: "He had total faith.": Author's interview with Bones Howe, 1/16/94.

page 144: "Don't be stupid": Quoted in Crosby and Gottlieb, *Long Time Gone*, p. 145.

page 144: "a cat who is like us": Quoted in Ben Fong-Torres, "David Crosby: The Rolling Stone Interview," *Rolling Stone*, 7/23/70.

page 145: "I knew that MGM": Quoted in Pelissero and Cornyn.

page 145: "I think Ahmet was concerned": Quoted in Pelissero and Cornyn. Subsequent Ostin quotes in this chapter are from this source unless otherwise noted.

page 146: "Ahmet wasn't listening to Ted Ashley": Quoted in Pelissero and Cornyn.

page 148: Browne and Doheny skinny-dipping at Rothchild's house: Taken from Cameron Crowe, "A Child's Garden of Jackson Browne," *Rolling Stone,* 5/23/74.

page 148: "There was a lot of sharing going on": Author's interview with Barry Friedman, 5/13/93.

page 148: "[He's] a stunner": Fong-Torres, op. cit.

page 149: Description of Geffen's introduction to Browne: Richard Meltzer, "Young Jackson Browne's Old Days," *Rolling Stone,* 6/22/72.

page 149: Geffen's unsuccessful attempts to get Browne a deal: From the transcript of Cameron Crowe's interview with Jackson Browne for *Rolling Stone,* undated.

page 149: "I'm telling you": Smith, *Off the Record,* p. 305. This is also the source of the subsequent exchange between Geffen and Ertegun.

page 149: Details of the Atlantic/Stax distribution agreement are dealt with extensively in Peter Guralnick, *Sweet Soul Music: Rhythm and Blues and the Southern Dream of Freedom* (New York: Harper & Row, 1986).

page 150: "Some people would never get on record.": Transcript of Crowe interview with Browne, op. cit.

page 151: "David grabbed this L.A. sound": Author's interview with Irving Azoff, 6/23/92.

8. Brothers and Sisters, I Give You a Testimonial: The MC5 (pages 152–182)

page 154: "Jerry truly believed in Jon Landau": Author's interview with Danny Fields, 9/5/92.

page 154: "Every few months": Author's interview with Wayne Kramer, 11/12/92. All subsequent quotes are from this interview unless otherwise noted.

page 158: "I spent two or three years": Author's interview with John Sinclair, 11/3/92. All Sinclair quotes are from this interview unless otherwise noted.

page 158: "I'd gone there a couple of times": Quoted in "MC5 on the Cusp," *Creem,* vol. 2, #4, 1969.

page 160: Background on Russ Gibb and the Grande: Author's interview with Kramer.

page 161: "LSD . . . was the catalyst": John Sinclair, *Guitar Army: Street Writings/Prison Writings* (New York: Douglas Books, 1972), p. 22.

page 162: Details of the May 31 show at the Hideout and the subsequent show at the Grande are detailed in Michael D. Cary, *"The Rise and Fall of the MC5: Rock Music and the Counterculture Politics in the Sixties"* (Ph.D. diss., Lehigh University, 1985). Cary's paper is a thorough and insightful account of the MC5's career and a valuable source for confirming many of the principals' statements to the author.

page 164: The Loft show and arrest of Sinclair and Smith: Ibid.

page 165: Crawford introduction taken from the Elektra album *Kick Out the Jams,* 1969.

page 166: Biographical sketch of Fields: Author's interview with Fields, 9/5/92, and "Who Bridges the Gap Between the Record Executive and the Rock Musician? I Do. (An interview with Danny Fields)," *Scenes,* July 1969.

page 167: Conversation between Fields and Holzman: Author's interview with Fields, 9/5/92.

page 168: "the white honkie culture": Sinclair, *Guitar Army*, p. 104.

page 168: "the best goddamn band in the world": Quoted in *Scenes*, op. cit.

page 168: "I never met anybody like Sinclair": Quoted in "Fusion Interview," op. cit.

page 169: "Stop right there, man": Ibid.

page 169: Letter to Holzman: Ibid.

page 169: Landau's role in *Rolling Stone* cover story: Fields, quoted in *Scenes*, op. cit.

page 169: The MC5 presented Landau: Confidential source.

page 169: East Coast tour, problems with promoters, and involvement with the Motherfuckers: Author's interviews with Kramer and Sinclair as well as Cary, "The Rise and Fall of the MC5."

page 171: Gavin's reaction noted in Cary, "The Rise and Fall of the MC5." Although unable to date the newsletter, Cary reports it appeared in the spring of '69 and cites a mention of the Gavin review in the 4/19/69 issue of *Rolling Stone.*

page 172: MC5's reaction to Elektra changing the album: Author's interview with Kramer.

page 172: "The MC5 had a hemorrhage": Author's interview with Jac Holzman, 12/15/92.

page 172: Exchange between Holzman and Sinclair: Ibid.

page 173: "It's all right for Morrison": Ibid.

page 173: "Look . . . I just got the word": "Fusion Interview," op. cit.

page 173: Conversation with Wexler about Atlantic Records recalled by Landau in "Fusion Interview," op. cit.

page 174: "He was an Otis Redding *fanatic*": Author's interview with Phil Walden, 9/1/92. Other quotes in this chapter are from this interview.

page 174: Landau's relationship with Walden and trip to Muscle Shoals: Ibid., and Jon Landau, "A History of the Development of Soul Music," senior honors thesis, Brandeis University, College of Arts and Sciences, 1969.

page 175: "The Elektra album": "Fusion Interview," op. cit.

page 176: Growing frictions between the MC5 and Trans-Love: Author's interviews with Kramer and Sinclair. Also Ben Fong-Torres, "Shattered Dreams: They Wanted to Be Bigger than the Beatles," *Rolling Stone*, 6/8/72.

page 176: "I'm picking up": Quoted in "Fusion Interview," op. cit.

page 176: "It's hard for me to conceive": Ibid.

page 176: "an amateurish manager": Quoted in Fong-Torres, op. cit.

page 177: "They're beginning to ask": Quoted in "Fusion Interview," op. cit.

page 177: "We basically fired them": Quoted in "Breaking Through the Terminal Stasis: MC5's Michael Davis," interview by Efram Turchick and Greg Langel, *Freakout USA,* spring 1993.

page 177: Details of proposal to Sinclair: Fong-Torres, op. cit.

page 177: "What do you think of all this?": Exchange between Sinclair and Landau reported in "Fusion Interview," op. cit.

page 178: "You guys wanted": Letter to Kramer quoted in Fong-Torres, op. cit. Confirmed by Kramer.

page 179: "Landau was really inflexible": Quoted in Turchick and Langel, op. cit.

page 179 "not a thoroughly bad album": Bill Benoit, "Cultural Revisionism of 'Kick Out the Jams Revisited,' " *Big Fat,* vol. 1, #2, 3/19/70.

page 181: "It will be the regular scene": Quoted in Fong-Torres, op. cit.

page 181: "It's nights like this": Ibid.

page 182: Conversation between Kramer and Sinclair: Author's interview with Kramer.

9. Coronations and Beheadings (pages 183–207)

page 183: "When you are making records": Jon Landau, "On Producing Records," November 1970. Reprinted in *It's Too Late to Stop Now.*

page 184: "Everyone had already decided": Author's interview with James Isaacs, November 1993.

page 184: Underground Camera suit: Author's interview with Danny Schecter, 7/15/93.

page 185: "We imagined that this was solidarity": Author's interview with Joe Rogers, 10/18/93. All subsequent Rogers quotes are from this interview.

page 185: "These guys hated promotion men": Author's interview with Mario Medious, 11/12/92. All subsequent Medious quotes are from this interview.

page 186: "Mario was the first guy": Author's interview with Peter Wolf, 8/7/92. All subsequent Wolf quotes are from this interview.

page 187: "a new style of promotion man": Jerry Hopkins, "Los Angeles Scene," *Rolling Stone,* 6/22/68.

page 187: Keeping the members of Led Zeppelin stoned: Author's interview with Mario Medious.

page 187: "and maybe something for his nose.": Stu Werbin, "The Big M Is Taking Care of Business," *Rolling Stone,* 10/12/72.

page 187: "anything from hash brownies": Author's interview with Bob Garcia, 12/9/92.

page 188: "It really was Mario's personality": Author's interview with Stu Werbin, 8/18/93. All Werbin quotes are from this interview unless otherwise noted.

page 188: Exchange between Medious and Wolf. Author's interview with Medious. Confirmed by Wolf.

page 189: "The band felt": Author's interview with Fred Lewis, 5/3/94.

page 190: "He called me after two or three weeks": Author's interview with Jerry Wexler, 3/6/93.

page 190: Album recorded in three days: Tony Glover, "For the Little Ladies of the Night and All the Ships Out at Sea, for the Kid from Alabama Keepin' All Hid, for the Master-Blaster—Gonna Do It Right, We're Gonna Start It Off Tonight!!!" *Creem,* vol. 4, #4, September 1972.

page 190: "The best album I've heard": Jon Landau, "*The J. Geils Band* (Atlantic SD 8275)," *Rolling Stone,* 1/21/71.

page 191: "I was sort of a puppet promoter": Author's interview with Howard Stein, 4/28/93.

page 192: so he wouldn't have to go to Boston: Barsalona, quoted in "Frank Barsalona: The Lisa Robinson Interview," in "Premier: Twenty Years of Rock 'n' Roll," *Billboard,* 8/18/84.

pages 192–193: Dee Anthony and Joe Pagano: Author interview with Dee Anthony, 9/16/96. Pagano and Valachi noted in Virgil W. Peterson, *The Mob: 200 Years of Organized Crime in New York* (Ottawa, Ill.: Greenhill, 1983), pp. 380–82.

page 193: Anthony threatened Garcia: Author's interview with Garcia, 12/9/92.

page 193: British managers who were eager: Author's interview with Doug D'Arcy, formerly of Chrysalis management, 3/31/93.

page 193: "Their promises were very down to earth": Author's interview with Jerry Shirley, 9/9/93. All subsequent Shirley quotes are from this interview.

page 194: "Little Angelo" and backstage pep talks: Author's interview with Jerry Shirley.

page 195: "Kids just weren't interested": Quoted in "He's Not Quite Emperor of a Boston Empire," *Boston Globe,* 1/21/71. This article is also the source of the financial information regarding the Tea Party's problems.

page 195: Closing of the Tea Party: "The Tea Party, Boston's Rock Core, Closes Doors from Lack of Funds," *Boston Globe,* 1/5/71.

page 196: "The staff retains editorial and esthetic autonomy": "Coming Distractions," *Cambridge Phoenix,* vol. 2, #10, 4/30/70.

page 196: "Landau was always": Author's interview with Bob Williams, 6/27/93.

page 196: "He had so much prestige": Author's interview with Harper Barnes, 10/11/93.

page 197: "Ray's basic problem": Author's interview with Jeff Albertson, 11/19/93.

page 198: Telephone system taps: Author's interview with Ray Riepen, 3/11/93.

page 199: "I decided I didn't want": Author's interview with Bo Burlingham, 10/6/93. This is also the source for the background on Burlingham and how he came to WBCN.

page 199: Exchanges between Laquidara and Burlingham and Riepen and Burlingham: Author's interview with Burlingham, 10/9/93.

page 201: "Meetings are so stupid": Quoted in The Black Shadow, "The Media Freaks Meet the Movement," *Rolling Stone,* 7/23/70. This article, as well as Larry Yurdin, "The Alternative Media Conference of 1970," in *The AOR Story,* a 1978 supplement to *Radio & Records,* provided many of the background details on the conference. Additional information was gleaned from author's interviews with Peter Wolf and Stu Werbin.

page 201: Incident involving Brodie, Laquidara, and Riepen: Author's interview with Charles Laquidara, 9/21/93. All Laquidara quotes are from this interview unless otherwise noted.

page 202: Wolf's departure from WBCN: Author's interview with Wolf, 8/7/92.

page 204: "It was like an auto plant": Author's interview with Danny Schecter, 7/15/93.

page 205: "I betrayed him" and "I had lunch": Author's interview with Harper Barnes, 10/11/93.

page 206: Twenty-fifth anniversary reunion: Details and conversation are from author's interview with Bo Burlingham, 10/9/93.

10. Rock and Roll Future (pages 211–228)

page 211: "When I went to *The Phoenix*": Author's interview with Larry Durocher, 12/7/93. All subsequent Durocher quotes are from this interview unless otherwise noted.

page 212: "Larry is one of the most": Author's interview with Jeff Albertson, 11/19/93. All subsequent Albertson quotes are from this interview.

page 213: "Jon was obviously": Author's interview with Harper Barnes, 10/11/93.

page 213: "[Durocher] and Jon would get on the phone": Confidential source. Confirmed by Harper Barnes.

page 213: "to protect the editorial product": Charlie McCollum and Paul Solman, "BAD News: Take the Money and Run," *The Real Paper,* 8/2/72.

page 214: "I know that if I write": Jon Landau's "Harper Barnes," *The Phoenix,* 5/31/72.

page 216: Criticism of Coppola: Jon Landau, "The Peeper Principle," *Rolling Stone,* 5/23/74.

page 216: Landau's meeting with Milius and introduction to John Ford's films: John Landau, " 'Dillinger': Cops, Robbers & Superstardom," *Rolling Stone,* 8/30/73. The article is also the source for Landau's quote on the heroes in Milius's movies.

page 217: "lonely men with egos so big": Jon Landau, "John Ford: An American Director," *Rolling Stone,* 10/11/73.

page 217: "left as we found him": Ibid.

page 218: "Missner's employees": Quoted in Paul Solman, "The Story of the Phoenix, BAD, and the Real Paper," *The Real Paper,* 9/20/72.

page 218: "He was just a jerk": Author's interview with Don Law, 3/4/93.

page 219: An "antibusiness business": Paul Solman and Thomas Friedman, *Life and Death on the Corporate Battlefield* (New York: Simon & Schuster, 1982). This book is the source for information on the cooperative pay structure of *The Real Paper.*

page 219: "The [music] industry started *The Real Paper*": Author's interview with Bob Williams, 6/27/93.

page 220: "We all thought he was the only important name": Author's interview with Paul Solman, 6/26/93.

page 220: "a small band of heroes": Jon Landau, "The Guns of August," *The Real Paper,* 9/13/72.

page 221: "I could always write": Wendy Smith, "*PW* Interviews Dave Marsh," *Publishers Weekly,* 10/21/83.

page 221: "He was a kid": Author's interview with John Sinclair, 11/3/92.

page 221: Marsh's assessment that the White Panthers had grown irrelevant: Dave Marsh, "Guitar Army/John Sinclair," *Creem,* vol. 4, #10, March 1973.

page 221: Landau helped Marsh get a job at *Rolling Stone*: Author's interview with Dave Marsh, 12/22/95.

page 222: Factions at *The Real Paper*: Author's interviews with Marsh, 12/22/95, and Albertson, 11/19/93, and in Solman and Friedman, op. cit.

page 223: "You know how it is": Author's interview with James Isaacs, November 1993.

page 223: "a totally brilliant": Quoted in performance appendix to Charles R. Cross and the Editors of *Backstreets* magazine, *Backstreets: Springsteen, the Man and His Music* (New York: Harmony Books, 1989).

page 223: "at the start of something large": Henry Armetta James Isaacs, "In Concert: Bruce Springsteen at Joe's Place," *The Real Paper,* 1/23/74.

page 223: "Let me put it to you": Quoted in Cross, *Backstreets,* p. 171.

page 224: "Mike and I watched": Author's interview with Bob Spitz, 7/28/93.

page 224: "Clive sent over the record": Author's interview with Stu Werbin, 8/18/93.

page 225: "I reviewed the album": Sworn deposition of Jon Landau before Ellen K. Leifer, Notary Public, at the offices of Gold, Farrell & Marks, 595 Madison Ave, New York, 1/12/77, in the case of *Laurel Canyon Ltd.* v. *Bruce Springsteen, CBS Inc. and Jon Landau.*

page 225: "the most impressive new singer-songwriter": Jon Landau, "Loose Ends: Bruce Springsteen's Inspired Street Fantasy," *The Real Paper,* 4/10/74.

page 226: "In my own moments": Jon Landau, "Growing Young with Rock 'n' Roll," *The Real Paper,* 5/22/74.

page 227: "I'm not yet ready": Ellen Willis, *The New Yorker,* 11/4/74.

page 228: "Listen, I got a question for you": Confidential source.

page 228: Landau and Springsteen locked in conversation: Author's interview with James Isaacs, cohost of the party, 11/16/93.

11. Eagles Aerie: Hoot Night at the Troubadour (pages 229–253)

page 229: "We were all going": Author's interview with Glenn Frey, 9/21/93. All subsequent Frey quotes are from this interview unless otherwise noted.

page 230: "It wasn't really their world": Author's interview with J. D. Souther, 8/19/93. All subsequent Souther notes are from this interview unless otherwise noted.

page 230: "We were constantly challenging": Author's interview with Ned Doheny, 3/17/93. All subsequent Doheny quotes are from this interview unless otherwise noted.

page 230: "David Crosby is in a band": Author's interview with Frey.

page 231: "When I first got to town": Author's interview with Irving Azoff, 6/23/92. All subsequent Azoff quotes are from this interview unless otherwise noted.

page 231: "On any given night": Author's interview with John Boylan, 12/10/92. All subsequent Boylan quotes are from this interview.

page 231: "Linda [Ronstadt] would go down": Author's interview with Peter Asher, 8/20/93. All subsequent Asher quotes are from this interview.

page 232: "Geffen himself couldn't carry a tune . . ." Cameron Crowe, "Chips Off the Old Buffalo: Perched on the Million-Dollar Border Between Boredom and Laidbackness, the Eagles Perceive a Hardening of the Artistry and the Industry," *Rolling Stone,* 9/25/75.

page 232: "Geffen had this saying": Author's interview with John Hartmann, 8/26/93.

page 233: "At that point, David knew very little": Author's interview with Paul Ahern, 4/1/93.

page 234: Landau flattering Geffen: Jon Landau, "A Rat; A Mensch," *The Real Paper,* 9/26/73.

page 234: "The difference was Geffen/Roberts": Author's interview with Elliot Mazer, 1/24/94.

page 234: "John Hartmann and I": Author's interview with Harlan Goodman, 8/20/93. All Goodman quotes are from this interview.

page 236: "David's talent": Author's interview with Bones Howe, 1/6/94.

page 236: "Elliot was the happy": Author's interview with Don Henley, 12/10/92. All subsequent Henley quotes from this interview unless noted.

page 238: "It's the old sauna story": Quoted in Cameron Crowe, "Chips Off the Old Buffalo . . ."

page 239: "at Neil's beck and call": Author's interview with Jack Nitzsche, 9/19/93.

page 240: Details of Asylum sale: A. D. Murphy, "Geffen Now Exec Assistant to WCI Chief Steve Ross," *Variety,* 11/11/76.

page 241: Details of 75 percent turnover: Julie Baumgold, "The Winning of Cher," *Esquire,* February 1975.

page 242: Conversation between Goodman and Azoff: Author's interview with Harlan Goodman.

page 244: Details of drug search: Cameron Crowe, "They Call Him Big Shorty," *Rolling Stone,* 6/15/78. Confirmed by Irving Azoff.

page 246: "Geffen failed and refused": In *Glen* [sic] *Frey, Randy Meisner, Bernie Leadon, Don Henley and Don Felder* v. *Warner Bros. Inc., WB Music Corp., David Geffen, Companion Music, Benchmark Music, et al.,* Case #C199570. Filed 9/8/77 in Superior Court of the State of California, County of Los Angeles.

page 246: kissing sounds in the press: Mikal Gilmore, "Eagles Sue Geffen & Warner Bros.," *Rolling Stones,* 6/30/77.

page 248: Details of stock value and Ross's reaction: Bruck, *Master of the Game,* p. 77.

page 248: "I did much better for Ross": Author's interview with Jac Holzman, 12/15/92.

page 249: "One day you'll cry tears": Jerry Wexler and David Ritz, *Rhythm and the Blues: A Life in American Music* (New York: Knopf, 1993), p. 254.

page 250: Geffen's beach house: "David Geffen," *Current Biography,* January 1992.

page 250: "Dylan doesn't seem to realize": Quoted in David Felton, "Bob Dylan Sells Out," *Rolling Stone,* 1/3/74.

page 251: "He thought Geffen": Quoted in Judith Sims, "Dylan Back to Columbia," *Rolling Stone,* 12/12/74.

page 251: "Bob Dylan has made a decision": Quoted in Sims, op. cit.

page 251: "He lost enthusiasm for Elektra": Author's interview with Joe Boyd, 3/22/93. All subsequent Boyd quotes are from this interview.

page 251: "Mo kind of sided with him": Ibid.

page 251: "David Geffen wanted": Pelissero and Cornyn.

page 252: lobbying in the press: "Life in the Vinyl Jungle," *Forbes,* 11/15/74.

page 252: "I hated those meetings": Quoted in Shewey, op. cit.

page 252: "This wasn't one of those": Author's interview with Ted Ashley, 9/9/93.

page 253: "I have no plans": Quoted in "David Geffen Has No Intention for Now of Music Biz Return," *Variety,* 12/23/77.

page 253: "There was . . . a brief vogue": Trow, op. cit.

12. The Player (pages 254–274)

page 254: The background on Appel's career is drawn from author's interview with Mike Appel, 6/7/93, as well as "Mike Appel: Interview by Charles R. Cross, November 1990," originally published in *Backstreets* magazine and reprinted in

Cross, *Backstreets: Springsteen, the Man and His Music* (New York: Harmony Books, 1989), and Mark Eliot with Mike Appel, *Down Thunder Road: The Making of Bruce Springsteen* (New York: Simon & Schuster, 1991).

page 255: "He says he thinks": Author's interview with Mike Appel, 6/7/93. All subsequent quotes are from this interview unless otherwise noted.

page 255: Dee Anthony's recollection of his dealings with Appel and Sir Lord Baltimore: author interview with Dee Anthony, 9/16/96.

page 255: "pus": Quoted in Graham and Greenfield, *Bill Graham Presents,* pp. 324–25.

page 255: "horrible": Ibid.

page 255: "They were the worst two songs": Cross, *Backstreets.*

page 256: "The second time": Cross, *Backstreets.*

page 256: "They were scamming": Author's interview with Bob Spitz, 7/28/93. All subsequent Spitz quotes are from this interview.

page 257: "Bruce was incredibly energetic": Quoted in "Danny Federici: Interview by Robert Santelli," *Backstreets,* November 1990.

page 258: "Were you brought up by nuns?": Quoted in John Hammond and Irving Townsend, *John Hammond on Record* (New York: Summit, 1977), p. 391.

page 258: Description of Springsteen's schooling: Quote and details in Peter Knobler, "You Want It, You Take It, You Pay the Price: Bruce Springsteen's Rites of Passage," *Crawdaddy!,* March 1978.

page 259: "Nothing hit me": Quoted in Peter Knobler, "Who Is Bruce Springsteen and Why Are We Saying All These Wonderful Things About Him?," *Crawdaddy!,* March 1973.

page 259: "When I was growing up": Quoted in Paul Gambaccini, *Bruce Springsteen* (New York: Perigree/Delilah, 1979), p. 13.

page 259: Graduation story: Knobler, "You Want It," op. cit.

page 260: Evicted from the house: Knobler, "Who Is," op. cit.

page 260: "for reasons of weirdness": Quoted in Stuart Werbin, "Bruce Springsteen: It's Sign Up a Genius Month," *Rolling Stone,* 4/26/73.

page 261: Details of initial CBS royalty payments totaling $25,000: *Recording Agreement Between CBS Records and Laurel Canyon Production,* 6/9/72. Offered in the amended complaint of *Bruce Springsteen* v. *Michael Appel, Laurel Canyon Management Inc., Laurel Canyon Ltd. and Laurel Canyon Music Inc.,* U.S. District Court, Southern District of New York, #76 Civ. 3334. Filed 3/15/77.

page 261: Didn't bother to open a business account: Author's interview with Bob Spitz, who kept the books at Laurel Canyon.

page 261: Details of Hammond's fears that Springsteen had signed "a slave contract" and other quotes in this paragraph are taken from Lou Cohan and Ken Viola, "Meet John Hammond, the Man Who Brought You Bruce Springsteen," *Thunder Road* #5, Bogota, N.J., 1980.

page 262: $12,000 for office furniture: Author's interview with Spitz.

page 262: Unlimited time and credit at 914: Cohan and Viola, op. cit.

page 262: Exchange between Spitz and McKeith: Author's interview with Spitz. Confirmed by McKeith.

page 263: "I could tell": Author's interview with Sam McKeith, 8/23/93. All subsequent McKeith quotes are from this interview unless otherwise indicated.

page 263: William Morris Agency and African-Americans: Author's interviews with McKeith, 8/23/93, and Steve Leber, 5/20/93.

page 263: "Were they going to make a black guy a movie agent?": Author's interview with Steve Leber, 5/20/93.

page 266: "So frequently the artistic need": Author's interview with Jeff Albertson, 11/19/93.

page 266: Details of Springsteen's last-minute perseveration: Author's interview with Spitz.

page 267: "Bobby . . . go make a tape copy": The source for shopping Springsteen is author's interview with Spitz.

page 268: "I thought, 'Great' ": Author's interview with Peter Philbin, 5/26/93. All subsequent Philbin quotes in this chapter are from author's interview.

page 268: Asbury Park sold twenty thousand copies: Author's interview with Philbin.

page 268: "the obvious heir-apparent to the throne of Scuzz King of Rock 'n' Roll": Dave Marsh, "Elvis: *Aloha from Hawaii via Satellite* (RCA); Bruce Springsteen: *Greetings from Asbury Park, N.J.* (Columbia)," *Creem,* vol. 4, #12, May 1973.

page 269: "a disaster": Cohan and Viola, op. cit.

page 270: "WABC!" Quoted in Peter Knobler, "Running on the Backstreets with Bruce Springsteen," *Crawdaddy!,* October 1975.

page 271: "How big will Bruce be?": The exchange between Appel and Philbin is from the author's interview with Philbin.

page 272: "an all-consuming artist": Eliot and Appel, *Down Thunder Road.*

13. The Guru (pages 275–298)

page 275: Landau's increasing focus on the record business is particularly evident in Jon Landau, "Top Twenty: The Times They Are A-Middlin'," *Rolling Stone,* 6/6/74.

page 275: Landau's relationship with Springsteen: Ibid.

page 276: "The whole episode": Quoted in "Springsteen's Fight: Born to Rock 'n' Roll," *Melody Maker,* 11/15/75.

page 276: CBS $150,000 in the red: "Springsteen: The Merchandising of a Superstar," *Business Week,* 12/1/75.

page 276: "The only concept": Quoted in Peter Knobler, "Running on the Backstreets with Bruce Springsteen," *Crawdaddy!,* October 1975.

page 276: Details of the conversation between Landau and Springsteen are taken from the depositions of Jon Landau and Mike Appel in the cases of *Bruce Springsteen* v. *Michael Appel, Laurel Canyon Management Inc. et al.* and *Laurel Canyon Ltd.* v. *Bruce Springsteen, CBS Inc., and John Landau* as quoted in Eliot and Appel, *Down Thunder Road,* p. 137.

page 277: "Duke Ellington used to say": Author's interview with Mike Appel, 6/7/93. All subsequent Appel quotes are from this interview unless otherwise noted.

page 277: "Well . . . I was trying": Author's interview with Appel.

page 277: Telephone conversation between Landau and Springsteen: Confidential source.

page 278: "He don't know nothing": Quoted in Bart Bull, "Casing the Promised Land," *Backstreets,* summer 1991.

page 278: "He came up with the idea": Quoted in John Rockwell, "New Dylan from New Jersey? It Might as Well Be Springsteen," *Rolling Stone,* 10/9/75.

page 278: Landau's producer "points": Landau deposition, op. cit.

page 279: "Jon had produced": Author's interview with Larry Durocher, 12/7/93.

page 279: Details of *Born to Run* recording sessions are taken from Rockwell, op. cit., and Knobler, op. cit.

page 280: "Bruce was not": Author's interview with Karen Darvin, 9/5/94.

page 280: "I know what's on there": Quoted in Coleman, op. cit.

page 281: "the living culmination": Dave Marsh, "Bruce Springsteen: A Rock 'Star Is Born,' " *Rolling Stone*, 9/25/75.

page 282: "Is it all publicity?": Quoted in *Business Week*, op. cit.

page 282: "He had no idea I was coming": Author's interview with Maureen Orth, 4/22/93. All Orth quotes are from this interview unless otherwise noted.

page 282: "the sound of universes colliding": Ibid.

page 283: Appel suspected Orth : Eliot and Appel, op. cit.

page 283: "her style is about as compatible": Dave Marsh, *Born to Run: The Bruce Springsteen Story* (New York: Dolphin/Doubleday/Delilah, 1979), p. 119.

page 283: Landau's continuing relationship with *Rolling Stone* is evident in the work published during this period, as well as his own deposition of 1/12/77 in *Laurel Canyon Ltd.* v. *Bruce Springsteen, CBS Inc., and Jon Landau.*

page 284: Sinclair's opinion of Marsh and Landau's role in shaping a critical consensus for Springsteen is taken from the author's interview with Sinclair ("They were the conspirators on the Springsteen hype."), 11/3/92.

page 284: "Springsteen's are not songs": John Sinclair, "Bob Seger/Bruce Springsteen: Which Is the Real B.S.?," *Ann Arbor Sun*, 10/1–15/75.

page 285: Landau suddenly told the labels: Confidential source.

page 286: Screaming match between Appel and Landau at the Record Plant: Eliot and Appel, *Down Thunder Road.*

page 286: Landau aided in recording Roxy shows: Ray Coleman, "Interview with Jimmy Iovine," *Melody Maker*, 11/15/75.

page 286: "It was a different thing": Author's interview with Peter Philbin, 11/6/94.

page 286: "a hodgepodge of California studio effects": Dave Marsh, "Stalking the Great Pretender," *Rolling Stone*, 1/27/77.

page 287: Details of Springsteen's royalty agreement are taken from "Exclusive Recording Agreement Between Bruce Springsteen and Laurel Canyon Production, March '72," Exhibit B in *Bruce Springsteen* v. *Michael Appel, Laurel Canyon Management Inc., Laurel Canyon Ltd. and Laurel Canyon Music Inc.*, amended complaint, U.S. District Court, Southern District of New York, 76 Civ. 3334 (LG).

page 288: Details of Springsteen's disenchantment and hiring of Mayer: Author's interview with Mike Mayer, 10/12/94. All Mayer quotes are from this interview.

page 289: "It was our take": Ibid.

page 289: "This was the moment": Eliot and Appel, *Down Thunder Road.*

page 290: Details of suit are from verified complaint in *Bruce Springsteen* v. *Michael Appel et al.* Filed 7/27/76 in U.S. District Court, Southern District of New York.

page 291: "There's no money left": Details and conversations with Springsteen and Appel are from author's interview with Bob Spitz, 7/28/93.

page 291: "I called Appel up": Author's interview with Sam McKeith, 8/23/93.

page 291: "Look, I like Mike": Ibid.

page 292: "When Bruce left him": Author's interview with Steve Leber, 5/20/93.

page 293: "I knew Landau through Paul": Author's interview with Michael Tannen, fall 1992. All subsequent Tannen quotes are from this interview.

page 294: "The pressures of the business . . .": Quoted in Paul Williams, "Lost in the Flood," copyright 1988. Reprinted in Cross, *Backstreets: Springsteen*, p. 62.

page 294: "Bruce and the rest of us": Quoted in Ray Coleman, "Success Can Never Affect Us," *Melody Maker*, 11/15/75.

page 295: "I wasn't real thrilled": Author's interview with David McGee, 3/25/93. All subsequent McGee quotes are from this interview unless otherwise noted.

page 295: "Bruce was really sweet": Author's interview with Marc Brickman, 8/22/93. All subsequent Brickman quotes are from this interview unless otherwise noted.

page 296: "I had to listen to that bullshit": Author's interview with Durocher, 12/7/93.

page 297: Marks's assessment of the case: Author's interview with Leonard Marks, 2/17/93.

page 297: "A series of advisers and producers": Ibid.

page 298: Details of legal maneuvers from the amended answer of Bruce Springsteen are in *Laurel Canyon Ltd.* v. *Bruce Springsteen, CBS Inc. and Jon Landau*, Index #13908/76. Filed 4/14/77 in Supreme Court of the State of New York, County of New York, and from David McGee, "Bruce Springsteen Reclaims the Future," *Rolling Stone*, 8/11/77.

page 298: Details of settlement: Confidential source. Confirmed in Eliot and Appel, *Down Thunder Road*.

14. Dee Anthony's Three Rules of Success (pages 299–317)

page 300: "I think Bruce saw something": Author's interview with Marc Brickman, 8/22/93. All Brickman quotes are from this interview unless otherwise noted.

page 301: "homeless, without family or roots": Landau, "John Ford: An American Director," op. cit.

page 302: "The guy that Mike Appel met": Author's interview with Peter Philbin, 11/6/94.

page 302: CBS support of Springsteen: Figures taken from John Lombardi, "St. Bruce: The Sanctification of Bruce Springsteen and the Rise of Mass Hip," *Esquire*, December 1988.

page 302: "It's okay as long as": Quoted in Ray Coleman, "Bruce Springsteen: Born to Rock 'n' Roll," *Melody Maker*, 11/15/75.

page 302: "This is the reason": Ibid.

page 303: "his personal credo": Jon Landau, "A History of the Development of Soul Music: 1930 to the Present," a senior honors thesis in history, Brandeis University, College of Arts and Sciences, 1969.

page 304: "I couldn't play": Quoted in Paul Williams, "Lost in the Flood," copyright 1988. Reprinted in Cross, *Backstreets: Springsteen*.

page 304: "Bruce has already said": Quoted in Ray Coleman, "Success Can Never Affect Us: Interview with Steve Van Zandt," *Melody Maker*, 11/15/75.

page 304: Springsteen refused to let Appel sell T-shirts: Author's interview with Brickman.

page 305: "We were doing eight, nine months": Author's interview with Steve Van Zandt, 12/29/94.

page 305: Information on Don Law's career and legal problems: Michael Matza and Kit Rachlis, "The Law and Mr. Law," *The Boston Phoenix*, 12/1/81, and "Don Law, Superpromoter, Turns Tickets to Cash," *Boston Globe*, 9/20/92.

page 307: Details of Frampton's early career are from Elizabeth Kay, "The Peter Principle," *Rolling Stone*, 7/3/86, and Cameron Crowe, "The Year of the Face," *Rolling Stone*, 4/22/76.

page 307: "We were very impressed": Author's interview with Jerry Shirley, 9/9/93. All subsequent Shirley quotes are from the author's interview unless otherwise noted.

page 308: Marriott's free spending: Author's interview with John Doumainian, 7/28/93. All subsequent Doumainian quotes are from this interview.

page 309: "Tremendous money": Author's interview with Vince Mauro, fall 1993.

page 309: "Dee might have messed over his acts": Author's interview with Mario Medious, 11/12/92. Medious is the source of his conversation with Anthony.

page 310: Details of Oven Development: Author's interview with Shirley.

page 311: "It got to the point": Crowe, "The Year of the Face," op. cit.

page 312:: $175,000 in the hole: Author's interview with Dee Anthony, 3/1/93.

page 312: Details of promotion for Frampton: Author's interview with Mauro, fall 1993.

page 312:: *Billboard* chart and sales for *Frampton Comes Alive!* A&M Records, *A&M Records: The First 25 Years* (Hollywood: A&M Records), 1987.

page 312:: "I don't really realize": Quoted in Cameron Crowe, "The One and Only Peter Frampton," *Rolling Stone*, 2/10/77.

page 312:: Second concert at Oakland Coliseum: Ibid.

page 313: 118,000 tickets: Author's interview with Anthony, 3/1/93.

page 313: "They were very ethical": Author's interview with Don Law, 3/4/93.

page 314: "Peter's take": Author's interview with Dee Anthony, 3/1/93. All subsequent Anthony quotes are from this interview unless otherwise noted.

page 314: Anthony insisted Frampton cut a follow-up: Author's interview with Mauro, who recalls urging that Frampton make a blues album instead of trying to replicate the success of *Frampton Comes Alive!*, fall 1993.

page 314: "No one really thought": Quoted in Kay, op. cit.

page 315: "duller than nails": Merrill Shindler, "Vegas Barely Comes Alive: Peter Frampton, Aladdin Theatre for the Performing Arts, Las Vegas, 7.12.77," *Rolling Stone*, 9/8/77.

page 315: Anthony preferred the bungalow Elizabeth Taylor used: Author's interview with Doumainian. "Took to greeting guests in a toga": Two confidential sources.

page 316: "This isn't a movie": Janet Maslin, "Screen: Son of 'Sgt. Pepper,' " *New York Times*, 7/21/78.

15. King David, Act Two (pages 318–331)

page 318: "It's a way": Quoted in Cynthia Kirk, "David Geffen Joins WCI Record Group as Consultant-Advisor," *Variety*, 2/22/79.

page 319: "I felt then, as I do now": Fredric Dannen's interview with David Geffen, 7/27/87.

page 319: "When Steve Ross came in": Author's interview with Stan Cornyn, 12/7/92.

page 320: Growth figures for Warner Music operation: Warner Bros. Records press release, 11/1/94.

page 321: "excruciating pressure" and subsequent Smith remark: Author's interview with Joe Smith, 12/21/94.

page 321: $17 million Geffen distribution deal: Dannen, *Hit Men* (New York: Times Books, 1990), p. 156 (paperback).

page 322: Meeting on Warners back lot between Ostin and Young: Robert Hilburn and Chuck Phillips, "Quotations From Chairman Mo," *Los Angeles Times,* 12/11/94.

page 323: "Frank . . . this is one of those times": Author's interview with Cornyn, 12/7/92.

page 323: "Travelling there soon became a bore": Neil Young's liner notes for the album *Decade.*

page 323: "Nobody expected *Time Fades Away*": Quoted in Crowe, "So Hard to Make Arrangements for Yourself," op. cit.

page 324: Story of *American Stars 'n' Bars:* Cameron Crowe, "Neil Young: The Last American Hero," *Rolling Stone,* 2/8/79.

page 324: "Rather than release an album": Cameron Crowe, "Neil Young: Still Expecting to Fly," *Musician,* November 1982.

page 325: "For my money . . . Neil Young": Paul Nelson, "Every Promise Fulfilled: *Rust Never Sleeps* by Neil Young," *Rolling Stone,* 10/18/79.

page 325: "Neil never sold out": Author's interview with John Hartmann, 8/26/93.

page 326: "Other companies": Quoted in P. Makos, "Interview with Elliot Roberts," *Broken Arrow,* #7, August 1982, London.

page 328: "never even been sick at all": Christian Williams, "David Geffen's Touch of Gold," *The Washington Post,* 5/6/82.

page 328: "If they think": Robert Sam Anson, "David Geffen Talks a Little," *Esquire,* November 1982.

page 328: "It's a hard one": Author's interview with Ted Ashley, 9/9/93.

page 329: "When David feels maligned": Quoted in Patrick Goldstein, "Geffen: From a Minor to a Mogul," *Los Angeles Times,* 12/12/82.

page 329: Details of Towne charges are taken from *Towne* v. *Geffen, Geffen Films, Warner Bros. WCI, and Steven Ross,* #C407184. Filed 4/13/82 in California Supreme Court.

page 330: Geffen's deposition in the Towne divorce case is detailed in Dennis McDougal, "MCA Deal Caps Geffen's Climb from Mail Room," *Los Angeles Times,* 3/15/90.

page 330: "This is not an isolated instance": *Towne* v. *Geffen* et al, op. cit.

page 330: "You're looking at the man": Quoted in Goldstein, op. cit.

page 330: Personal Best cleared $7 million for Geffen: Lisa Gubernick, "For Me, This Is Tennis," *Forbes,* 5/30/88.

16. A Great Marketing Experience (pages 332–352)

page 332: "The first thing I produced": Author's interview with Steve Van Zandt, 12/29/94.

page 332: "Hungry Heart" included on *The River* at Landau's insistence: In Fred Schruers, "Bruce Springsteen and the Secret of the World," *Rolling Stone,* February 1981.

page 333: CBS sales figures: Dannen, *Hit Men,* p. 5.

page 333: "finish the fucking record": Quoted in Fred Goodman, "Walter Yetnikoff: The Most Powerful Man in the Record Business," *Rolling Stone,* 12/15/88.

page 333: "I'm sitting there thinking": Author's interview with Peter Philbin, 11/6/94. All subsequent Philbin quotes are from author's interview unless otherwise noted.

page 334: "Unrequited love": Author's interview with Marc Brickman, 8/22/93. All subsequent Brickman quotes are from this interview.

page 335: Landau was feared: Asked if Landau got along with the band, Marc Brickman had this to say: "No. He was there, and everyone was obviously afraid of him."

page 335: Landau and Van Zandt fighting over royalties and credits: Lombardi, op. cit.

page 335: "Why didn't you get him": Author's interview with David McGee, 3/25/93.

page 335: Springsteen/Brickman exchange over lights: Author's interview with Brickman.

page 336: Conversation between Springsteen, Albertson, and Landau: Author's interview with Albertson, 11/19/93.

page 336: "I never aspired": Ibid.

page 337: "help inspire the country": John Rockwell, "Rock: Bruce Springsteen at the Garden," *The New York Times,* 11/29/80.

page 337: Landau gave Springsteen a copy of Klein book: Author's interview with Brickman.

page 337: The River show in Spain: Ibid.

page 338: "you made in your garage": Author's interview with Walter Yetnikoff, 1/5/95.

page 338: Springsteen and Landau's private concerns over loss of audience: Andrea Klein, the graphic designer who worked closely with Landau and Springsteen on the covers for several albums, told *Backstreets* magazine that "Bruce actually had a fear—he expressed that he didn't think he had any fans out there . . . His fans had grown up, had gone to college and graduated. That's how both he and Jon felt. So they were very much ready to establish him again commercially." From "Cover Me: Behind the Design of *Born in the U.S.A.*," reprinted in Cross, *Backstreets: Springsteen.*

page 339: "Record companies earn their way": Author's interview with Al Teller, 11/11/94. All subsequent Teller quotes are from this interview unless otherwise noted.

page 340: Growth of MTV: Viewership figures are those claimed by MTV.

page 344: Landau fretted: Author's interview with Teller.

page 345: "We started out as a band": Quoted in Robert Santelli, "Interview with Danny Federici," *Backstreets Magazine,* #34/35, winter 1991.

page 346: Number of tour dates taken from appendix to Cross, *Backstreets, Springsteen.* Gross estimate in David McGee, "Fooled in the USA? Behind the Public Image of Bruce Springsteen," *New Musical Express,* 7/18/87. Source for estimated merchandising gross is confidential.

page 347: "Naturally, the intelligent groups": Jon Landau, "Rock Trends: Where Have All the Dollars Gone?," *The Phoenix,* 7/4/70.

page 347: "Promotion is": Richard Goldstein, "Autohype: Context as Criterion," originally published in *The Village Voice.* Reprinted in *Goldstein's Greatest Hits: A Book Mostly About Rock 'n' Roll* (New York: Prentice-Hall, 1970), p. 189.

page 347: "Let freedom ring": Quoted in Chet Flippo, "Bruce Springsteen: A Pure Patriot Keeps His Promise," *Musician,* November 1984.

page 347: Springsteen's voting habits: In Kurt Loder's "Bruce Springsteen: The Rolling Stone Interview," *Rolling Stone,* 12/6/84.

page 348: Springsteen implied he had been rejected as psychologically unfit for service in the first story to appear on him in *Rolling Stone,* Stuart Werbin's "Bruce Springsteen: It's Sign Up a Genius Month," *Rolling Stone,* 4/26/73.

page 348: "Bruce actually beat the draft": Marsh, *Born to Run,* p. 12.

page 349: "an extremely bold choice," and "the one song that could make every implication": Dave Marsh, *Glory Days: Bruce Springsteen in the 1980s* (New York: Pantheon, 1987), pp. 387–88.

page 349: Comparison of "If I Should Fall Behind" to Rousseau's social contract appeared in Marsh's newsletter, *Rock & Rap Confidential,* undated. The remark was part of a review of a showcase that Springsteen played at New York's Bottom Line for Sony Music staffers and a handful of invited journalists on the eve of the release of *Human Touch* and *Lucky Town.* Although it was closed to the public, Marsh, who had made much of Springsteen's avowal never to play another industry showcase in his first book, characterized the show as a public performance.

page 349: Quotes and details of Moore's meeting with Marsh appear in Moore's foreword to Ben Hamper, *Rivethead: Tales from the Assembly Line* (New York: Warner Books, 1992). Hamper's send-up of rock-star pretensions is also included in the book.

page 349: Marsh staked no claim: Marsh, *Glory Days,* p. xiii.

page 350: Alternative press's rejection of mainstream tenets, including objectivity: See Peck, *Uncovering the Sixties,* pp. 23–24. Peck offers a detailed analysis of objectivity and its challenge by the underground press.

page 350: "History . . . will prove me right": Author's interview with Dave Marsh, 12/22/95.

page 350: Rolling Stone's criticism of Marsh's relationship with Springsteen: Anthony DeCurtis's review of *Glory Days,* "Bruce Bio: An Insider's Look at Springsteen," *Rolling Stone,* 6/4/87.

page 351: "Was it too much to think": Marsh, *Glory Days,* p. 450.

page 351: "There's an old saying": Dylan interview with Cameron Crowe in liner notes for *Biograph,* Columbia C5X 38830, released in November 1985.

17. A Captain of Industry (pages 353–379)

page 353: "The pressures of the business . . .": Williams in *Backstreets,* op cit.

page 355: Bragged that his role: Christian Williams, "David Geffen's Touch of Gold," *The Washington Post,* 5/6/82.

page 355: Details of Geffen's suit are taken from *The David Geffen Company* v. *Neil*

Young, Case #C174373. Filed 11/4/83 in Superior Court of the State of California, County of Los Angeles.

page 355: "The truth is": Transcript of Jeffrey Ressner's interview with David Geffen for *Rolling Stone,* May 1989.

page 356: "When he signed me": Quoted in Nick Kent, "This Young Will Run and Run," *Vox,* November 1990.

page 356: "It was too big": Quoted in Jimmy McDonough, "Too Far Gone: Fucking Up with Neil Young," *Village Voice Rock & Roll Quarterly,* winter 1989.

page 357: "*Trans* is about communication": Ibid.

page 357: Geffen Records' "secret intention": *Neil Young* v. *the David Geffen Company and David Geffen,* Case #C474373. Filed 5/7/84 in Superior Court of California, County of Los Angeles.

page 358: "I was trying to save Neil": Quoted in Patrick Goldstein, "David Geffen: The Rolling Stone Interview," *Rolling Stone,* 4/29/93.

page 358: Financial figures and estimate of worth for the David Geffen Company: Lisa Gubernick, "For Me, This Is Tennis," *Forbes,* 5/30/88.

page 359: "He was seminal": Author's interview with Don Henley, 12/10/92.

page 360: Goldstein's joke and Geffen's response: Author's interview with Patrick Goldstein, 4/11/95.

page 360: "Steve Ross wasn't willing": Quoted in Lisa Gubernick and Peter Newcomb, "The Richest Man in Hollywood," *Forbes,* 12/24/90.

page 360: Ross proposals rejected by Geffen: Geraldine Fabrikant, "The Record Man with Flawless Timing," *The New York Times,* 12/9/90.

page 360: "Steve never took a fatherly interest"; Quoted in Bernard Weinraub, "David Geffen: Still Hungry," *The New York Times Magazine,* 5/2/93.

page 360: "You can't make a deal": Author's interview with Ted Ashley, 9/9/93. All subsequent Ashley quotes are from this interview unless otherwise noted.

page 361: "Here I was an associate": Quoted in Gubernick and Newcomb, op. cit.

page 364: "too soon": The author, who attended the December 1985 press conference as a reporter for *Billboard,* posed the question to Welch.

page 364: Information on Tisch's rise at CBS: Sally Bedell Smith, *In All His Glory: The Life of William S. Paley, The Legendary Tycoon and His Brilliant Circle* (New York: Simon & Schuster, 1990), pp. 575–92.

page 365: Purchase price of SBK: Dannen, *Hit Men,* p. 328.

page 365: Paley agrees to record company sale: Smith, *In All His Glory,* p. 594.

page 365: *Newsweek* noted the sale: "CBS Records: If You Can't Beat 'em, Sell," *Newsweek,* 11/30/87.

page 365: *Newsweek* cover story on Columbia Pictures: "Japan Goes Hollywood," *Newsweek,* 10/9/89.

page 366: "I think Sony": Quotes and bonus figure are from Goodman, op. cit.

page 367: $10 million profit on Chrysalis: Transcript of Jeffrey Ressner's interview with David Geffen for *Rolling Stone,* May 1989.

page 367: "I don't think they considered": Ibid.

page 367: "I'm looking to own": Quoted in Fredric Dannen's interview with David Geffen, 7/27/87.

page 368: Dexter's assessment of the Beatles: Recalled by Alan Livingston, then president of Capitol Records, in the label's own in-house anniversary book,

Paul Grein's *Capitol Records Fiftieth Anniversary: 1942–1992,* copyright Capitol Records, Hollywood, 1992.

page 368: Ahern's failed attempt to sign Boston: Author's interview with Ahern, 4/1/93.

page 369: the leak appeared to help Geffen's lawyers: Details in Fred Goodman, "Who's the Biggest Man in Hollywood?" *Spy,* April 1991.

page 369: "If we had paid": Quoted in Fabrikant, op. cit.

page 369: Details of MCA stock arrangement are taken from S.E.C. form 8-K, filed 4/17/90 by MCA Inc.

page 369: Tax consequences of MCA deal: Jube Shiver, Jr., and Michael Cieply, "MCA Buys Out Last Major Independent Record Label," *Los Angeles Times,* 3/15/90.

page 369: "When I made the deal": Quoted in Fabrikant, op. cit.

page 370: Background on Matsushita/MCA negotiations in Peter J. Boyer, "Hollywood's King Cashes Out," *Vanity Fair,* February 1991.

page 371: The negotiations didn't stay: Richard Turner's "Thorn to Buy Geffen, Changing Key for Record Industry," *The Wall Street Journal,* 3/5/90.

page 371: "A leap in value of $197 million": Ibid.

page 371: "someone who knew": Ibid.

page 371: Geffen deliriously happy: Goodman, "Who's the Biggest Man," op. cit.

page 372: "He always sees": Ibid.

page 372: "I started the 1980s": Gubernick and Newcomb, op. cit.

page 372: "Really, it scared me": Quoted in Weinraub, op. cit.

page 372: Geffen's campaign contributions: David Lauter, "In Home Stretch, Clinton Topped Bush in Fund-Raising," *Los Angeles Times,* 3/4/93.

page 373: "I can't for the life of me": Quoted in Alan Citron, "The New Adventures of the Barefoot Billionaire," *Los Angeles Times Calendar,* 3/7/93.

page 373: Reader response to Geffen's remarks on the military: Letter by Robert Stirman, *Los Angeles Times Calendar,* 3/21/93.

page 373: "David will do anything": Quoted in Weinraub, op. cit.

page 373: *The Wall Street Journal* story suggesting Yetnikoff on his way out: Laura Landro, "CBS Chief Ready to Phase Out Managerial Duties," *The Wall Street Journal,* 8/17/90.

page 374: "Events will prove": Author's interview with Walter Yetnikoff, 8/21/90.

page 374: Geffen, Jackson, and *Moonwalker:* Dannen, *Hit Men,* p. 338.

page 374: Rumors that Jackson: Goodman, "Who's the Biggest Man," op. cit.

page 375: "Walter slit his own throat": Quoted in Peter J. Boyer, "David Is Goliath," *Vanity Fair,* March 1991.

page 375: "If you need a blood donor": Ron Givens, "With a Little Help from Their Friends," *Entertainment Weekly,* April 1990. This article is the source for details for AIDS benefit show.

page 376: "a bunch of assholes" and subsequent exchange from Michael Musto, "La Dolce Musto," *The Village Voice,* May 1990.

page 376: "a self-hating man": Michelangelo Signorile, "Gossip Watch," *Outweek,* 5/16/90.

page 377: "I'm not saying": Quoted in Goldstein, "David Geffen," op. cit.

page 377: $1 million donation to APLA: 3/1/92 press release from APLA.

page 377: "come a long way": Brendan Lemon, "David Geffen: Man of the Year," *The Advocate,* December 1992.

page 377: Signorile dubs Geffen "a hero": Michelangelo Signorile, *Queer in America: Sex, the Media, and the Closets of Power* (New York: Random House, 1993), p. 365.

page 377: the highest taxpayer in the country: Goldstein, "David Geffen," op. cit.

page 377: "I've made a billion dollars": Quoted in Kim Masters, "Hollywood Strikes Back! Cause Celebrities Defend Their Potomac Presence," *The Washington Post,* 5/25/93.

page 377: Geffen and Chinese trade: Jeffrey H. Birnbaum and Eric Pooley, "New Party Bosses," *Time,* 4/8/96.

page 378: Geffen's contributions to various Senate campaigns: Joe Battenfeld and Andrew Miga, "Bulk of Ted K's $2.2M War Chest Comes from Out of State," *Boston Herald,* 8/4/93; C. David Kotok, "Kerrey Campaign Fund Gets $862,578," *Omaha World-Herald;* David Lightman, "Lieberman Has $1.7 Million for Campaign," *Hartford Courant,* 8/3/93.

page 378: "No one's asked me": Quoted in Weinraub, op. cit.

page 379: Details of Geffen and Dreamworks' political contributions: Leslie Wayne, "A Hollywood Production: Political Money," *The New York Times,* 9/12/96.

page 379: "I don't want to present myself": Quoted in David Sheff, "Playboy Interview: David Geffen," *Playboy,* September 1994.

INDEX

ABOUT THE AUTHOR

FRED GOODMAN is a freelance journalist. A former *Rolling Stone* editor, his work has appeared in numerous publications, including *The New York Times*, *Vanity Fair*, *The Village Voice*, *New York*, *Spy*, *GQ*, *Us*, *Entertainment Weekly*, and *Worth*.